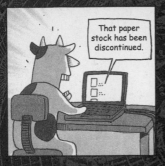

> That paper stock has been discontinued.

The paper that I've been using for my color illustrations all this time is no longer being made. This was the biggest shock of the year!

—*Hiromu Arakawa, 2009*

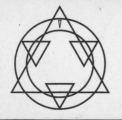

Born in Hokkaido (northern Japan), Hiromu Arakawa first attracted national attention in 1999 with her award-winning manga *Strdy Dog*. Her series *Fullmetal Alchemist* debuted in 2001 in Square Enix's monthly manga anthology *Shonen Gangan*.

FULLMETAL ALCHEMIST
VOL. 23

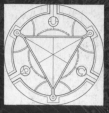

VIZ Media Edition

Story and Art by Hiromu Arakawa

Translation/Akira Watanabe
English Adaptation/Jake Forbes
Touch-up Art & Lettering/Wayne Truman
Design/Julie Behn
Editor/Alexis Kirsch

VP, Production/Alvin Lu
VP, Sales & Product Marketing/Gonzalo Ferreyra
VP, Creative/Linda Espinosa
Publisher/Hyoe Narita

Hagane no RenkinJutsushi vol. 23 © 2009 Hiromu Arakawa/SQUARE ENIX. First published in Japan in 2009 by SQUARE ENIX CO., LTD. English translation rights arranged with SQUARE ENIX CO., LTD. and VIZ Media, LLC.

Printed in the U.S.A.

Published by VIZ Media, LLC
P.O. Box 77010
San Francisco, CA 94107

10 9 8 7 6 5 4 3 2 1
First printing, July 2010

www.viz.com

鋼の錬金術師

FULLMETAL ALCHEMIST

23

荒川弘

HIROMU ARAKAWA

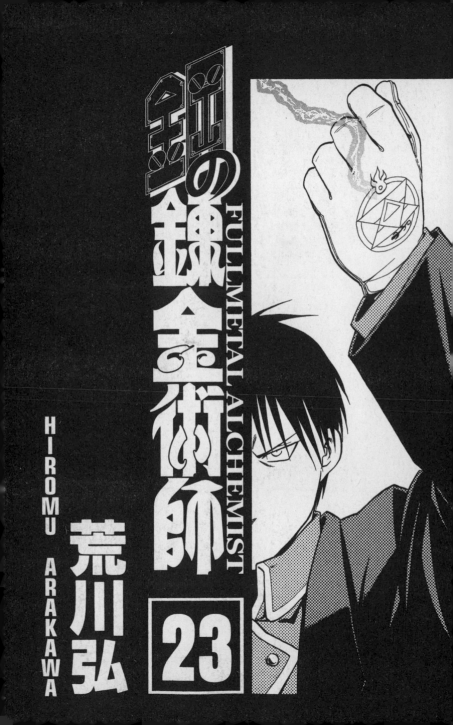

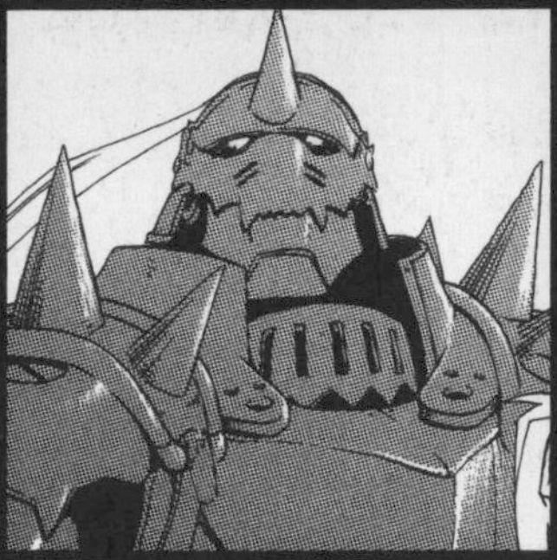

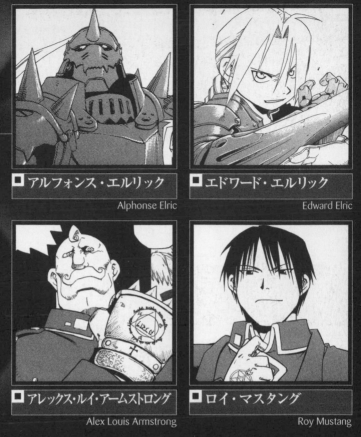

アルフォンス・エルリック

Alphonse Elric

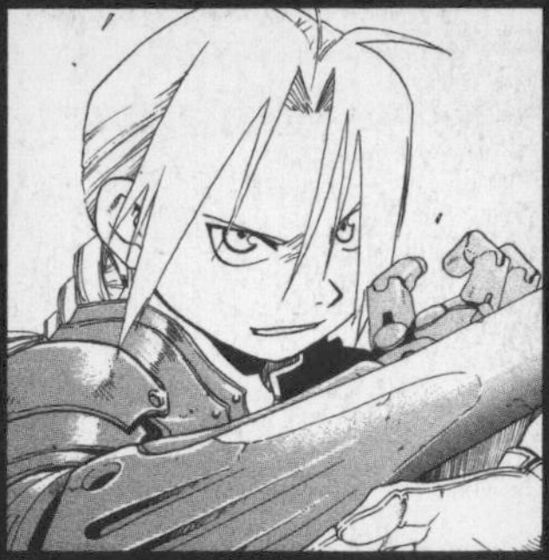

エドワード・エルリック

Edward Elric

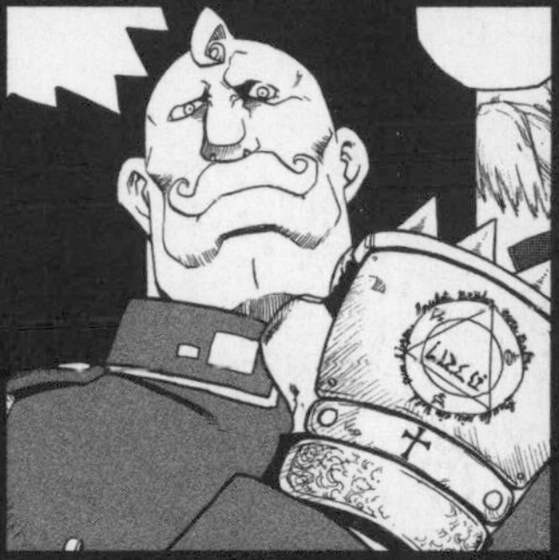

アレックス・ルイ・アームストロング

Alex Louis Armstrong

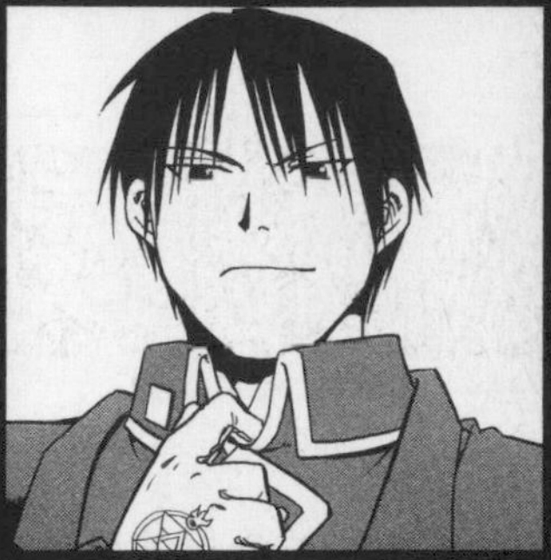

ロイ・マスタング

Roy Mustang

OUTLINE
FULLMETAL ALCHEMIST

Using a forbidden alchemical ritual, the Elric brothers attempted to bring their dead mother back to life. But the ritual went wrong, consuming Edward Elric's leg and Alphonse Elric's entire body. At the cost of his arm, Edward was able to graft his brother's soul into a suit of armor. Equipped with mechanical "auto-mail" to replace his missing limbs, Edward becomes a state alchemist in hopes of finding a way to restore their bodies. Their search embroils them in a deadly conspiracy that threatens to take the innocence, if not the lives, of everyone involved.

As the "Day of Reckoning" approaches, Central City has become a war zone! On one side, the Homunculi and the military leaders who have sold out their country for power; on the other, a rag-tag alliance of rebel soldiers loyal to Major General Armstrong and Roy Mustang, Ishbalan refugees and, of course, the Elric family and their allies. As things heat up on the streets, Ed, Hohenheim and Scar descend into "Father's" underground complex where they stumble upon the military's top-secret army of artificial humans. Meanwhile, on the outskirts of the capital, Al confronts the Homunculus Pride and the murderous alchemist Kimblee.

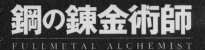

鋼の錬金術師
FULLMETAL ALCHEMIST

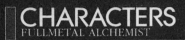

CHARACTERS
FULLMETAL ALCHEMIST

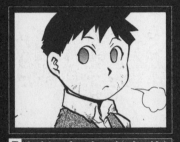

□ セリム・ブラッドレイ（プライド）

Selim Bradley (Pride)

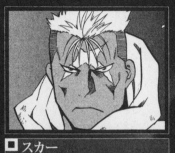

□ スカー

Scar

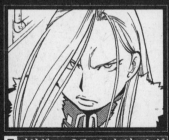

□ オリヴィエ・ミラ・アームストロング

Olivier Mira Armstrong

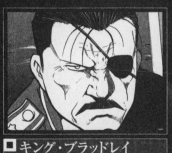

□ キング・ブラッドレイ

King Bradley

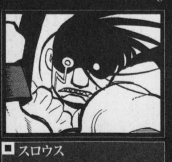

□ スロウス

Sloth

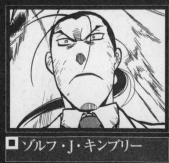

□ ゾルフ・J・キンブリー

Solf J. Kimblee

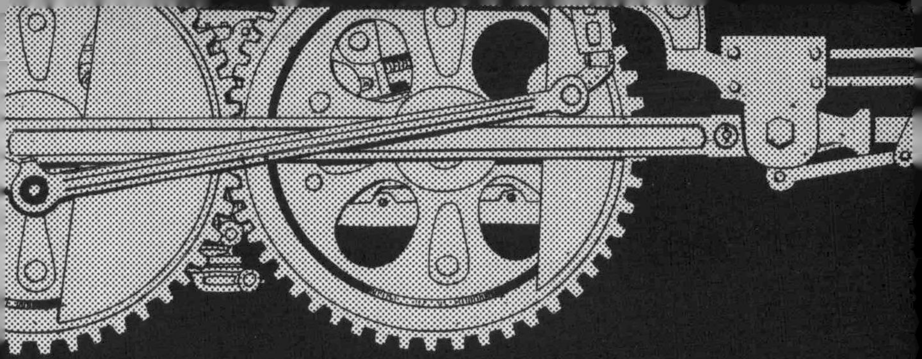

CONTENTS

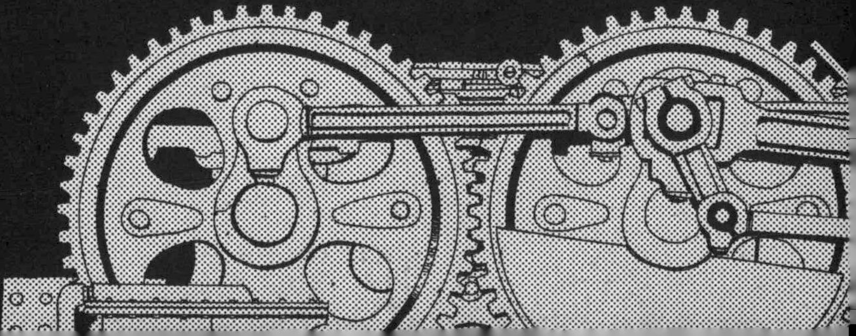

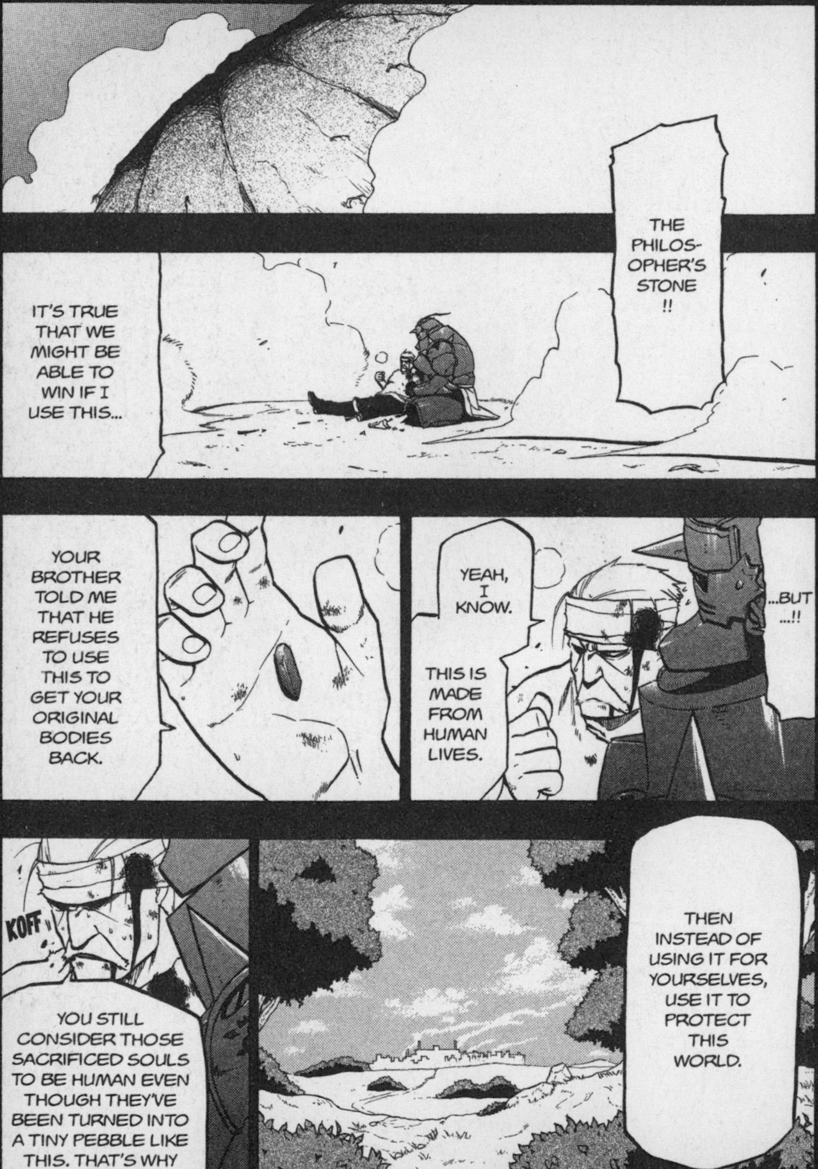
THE PHILOS-OPHER'S STONE !!
IT'S TRUE THAT WE MIGHT BE ABLE TO WIN IF I USE THIS...
YOUR BROTHER TOLD ME THAT HE REFUSES TO USE THIS TO GET YOUR ORIGINAL BODIES BACK.
YEAH, I KNOW.
THIS IS MADE FROM HUMAN LIVES.
...BUT ...!!
KOFF
YOU STILL CONSIDER THOSE SACRIFICED SOULS TO BE HUMAN EVEN THOUGH THEY'VE BEEN TURNED INTO A TINY PEBBLE LIKE THIS. THAT'S WHY I'M ASKING YOU TO USE IT.
THEN INSTEAD OF USING IT FOR YOURSELVES, USE IT TO PROTECT THIS WORLD.

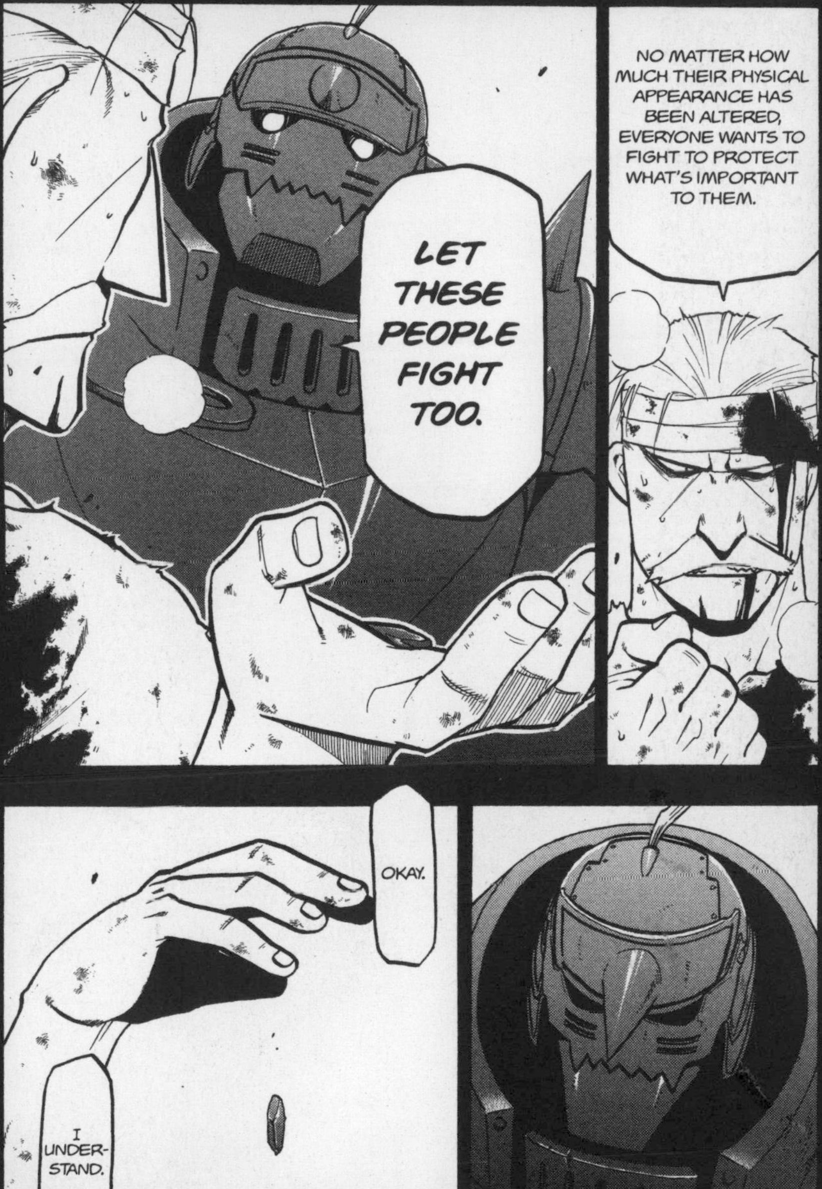
NO MATTER HOW MUCH THEIR PHYSICAL APPEARANCE HAS BEEN ALTERED, EVERYONE WANTS TO FIGHT TO PROTECT WHAT'S IMPORTANT TO THEM.
LET THESE PEOPLE FIGHT TOO.
OKAY.
I UNDER-STAND.

Chapter 92
With Everyone's Strength

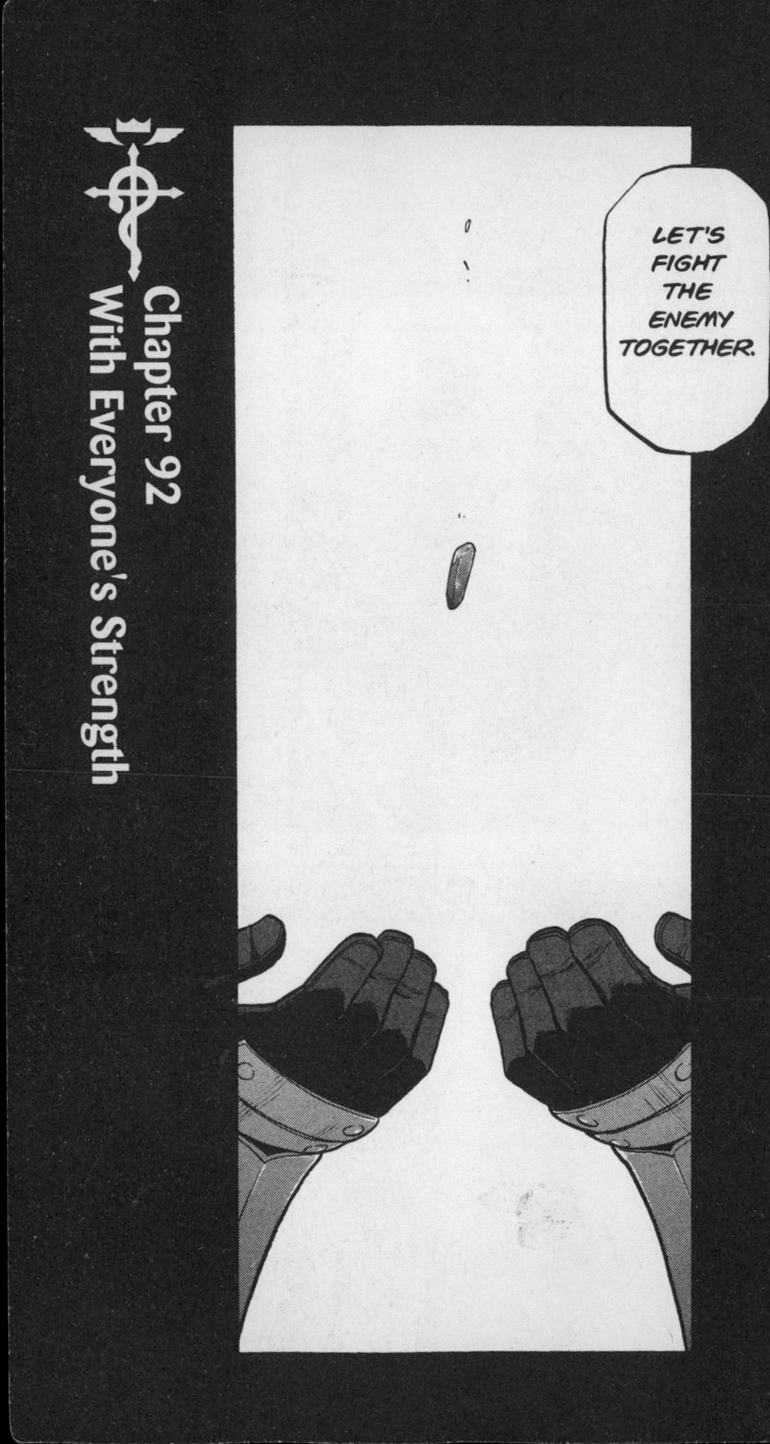
LET'S FIGHT THE ENEMY TOGETHER.

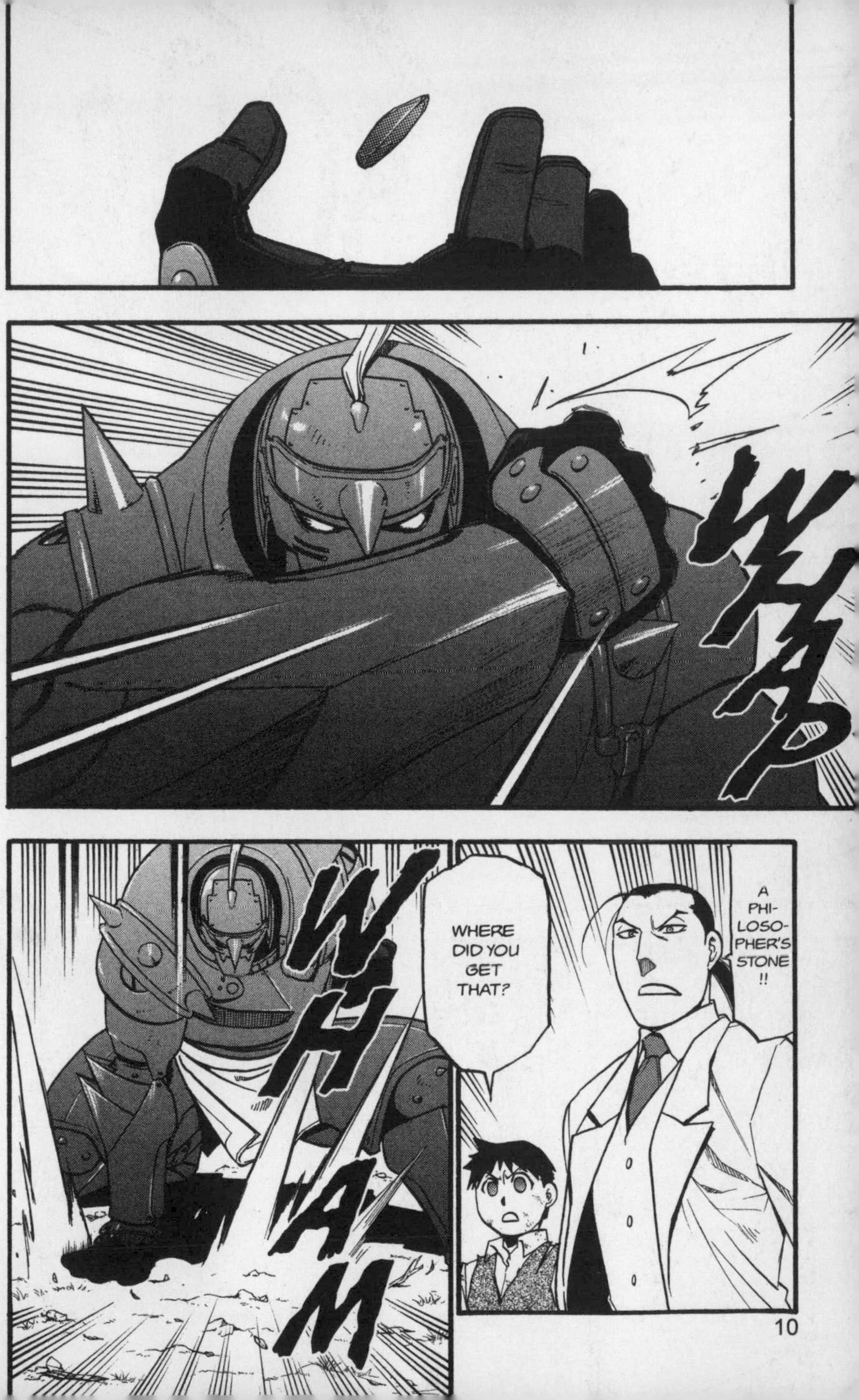
WHAP
A PHI-LOSO-PHER'S STONE !!
WHERE DID YOU GET THAT?
WHAM

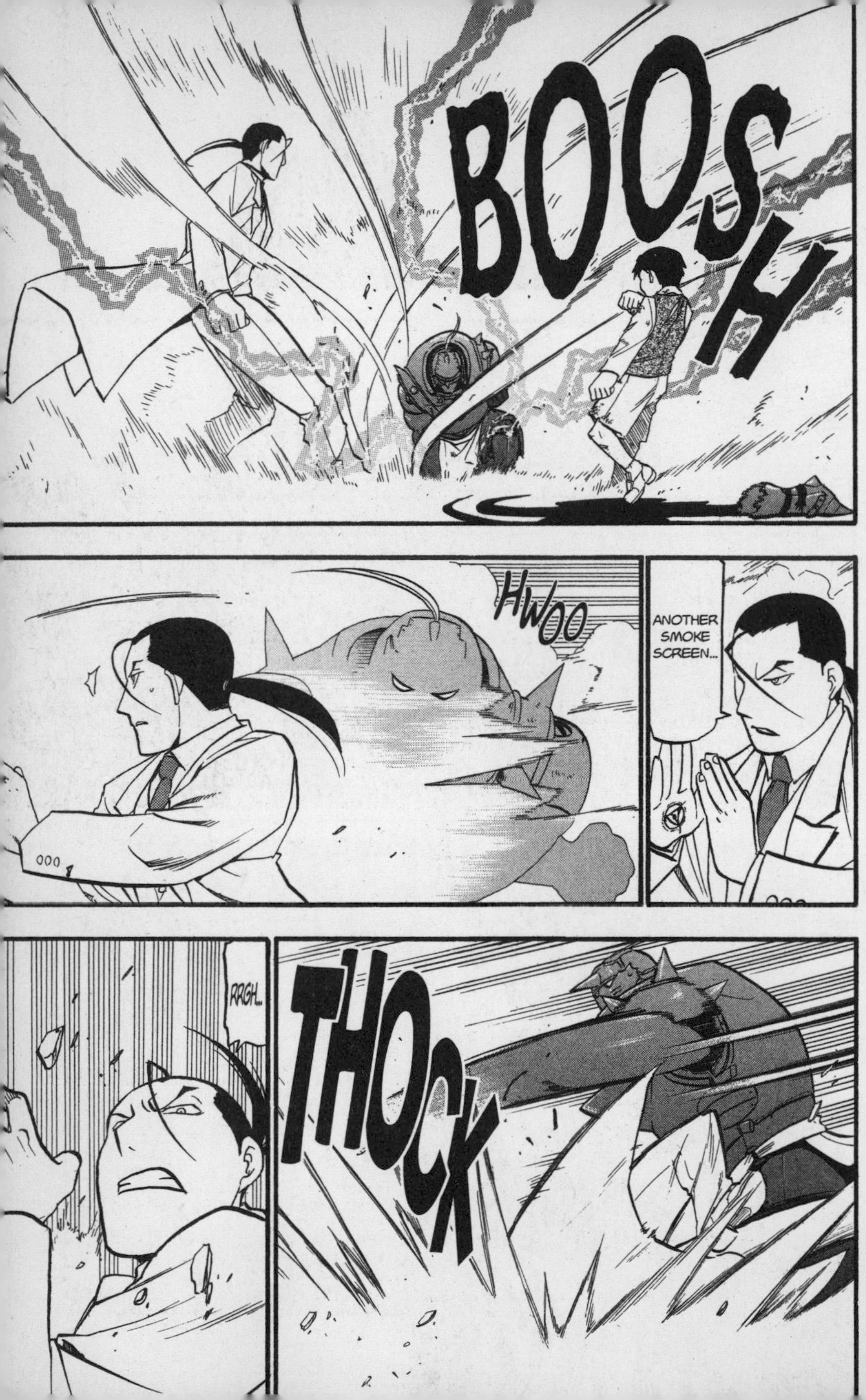
BOOSH
ANOTHER SMOKE SCREEN...
HWOO
THOCK
RRGH...

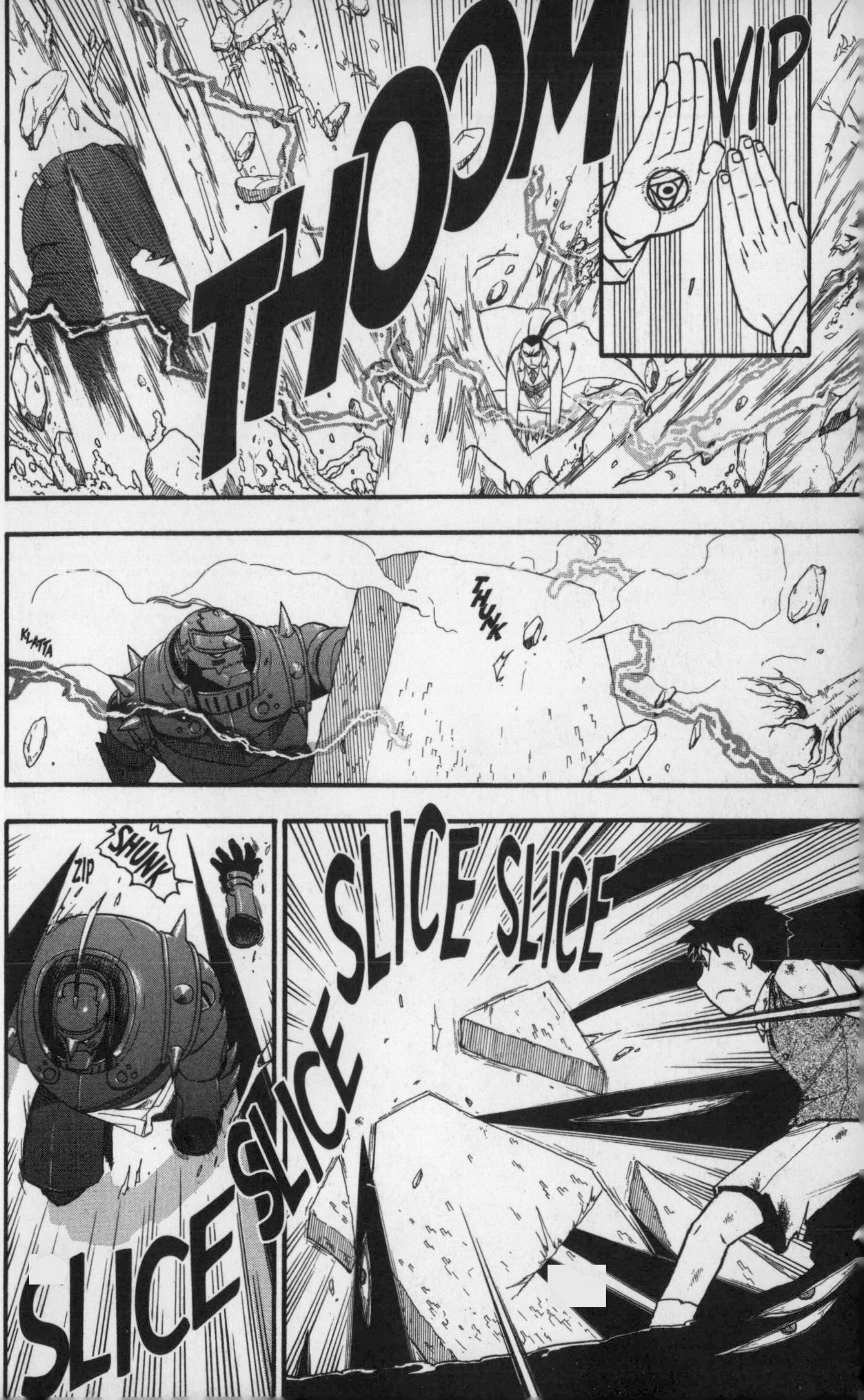
VIP
THOOM
THUNK
KLATTA
SLICE SLICE
SLICE SLICE
SHUNK
ZIP
SLICE

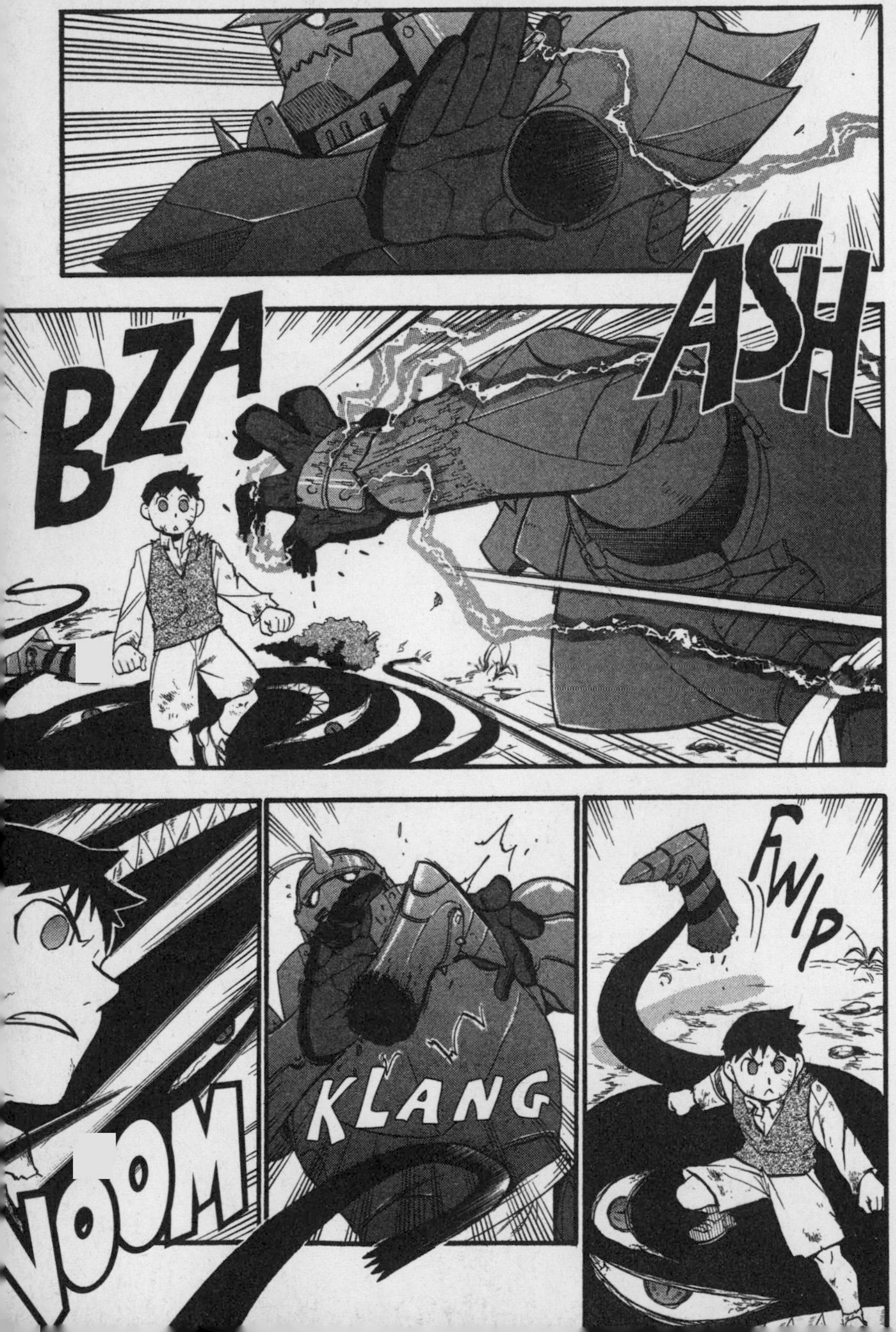
BZA
ASH
FWIP
KLANG
VOOM

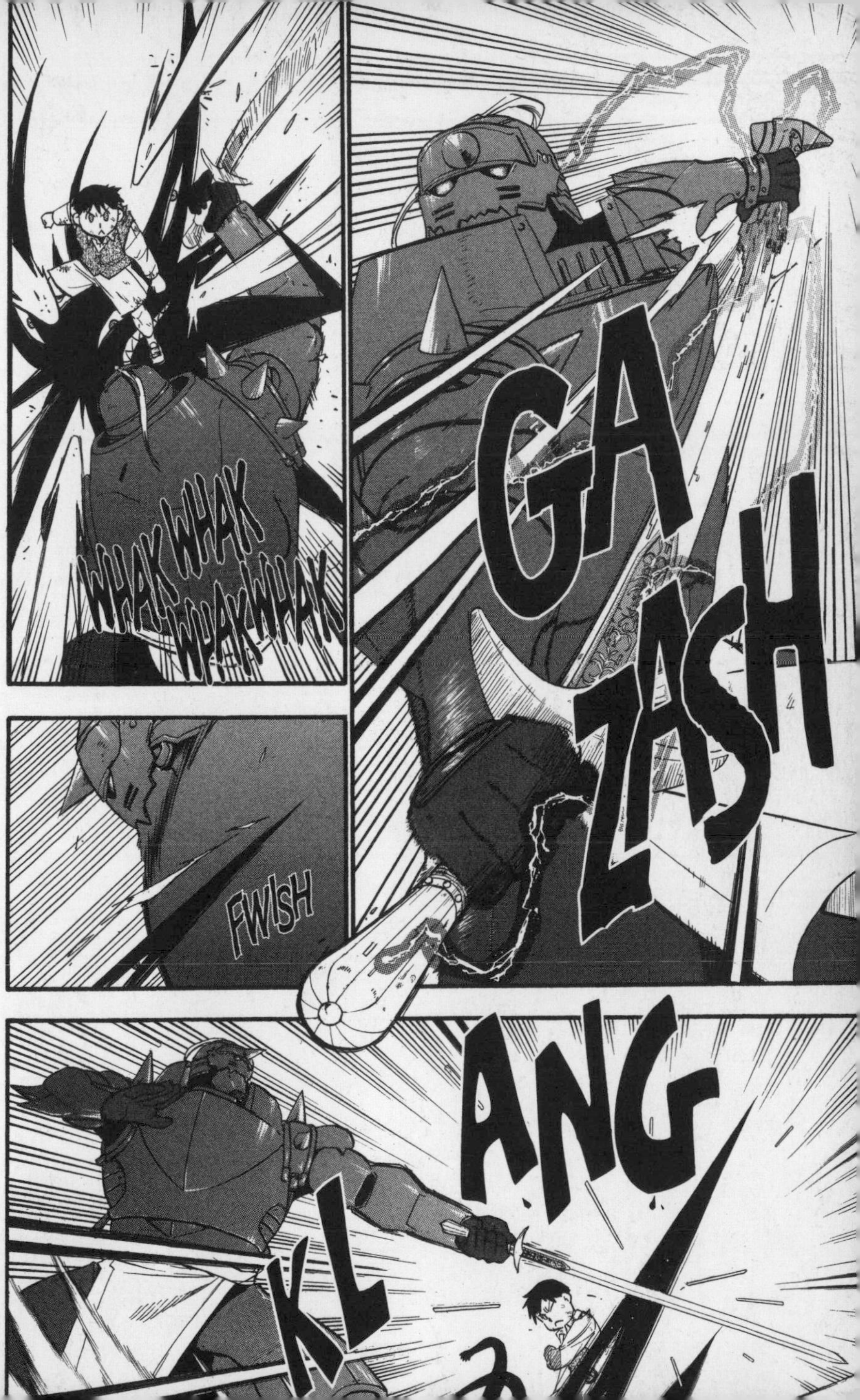
GA
ZASH
WHAK WHAK
WHAK WHAK
FWISH
KLANG

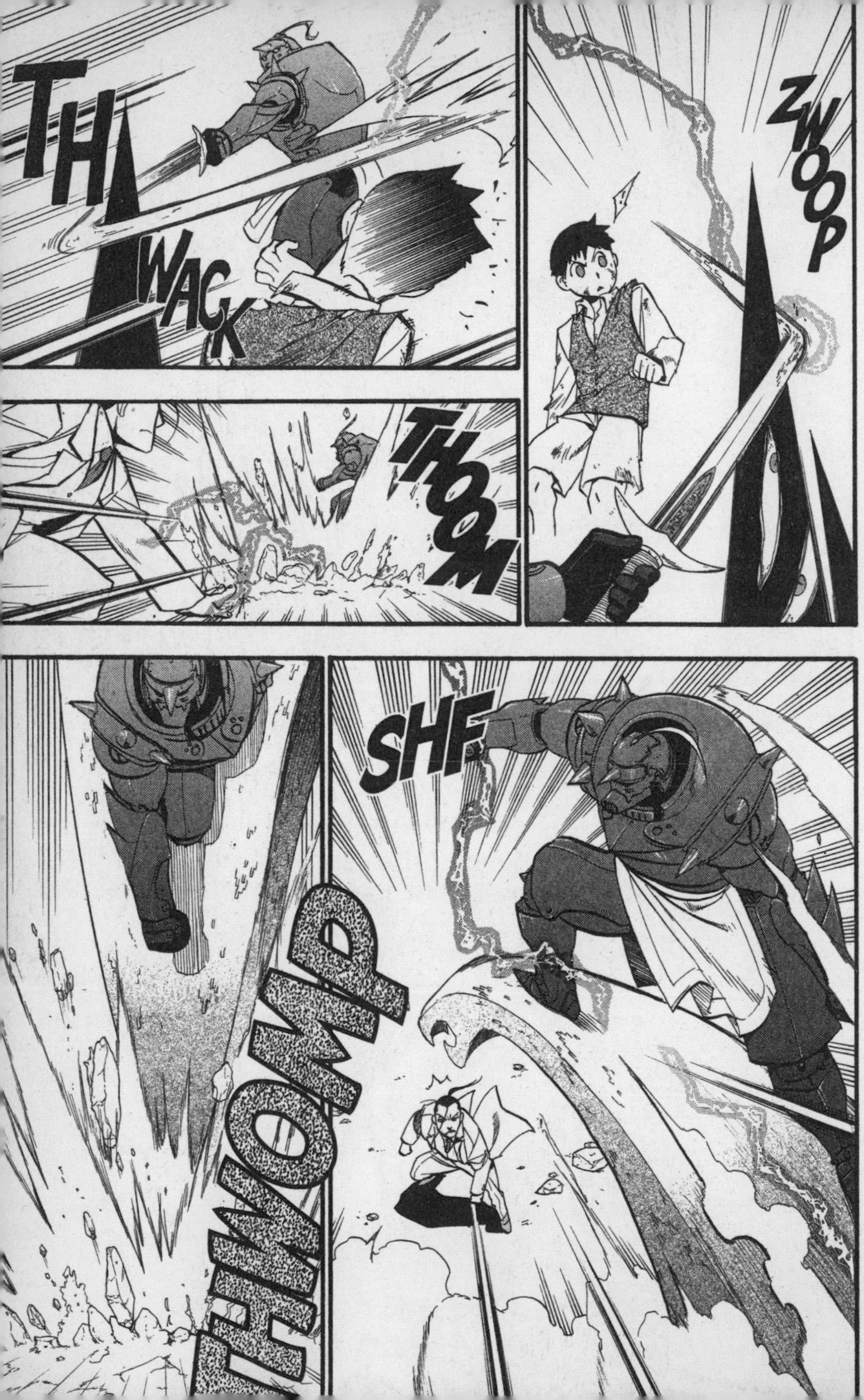
ZWOOP
THWACK
THOOM
SHF
THWOMP

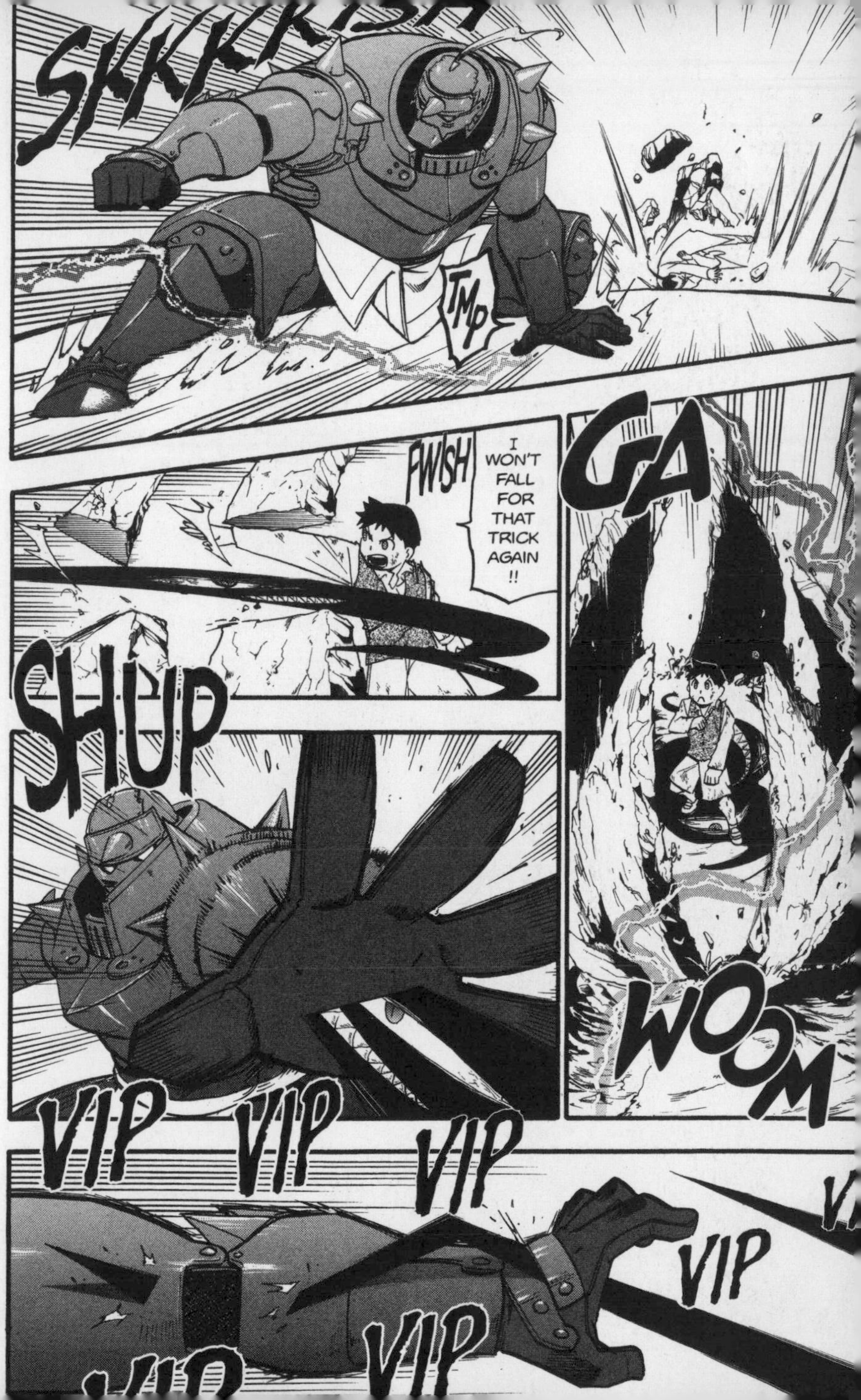
SKKKRSH
TMP
GA
WOOM
FWISH
I WON'T FALL FOR THAT TRICK AGAIN!!
SHUP
VIP
VIP
VIP
VIP
VIP

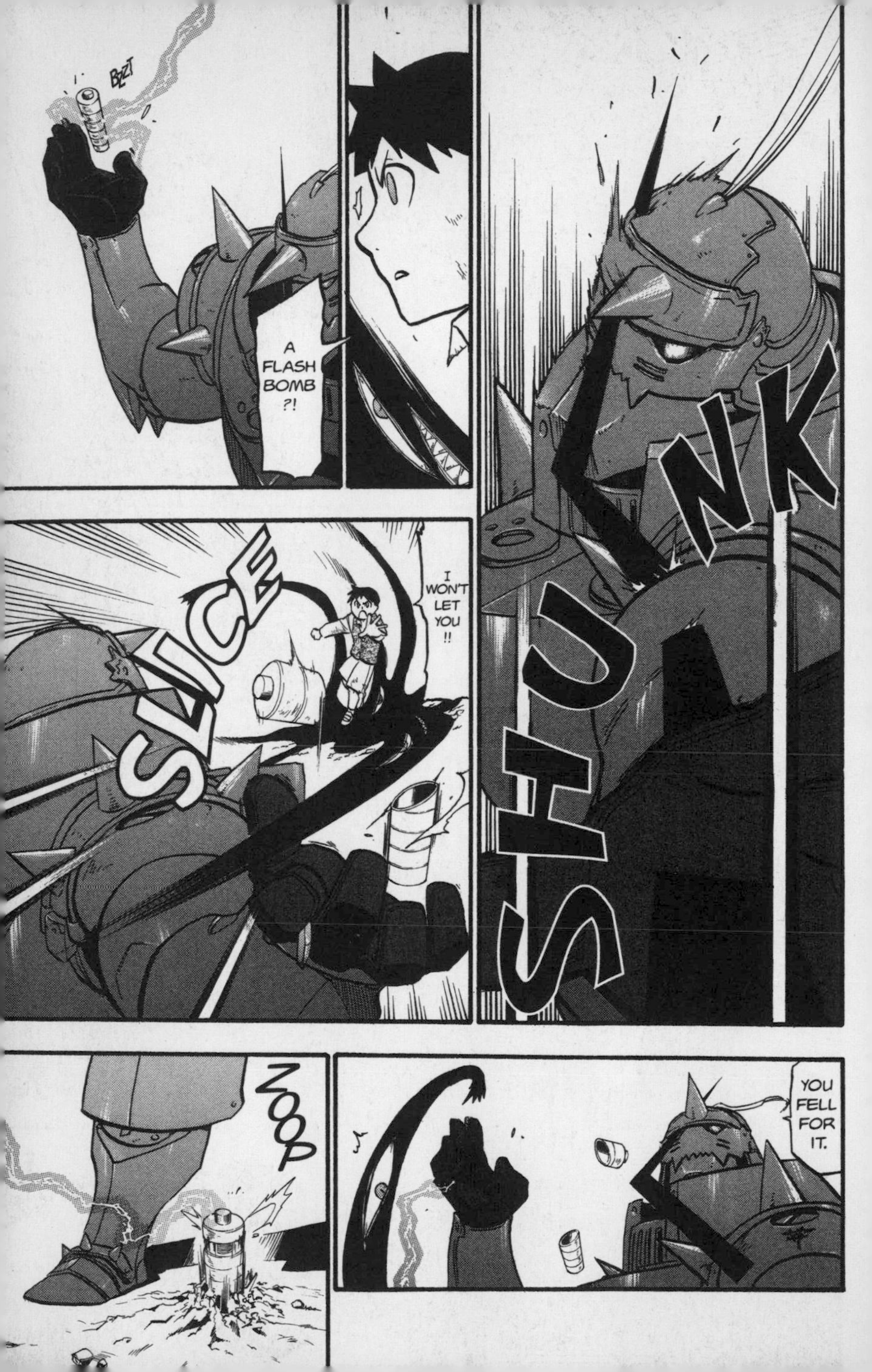
SHUNK
A FLASH BOMB ?!
BZZT
I WON'T LET YOU !!
SLICE
YOU FELL FOR IT.
ZOOP

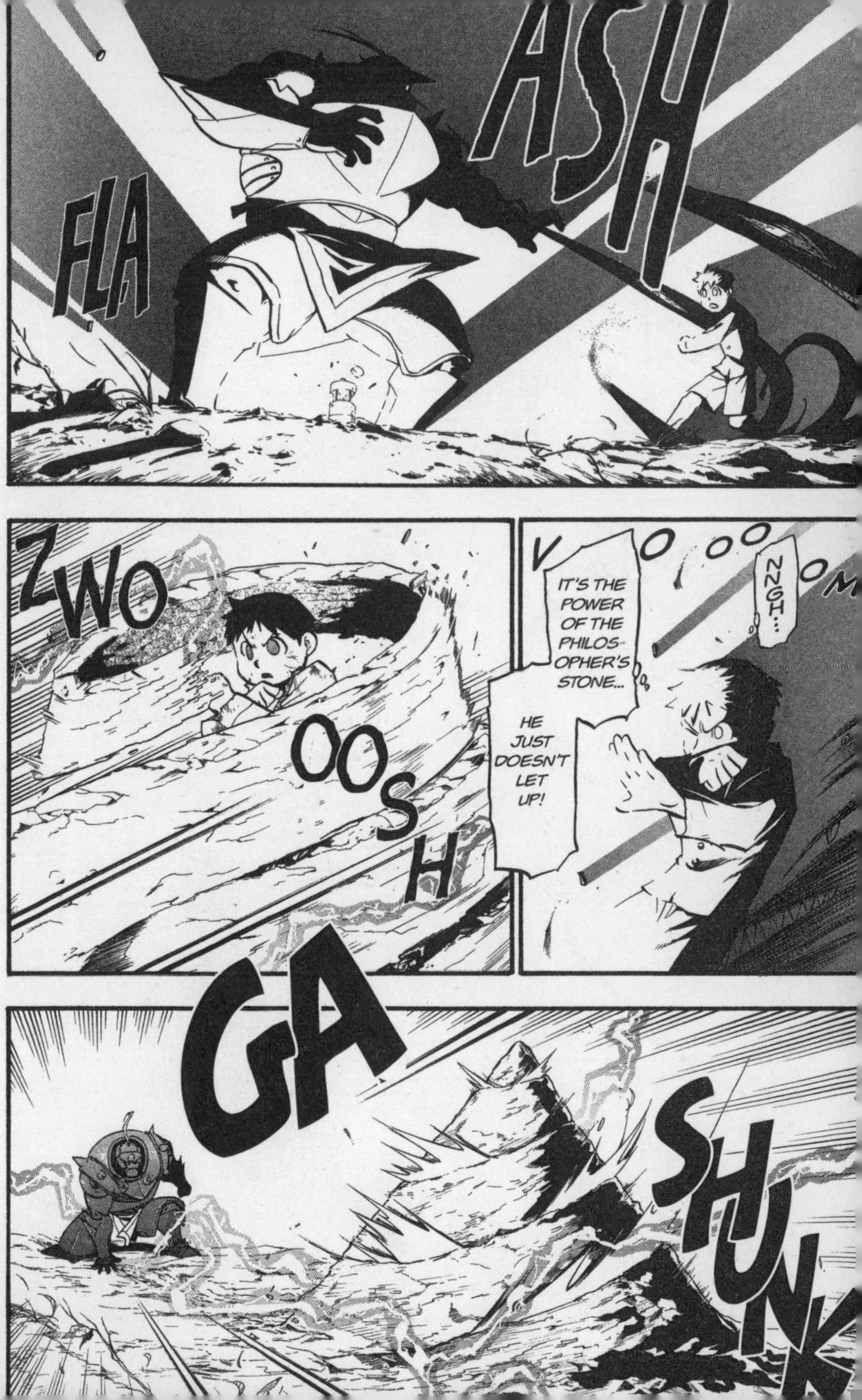
FLA
ASH
VOOOOOM
NNGH...
IT'S THE POWER OF THE PHILOSOPHER'S STONE...
HE JUST DOESN'T LET UP!
ZWO
OOSH
GA
SHUNK

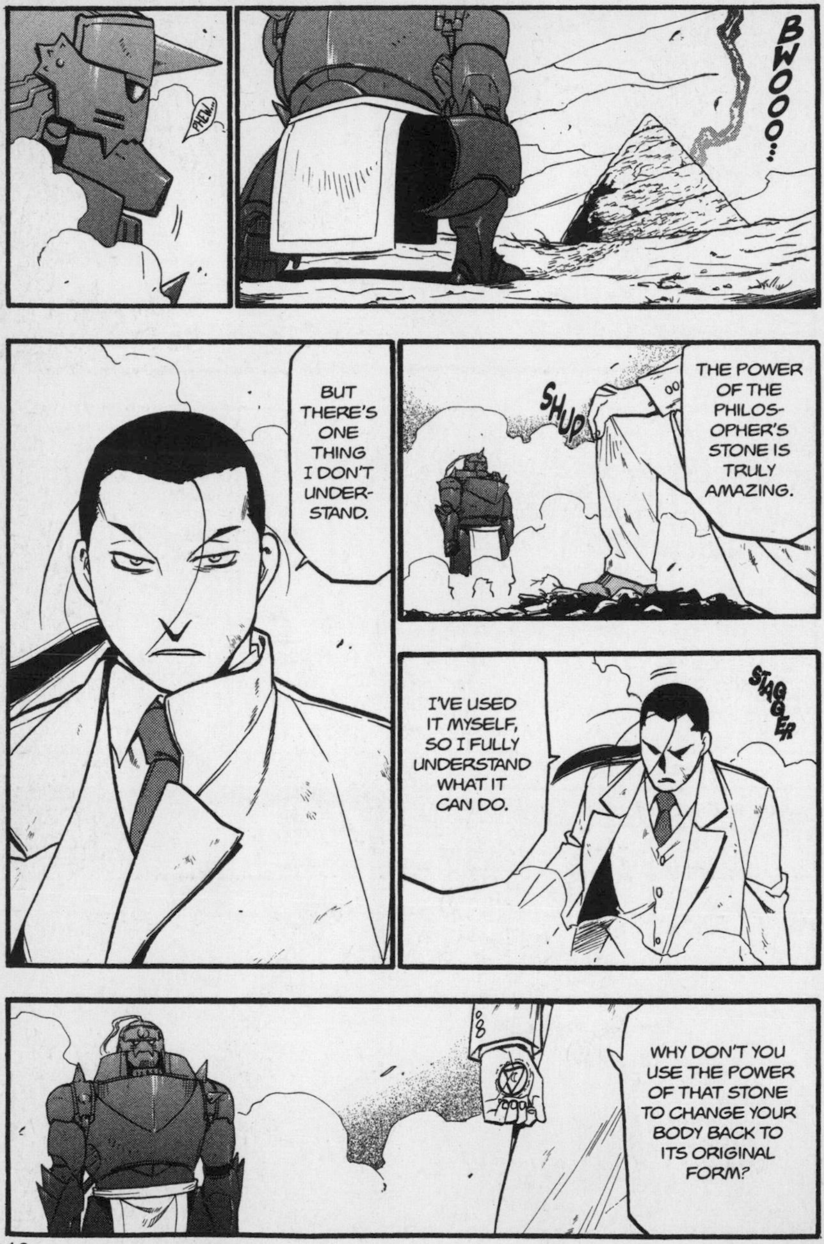
BWOOOO...
PHEW...
THE POWER OF THE PHILOS- OPHER'S STONE IS TRULY AMAZING.
SHUP
I'VE USED IT MYSELF, SO I FULLY UNDERSTAND WHAT IT CAN DO.
STAGGER
BUT THERE'S ONE THING I DON'T UNDER- STAND.
WHY DON'T YOU USE THE POWER OF THAT STONE TO CHANGE YOUR BODY BACK TO ITS ORIGINAL FORM?

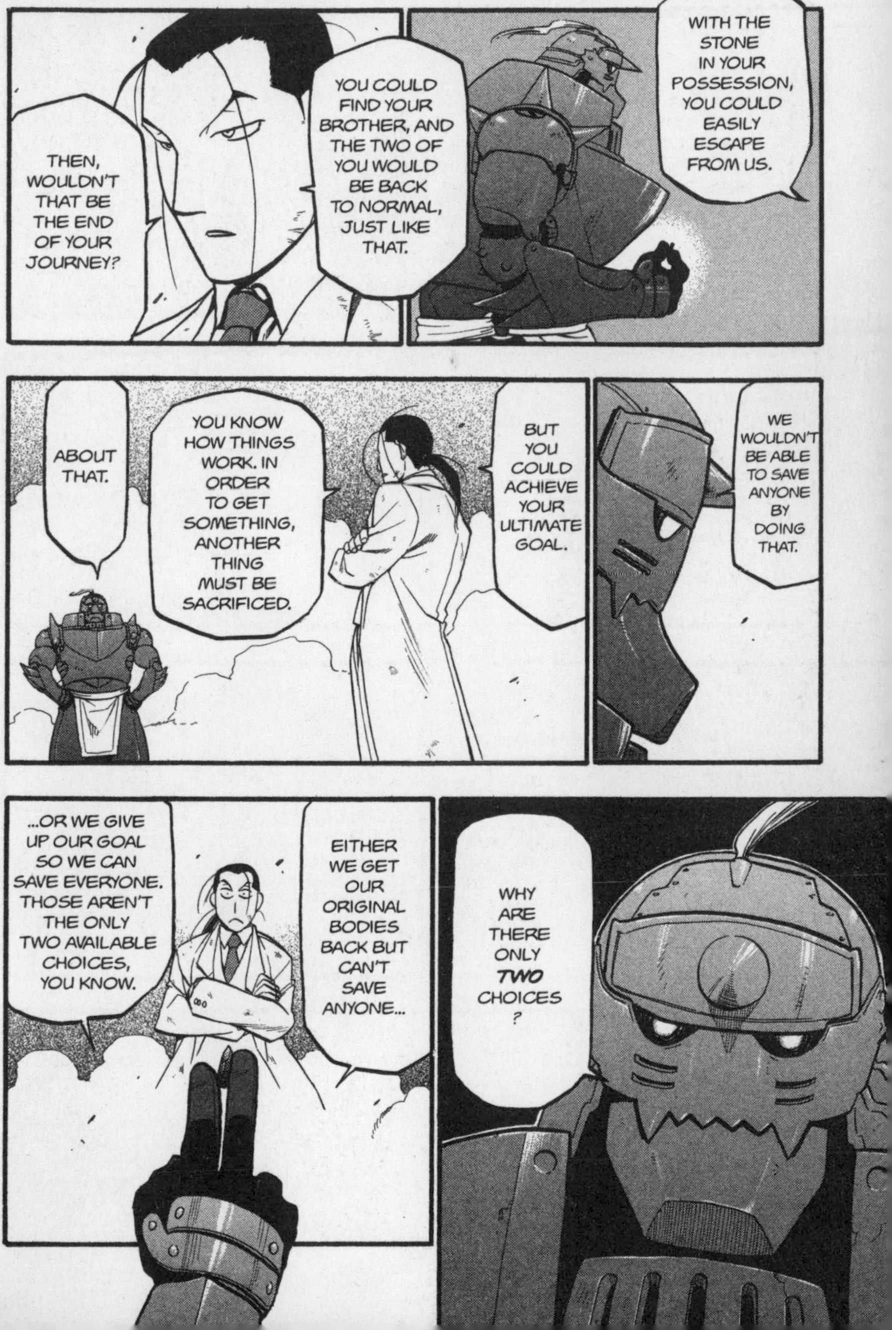
WITH THE STONE IN YOUR POSSESSION, YOU COULD EASILY ESCAPE FROM US.
YOU COULD FIND YOUR BROTHER, AND THE TWO OF YOU WOULD BE BACK TO NORMAL, JUST LIKE THAT.
THEN, WOULDN'T THAT BE THE END OF YOUR JOURNEY?
WE WOULDN'T BE ABLE TO SAVE ANYONE BY DOING THAT.
BUT YOU COULD ACHIEVE YOUR ULTIMATE GOAL.
YOU KNOW HOW THINGS WORK. IN ORDER TO GET SOMETHING, ANOTHER THING MUST BE SACRIFICED.
ABOUT THAT.
WHY ARE THERE ONLY *TWO* CHOICES?
EITHER WE GET OUR ORIGINAL BODIES BACK BUT CAN'T SAVE ANYONE...
...OR WE GIVE UP OUR GOAL SO WE CAN SAVE EVERYONE. THOSE AREN'T THE ONLY TWO AVAILABLE CHOICES, YOU KNOW.

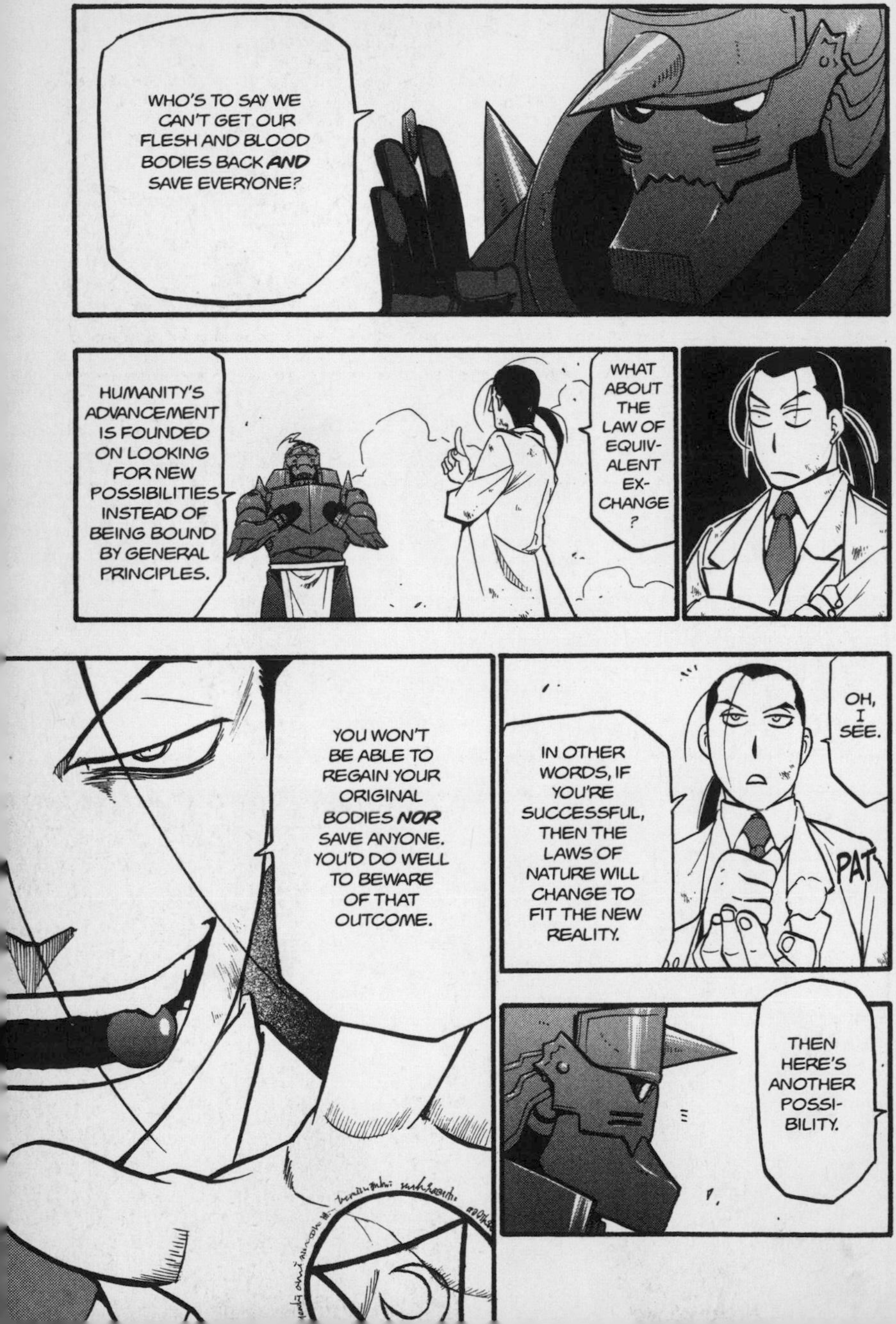
WHO'S TO SAY WE CAN'T GET OUR FLESH AND BLOOD BODIES BACK ***AND*** SAVE EVERYONE?
WHAT ABOUT THE LAW OF EQUIV-ALENT EX-CHANGE ?
HUMANITY'S ADVANCEMENT IS FOUNDED ON LOOKING FOR NEW POSSIBILITIES INSTEAD OF BEING BOUND BY GENERAL PRINCIPLES.
OH, I SEE.
IN OTHER WORDS, IF YOU'RE SUCCESSFUL, THEN THE LAWS OF NATURE WILL CHANGE TO FIT THE NEW REALITY.
PAT
THEN HERE'S ANOTHER POSSI-BILITY.
YOU WON'T BE ABLE TO REGAIN YOUR ORIGINAL BODIES ***NOR*** SAVE ANYONE. YOU'D DO WELL TO BEWARE OF THAT OUTCOME.

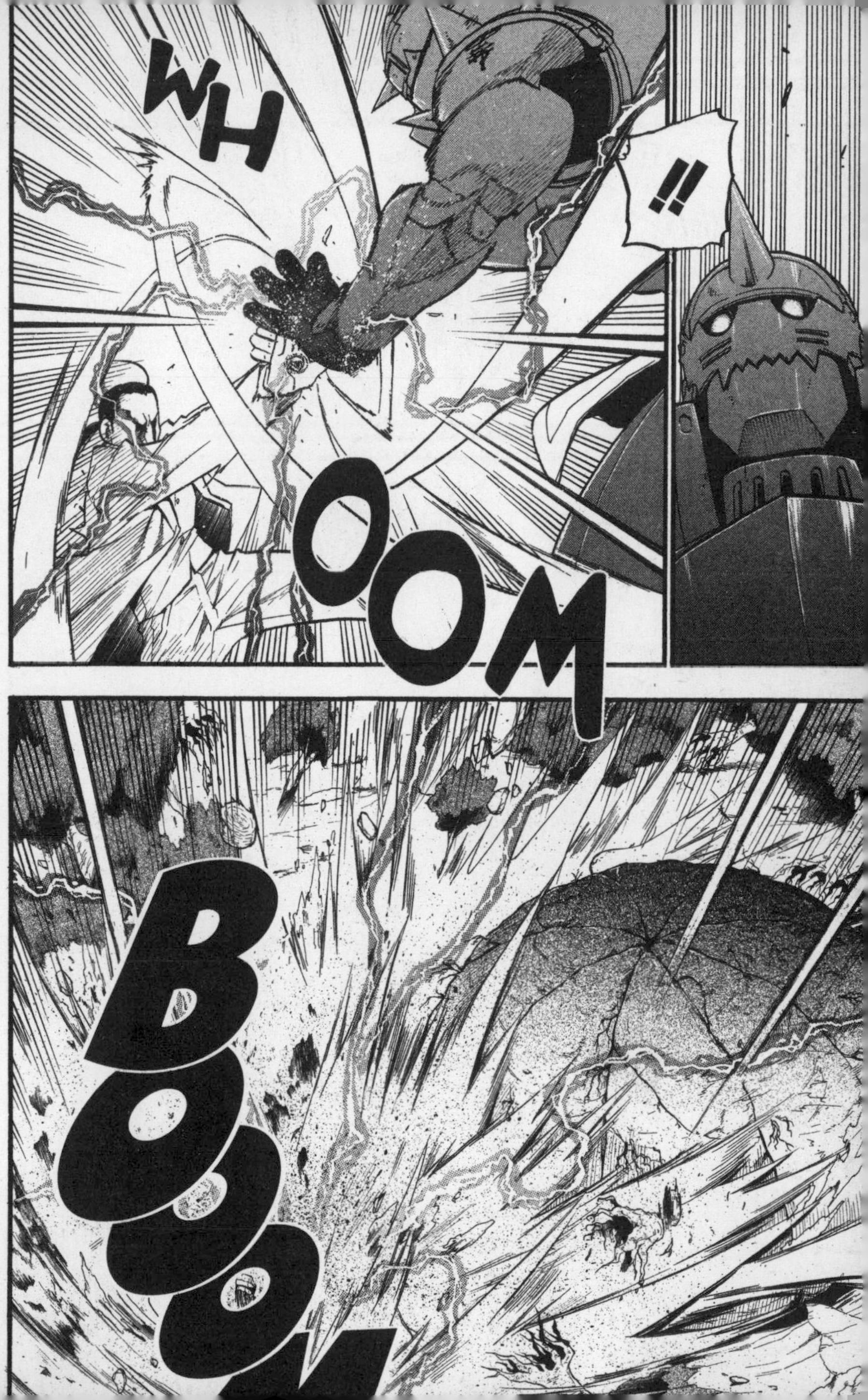
!!
WH
OOM
BOOOO

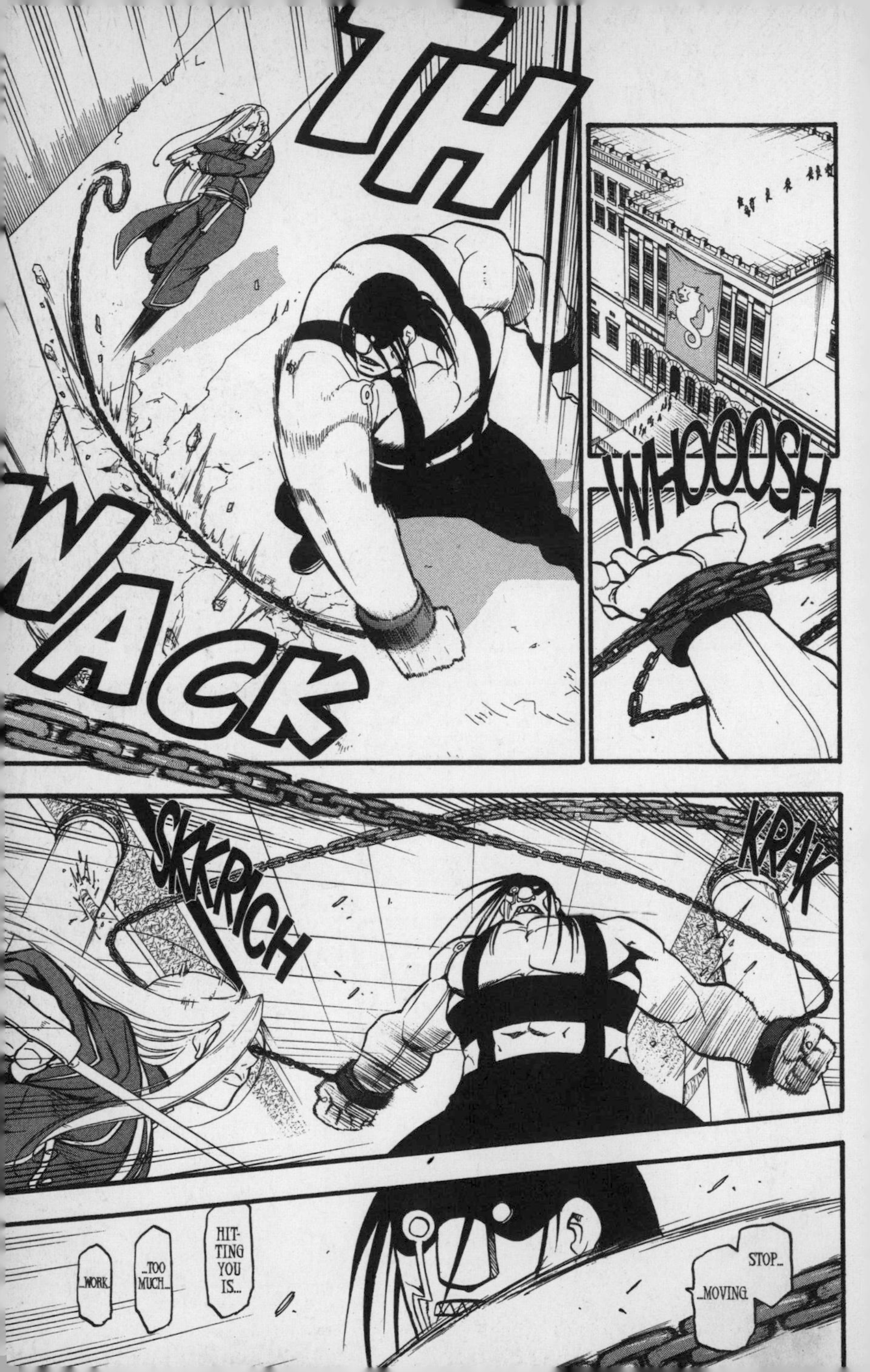
WHOOOSH
WHACK
KRAK
SKKRICH
STOP...
...MOVING.
HIT-TING YOU IS...
...TOO MUCH...
...WORK.

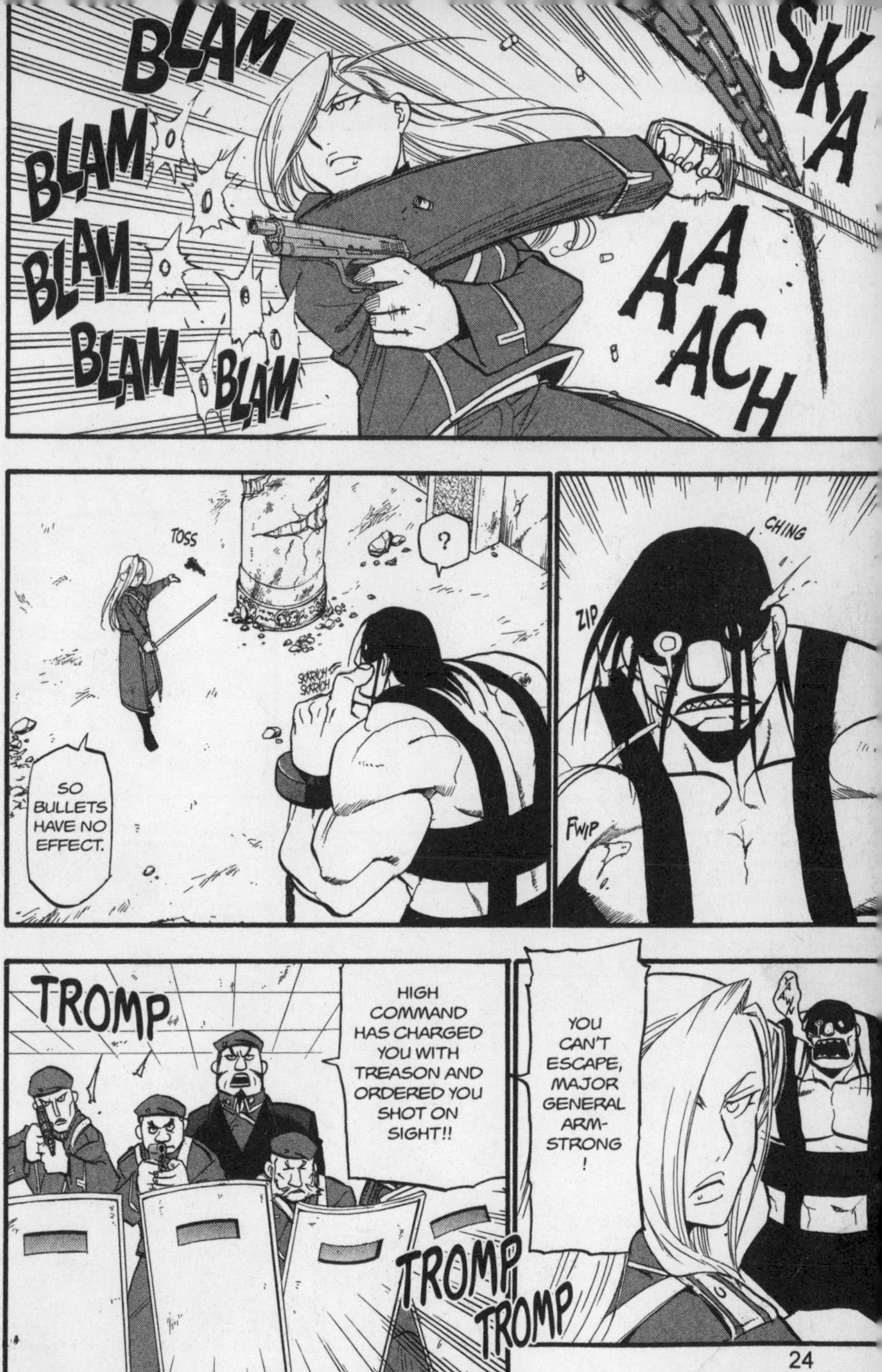
SKAAAACH
BLAM
BLAM
BLAM
BLAM
BLAM
CHING
ZIP
FWIP
?
TOSS
SKRRICH SKRRICH
SO BULLETS HAVE NO EFFECT.
YAWN
YOU CAN'T ESCAPE, MAJOR GENERAL ARM-STRONG!
TROMP
HIGH COMMAND HAS CHARGED YOU WITH TREASON AND ORDERED YOU SHOT ON SIGHT!!
TROMP
TROMP

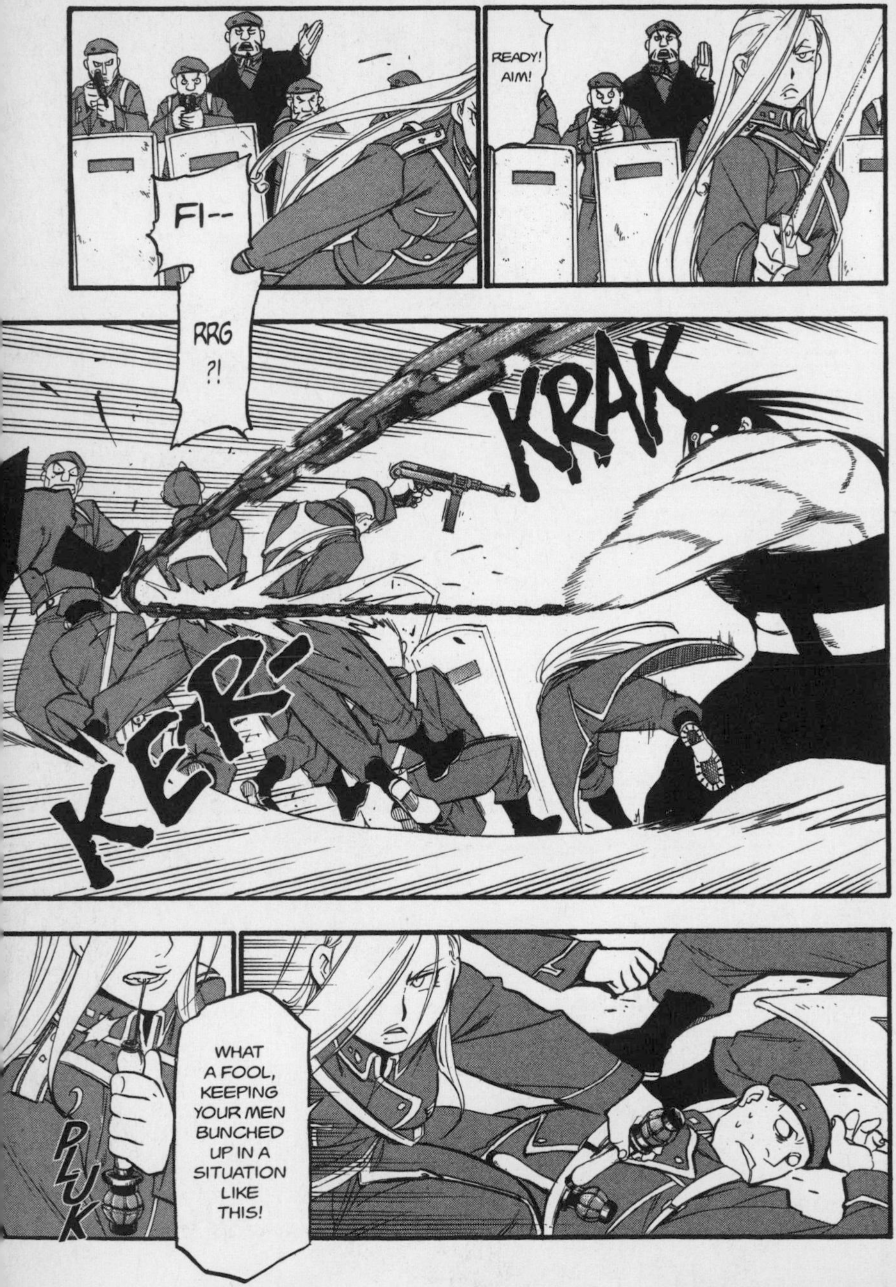
READY! AIM!
FI--
RRG ?!
KRAK
KER-
WHAT A FOOL, KEEPING YOUR MEN BUNCHED UP IN A SITUATION LIKE THIS!
PLUK

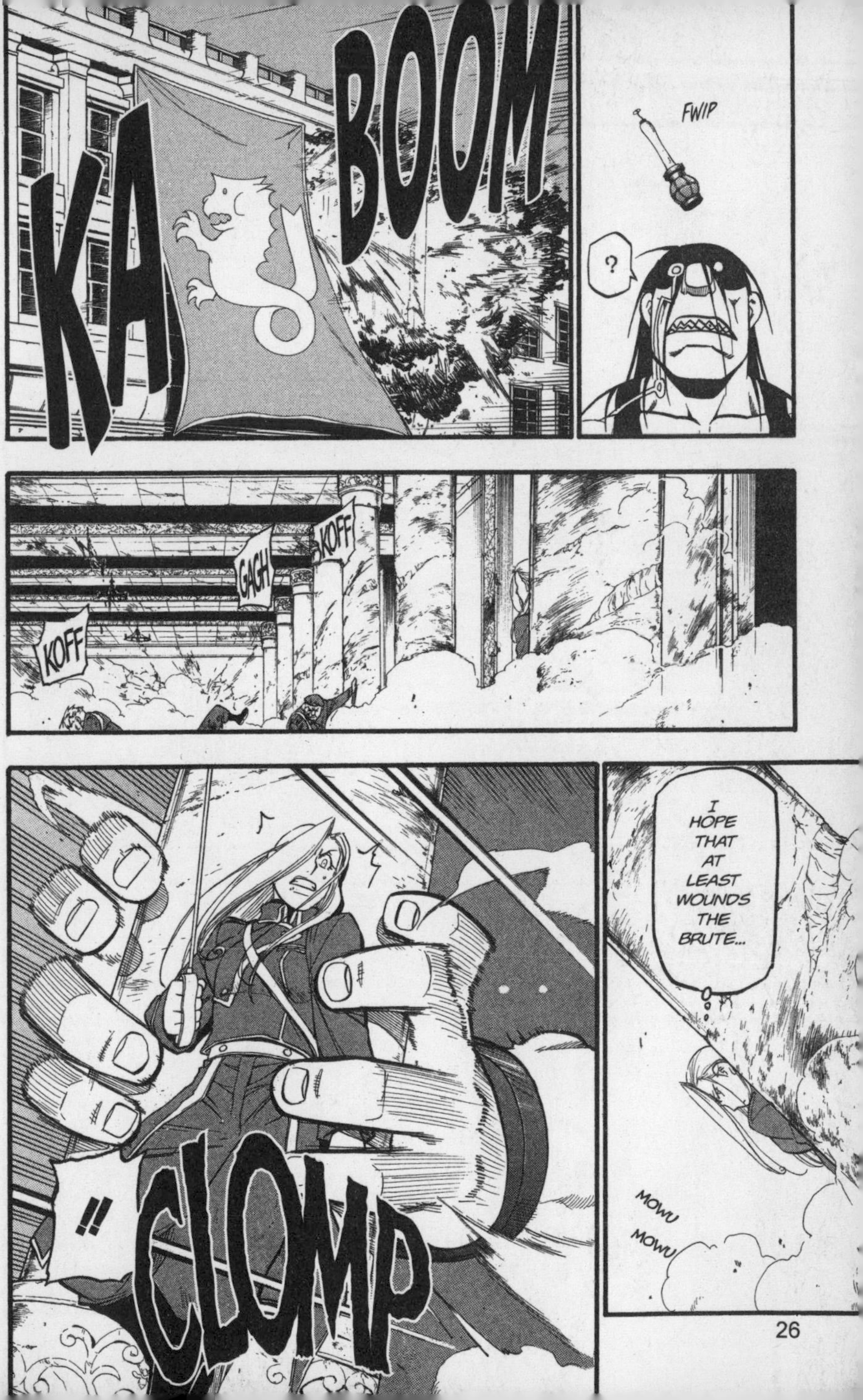
FWIP
?
KA
BOOM
KOFF
GAGH
KOFF
I HOPE THAT AT LEAST WOUNDS THE BRUTE...
MOWU
MOWU
!!
CLOMP

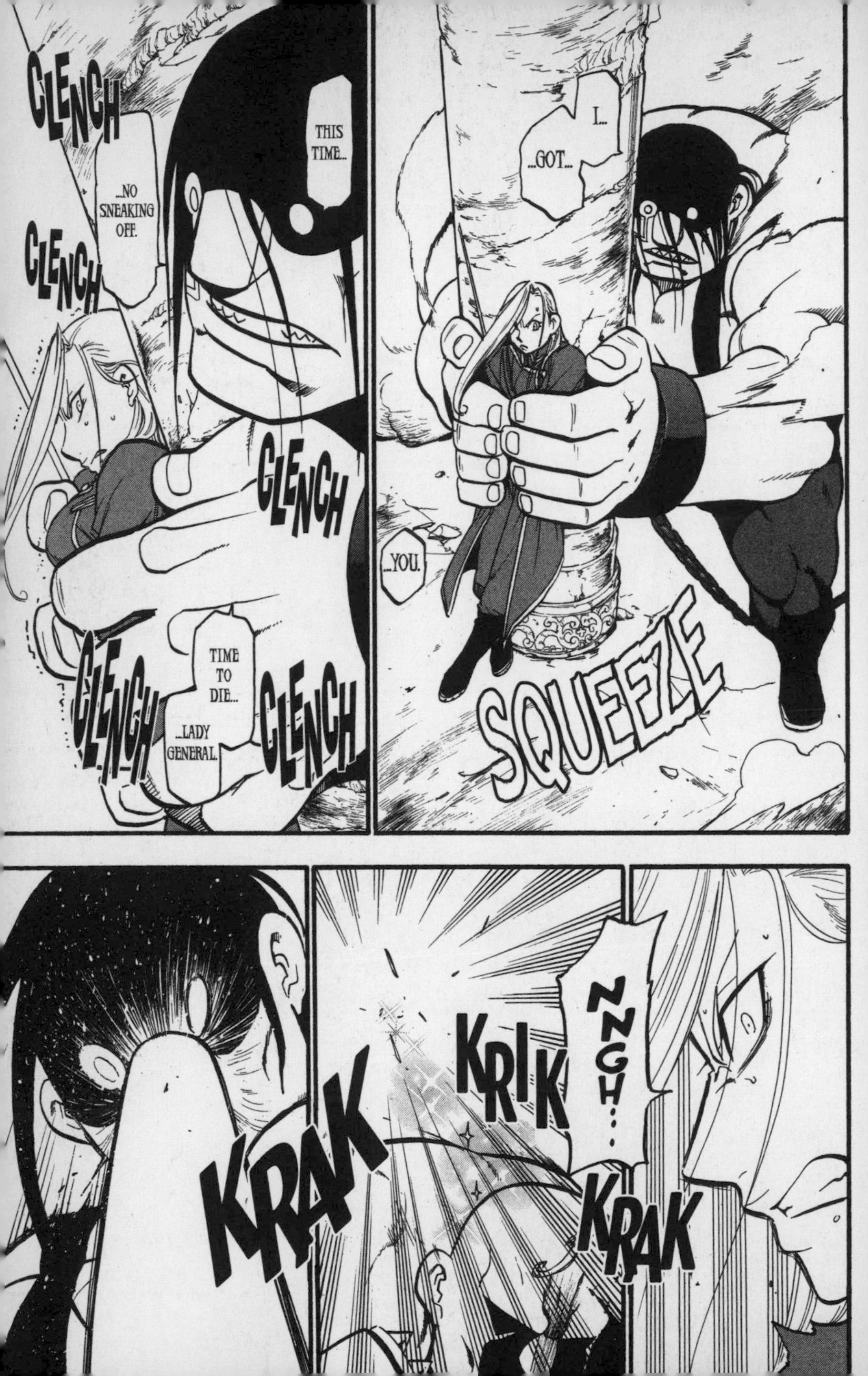
I...
...GOT...
...YOU.
SQUEEZE
THIS TIME...
...NO SNEAKING OFF.
CLENCH
CLENCH
CLENCH
TIME TO DIE...
...LADY GENERAL.
CLENCH
CLENCH
NNGH...
KRAK
KRIK
KRAK

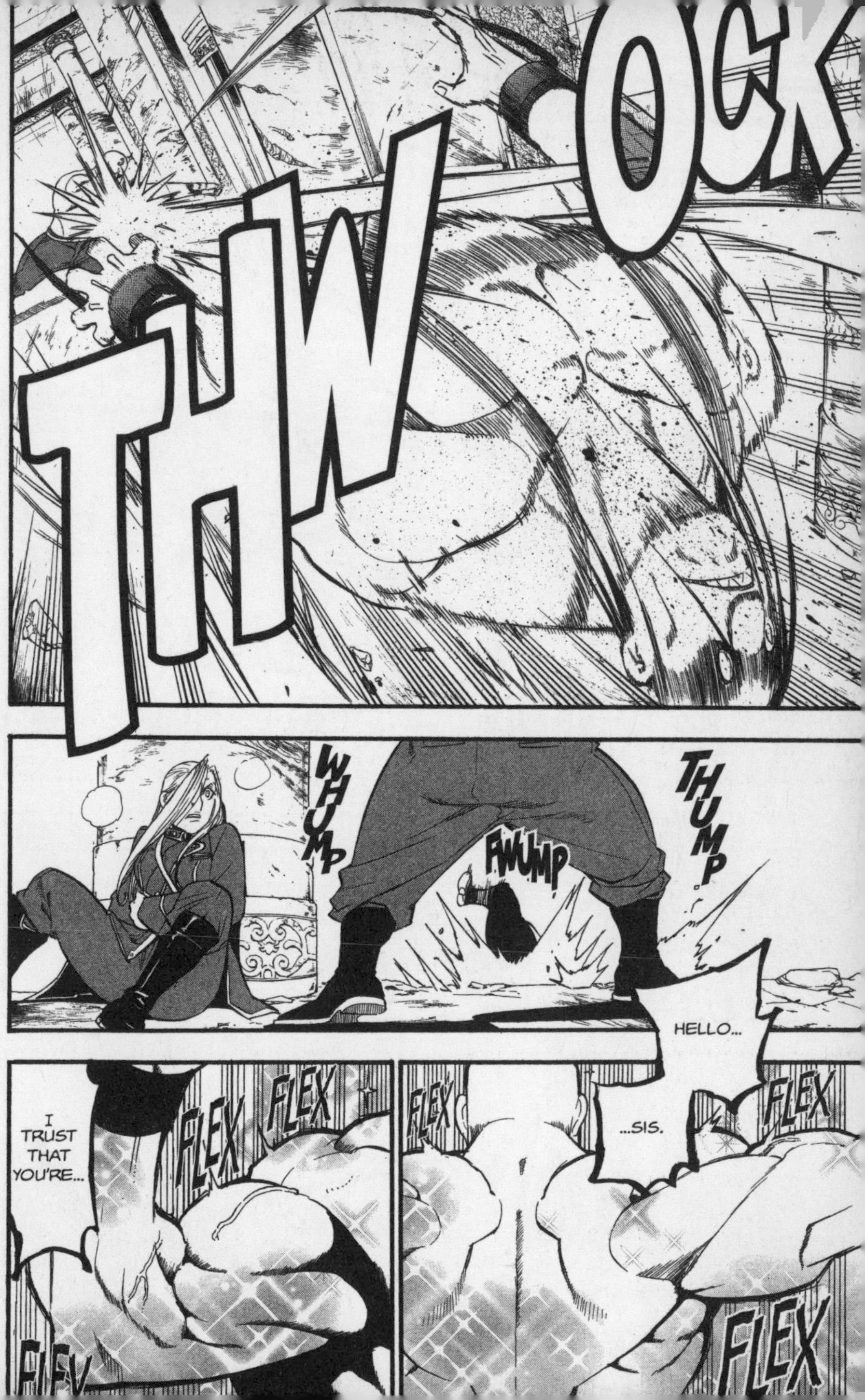
THWOCK
THUMP
FWUMP
WHUMP
HELLO...
...SIS.
FLEX
FLEX
FLEX
I TRUST THAT YOU'RE...
FLEX
FLEX

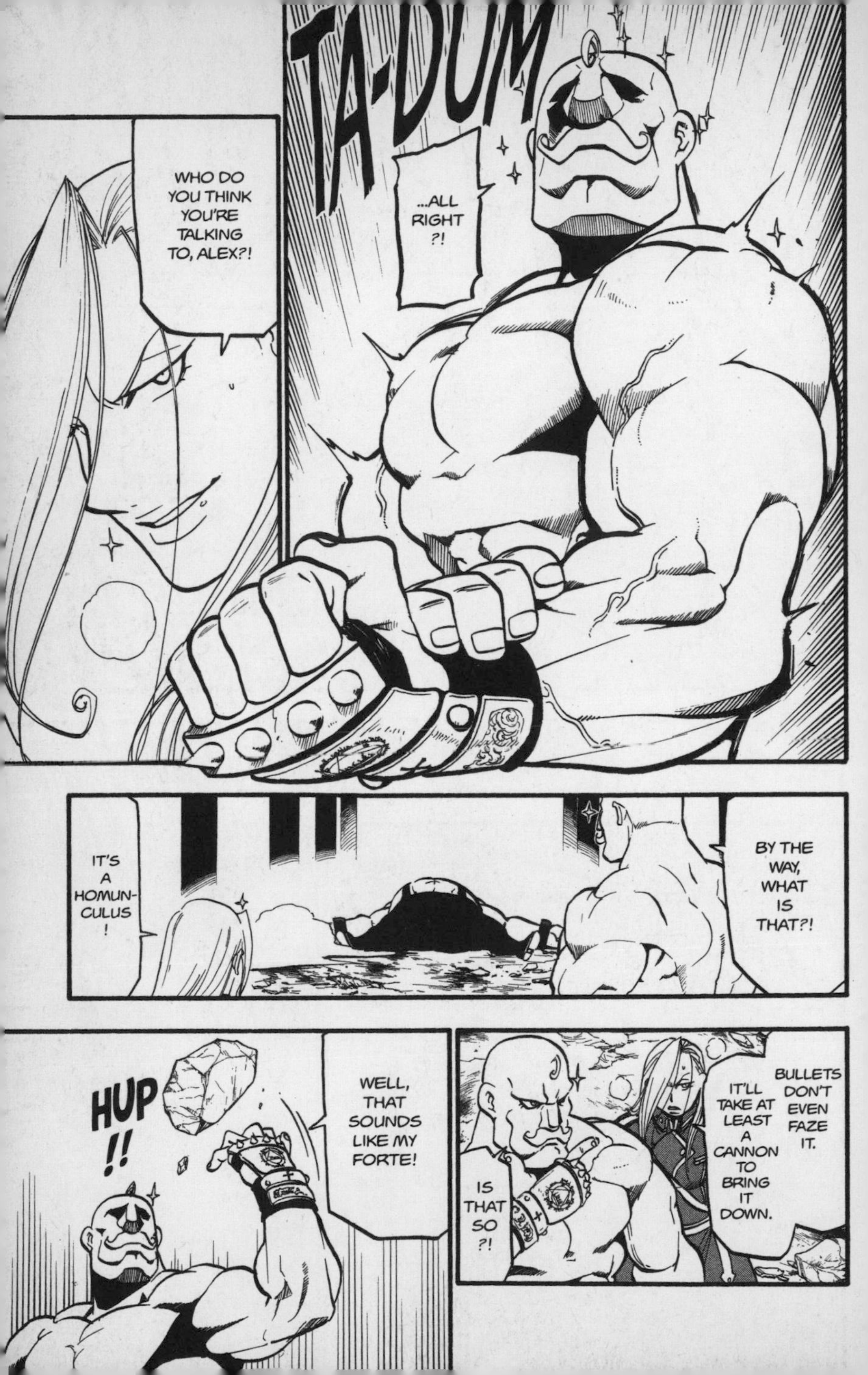
TA-DUM
...ALL RIGHT ?!
WHO DO YOU THINK YOU'RE TALKING TO, ALEX?!
BY THE WAY, WHAT IS THAT?!
IT'S A HOMUN-CULUS !
BULLETS DON'T EVEN FAZE IT.
IT'LL TAKE AT LEAST A CANNON TO BRING IT DOWN.
IS THAT SO ?!
HUP !!
WELL, THAT SOUNDS LIKE MY FORTE!

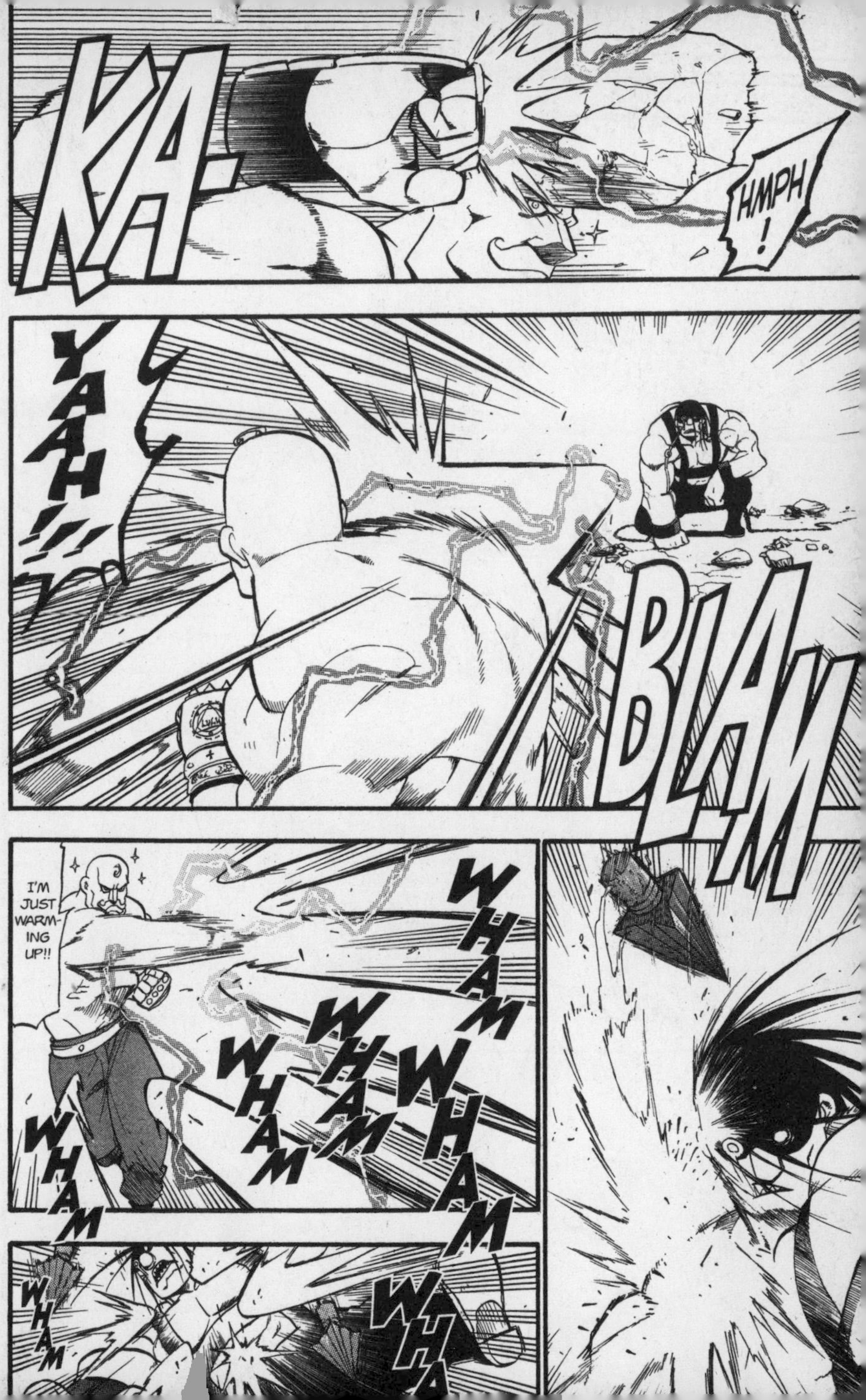
HMPH!
KA-
BLAM
YAAH!!!!!
WHAM
WHAM
WHA
I'M JUST WARMING-UP!!
WHAM
WHAM
WHAM
WHAM
WHAM
WHAM

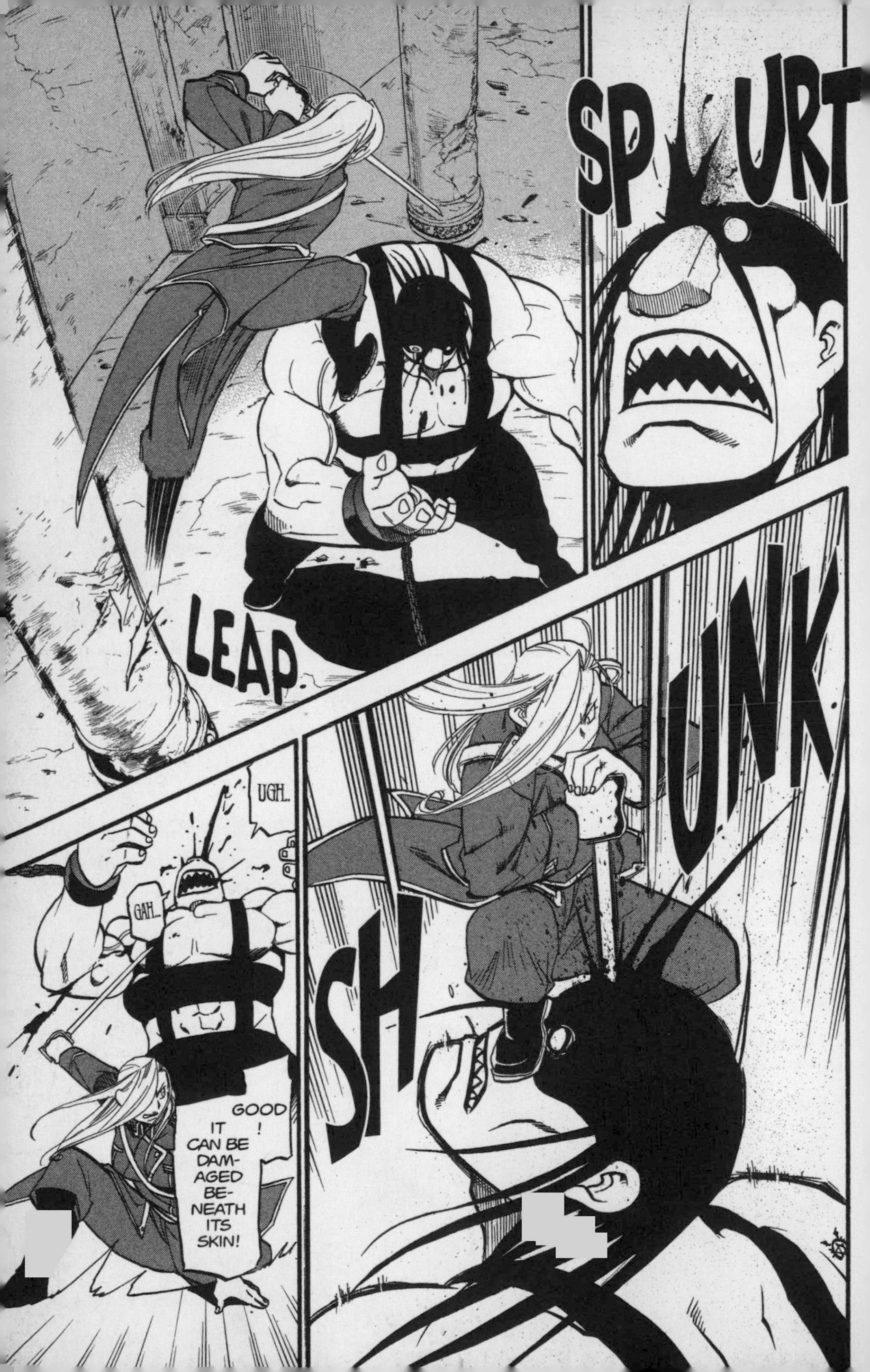
SP URT
LEAP
UNK
SH
UGH.
GAH...
GOOD! IT CAN BE DAM-AGED BE-NEATH ITS SKIN!

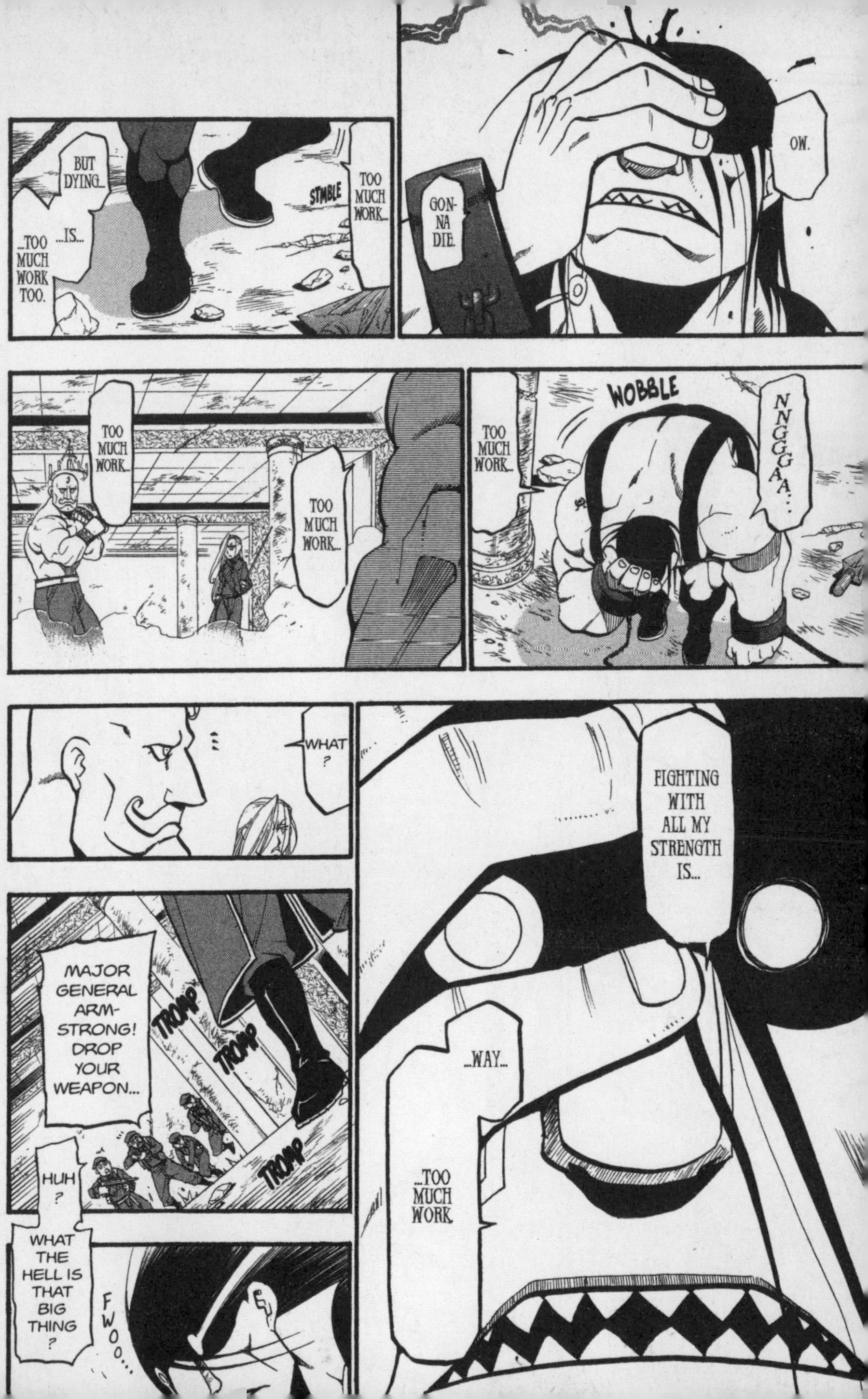
OW.
GON-NA DIE.
TOO MUCH WORK...
STMBLE
BUT DYING...
...IS...
...TOO MUCH WORK TOO.
NNGGAA...
WOBBLE
TOO MUCH WORK...
TOO MUCH WORK...
TOO MUCH WORK...
FIGHTING WITH ALL MY STRENGTH IS...
...WAY...
...TOO MUCH WORK.
WHAT?
MAJOR GENERAL ARMSTRONG! DROP YOUR WEAPON...
TROMP
TROMP
TROMP
HUH?
WHAT THE HELL IS THAT BIG THING?
FWOO...

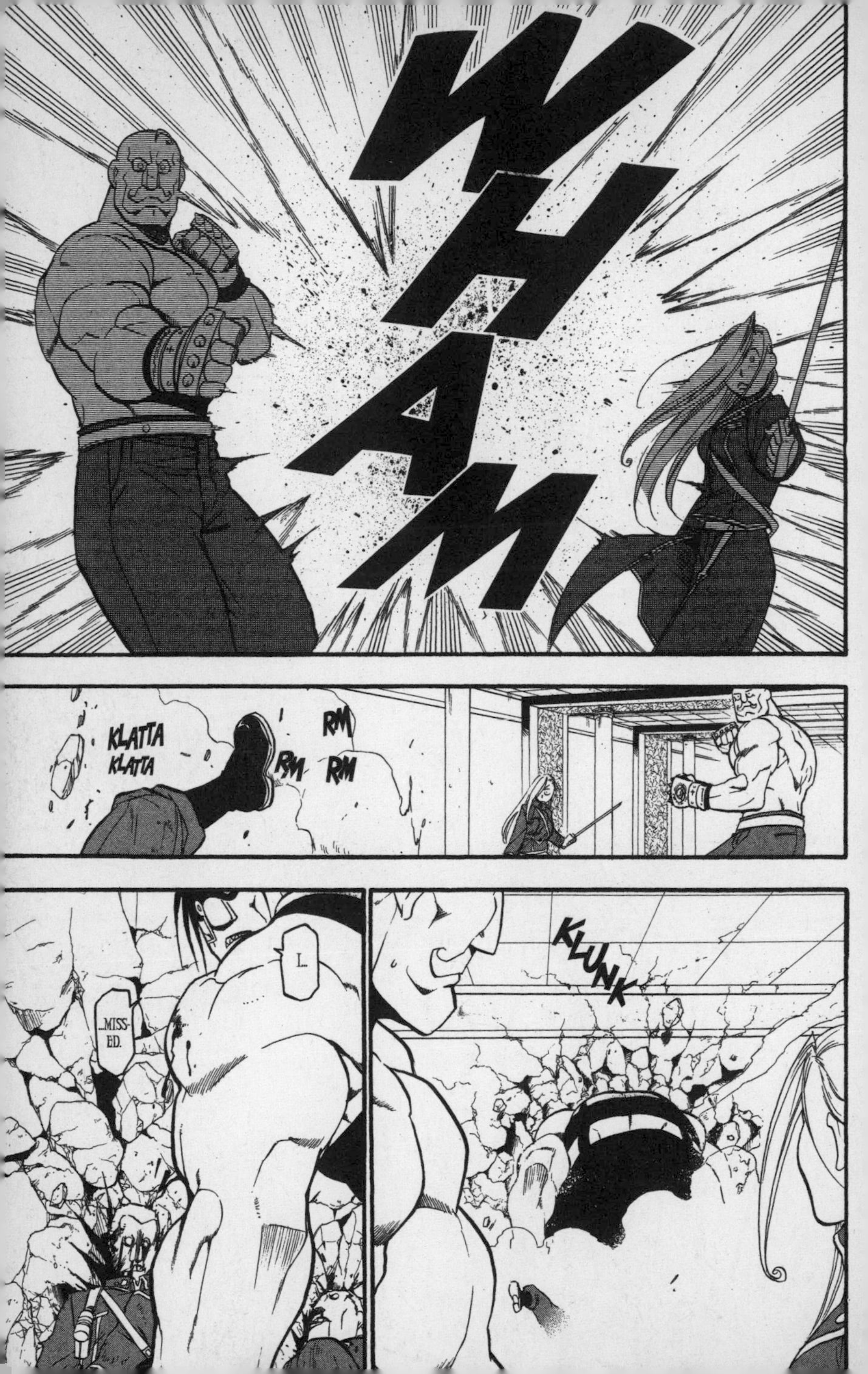
WHAM
RM RM RM
KLATTA KLATTA
KLUNK
L.
...MISS-ED.

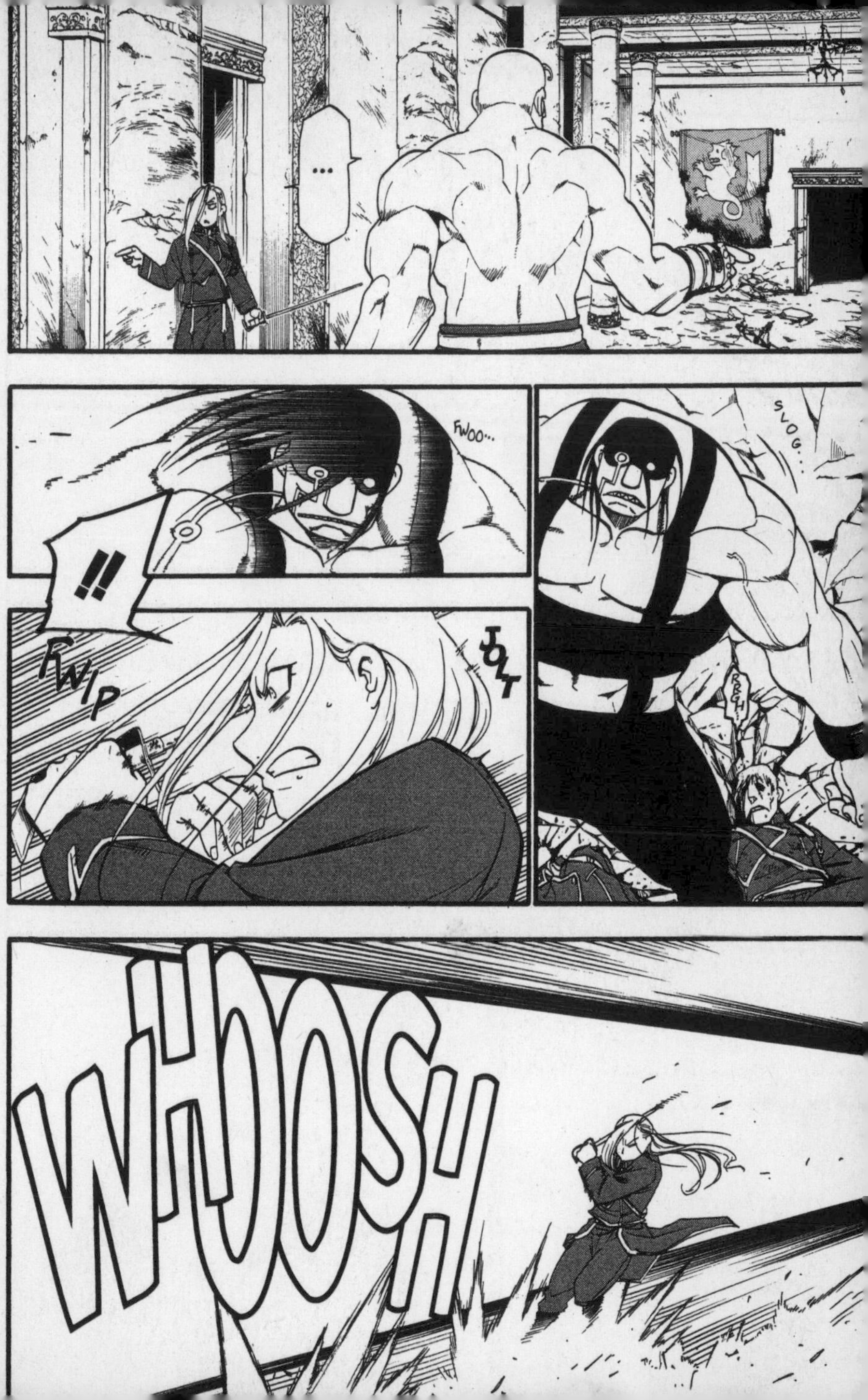
...
SLOG...
RRGH!
FWOO...
!!
FWIP
JOLT
WHOOSH

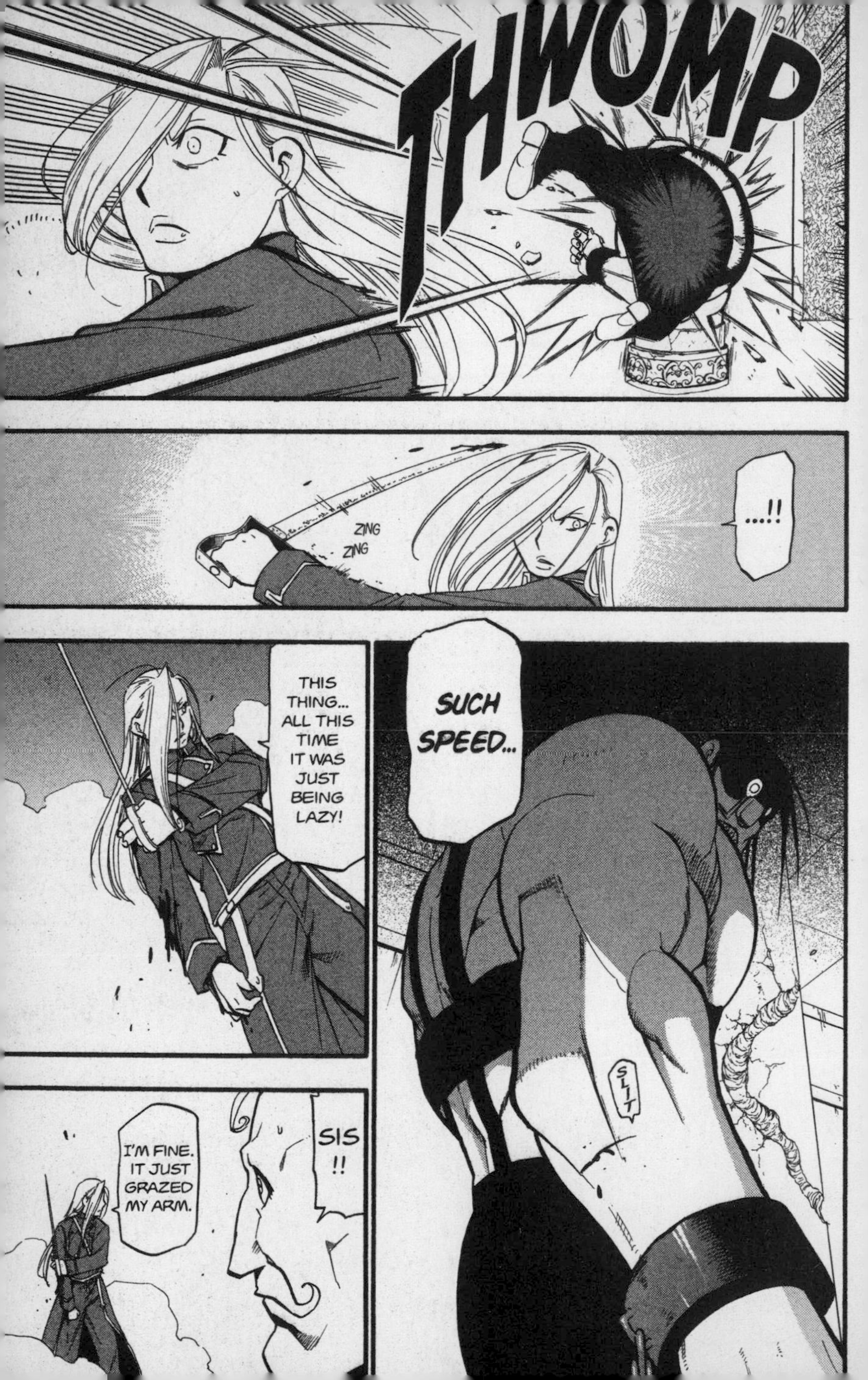
THWOMP
....!!
ZING
ZING
SUCH SPEED...
SLIT
THIS THING... ALL THIS TIME IT WAS JUST BEING LAZY!
SIS !!
I'M FINE. IT JUST GRAZED MY ARM.

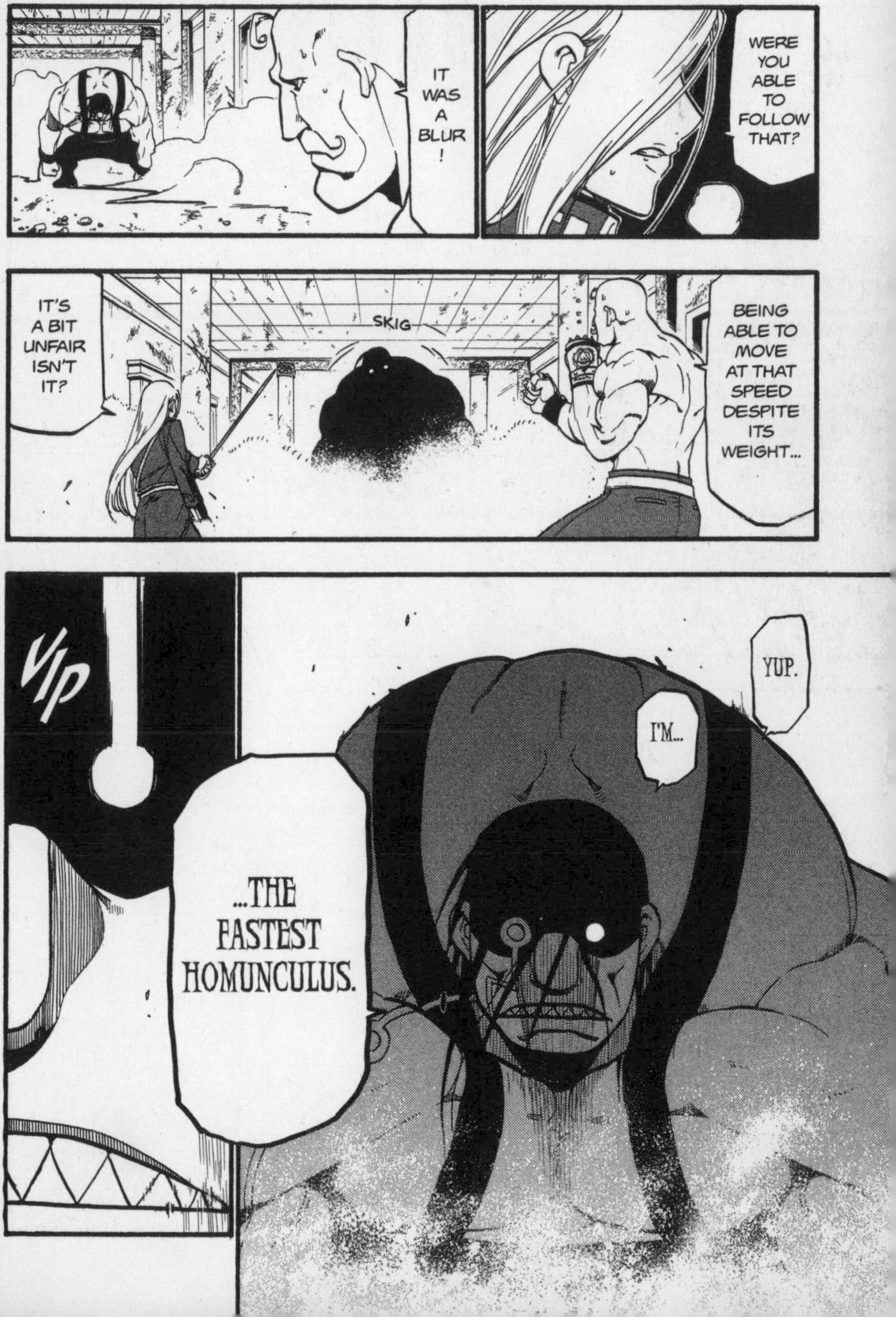
WERE YOU ABLE TO FOLLOW THAT?
IT WAS A BLUR!
BEING ABLE TO MOVE AT THAT SPEED DESPITE ITS WEIGHT...
SKIG
IT'S A BIT UNFAIR ISN'T IT?
YUP.
I'M...
...THE FASTEST HOMUNCULUS.
VIP

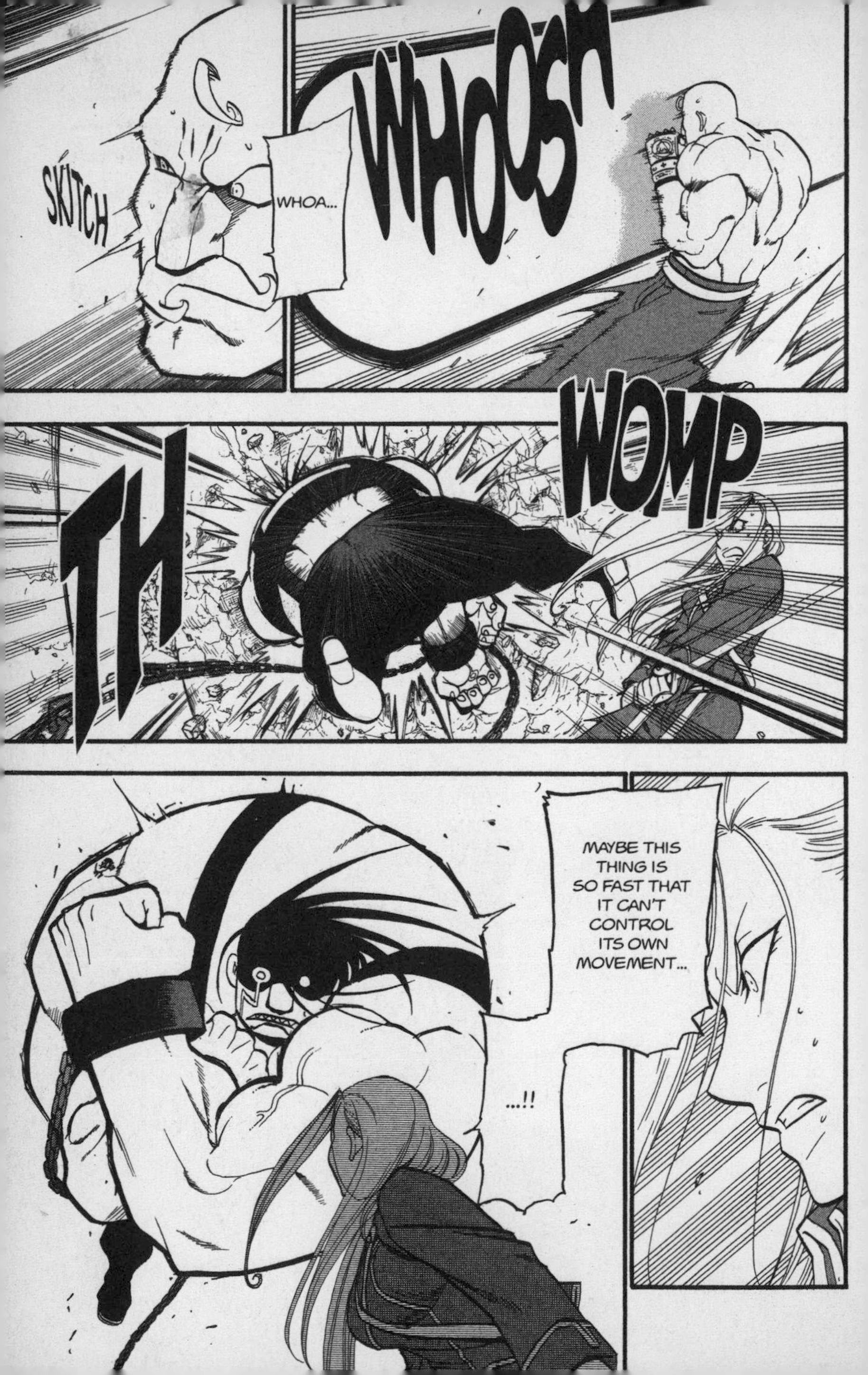
WHOOSH
WHOA...
SKITCH
WOMP
TH
MAYBE THIS THING IS SO FAST THAT IT CAN'T CONTROL ITS OWN MOVEMENT...
...!!

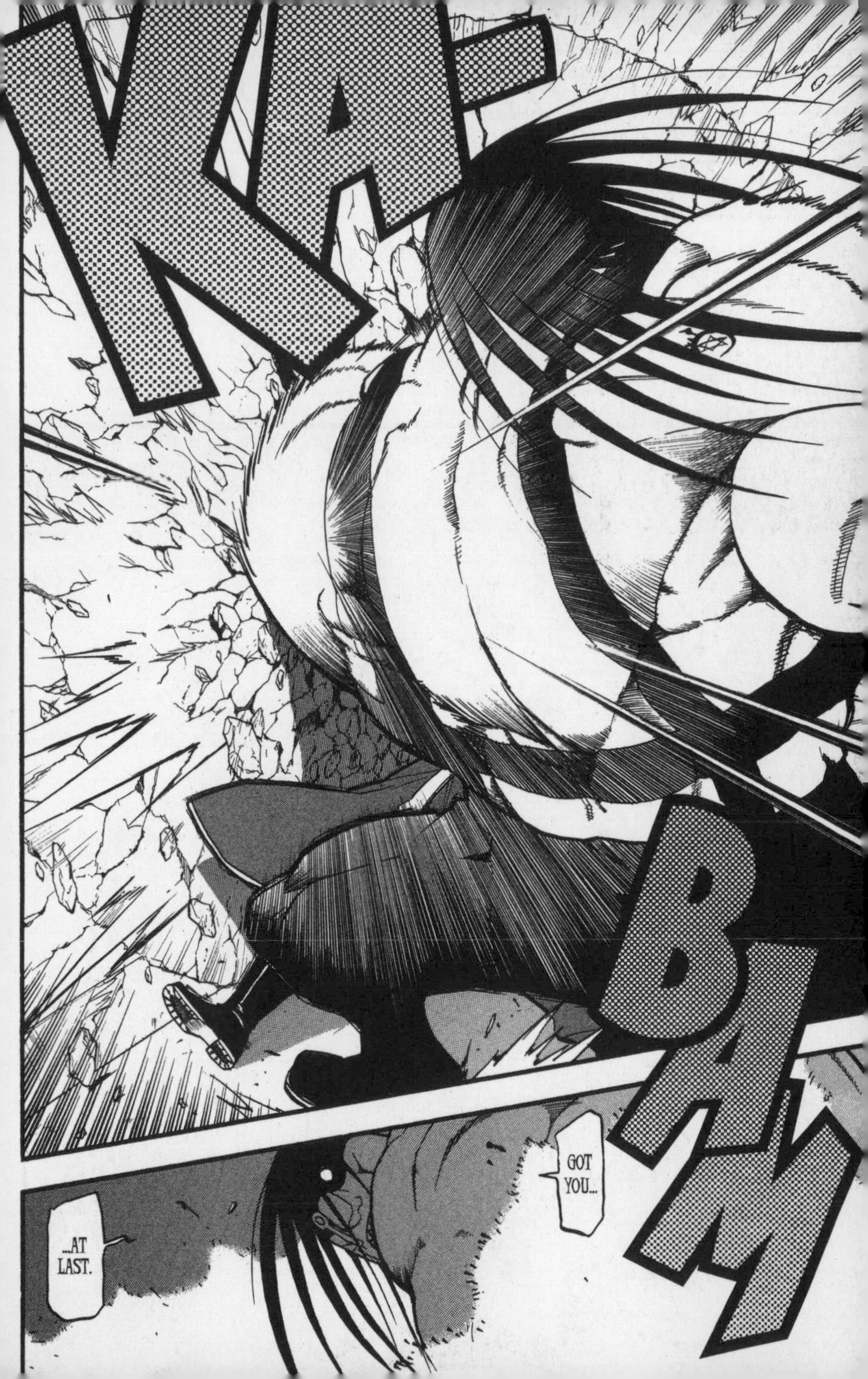
KA
GOT YOU...
...AT LAST.

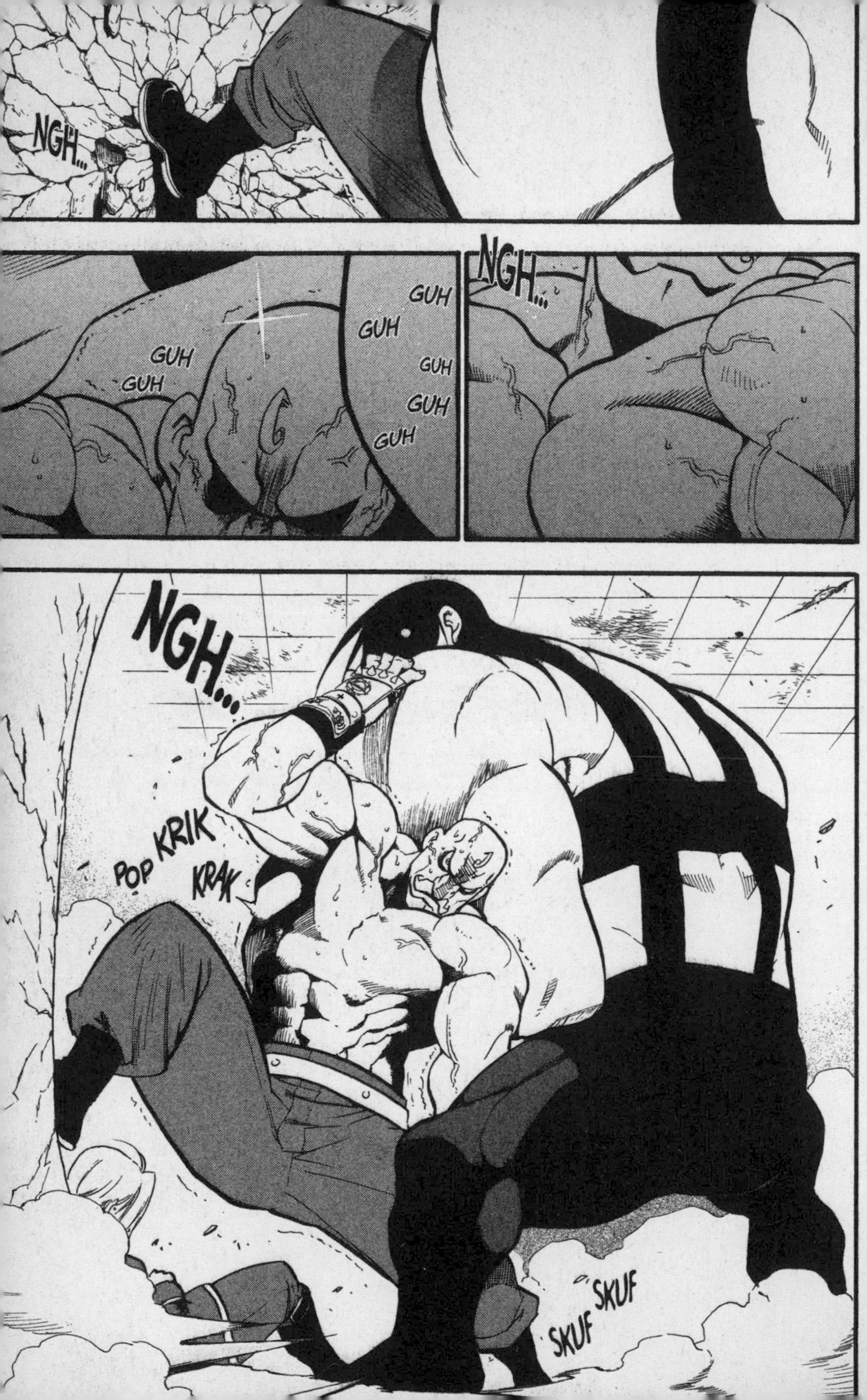
NGH...
NGH...
GUH
GUH
GUH
GUH
GUH
GUH
GUH
NGH...
POP
KRIK
KRAK
SKUF
SKUF

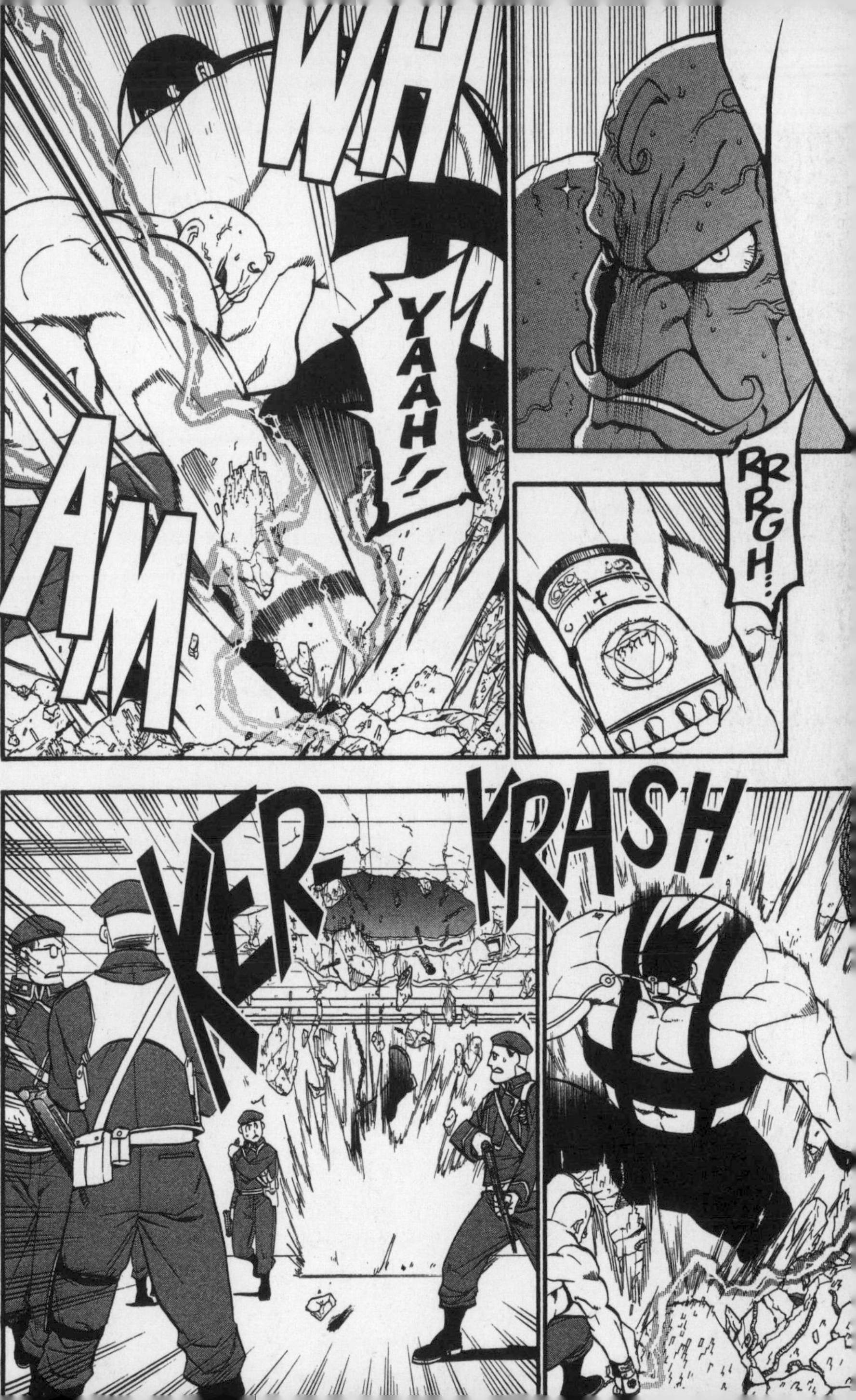
RRRGH!!
WHAM
YAAAH!!
KER-KRASH

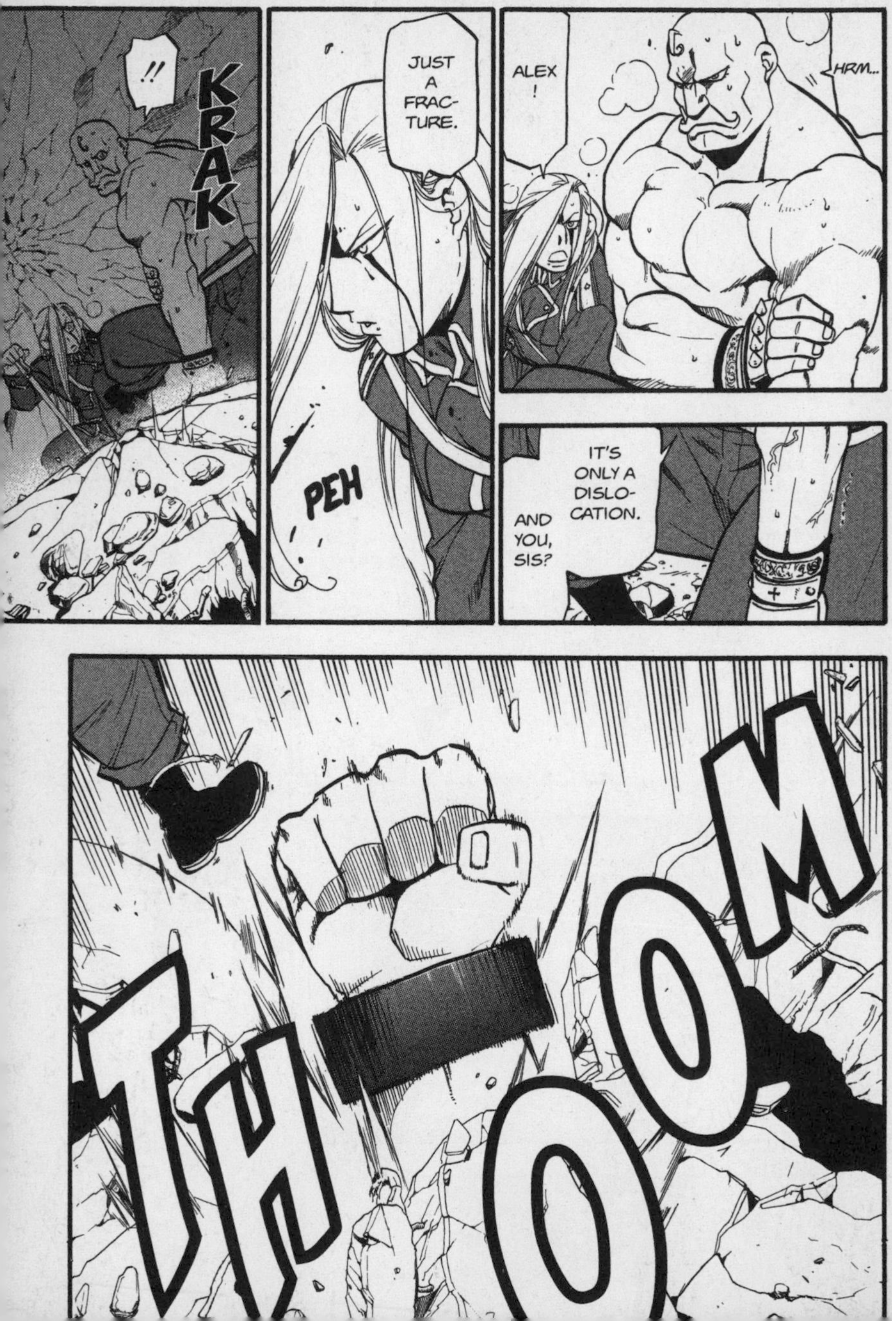
HRM...
ALEX!
IT'S ONLY A DISLOCATION.
AND YOU, SIS?
JUST A FRACTURE.
PEH
!!
KRAK
THOOOM

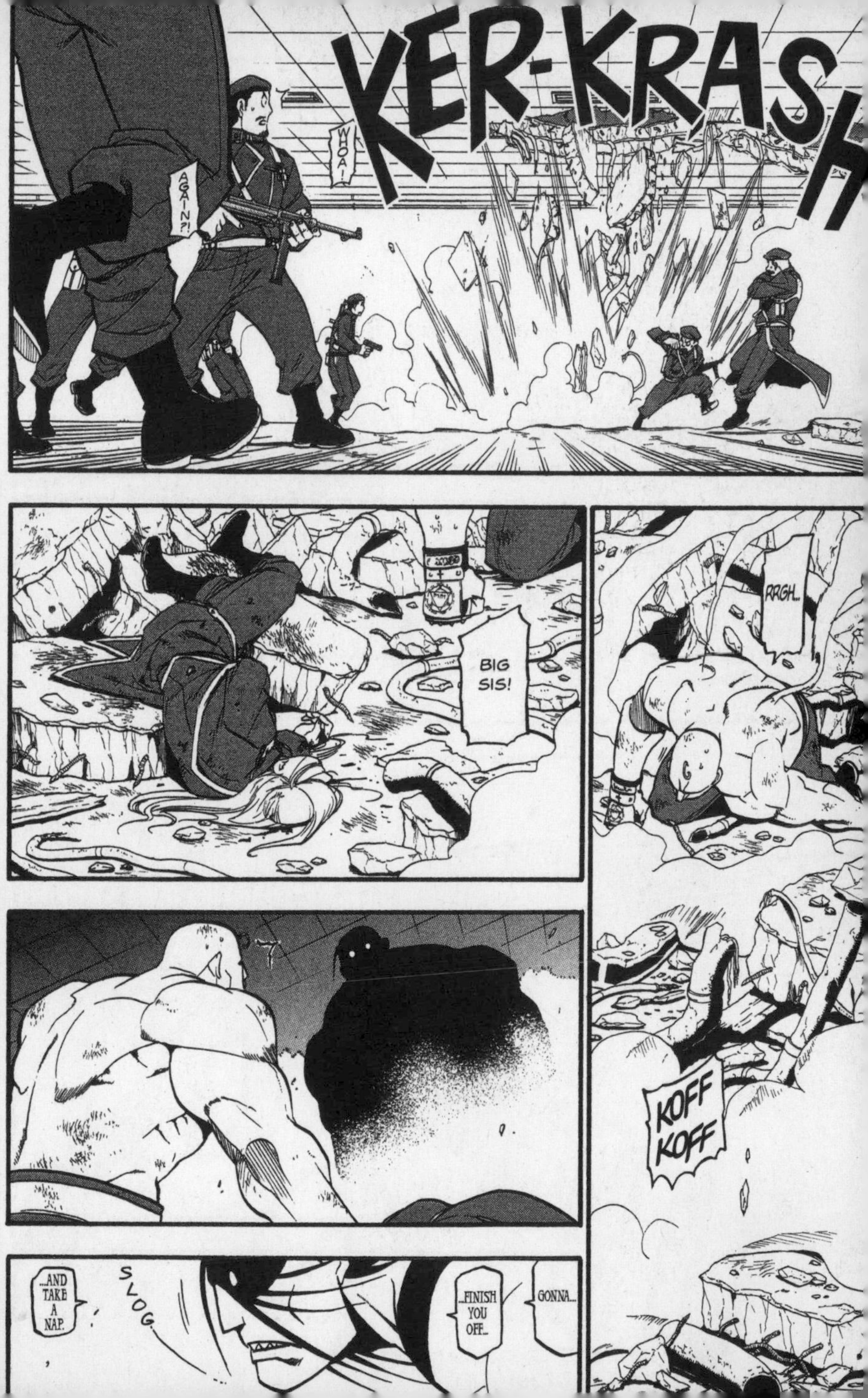
KER-KRASH
WHOA!
AGAIN?!
RRGH...
KOFF KOFF
BIG SIS!
GONNA...
...FINISH YOU OFF...
SLOG
...AND TAKE A NAP.

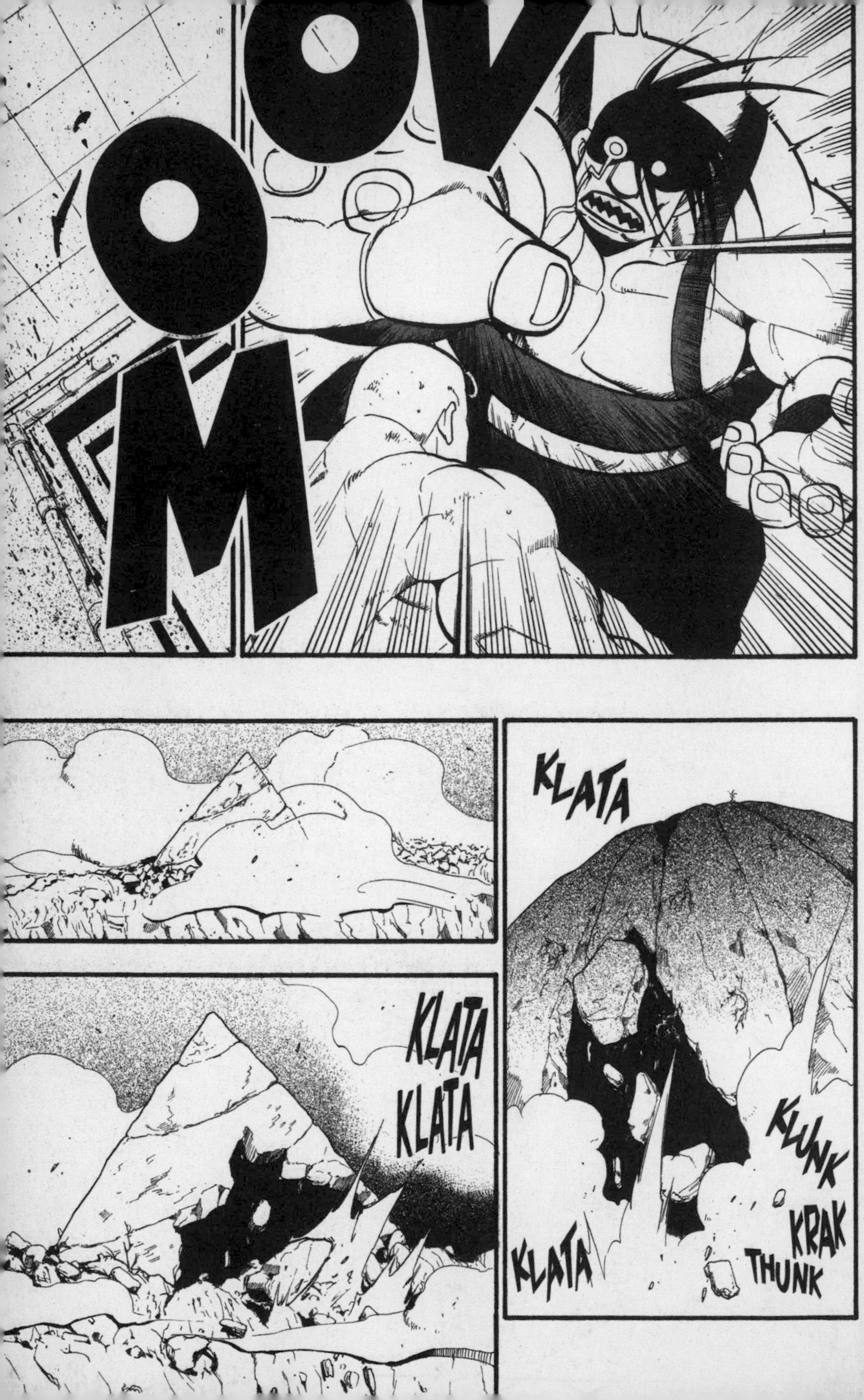
VOOM
KLATA
KLUNK
KRAK
THUNK
KLATA
KLATA
KLATA

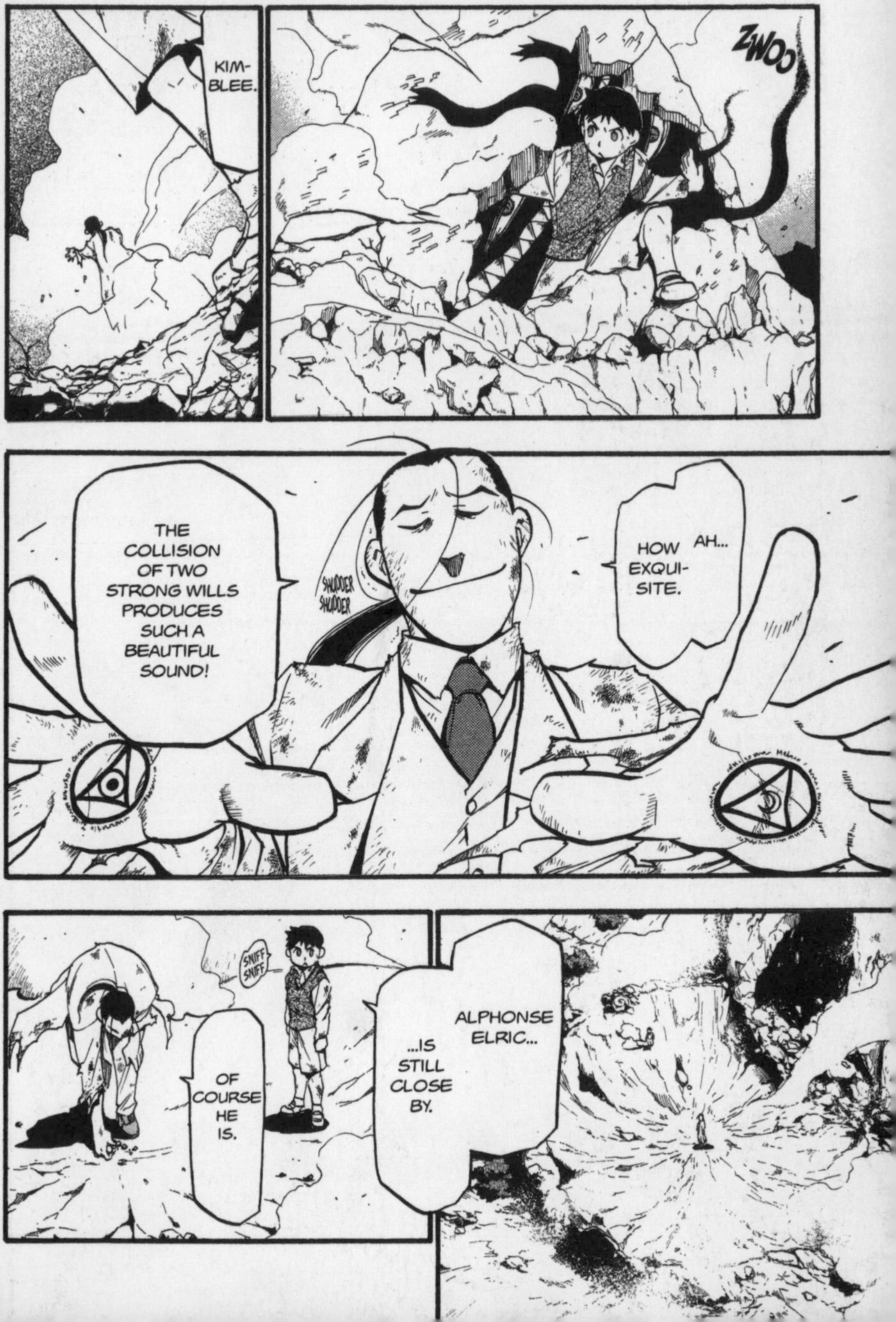
ZWOO
KIM-BLEE.
AH... HOW EXQUISITE.
SHUDDER SHUDDER
THE COLLISION OF TWO STRONG WILLS PRODUCES SUCH A BEAUTIFUL SOUND!
ALPHONSE ELRIC...
...IS STILL CLOSE BY.
SNIFF SNIFF
OF COURSE HE IS.

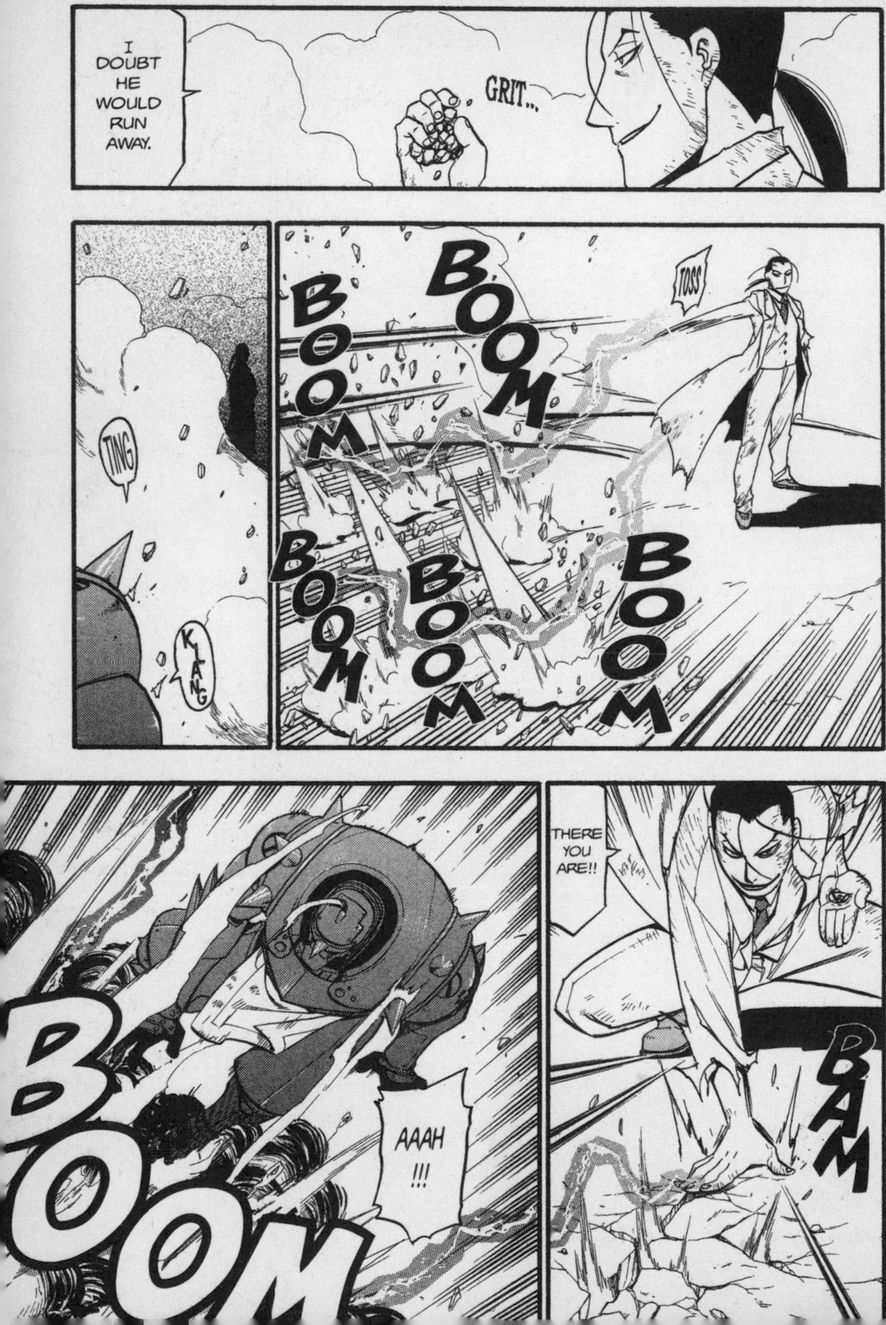
GRIT...
I DOUBT HE WOULD RUN AWAY.
TOSS
BOOM
BOOM
BOOM
BOOM
BOOM
TING
KLANG
THERE YOU ARE!!
BAM
AAAH !!!
BOOM

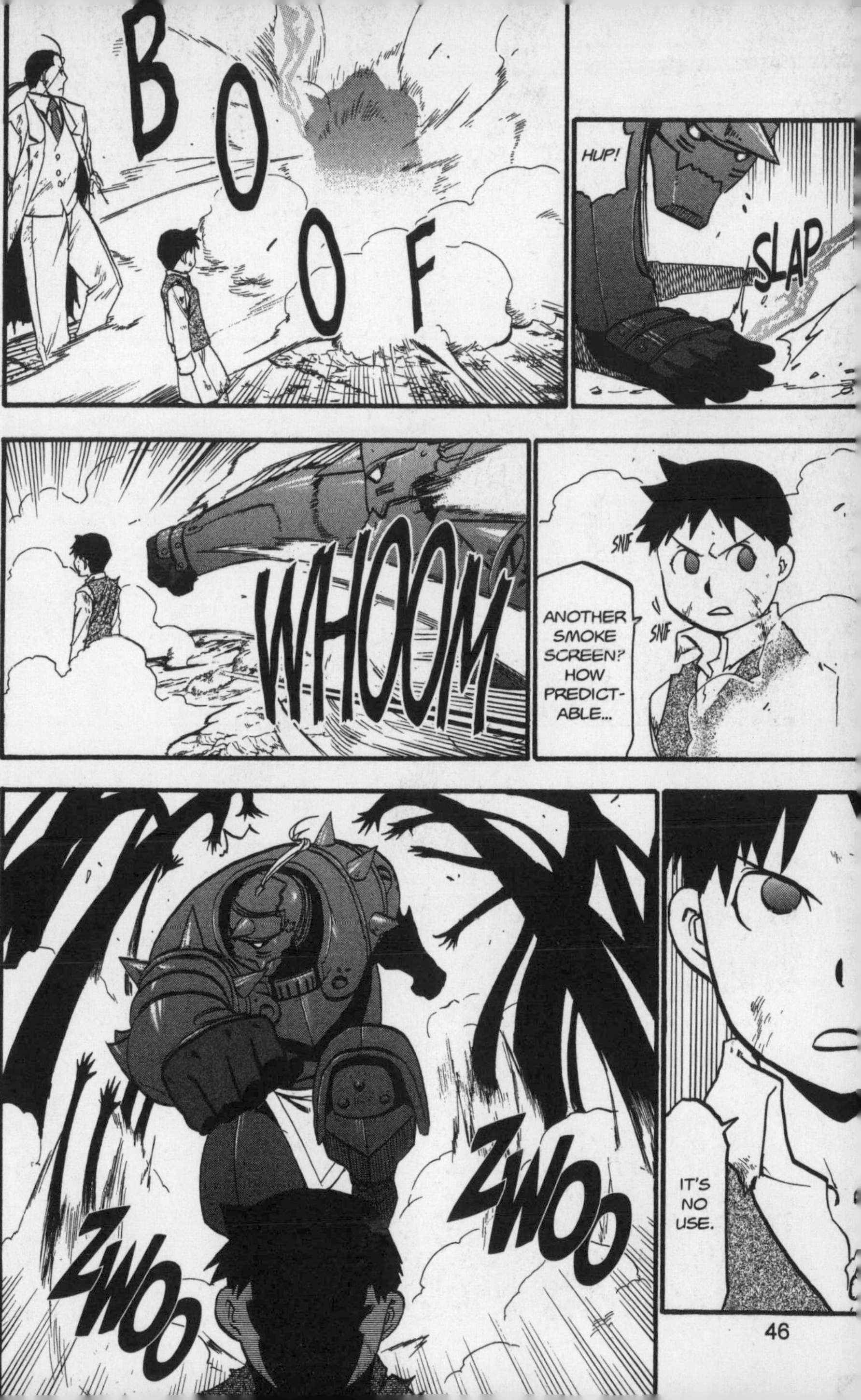
HUP!
SLAP
BOOOF
SNIF
ANOTHER SMOKE SCREEN? HOW PREDICT-ABLE...
SNIF
WHOOM
IT'S NO USE.
ZWOO
ZWOO

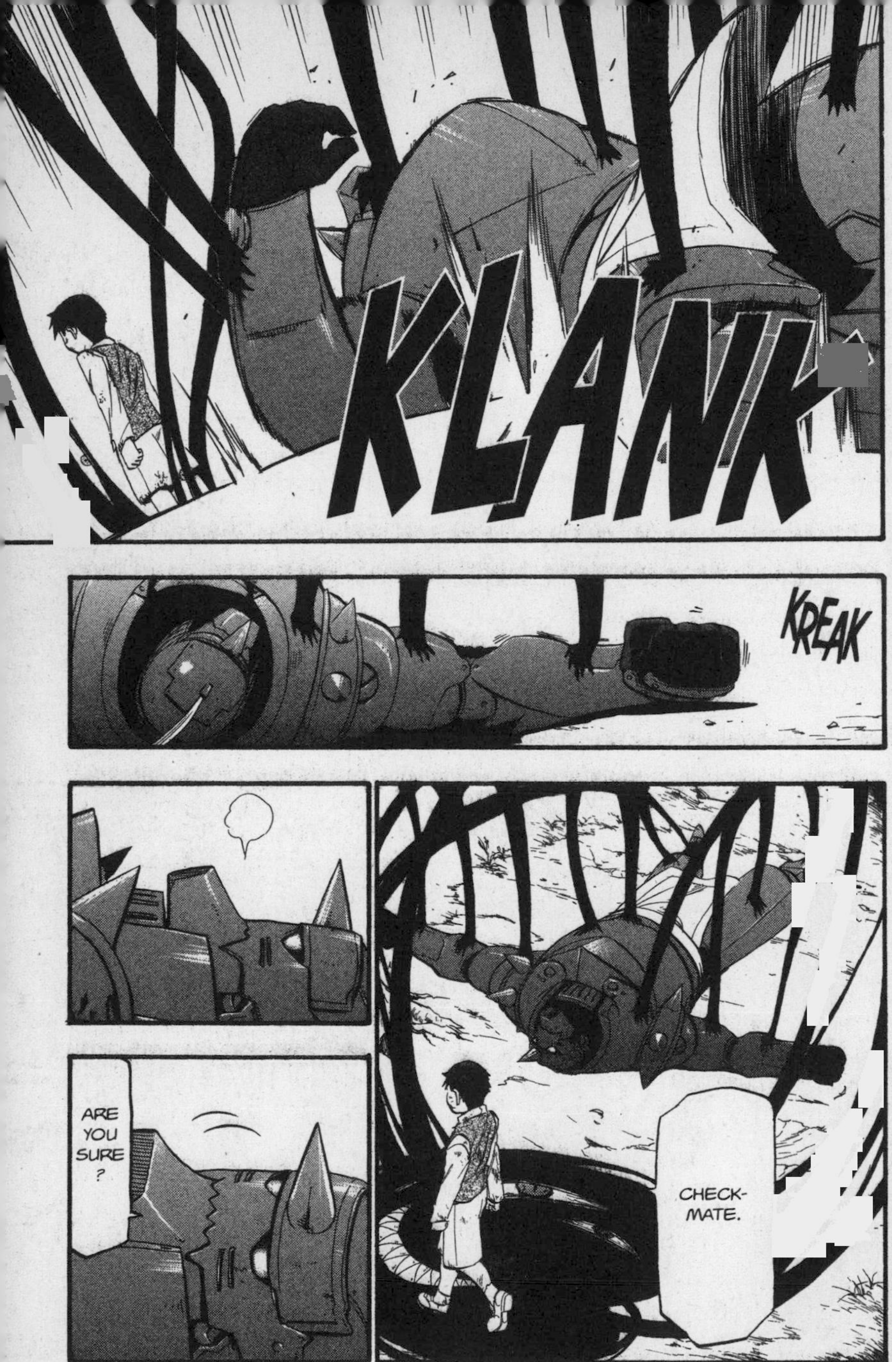
KLANK
KREAK
CHECK-MATE.
ARE YOU SURE?

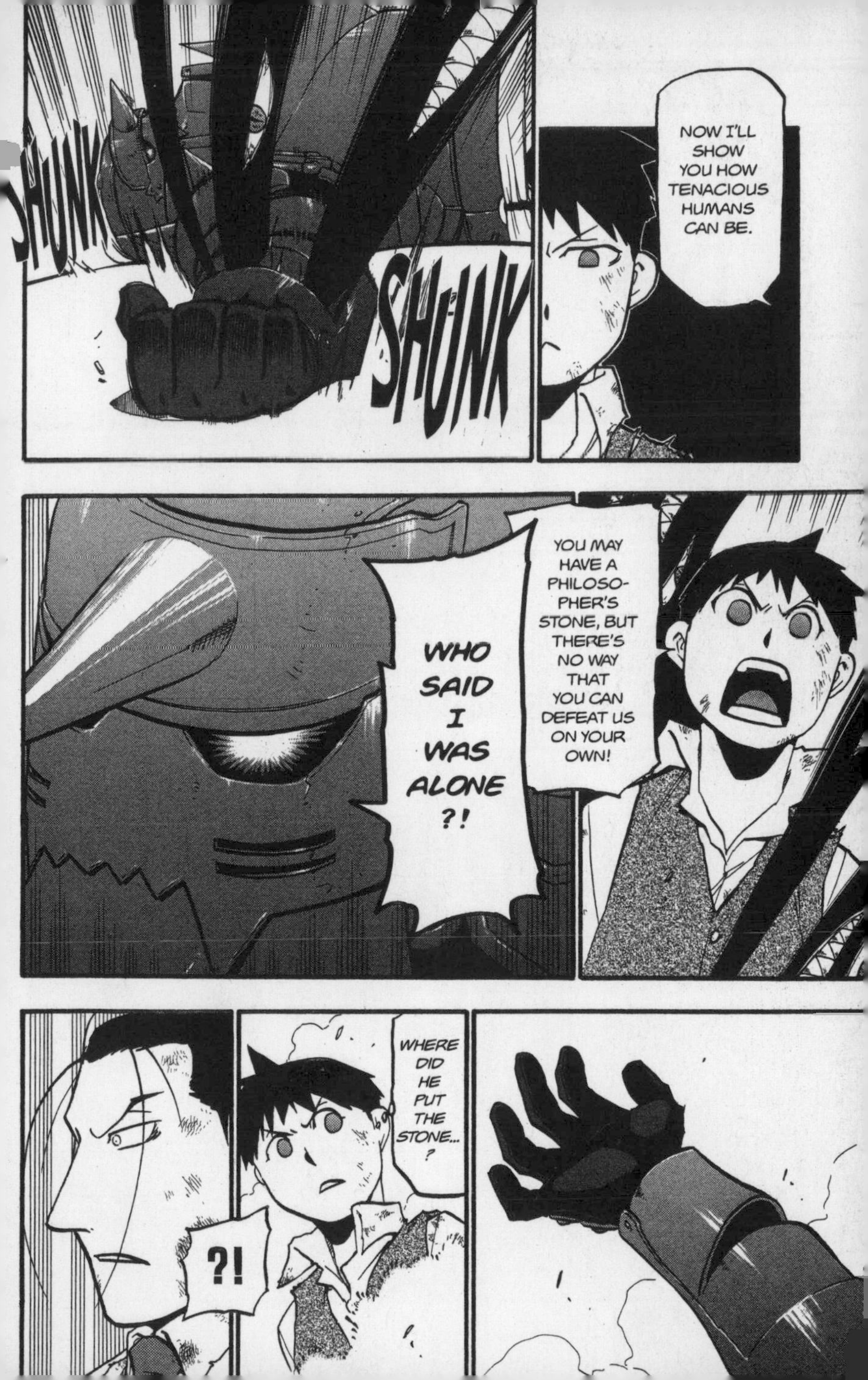
NOW I'LL SHOW YOU HOW TENACIOUS HUMANS CAN BE.
SHUNK
SHUNK
YOU MAY HAVE A PHILOSO-PHER'S STONE, BUT THERE'S NO WAY THAT YOU CAN DEFEAT US ON YOUR OWN!
WHO SAID I WAS ALONE ?!
WHERE DID HE PUT THE STONE... ?
?!

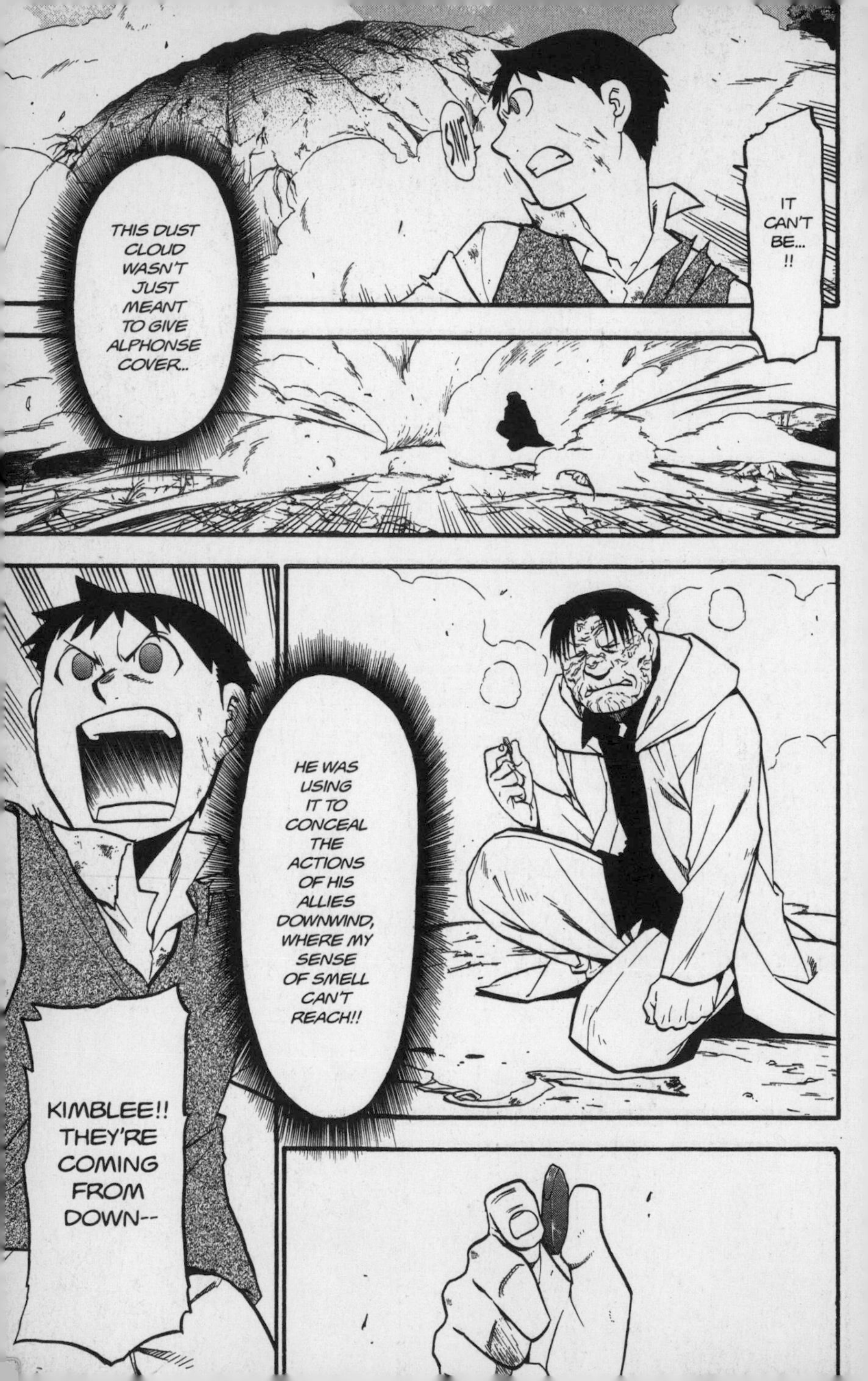

SNIFF
IT CAN'T BE... !!
THIS DUST CLOUD WASN'T JUST MEANT TO GIVE ALPHONSE COVER...
HE WAS USING IT TO CONCEAL THE ACTIONS OF HIS ALLIES DOWNWIND, WHERE MY SENSE OF SMELL CAN'T REACH!!
KIMBLEE!! THEY'RE COMING FROM DOWN--

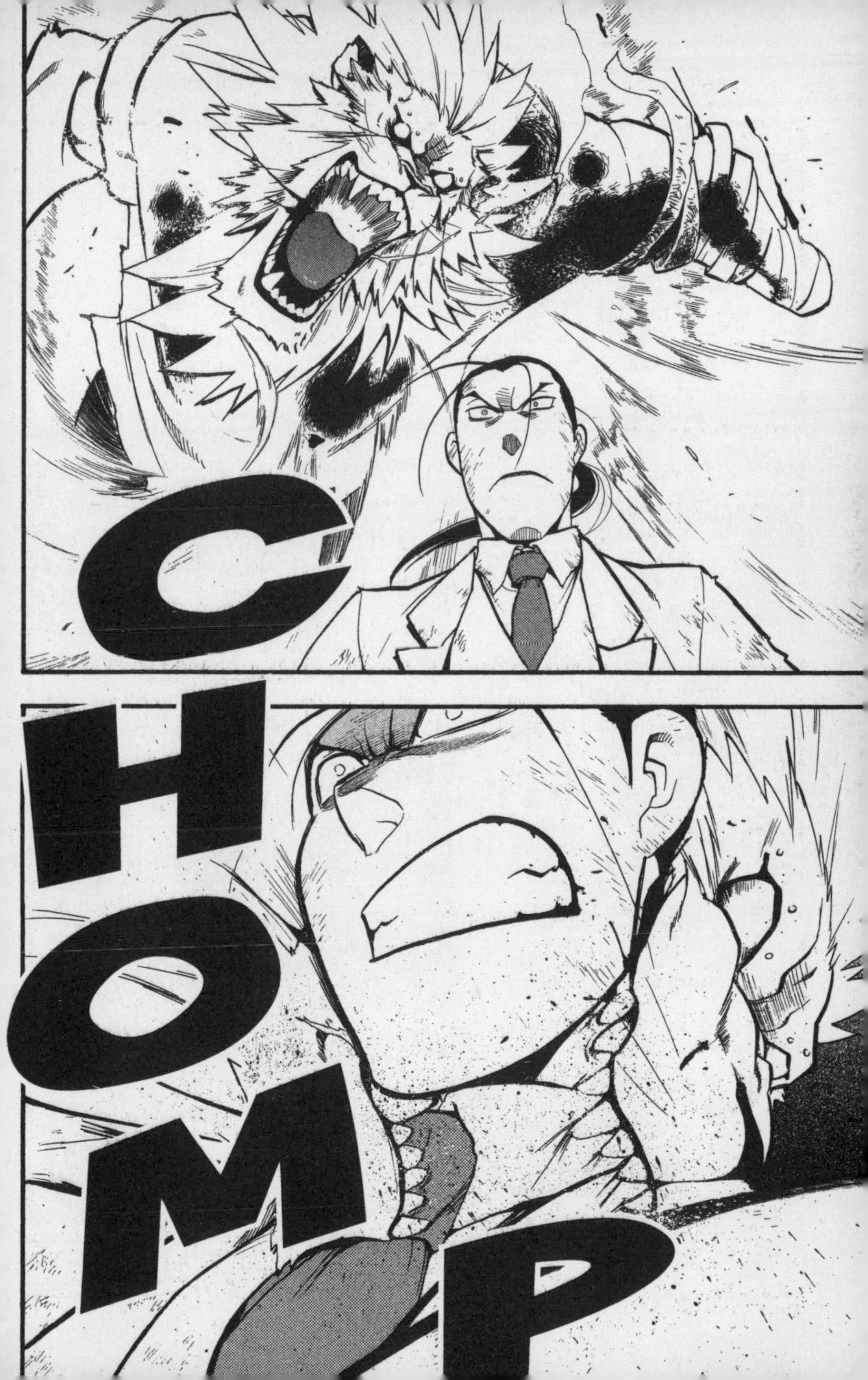
CHOMP

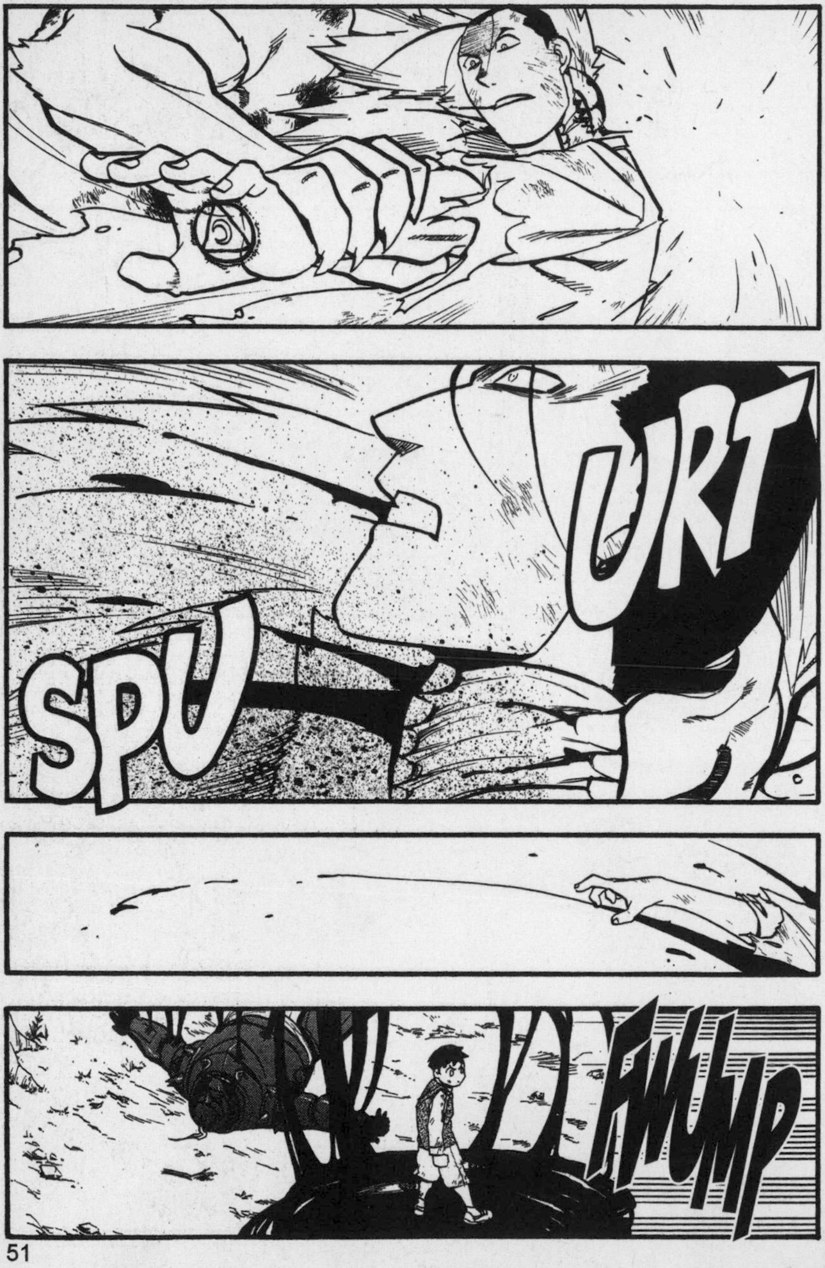
SPURT
FWUMP

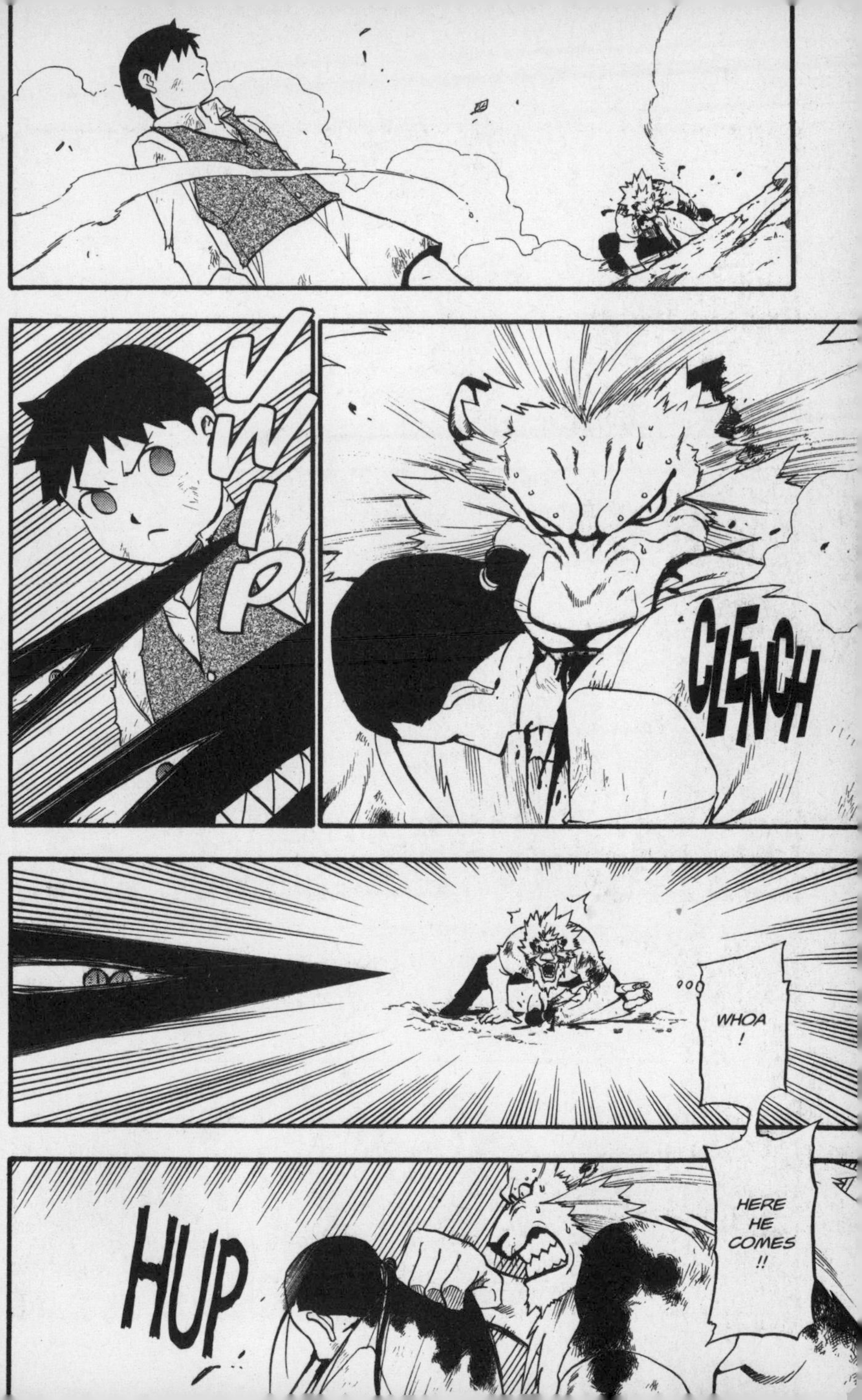
CLENCH
VWIP
WHOA!
HERE HE COMES!!
HUP

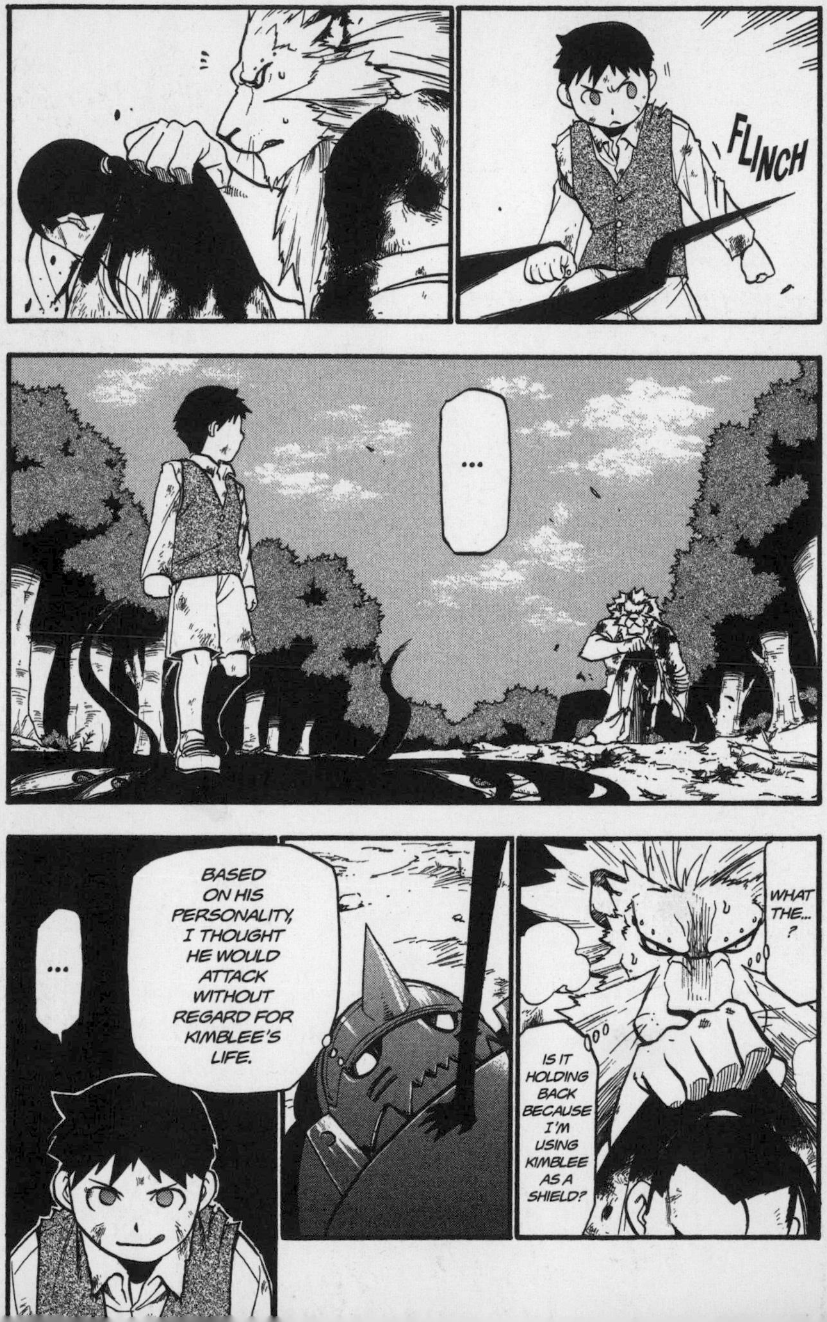
FLINCH
...
WHAT THE...?
IS IT HOLDING BACK BECAUSE I'M USING KIMBLEE AS A SHIELD?
...
BASED ON HIS PERSONALITY, I THOUGHT HE WOULD ATTACK WITHOUT REGARD FOR KIMBLEE'S LIFE.

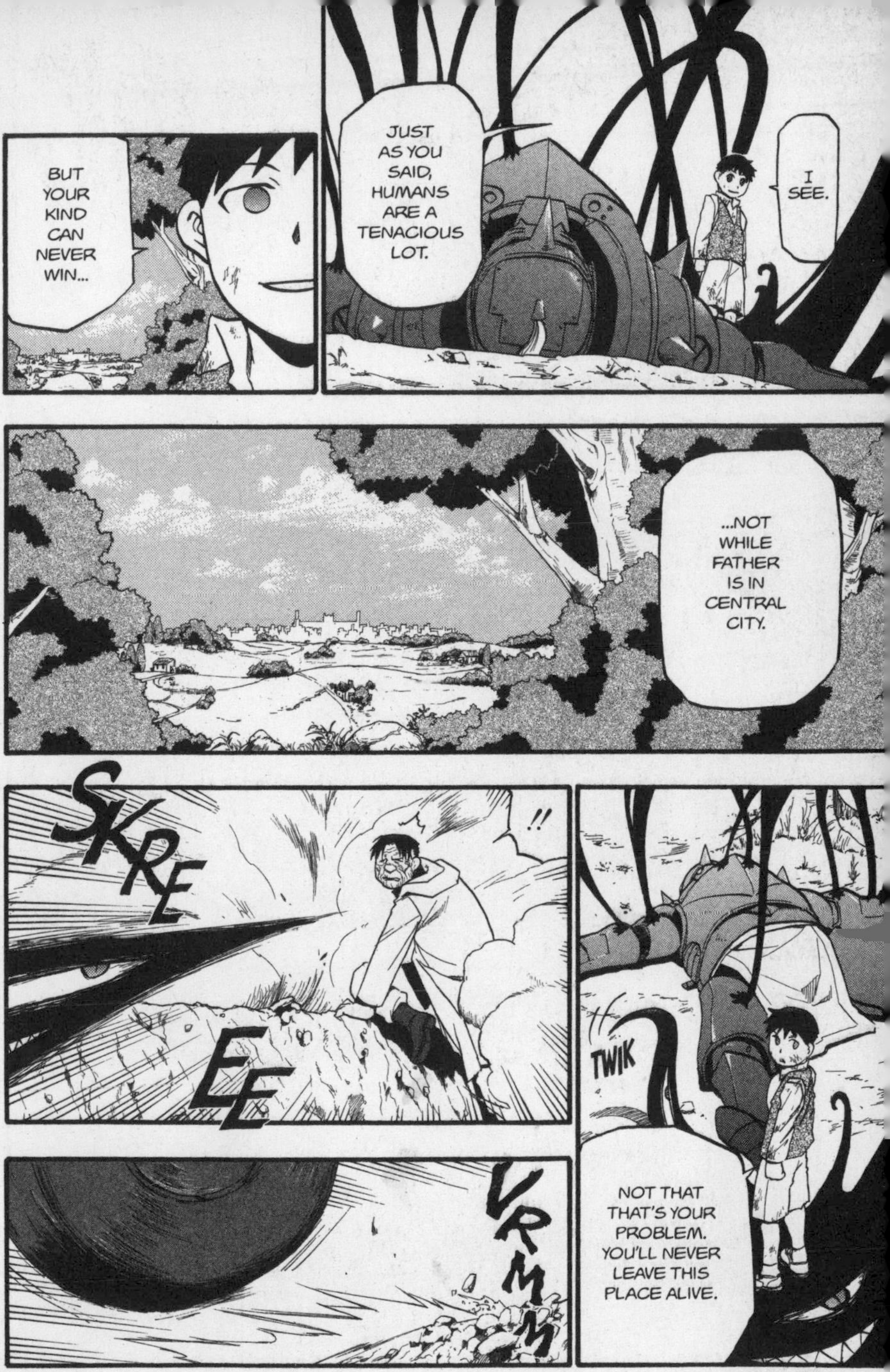
I SEE.
JUST AS YOU SAID, HUMANS ARE A TENACIOUS LOT.
BUT YOUR KIND CAN NEVER WIN...
...NOT WHILE FATHER IS IN CENTRAL CITY.
TWIK
NOT THAT THAT'S YOUR PROBLEM. YOU'LL NEVER LEAVE THIS PLACE ALIVE.
!!
SKREEE
VRMM

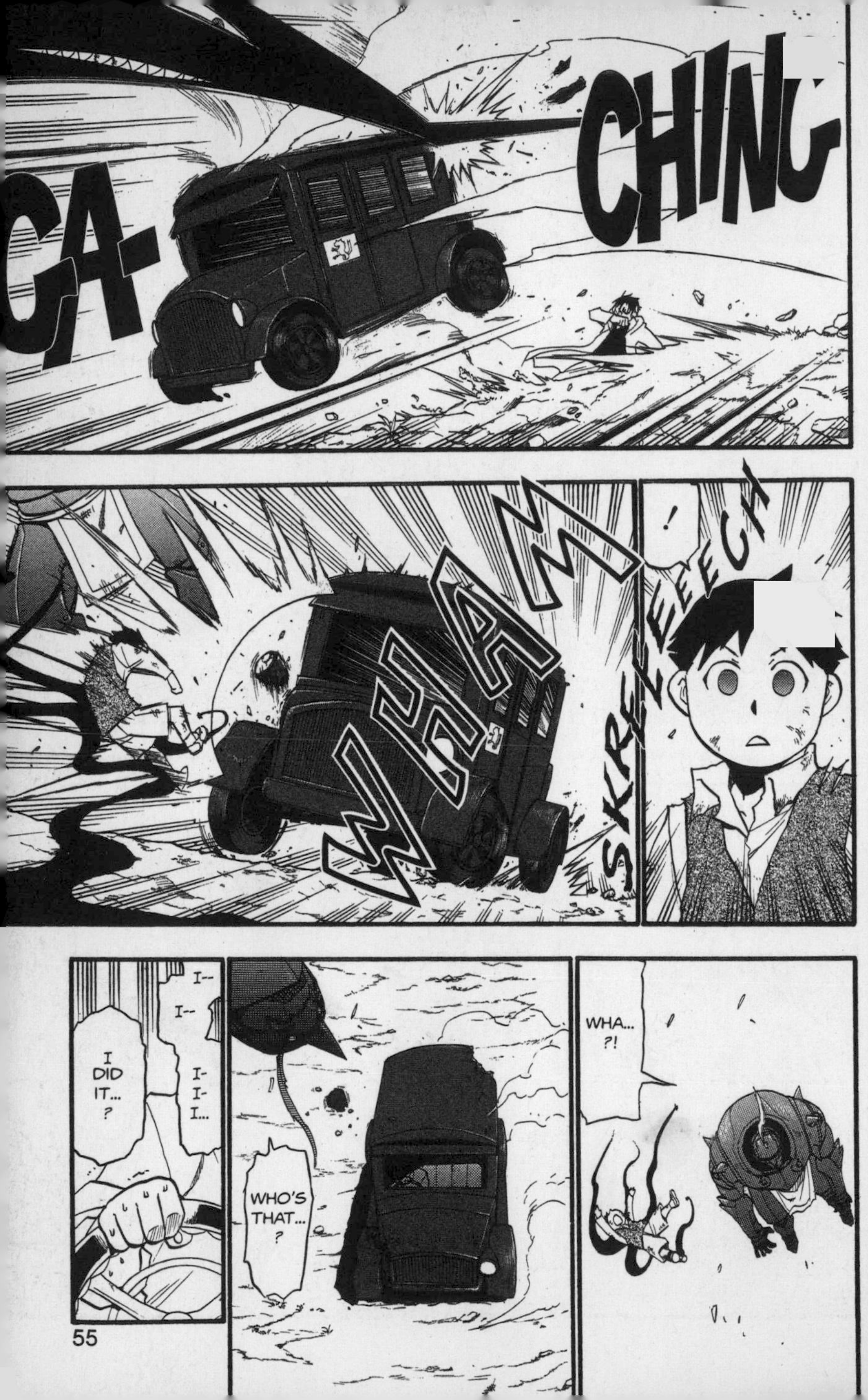
CA-CHING
!
SKREEEEECH
WHAM
WHA...?!
WHO'S THAT...?
I--
I--
I-I-I...
I DID IT...?

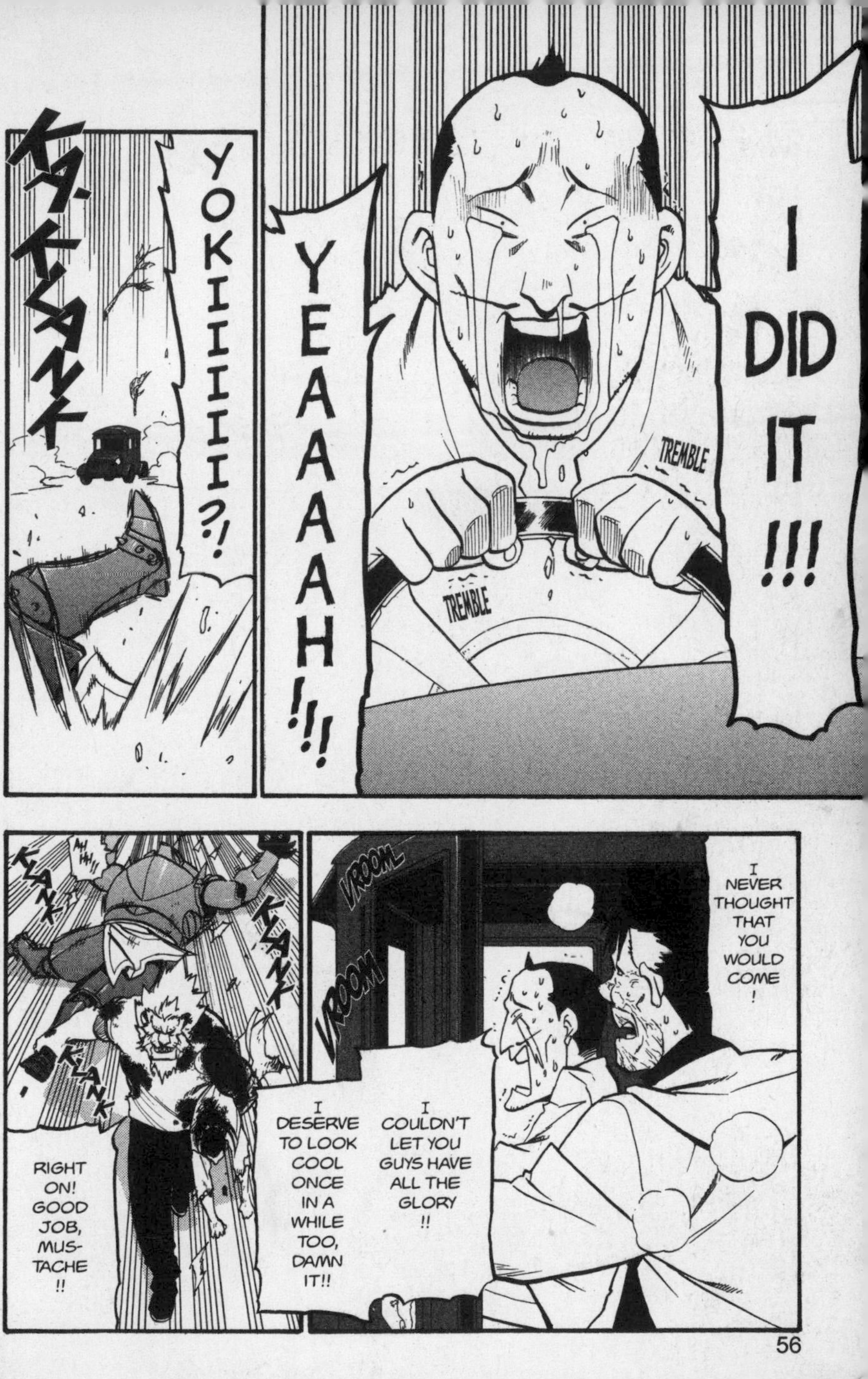
I DID IT!!!
YEAAAAAH!!!
TREMBLE
TREMBLE
YOKIIIIII?!
KA-KLANK
I NEVER THOUGHT THAT YOU WOULD COME!
VROOM
VROOM
I COULDN'T LET YOU GUYS HAVE ALL THE GLORY!!
I DESERVE TO LOOK COOL ONCE IN A WHILE TOO, DAMN IT!!
AH HH!!
KLANK
KLANK
KLANK
RIGHT ON! GOOD JOB, MUS-TACHE!!

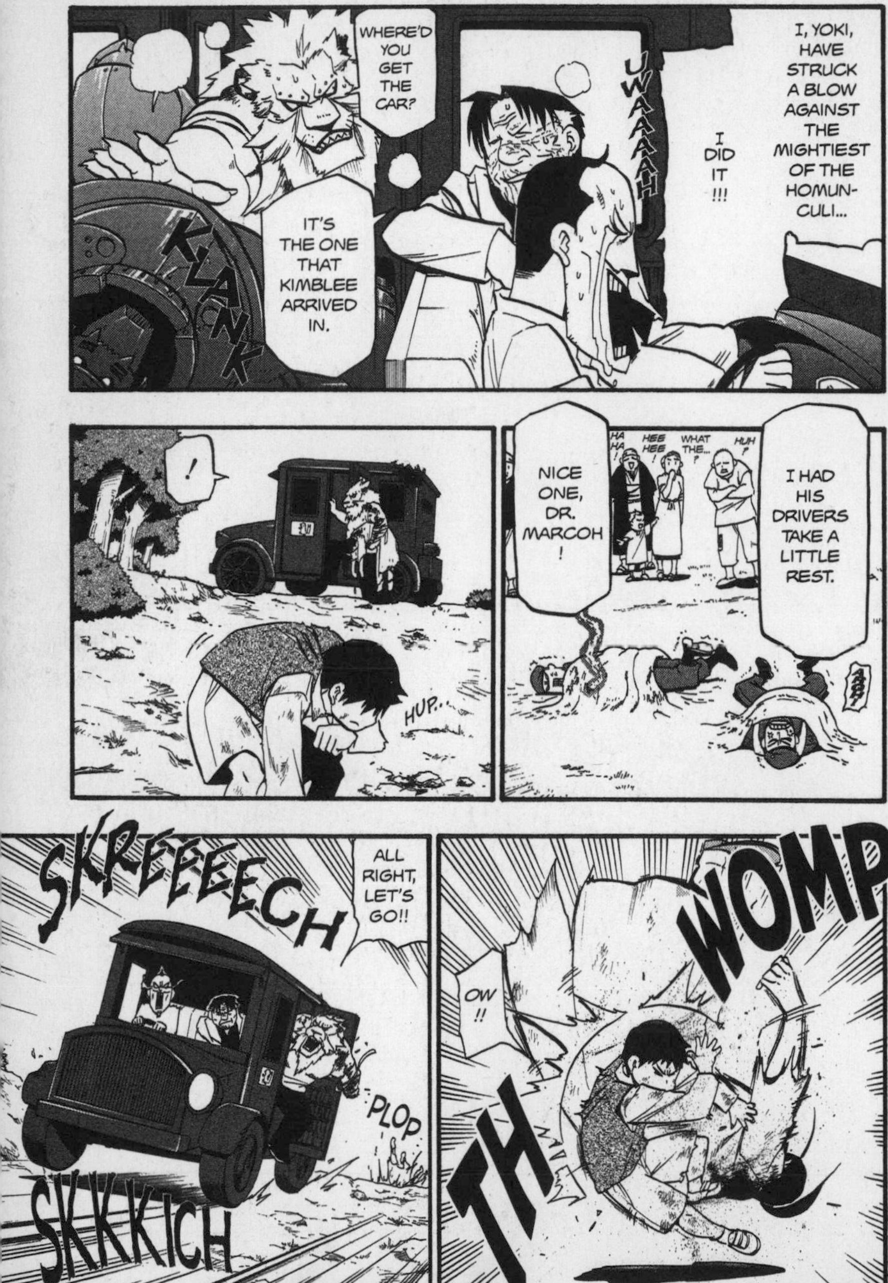
I, YOKI, HAVE STRUCK A BLOW AGAINST THE MIGHTIEST OF THE HOMUNCULI...
I DID IT !!!
JWAAAAAH
WHERE'D YOU GET THE CAR?
IT'S THE ONE THAT KIMBLEE ARRIVED IN.
KLANK
I HAD HIS DRIVERS TAKE A LITTLE REST.
HUH?
WHAT THE...?
HEE HEE!
HA HA!
NICE ONE, DR. MARCOH!
!
HUP...
WOMP
OW !!
TH
ALL RIGHT, LET'S GO!!
SKREEEECH
PLOP
SKKKICH

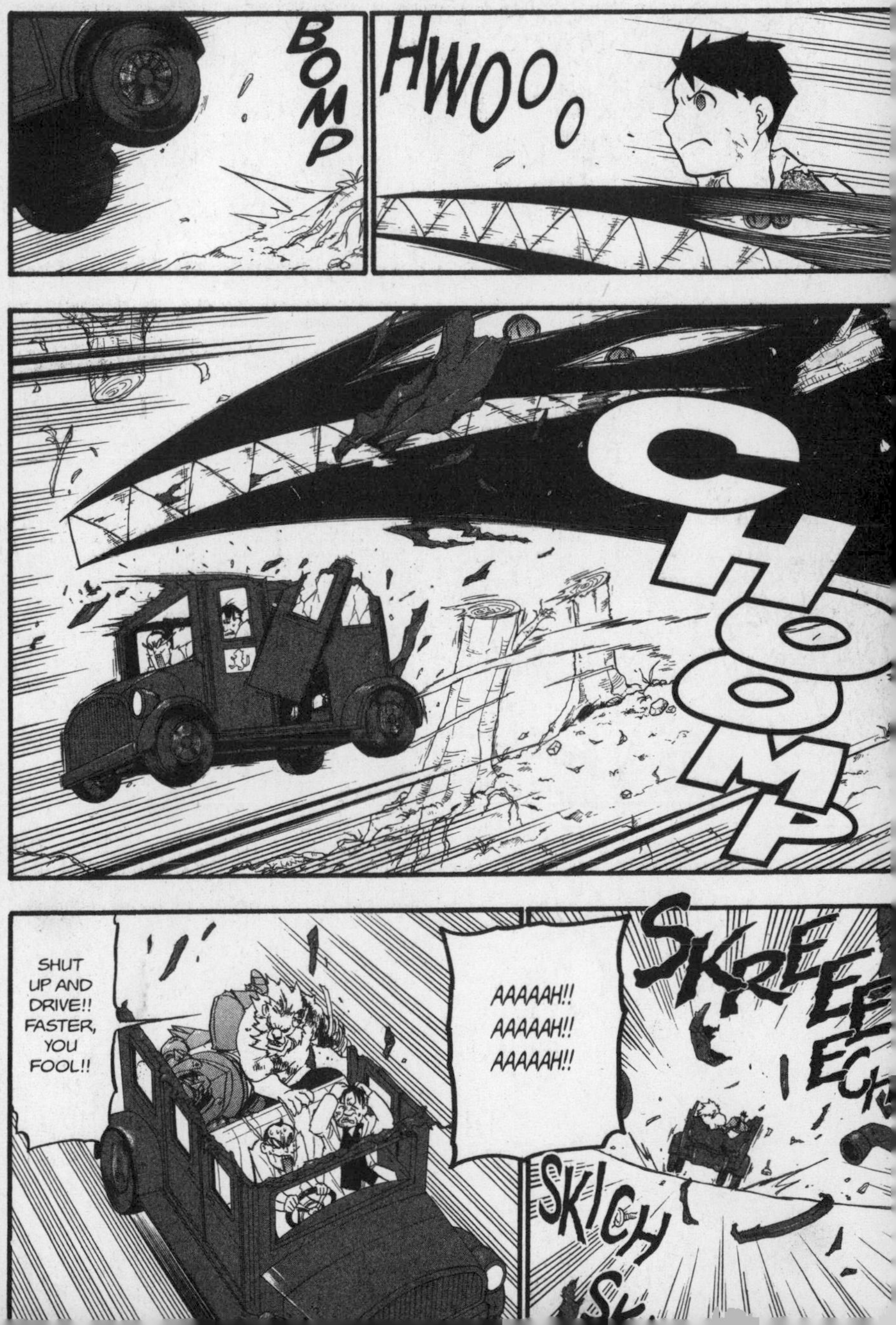
HWOOOO
BOMP
CHOMP
SKREEE
SKICH
AAAAAH!! AAAAAH!! AAAAAH!!
SHUT UP AND DRIVE!! FASTER, YOU FOOL!!

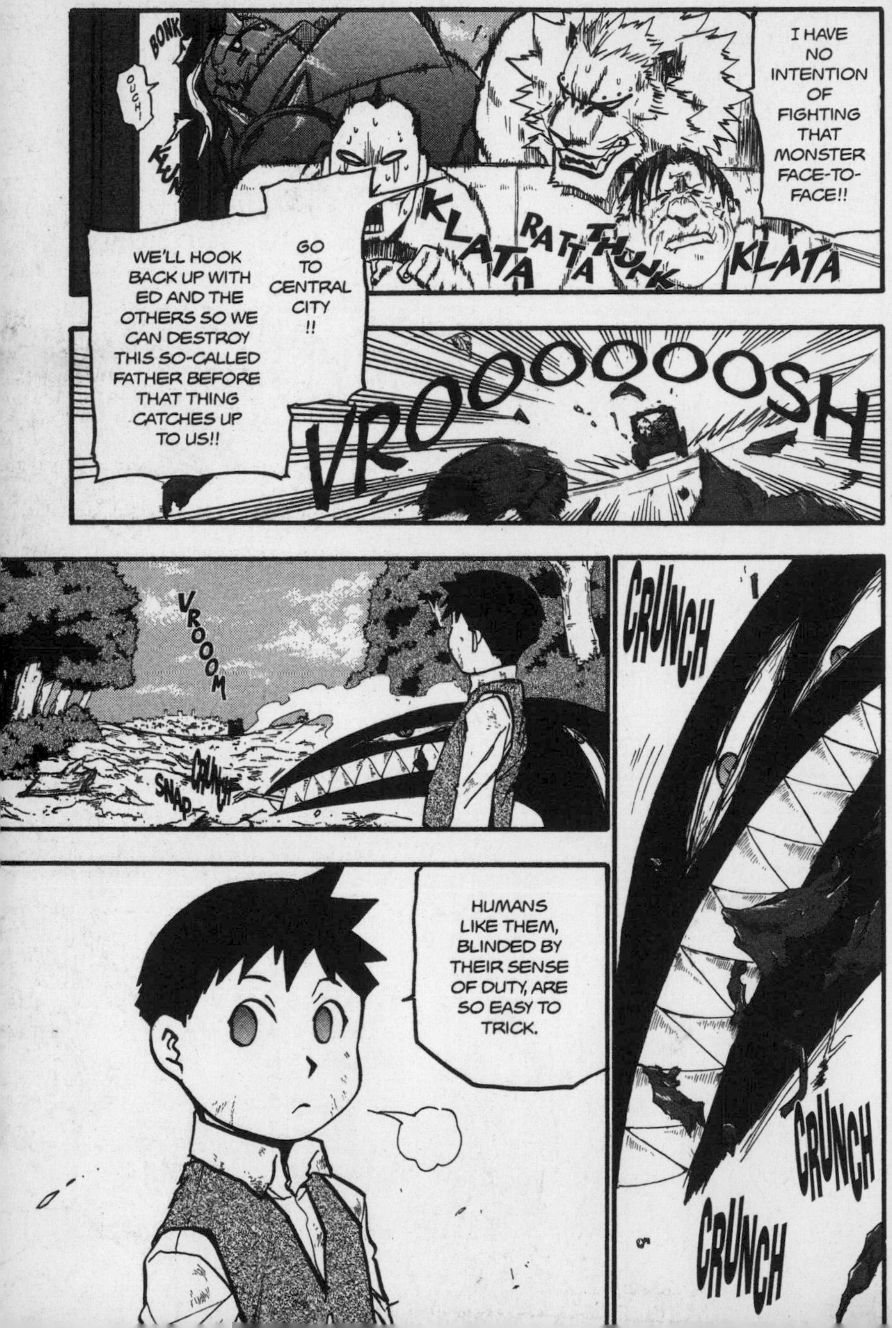
I HAVE NO INTENTION OF FIGHTING THAT MONSTER FACE-TO-FACE!!
KLATA
THUNK
RATTATA
KLATA
BONK
OUCH!
GO TO CENTRAL CITY!!
WE'LL HOOK BACK UP WITH ED AND THE OTHERS SO WE CAN DESTROY THIS SO-CALLED FATHER BEFORE THAT THING CATCHES UP TO US!!
VROOOOOOOSH
CRUNCH
CRUNCH
CRUNCH
VROOOOM
CRUNCH
SNAP
HUMANS LIKE THEM, BLINDED BY THEIR SENSE OF DUTY, ARE SO EASY TO TRICK.

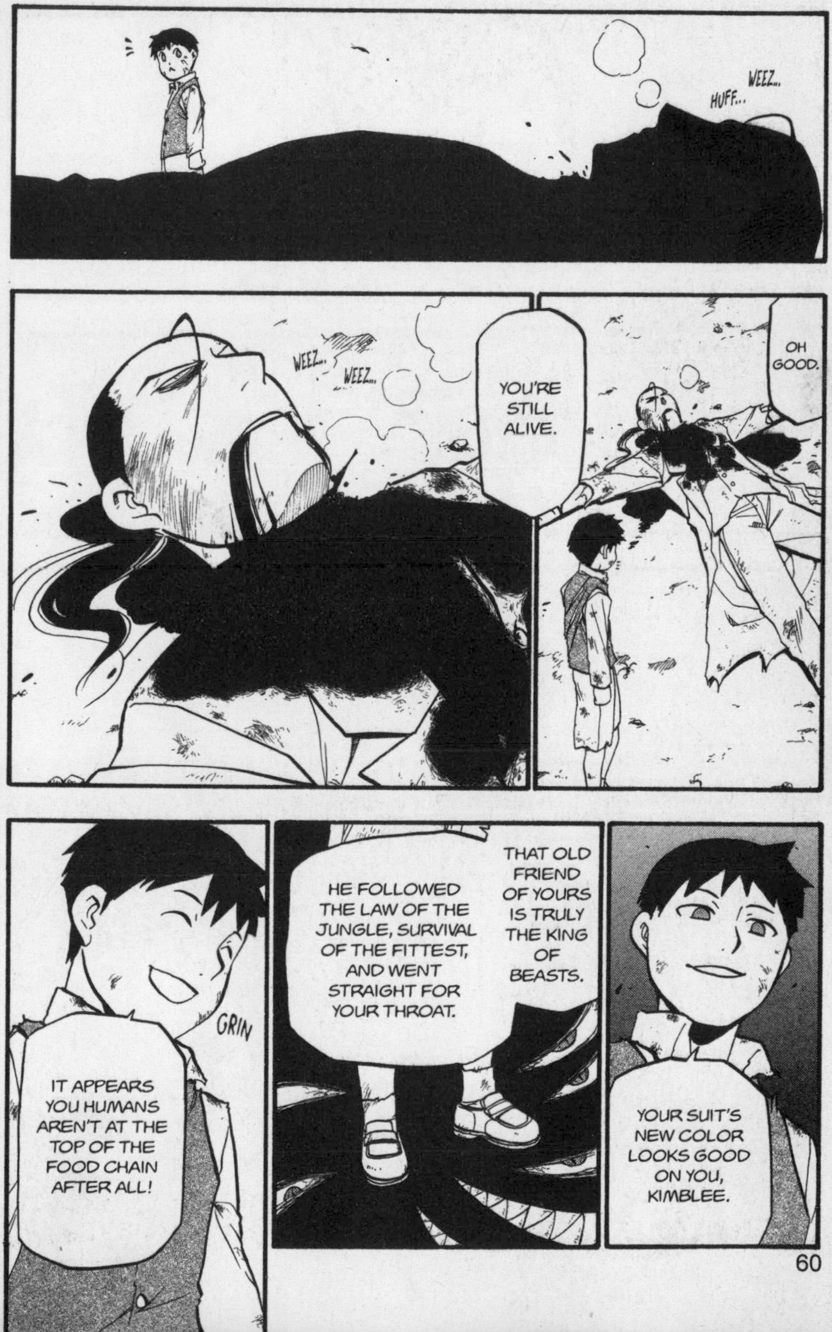
WEEZ...
HUFF...
OH GOOD.
YOU'RE STILL ALIVE.
WEEZ...
WEEZ...
YOUR SUIT'S NEW COLOR LOOKS GOOD ON YOU, KIMBLEE.
THAT OLD FRIEND OF YOURS IS TRULY THE KING OF BEASTS.
HE FOLLOWED THE LAW OF THE JUNGLE, SURVIVAL OF THE FITTEST, AND WENT STRAIGHT FOR YOUR THROAT.
GRIN
IT APPEARS YOU HUMANS AREN'T AT THE TOP OF THE FOOD CHAIN AFTER ALL!

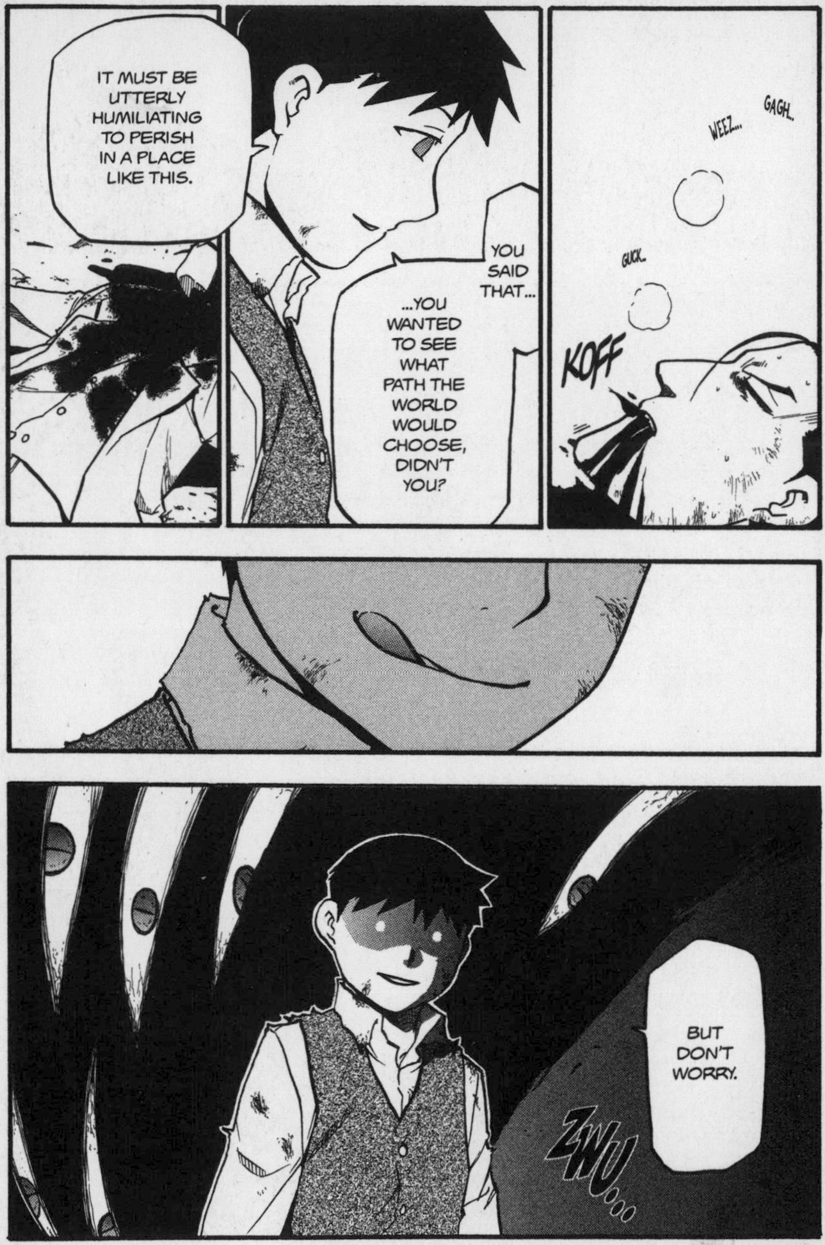
GAGH..
WEEZ...
GUCK.
KOFF
YOU SAID THAT...
...YOU WANTED TO SEE WHAT PATH THE WORLD WOULD CHOOSE, DIDN'T YOU?
IT MUST BE UTTERLY HUMILIATING TO PERISH IN A PLACE LIKE THIS.
BUT DON'T WORRY.
ZWU...

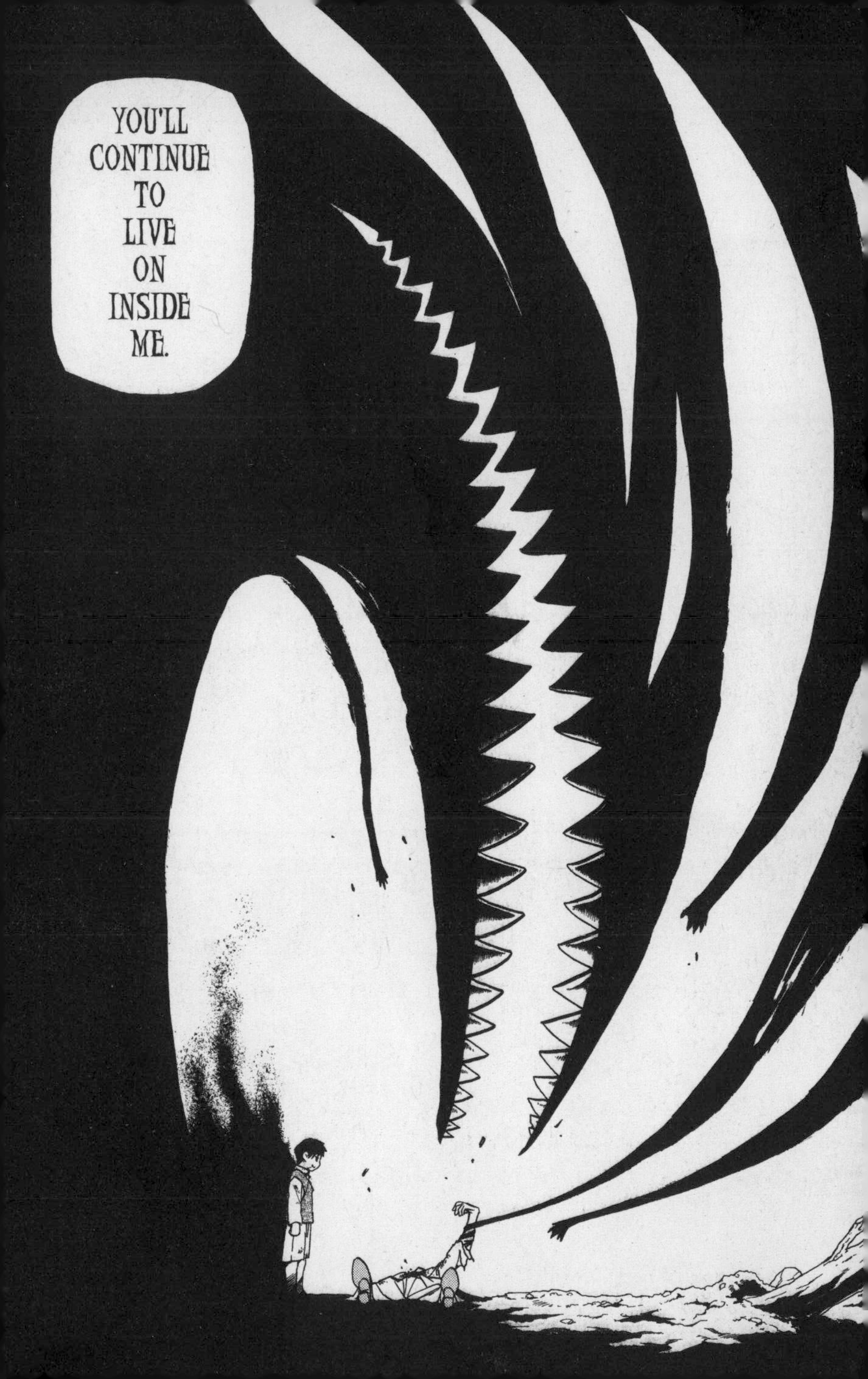
YOU'LL CONTINUE TO LIVE ON INSIDE ME.

Chapter 93 Archenemy

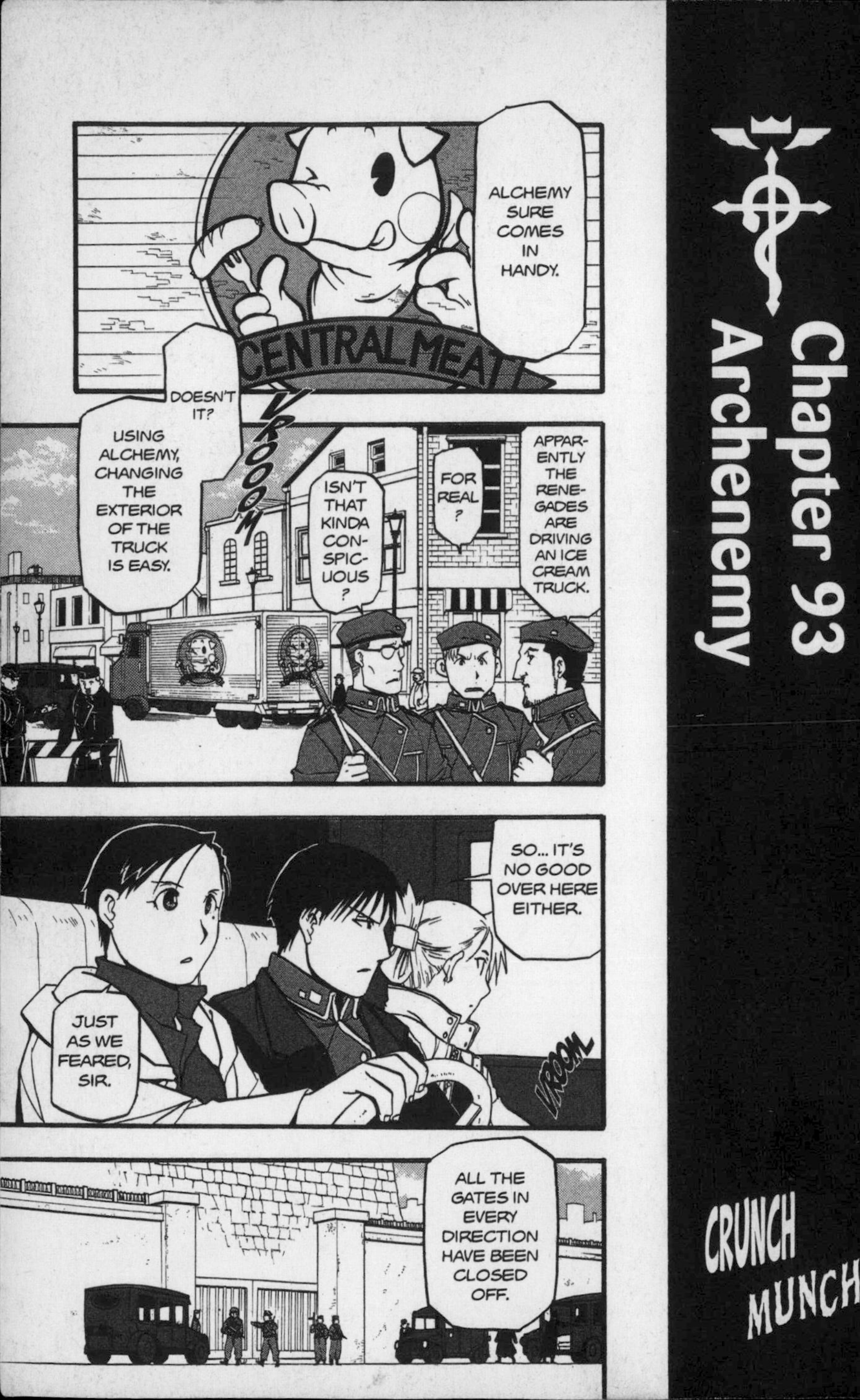
CENTRAL MEAT
ALCHEMY SURE COMES IN HANDY.
DOESN'T IT?
APPAR-ENTLY THE RENE-GADES ARE DRIVING AN ICE CREAM TRUCK.
FOR REAL?
ISN'T THAT KINDA CON-SPIC-UOUS?
USING ALCHEMY, CHANGING THE EXTERIOR OF THE TRUCK IS EASY.
VROOOOM
SO... IT'S NO GOOD OVER HERE EITHER.
JUST AS WE FEARED, SIR.
VROOM
ALL THE GATES IN EVERY DIRECTION HAVE BEEN CLOSED OFF.
CRUNCH
MUNCH

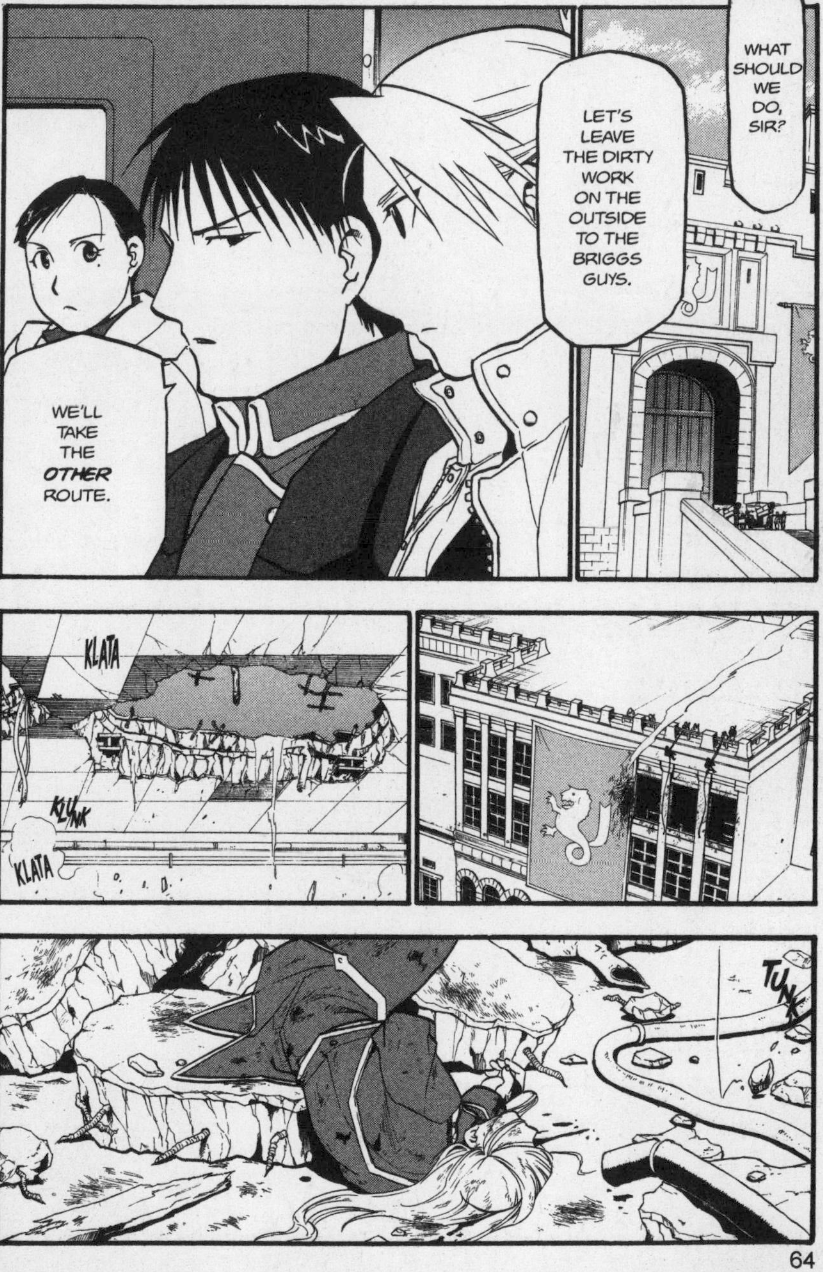
WHAT SHOULD WE DO, SIR?
LET'S LEAVE THE DIRTY WORK ON THE OUTSIDE TO THE BRIGGS GUYS.
WE'LL TAKE THE *OTHER* ROUTE.
KLATA
KLUNK
KLATA
TUNK

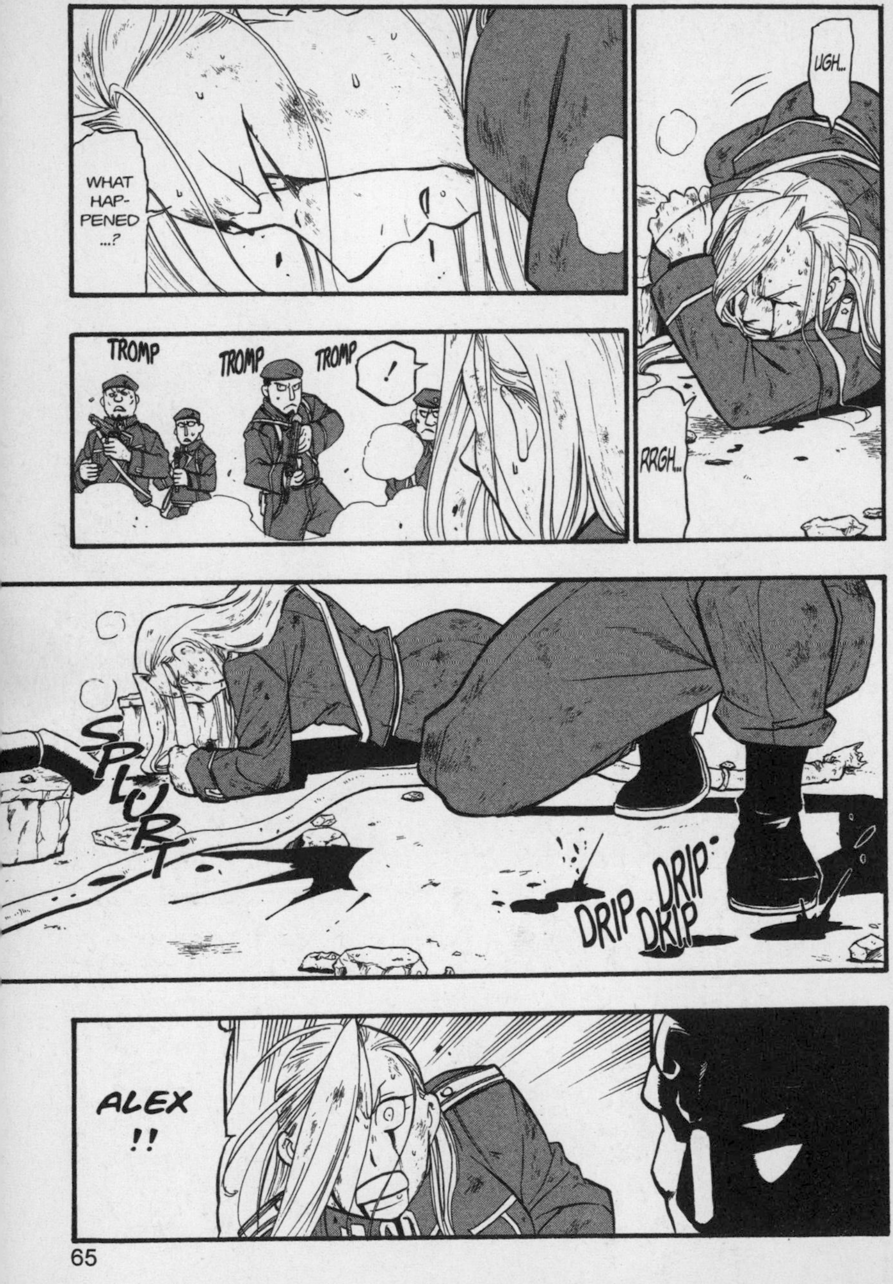
UGH...
RRGH...
WHAT HAP-PENED ...?
!
TROMP
TROMP
TROMP
DRIP DRIP DRIP
SPLURT
ALEX !!

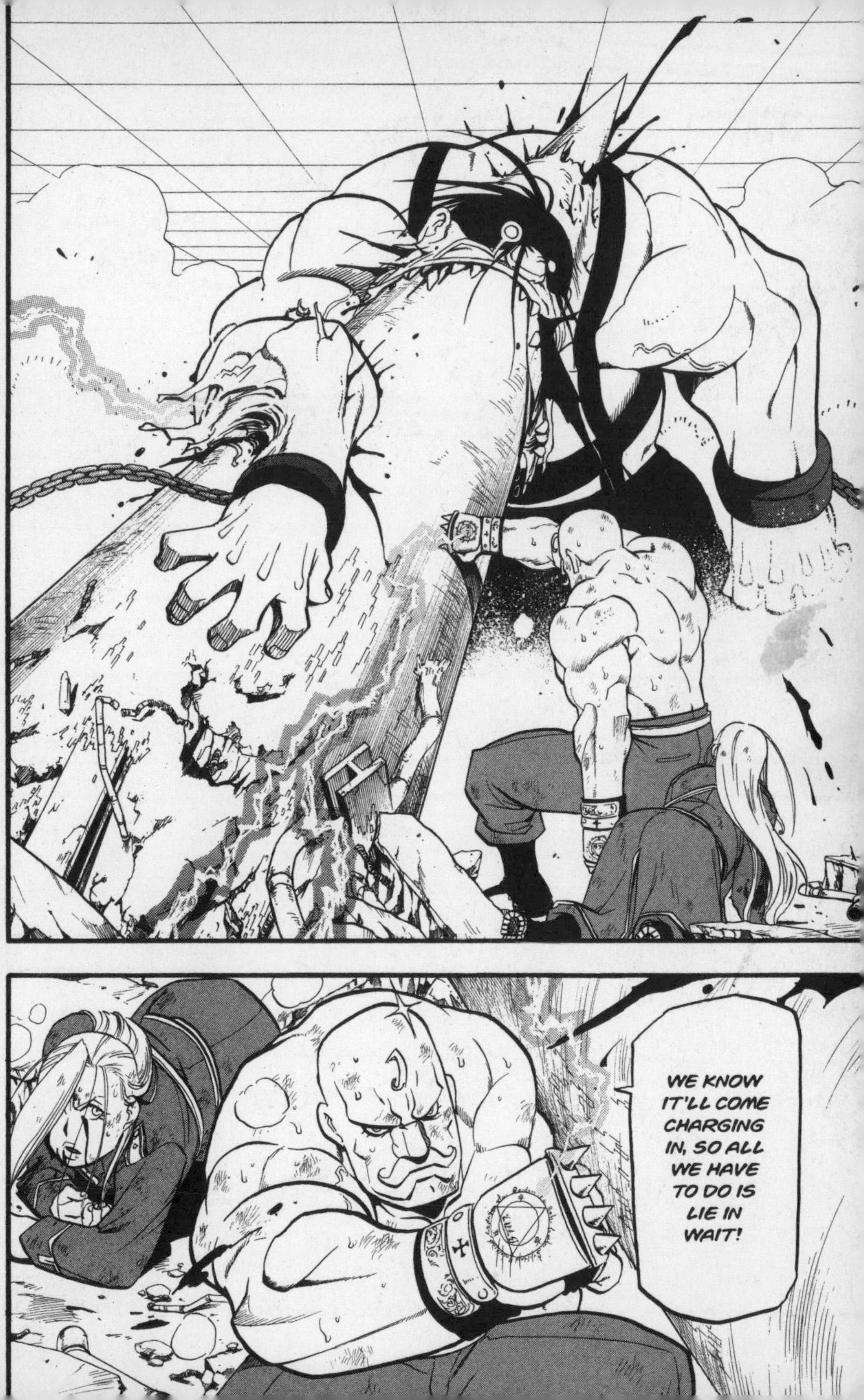
WE KNOW IT'LL COME CHARGING IN, SO ALL WE HAVE TO DO IS LIE IN WAIT!

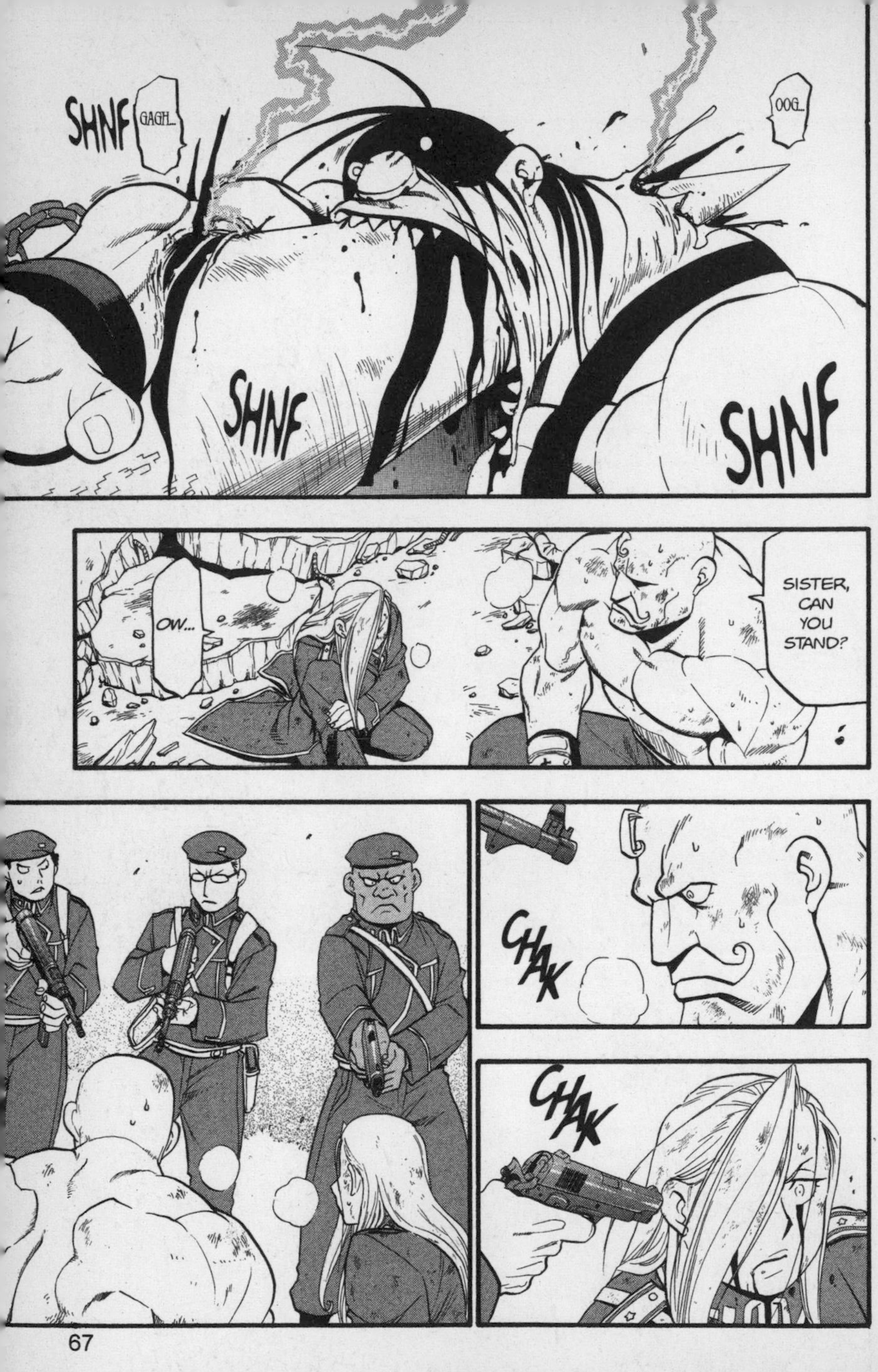
OOG...
GAGH...
SHNF
SHNF
SHNF
SISTER, CAN YOU STAND?
OW...
CHAK
CHAK

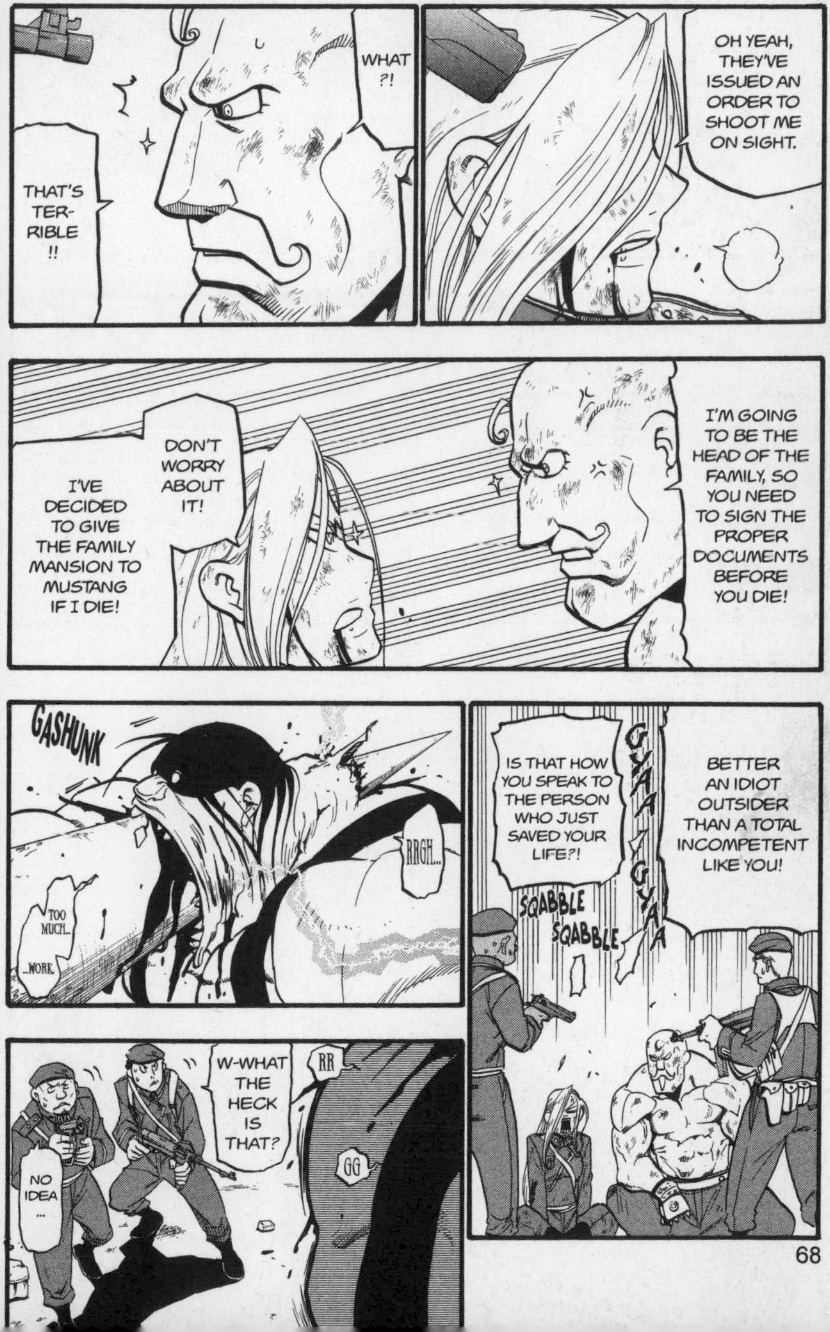
OH YEAH, THEY'VE ISSUED AN ORDER TO SHOOT ME ON SIGHT.
WHAT ?!
THAT'S TER-RIBLE !!
I'M GOING TO BE THE HEAD OF THE FAMILY, SO YOU NEED TO SIGN THE PROPER DOCUMENTS BEFORE YOU DIE!
DON'T WORRY ABOUT IT!
I'VE DECIDED TO GIVE THE FAMILY MANSION TO MUSTANG IF I DIE!
BETTER AN IDIOT OUTSIDER THAN A TOTAL INCOMPETENT LIKE YOU!
IS THAT HOW YOU SPEAK TO THE PERSON WHO JUST SAVED YOUR LIFE?!
GYAA GYAA
SQABBLE SQABBLE
GASHUNK
RRGH...
TOO MUCH...
...WORK
RR
W-WHAT THE HECK IS THAT?
GG
NO IDEA ...

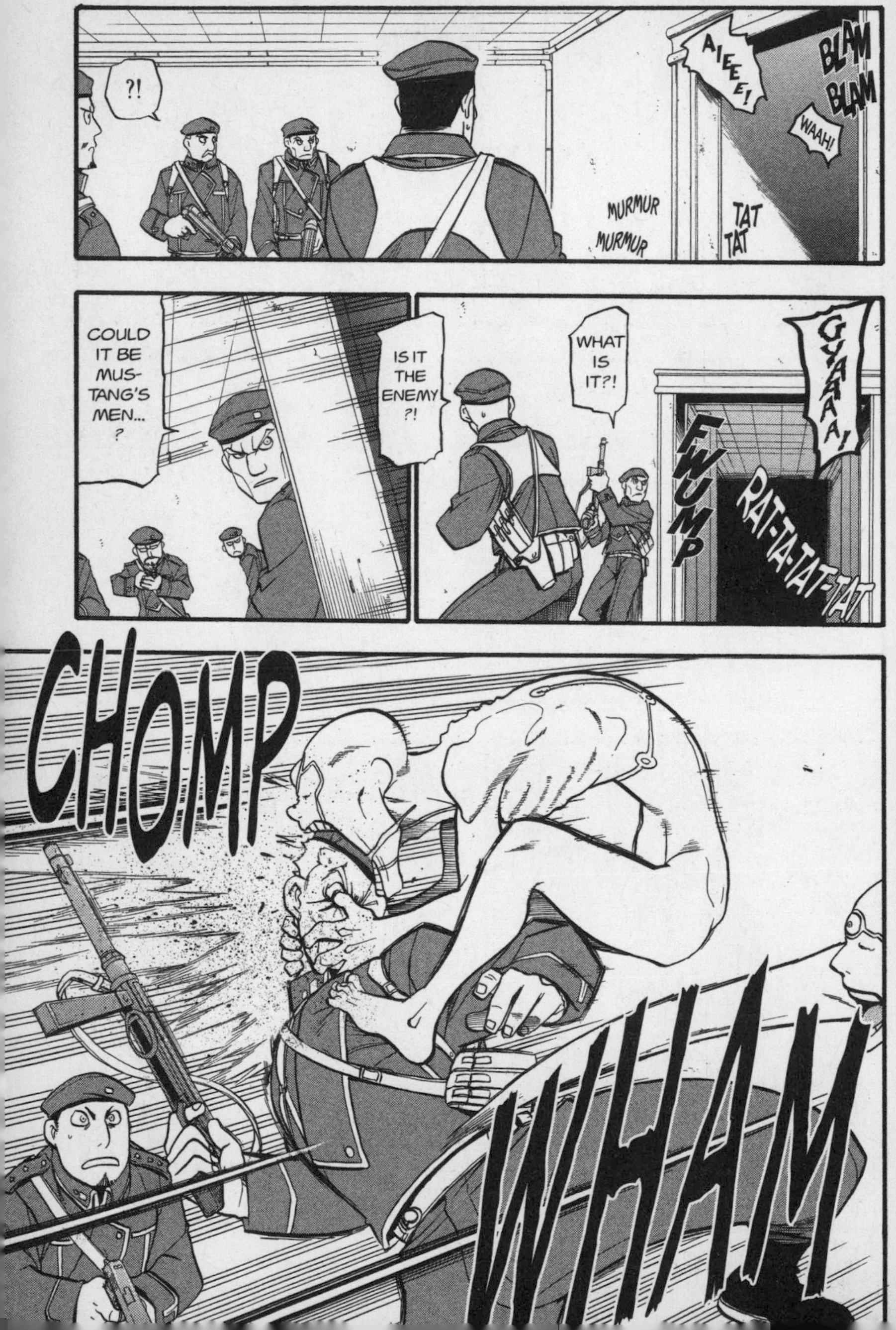
BLAM BLAM
AIEEE!
WAAH!
TAT TAT
MURMUR MURMUR
?!
GYAAAA!
RAT-TA-TAT-TAT
FWUMP
WHAT IS IT?!
IS IT THE ENEMY?!
COULD IT BE MUSTANG'S MEN...?
CHOMP
WHAM

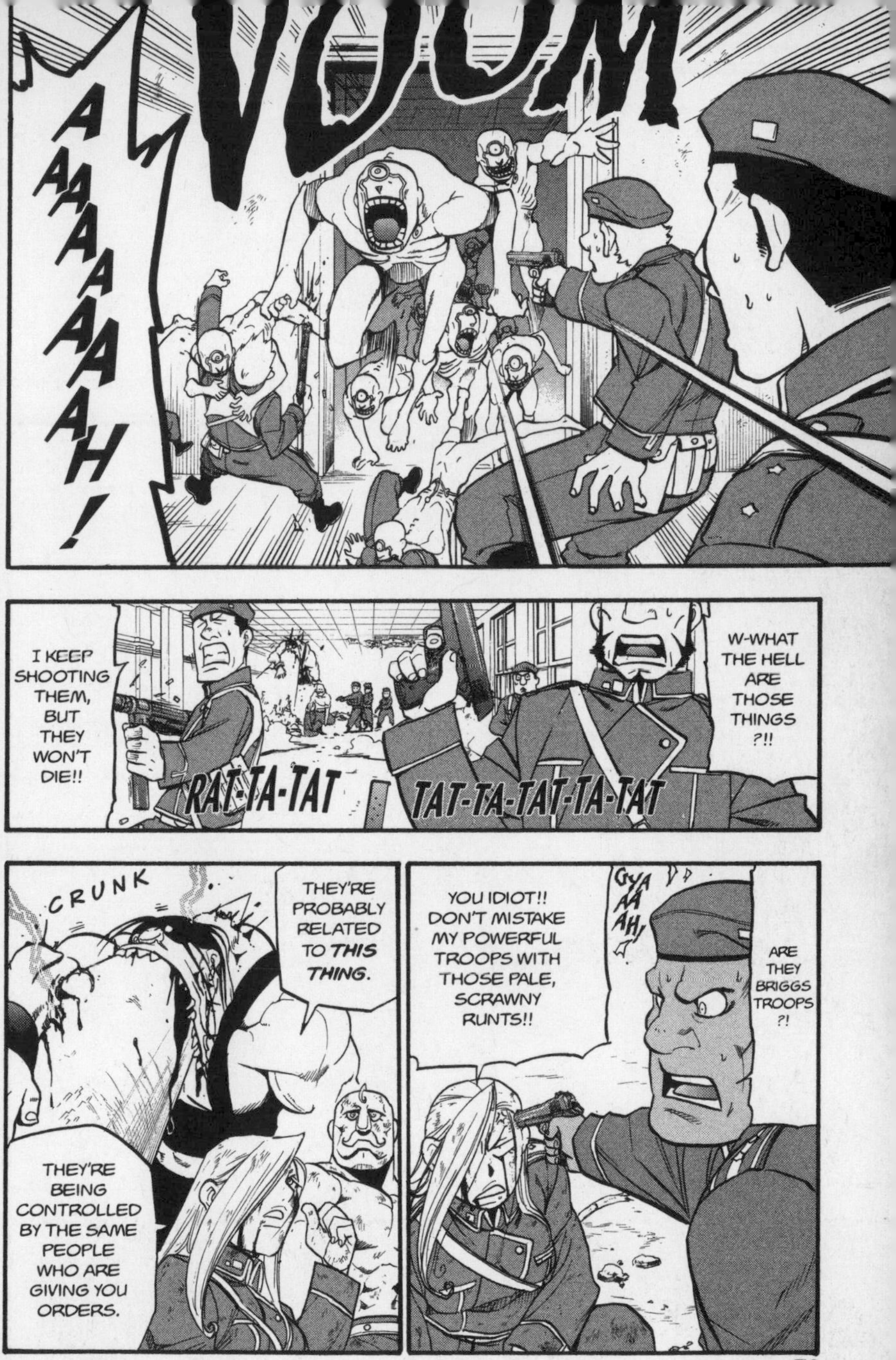
VOOM
AAAAAAAAAH!
W-WHAT THE HELL ARE THOSE THINGS?!!
I KEEP SHOOTING THEM, BUT THEY WON'T DIE!!
TAT-TA-TAT-TA-TAT
RAT-TA-TAT
GYAAAAH!
ARE THEY BRIGGS TROOPS?!
YOU IDIOT!! DON'T MISTAKE MY POWERFUL TROOPS WITH THOSE PALE, SCRAWNY RUNTS!!
THEY'RE PROBABLY RELATED TO THIS THING.
CRUNK
THEY'RE BEING CONTROLLED BY THE SAME PEOPLE WHO ARE GIVING YOU ORDERS.

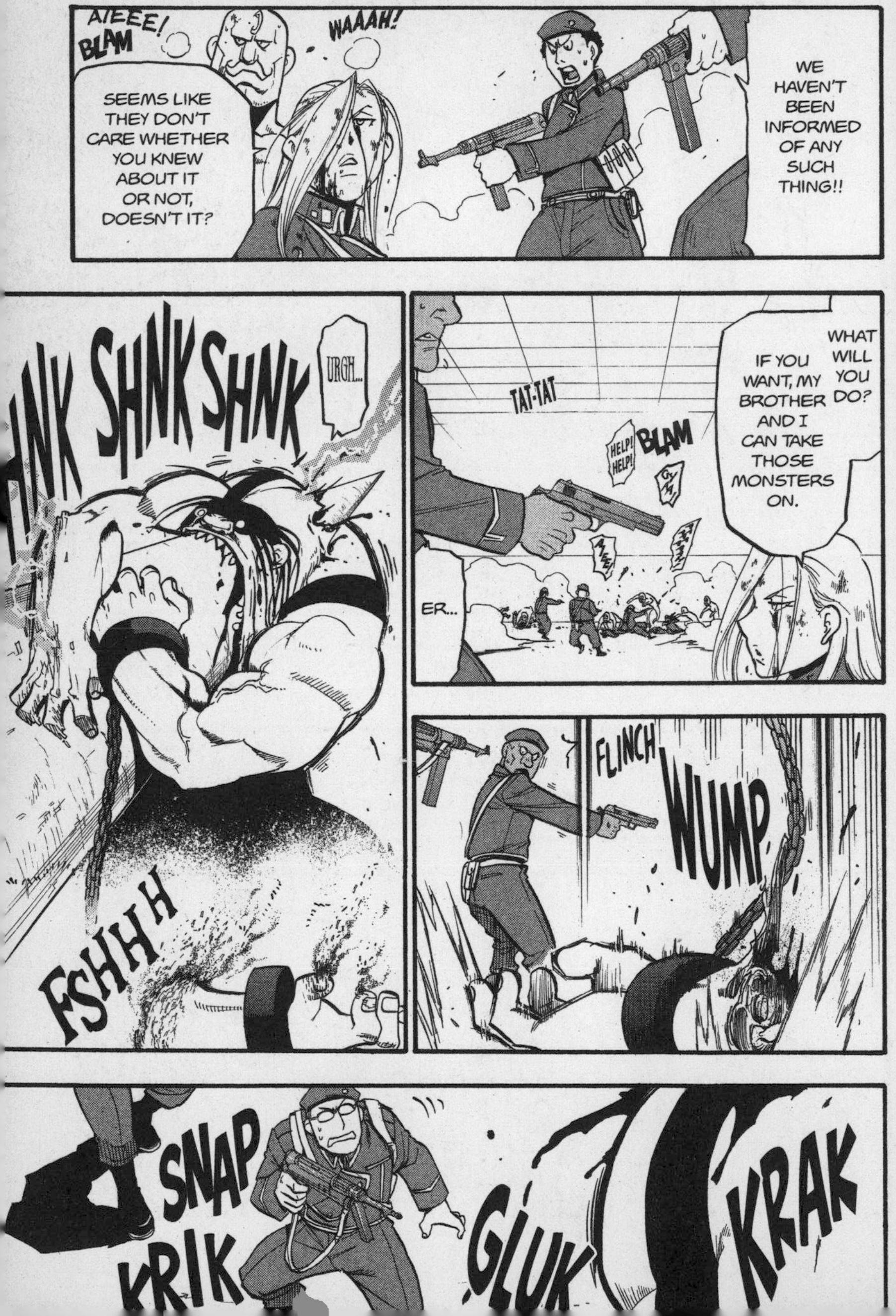
WE HAVEN'T BEEN INFORMED OF ANY SUCH THING!!
WAAAH!
AIEEE!
BLAM
SEEMS LIKE THEY DON'T CARE WHETHER YOU KNEW ABOUT IT OR NOT, DOESN'T IT?
WHAT WILL YOU DO?
IF YOU WANT, MY BROTHER AND I CAN TAKE THOSE MONSTERS ON.
TAT-TAT
BLAM
HELP! HELP!
ER...
WUMP
FLINCH
URGH...
SHNK SHNK SHNK
FSHHH
KRAK
GLUK
SNAP
KRIK

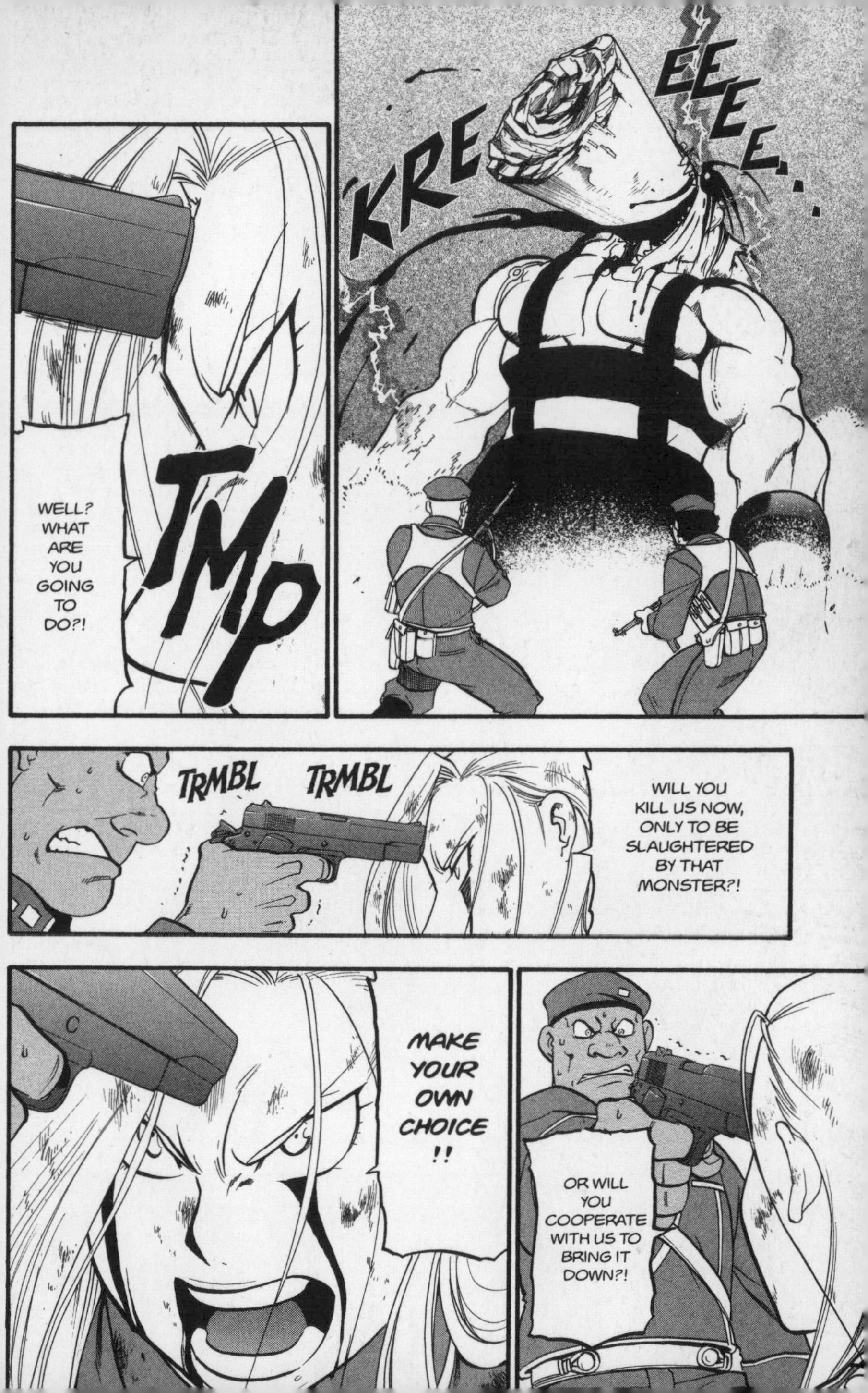
KREEEEEE...
TMP
WELL? WHAT ARE YOU GOING TO DO?!
WILL YOU KILL US NOW, ONLY TO BE SLAUGHTERED BY THAT MONSTER?!
TRMBL TRMBL
OR WILL YOU COOPERATE WITH US TO BRING IT DOWN?!
MAKE YOUR OWN CHOICE!!

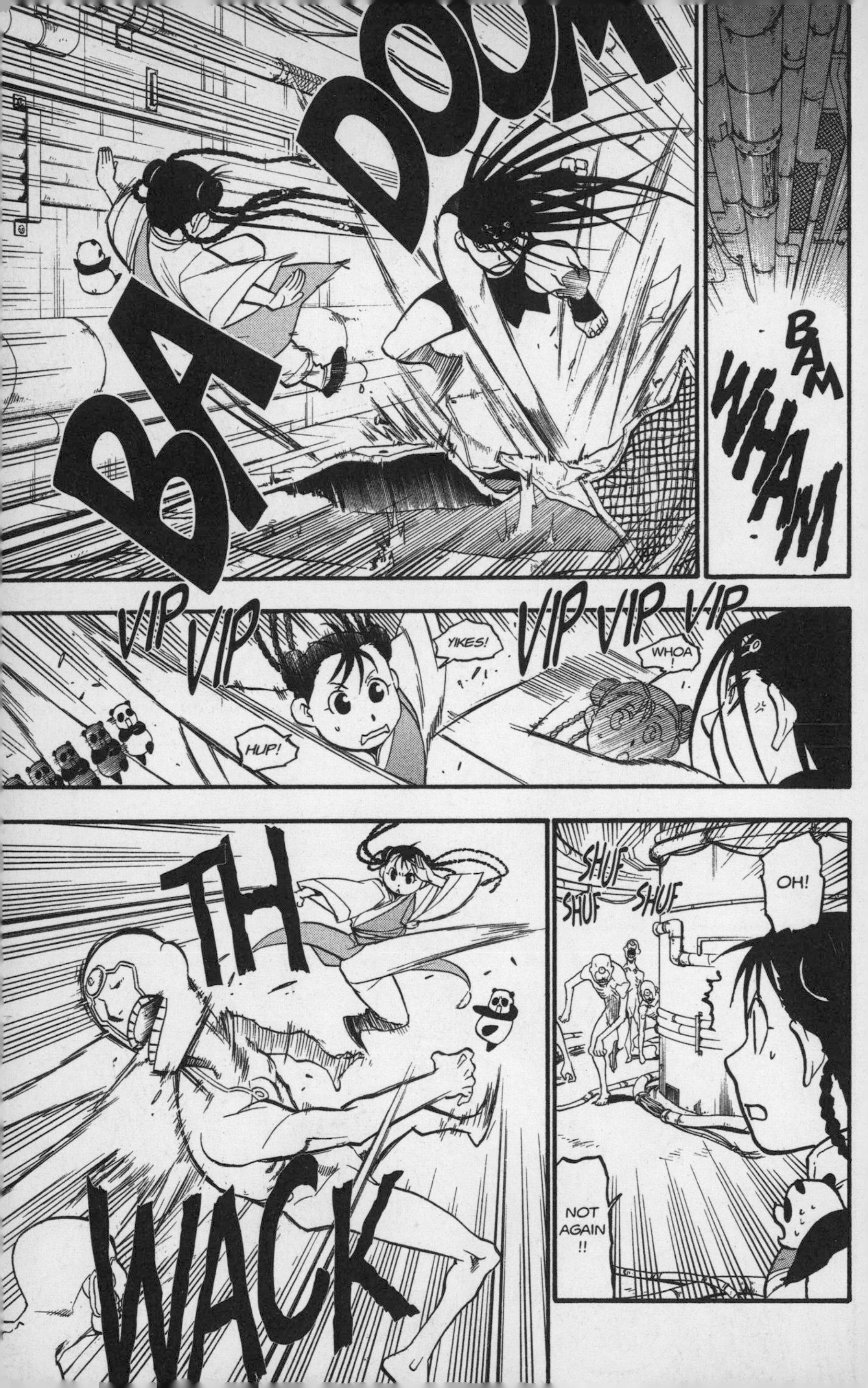
BAM
WHAM
DOOM
BA
WHOA!
VIP VIP VIP
YIKES!
VIP VIP
HUP!
OH!
SHUF SHUF
SHUF
NOT AGAIN!!
TH
WACK

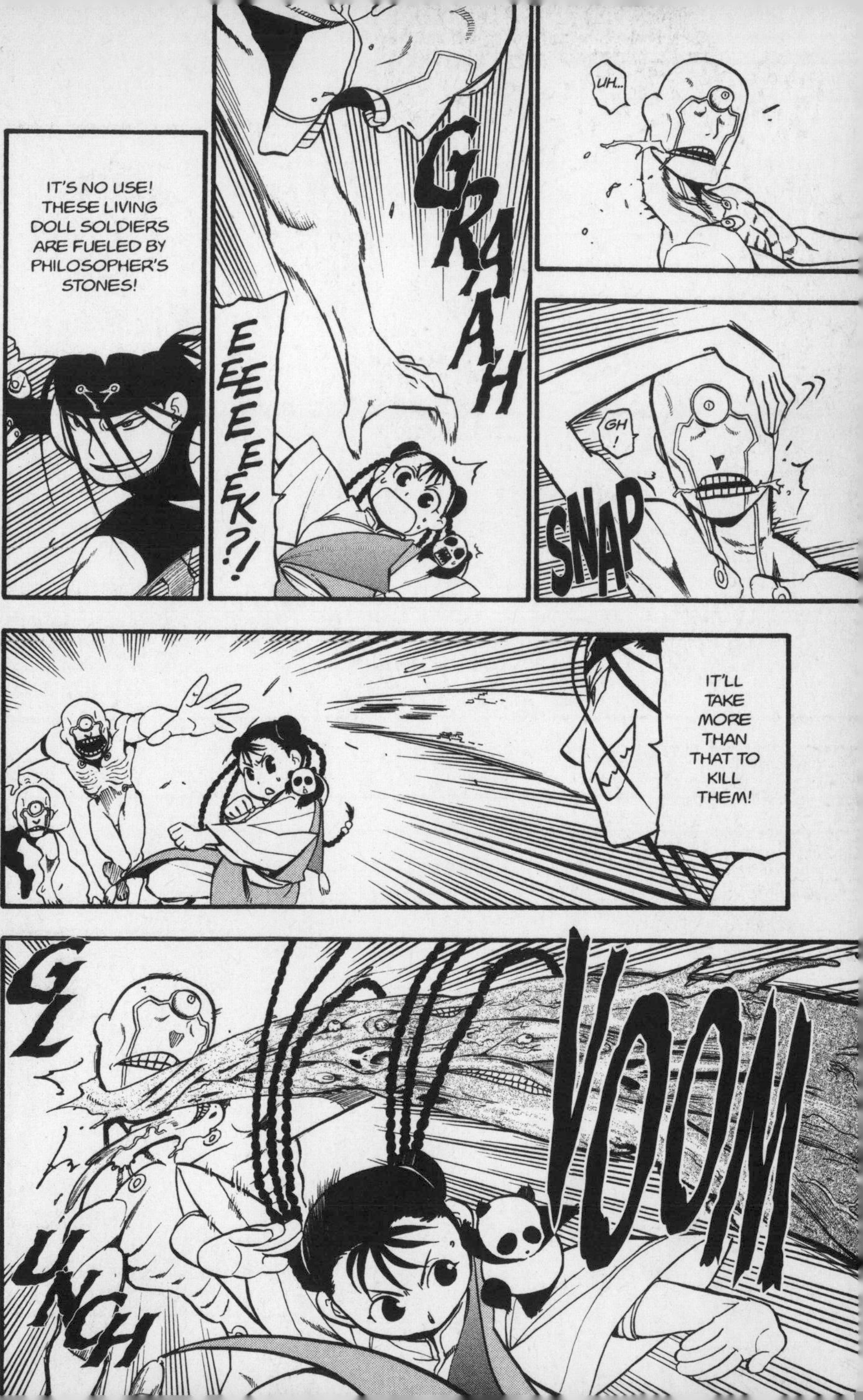
UH...
GH!
SNAP
GRAAH
EEEEEEK?!
IT'S NO USE! THESE LIVING DOLL SOLDIERS ARE FUELED BY PHILOSOPHER'S STONES!
IT'LL TAKE MORE THAN THAT TO KILL THEM!
VOOM
GLUNCH

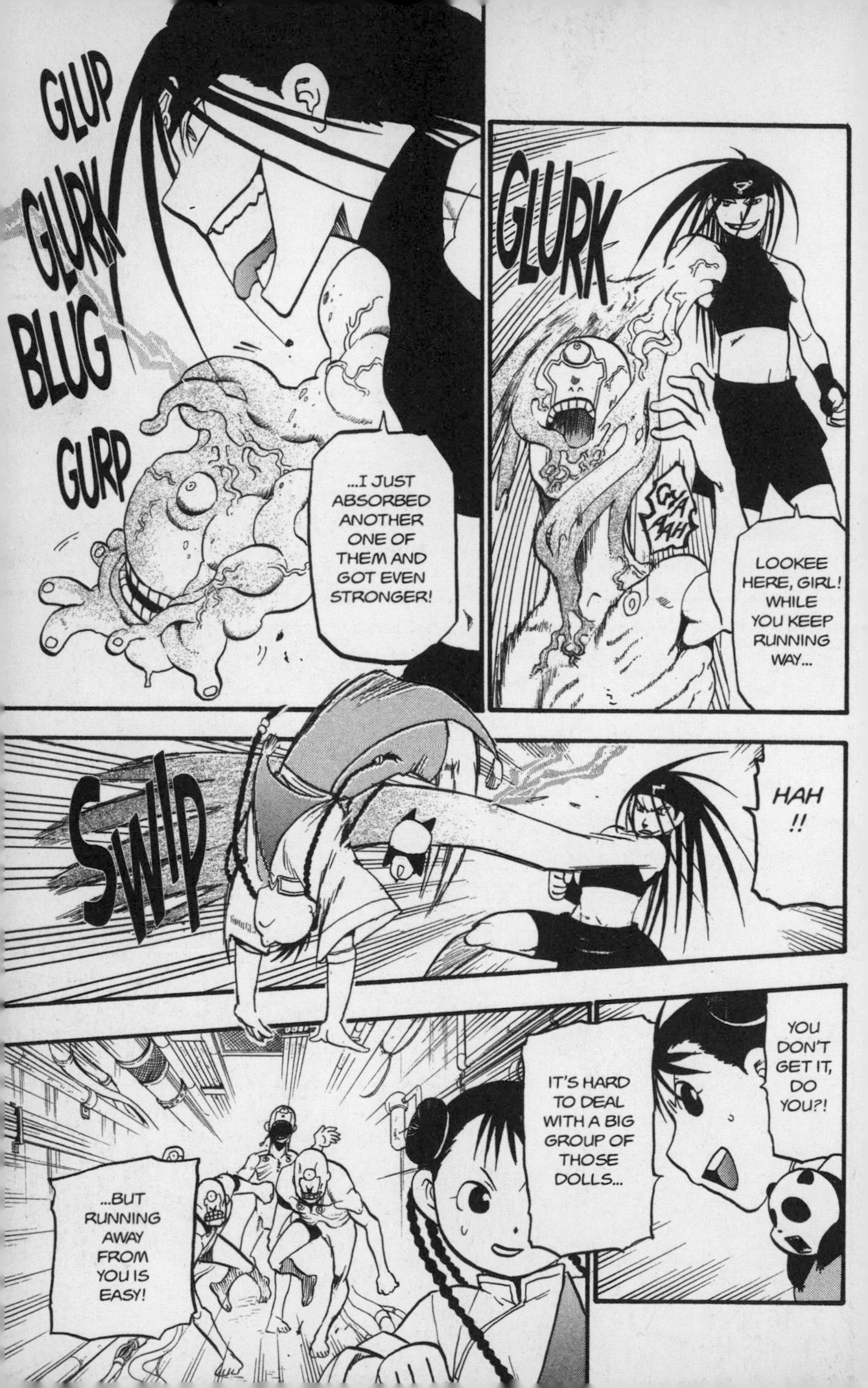
GLURK
LOOKEE HERE, GIRL! WHILE YOU KEEP RUNNING WAY...
GLUP
GLURK
BLUG
GURP
...I JUST ABSORBED ANOTHER ONE OF THEM AND GOT EVEN STRONGER!
HAH !!
SWIP
YOU DON'T GET IT, DO YOU?!
IT'S HARD TO DEAL WITH A BIG GROUP OF THOSE DOLLS...
...BUT RUNNING AWAY FROM YOU IS EASY!

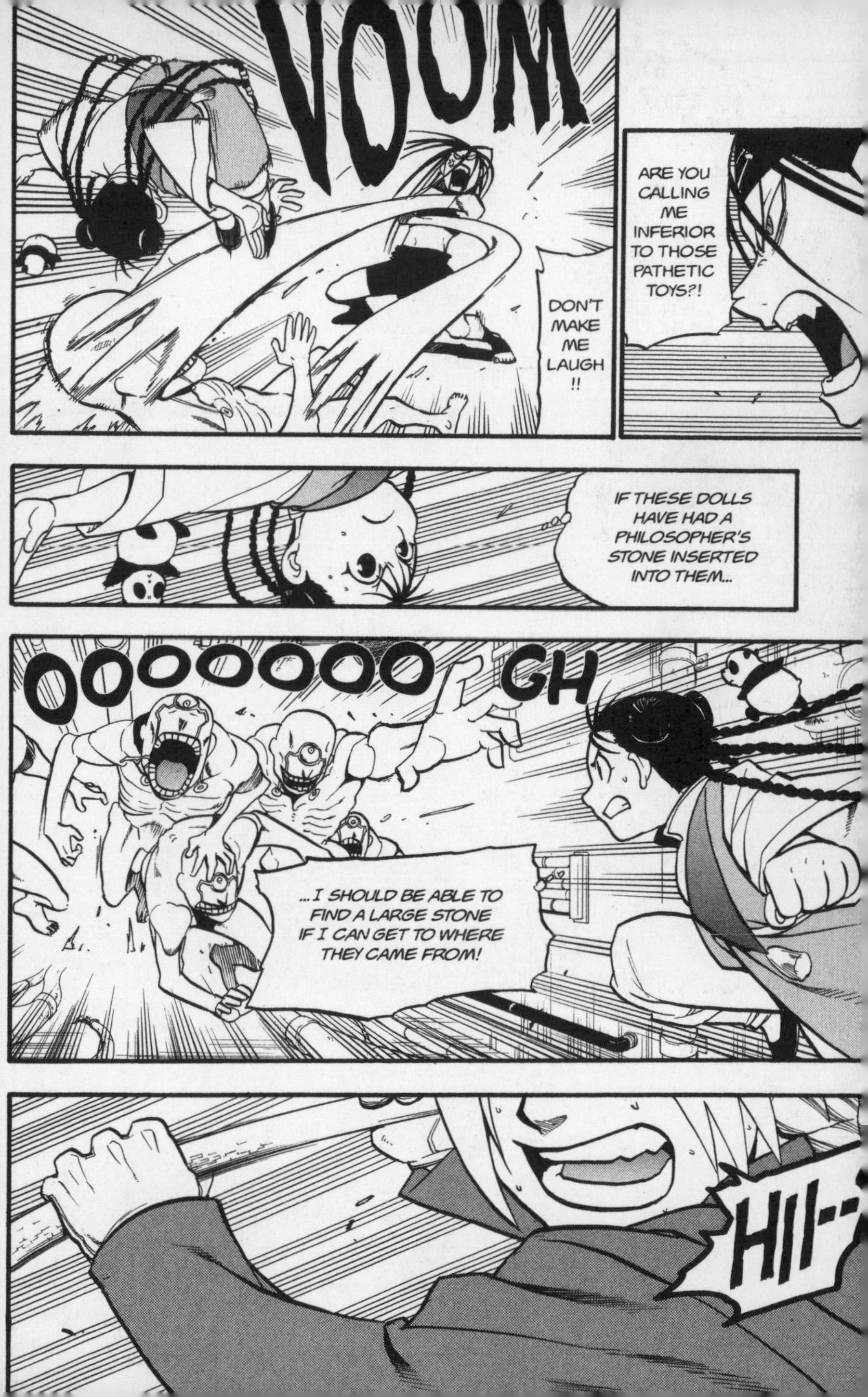
ARE YOU CALLING ME INFERIOR TO THOSE PATHETIC TOYS?!
VOOM
DON'T MAKE ME LAUGH !!
IF THESE DOLLS HAVE HAD A PHILOSOPHER'S STONE INSERTED INTO THEM...
OOOOOOOGH
...I SHOULD BE ABLE TO FIND A LARGE STONE IF I CAN GET TO WHERE THEY CAME FROM!
HII--

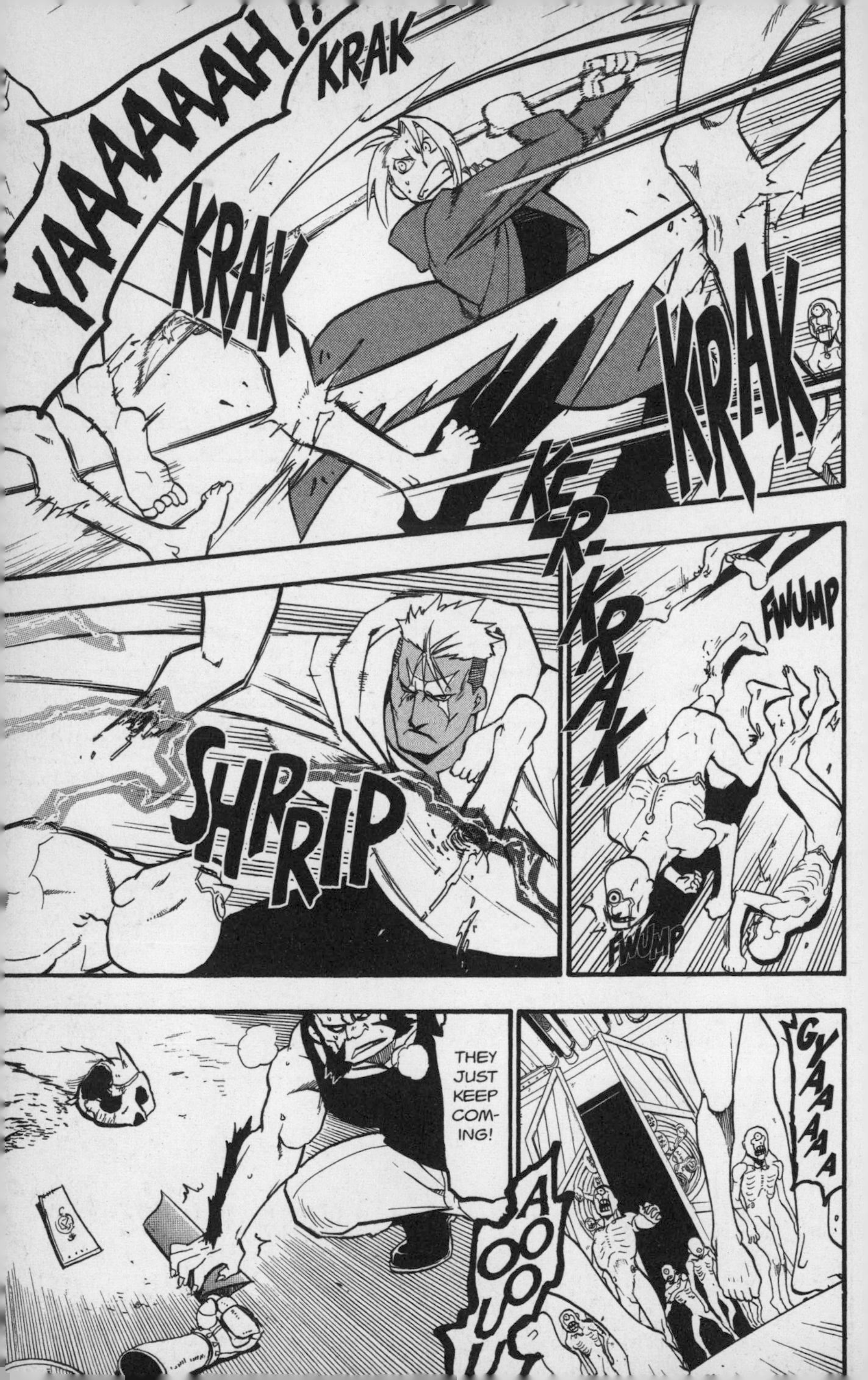
KRAK
YAAAAAH!!
KRAK
KRAK
KER-KRAK
FWUMP
FWUMP
SHRRIP
GYAAAAA
AOOOU
THEY JUST KEEP COM-ING!

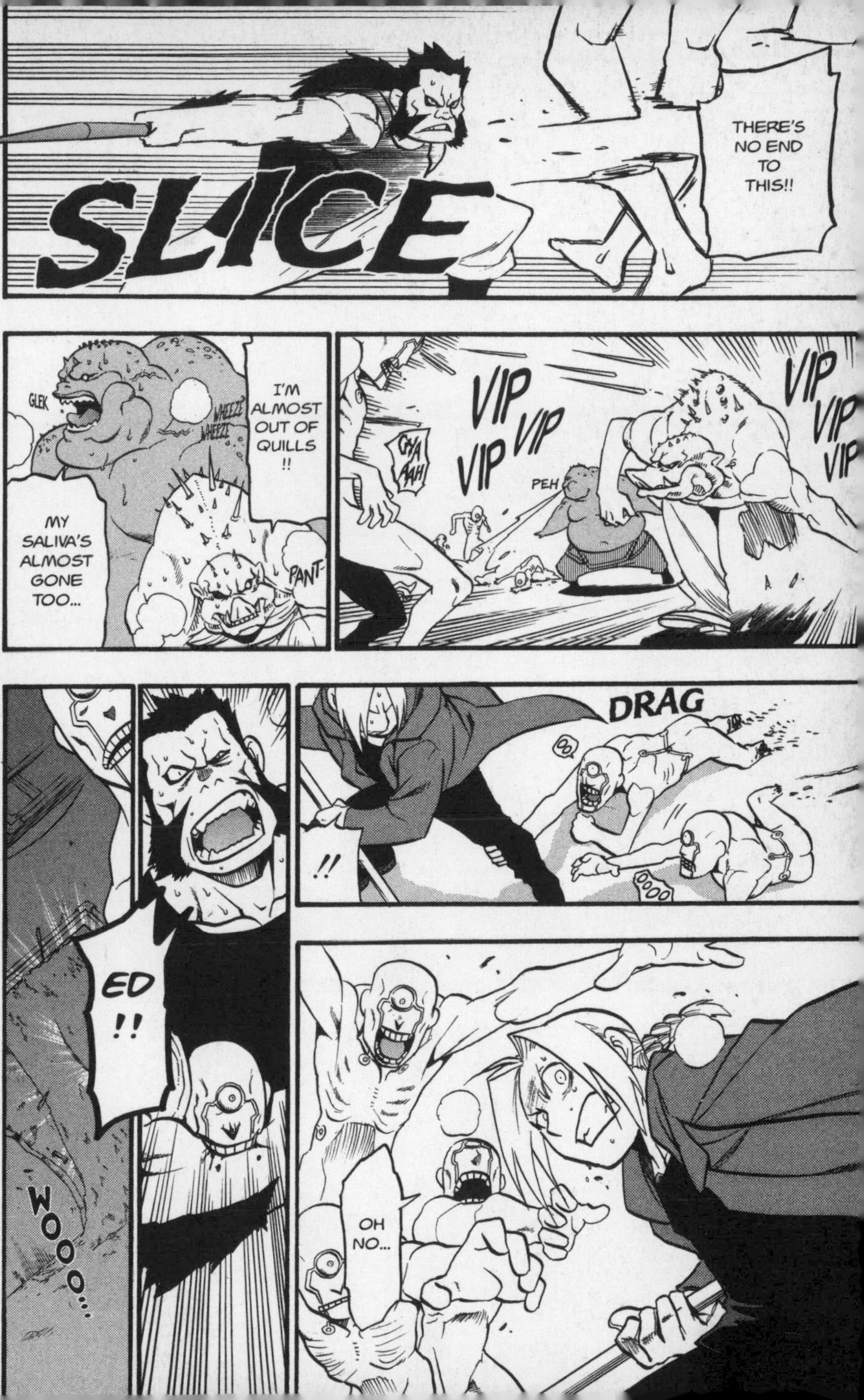
THERE'S NO END TO THIS!!
SLICE
VIP
VIP
VIP
GYAAAH
VIP
VIP
VIP
PEH
I'M ALMOST OUT OF QUILLS!!
WHEEZE
WHEEZE
GLEK
MY SALIVA'S ALMOST GONE TOO...
PANT
DRAG
!!
ED!!
WOOO...
OH NO...

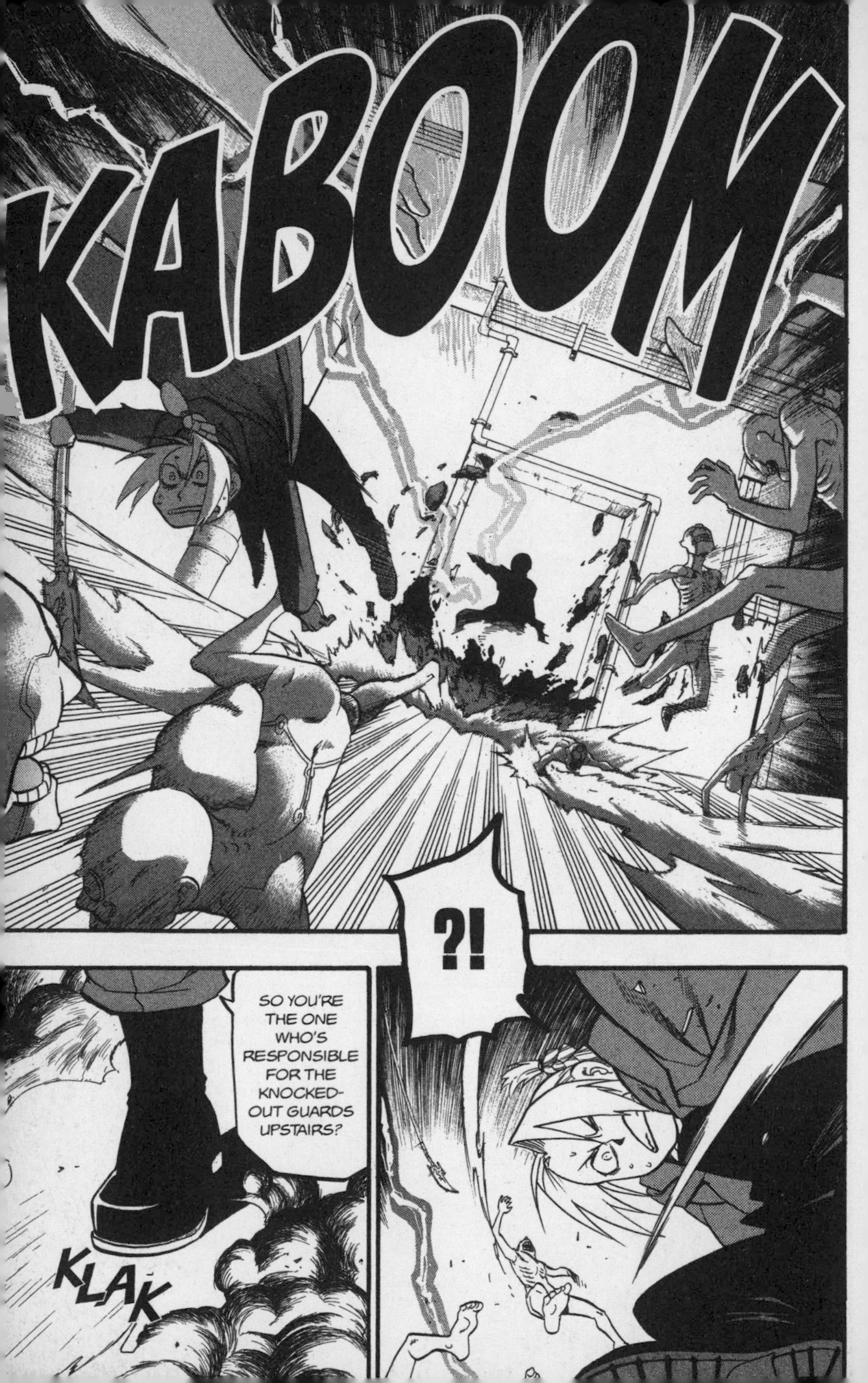
KABOOM
?!
SO YOU'RE THE ONE WHO'S RESPONSIBLE FOR THE KNOCKED-OUT GUARDS UPSTAIRS?
KLAK

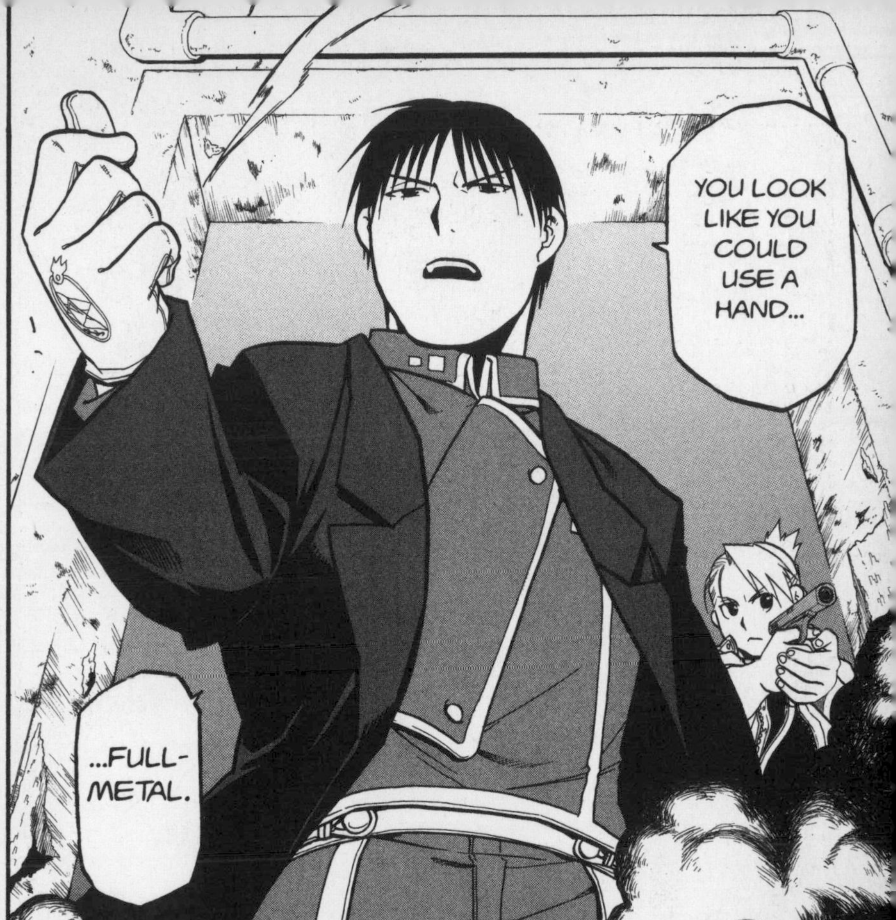
YOU LOOK LIKE YOU COULD USE A HAND...
...FULL-METAL.

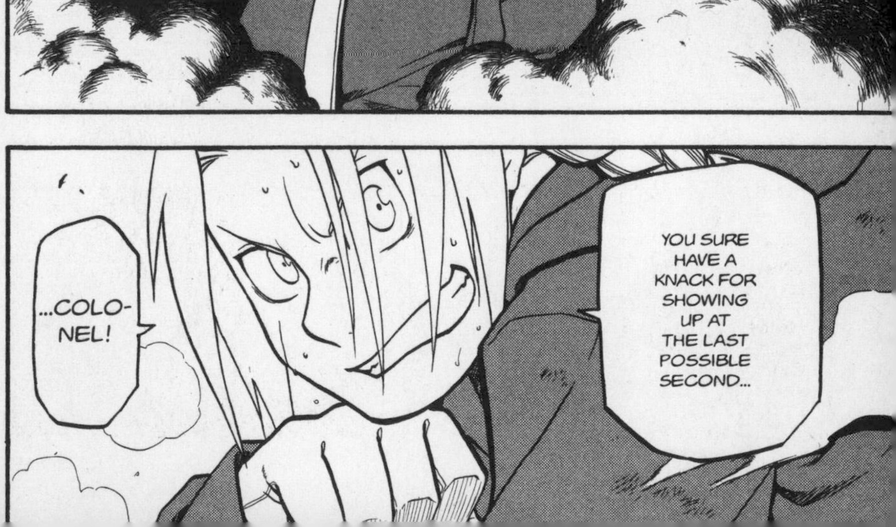
YOU SURE HAVE A KNACK FOR SHOWING UP AT THE LAST POSSIBLE SECOND...
...COLO-NEL!

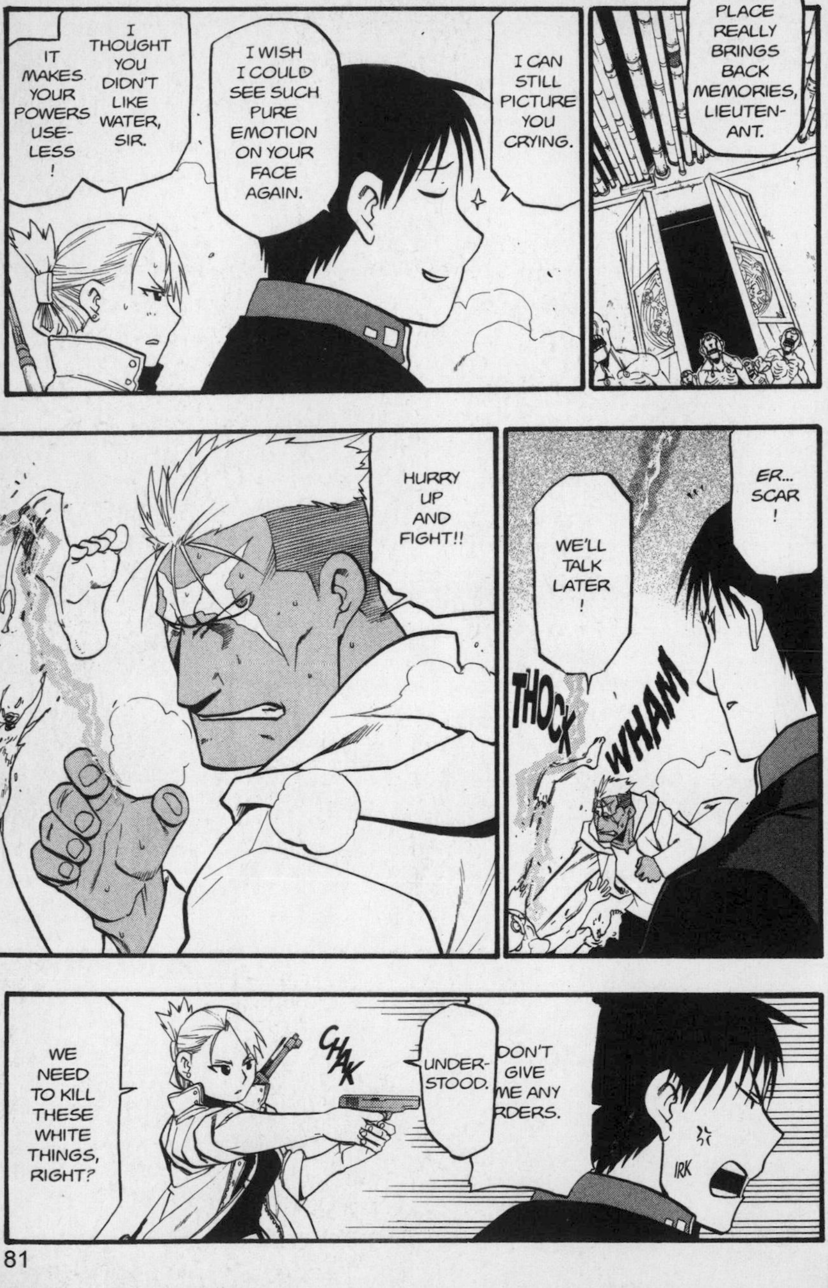
THIS PLACE REALLY BRINGS BACK MEMORIES, LIEUTENANT.
I CAN STILL PICTURE YOU CRYING.
I WISH I COULD SEE SUCH PURE EMOTION ON YOUR FACE AGAIN.
I THOUGHT YOU DIDN'T LIKE WATER, SIR.
IT MAKES YOUR POWERS USELESS!
ER... SCAR!
WE'LL TALK LATER!
THOCK
WHAM
HURRY UP AND FIGHT!!
DON'T GIVE ME ANY RDERS.
IRK
UNDERSTOOD.
CHAK
WE NEED TO KILL THESE WHITE THINGS, RIGHT?

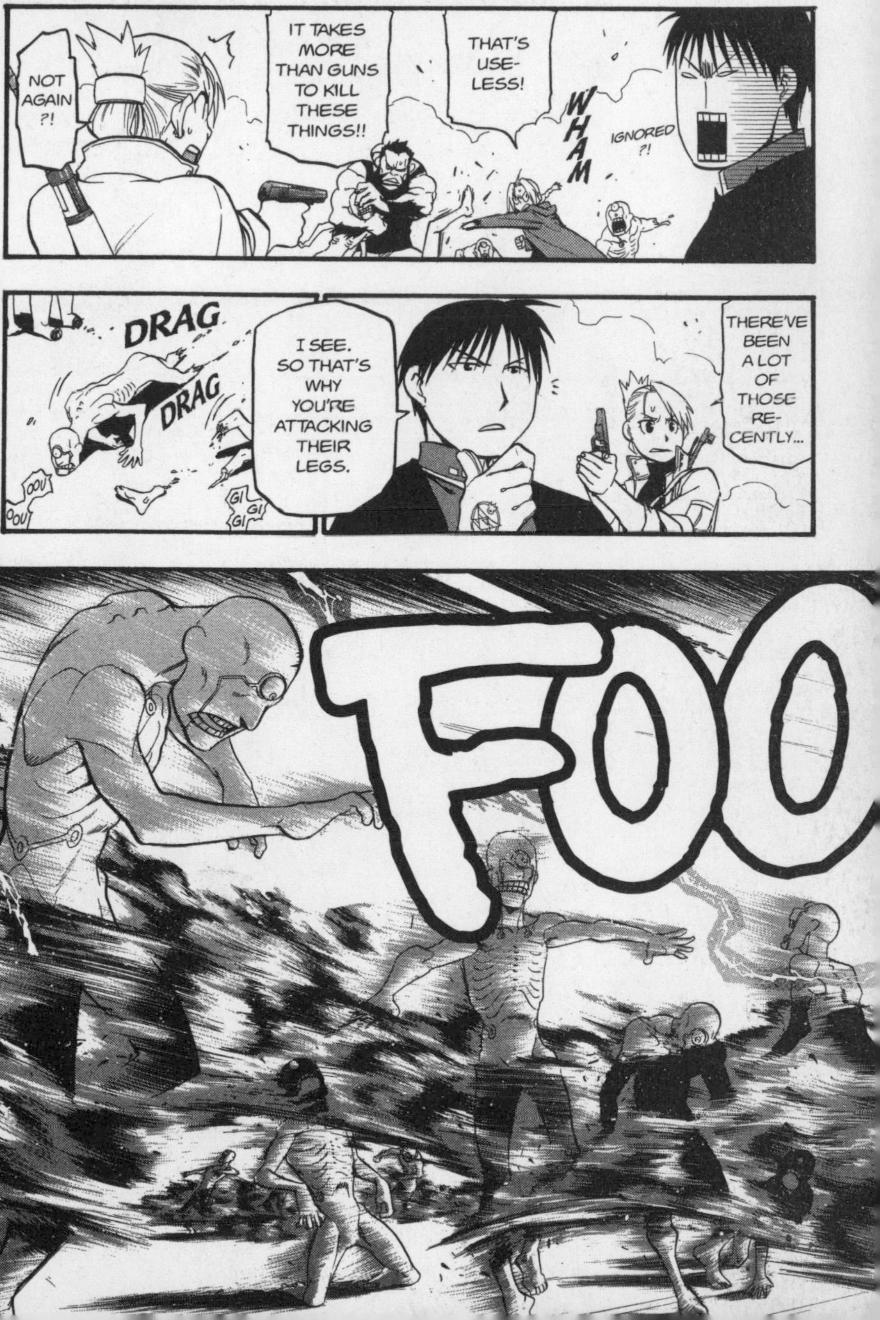
THAT'S USE-LESS!
WHAM
IGNORED ?!
IT TAKES MORE THAN GUNS TO KILL THESE THINGS!!
NOT AGAIN ?!
THERE'VE BEEN A LOT OF THOSE RE-CENTLY...
I SEE. SO THAT'S WHY YOU'RE ATTACKING THEIR LEGS.
DRAG
DRAG
GI GI GI
OOU OOU
FOO

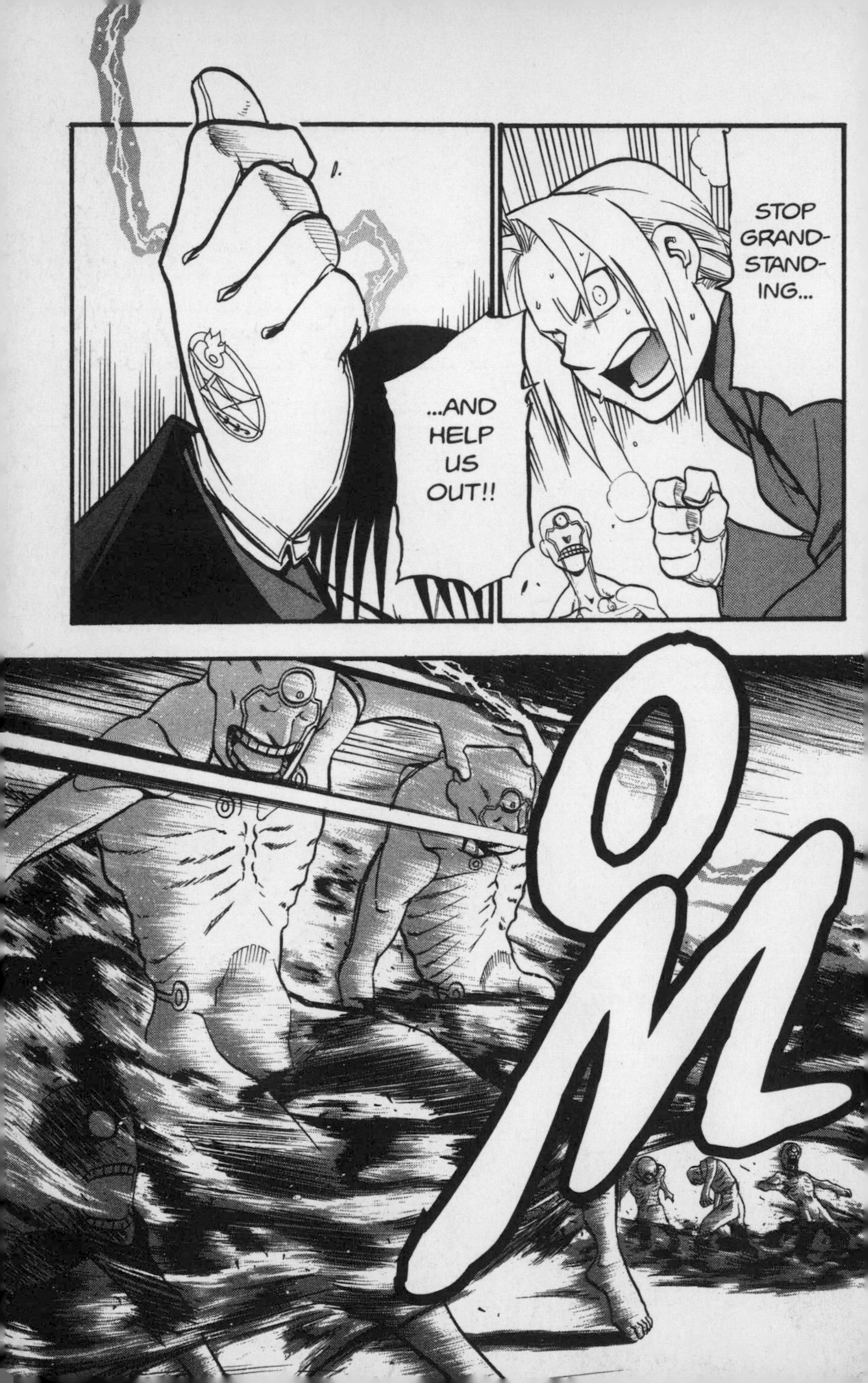
STOP GRAND-STANDING...
...AND HELP US OUT!!

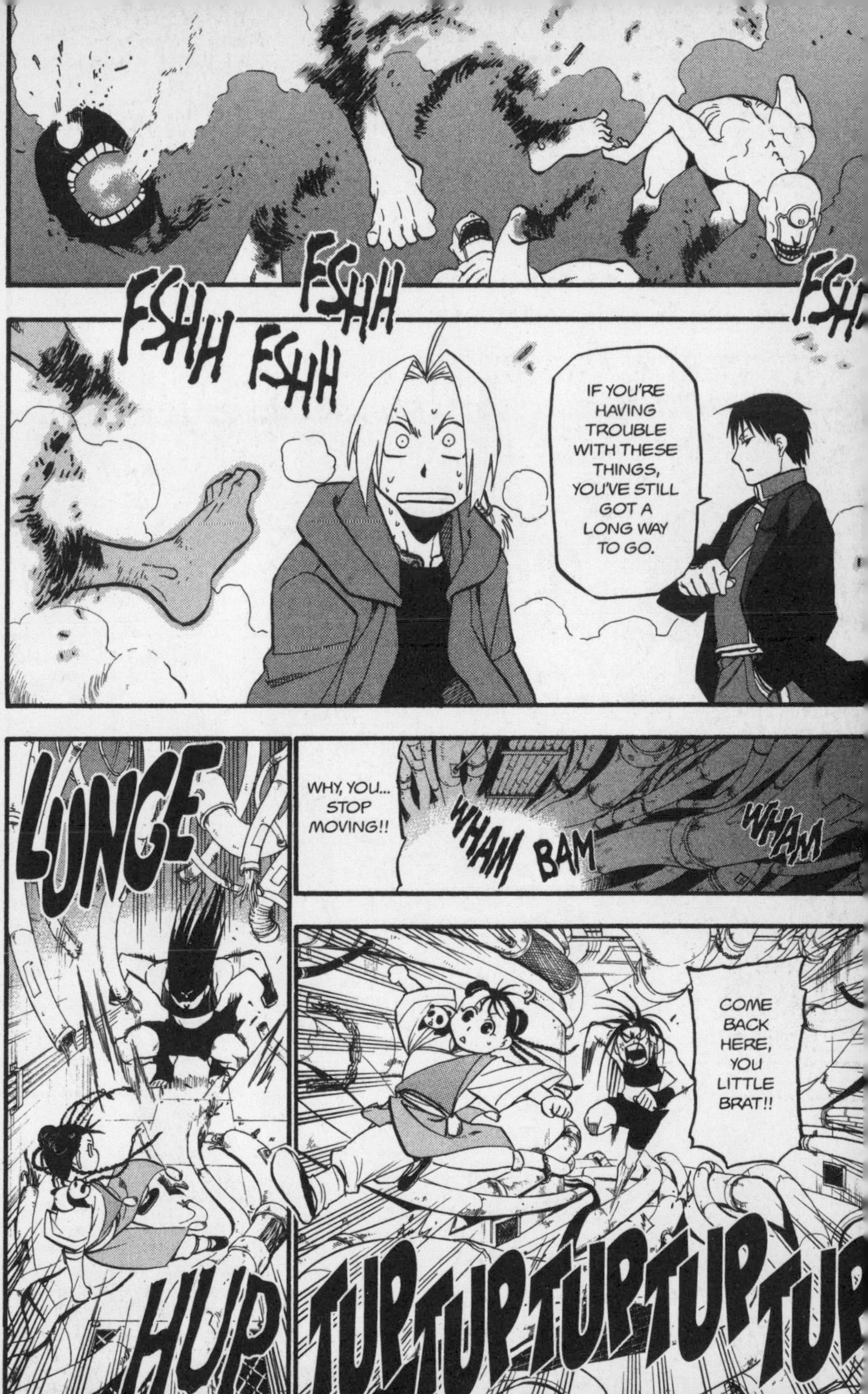
FSHH
FSHH
FSHH
FSHH
IF YOU'RE HAVING TROUBLE WITH THESE THINGS, YOU'VE STILL GOT A LONG WAY TO GO.
WHAM
BAM
WHAM
WHY, YOU... STOP MOVING!!
COME BACK HERE, YOU LITTLE BRAT!!
TUPTUPTUPTUPTUPTUP
LUNGE
HUP

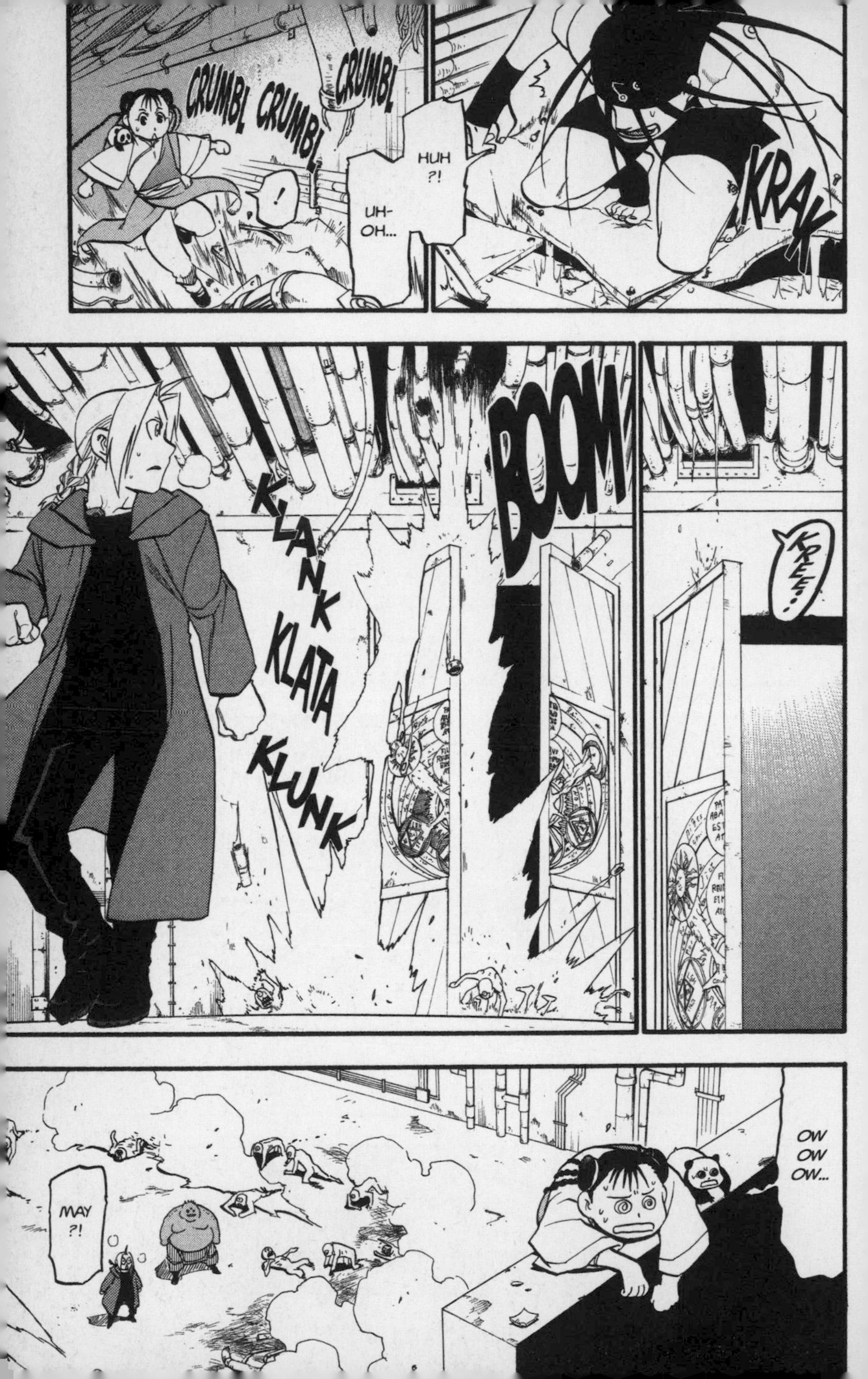
KRAK
CRUMBL
HUH ?!
UH-OH...
CRUMBL
CRUMBL
!
KREE...
BOOM
KLANK
KLATA
KLUNK
OW OW OW...
MAY ?!

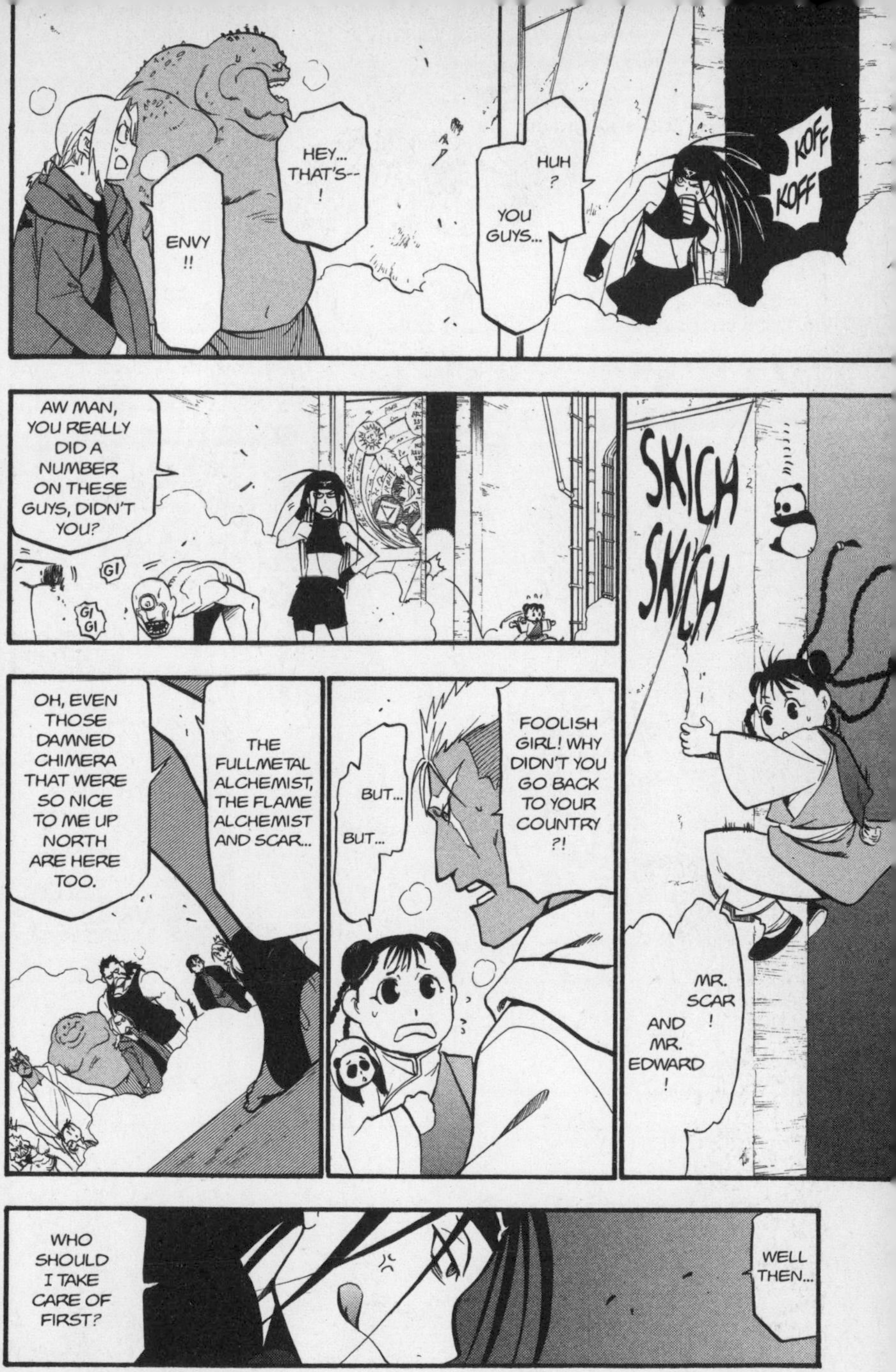
KOFF KOFF
HUH? YOU GUYS...
HEY... THAT'S--!
ENVY!!
SKICH SKICH
MR. SCAR!
AND MR. EDWARD!
AW MAN, YOU REALLY DID A NUMBER ON THESE GUYS, DIDN'T YOU?
GI
GI GI
FOOLISH GIRL! WHY DIDN'T YOU GO BACK TO YOUR COUNTRY?!
BUT... BUT...
THE FULLMETAL ALCHEMIST, THE FLAME ALCHEMIST AND SCAR...
OH, EVEN THOSE DAMNED CHIMERA THAT WERE SO NICE TO ME UP NORTH ARE HERE TOO.
WELL THEN...
WHO SHOULD I TAKE CARE OF FIRST?

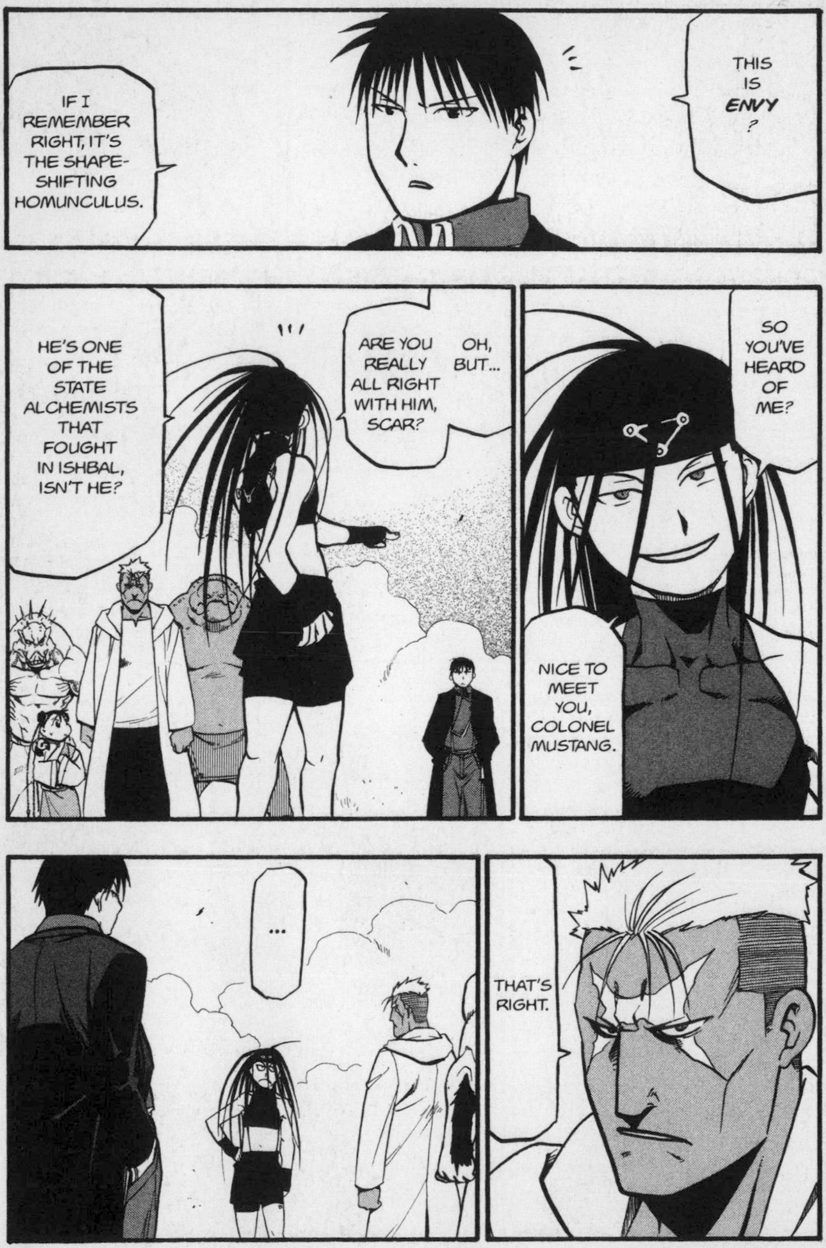
THIS IS ENVY?
IF I REMEMBER RIGHT, IT'S THE SHAPE-SHIFTING HOMUNCULUS.
SO YOU'VE HEARD OF ME?
NICE TO MEET YOU, COLONEL MUSTANG.
OH, BUT...
ARE YOU REALLY ALL RIGHT WITH HIM, SCAR?
HE'S ONE OF THE STATE ALCHEMISTS THAT FOUGHT IN ISHBAL, ISN'T HE?
THAT'S RIGHT.
...

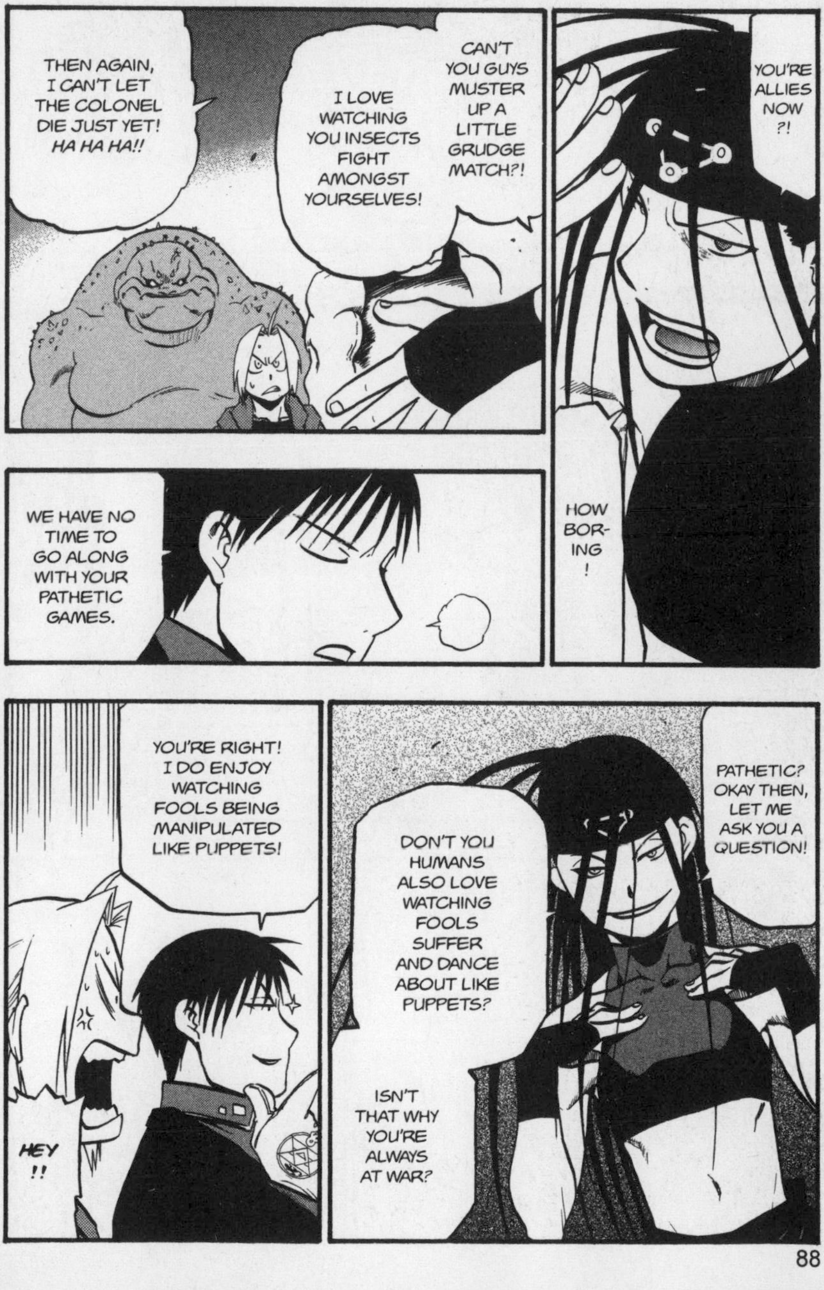
YOU'RE ALLIES NOW ?!
HOW BOR- ING !
CAN'T YOU GUYS MUSTER UP A LITTLE GRUDGE MATCH?!
I LOVE WATCHING YOU INSECTS FIGHT AMONGST YOURSELVES!
THEN AGAIN, I CAN'T LET THE COLONEL DIE JUST YET! *HA HA HA!!*
WE HAVE NO TIME TO GO ALONG WITH YOUR PATHETIC GAMES.
PATHETIC? OKAY THEN, LET ME ASK YOU A QUESTION!
DON'T YOU HUMANS ALSO LOVE WATCHING FOOLS SUFFER AND DANCE ABOUT LIKE PUPPETS?
ISN'T THAT WHY YOU'RE ALWAYS AT WAR?
YOU'RE RIGHT! I DO ENJOY WATCHING FOOLS BEING MANIPULATED LIKE PUPPETS!
HEY !!

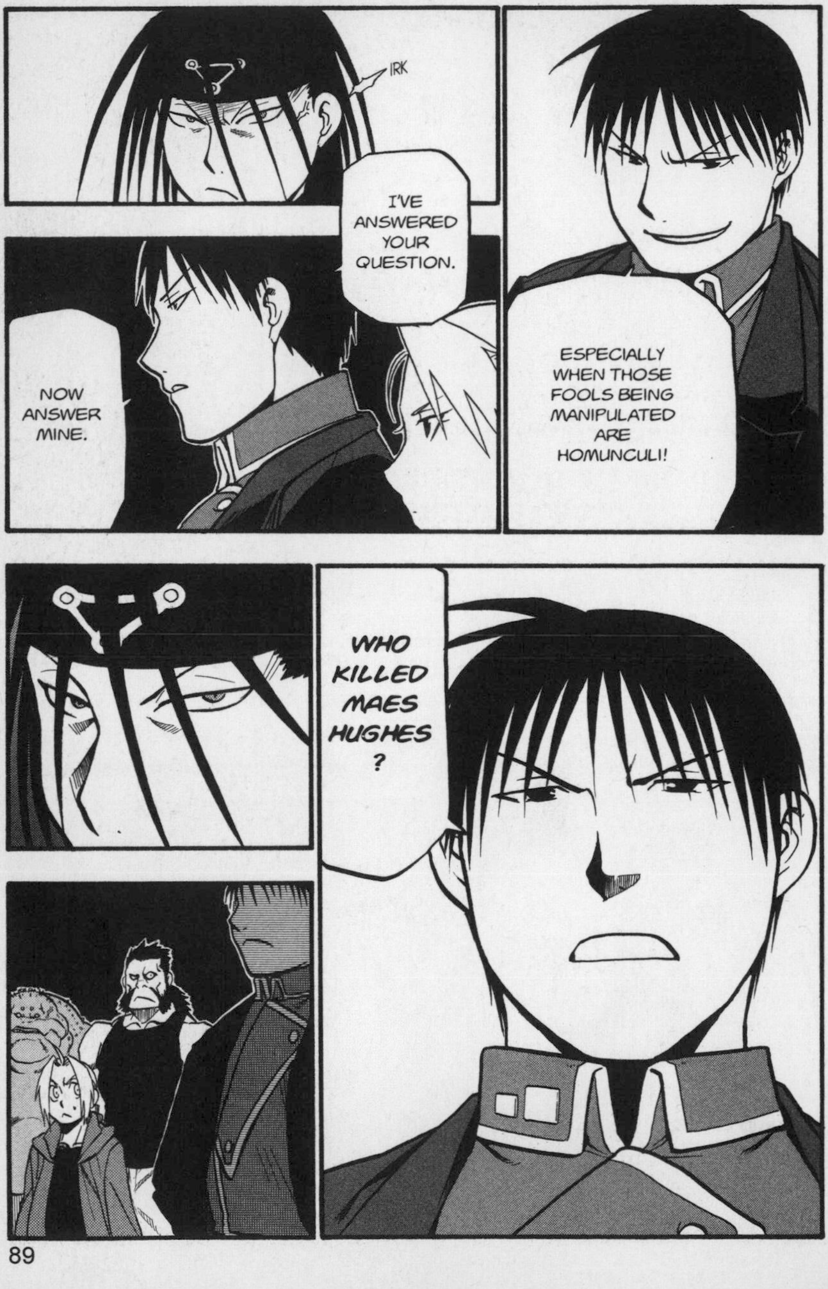
ESPECIALLY WHEN THOSE FOOLS BEING MANIPULATED ARE HOMUNCULI!
IRK
I'VE ANSWERED YOUR QUESTION.
NOW ANSWER MINE.
WHO KILLED MAES HUGHES ?

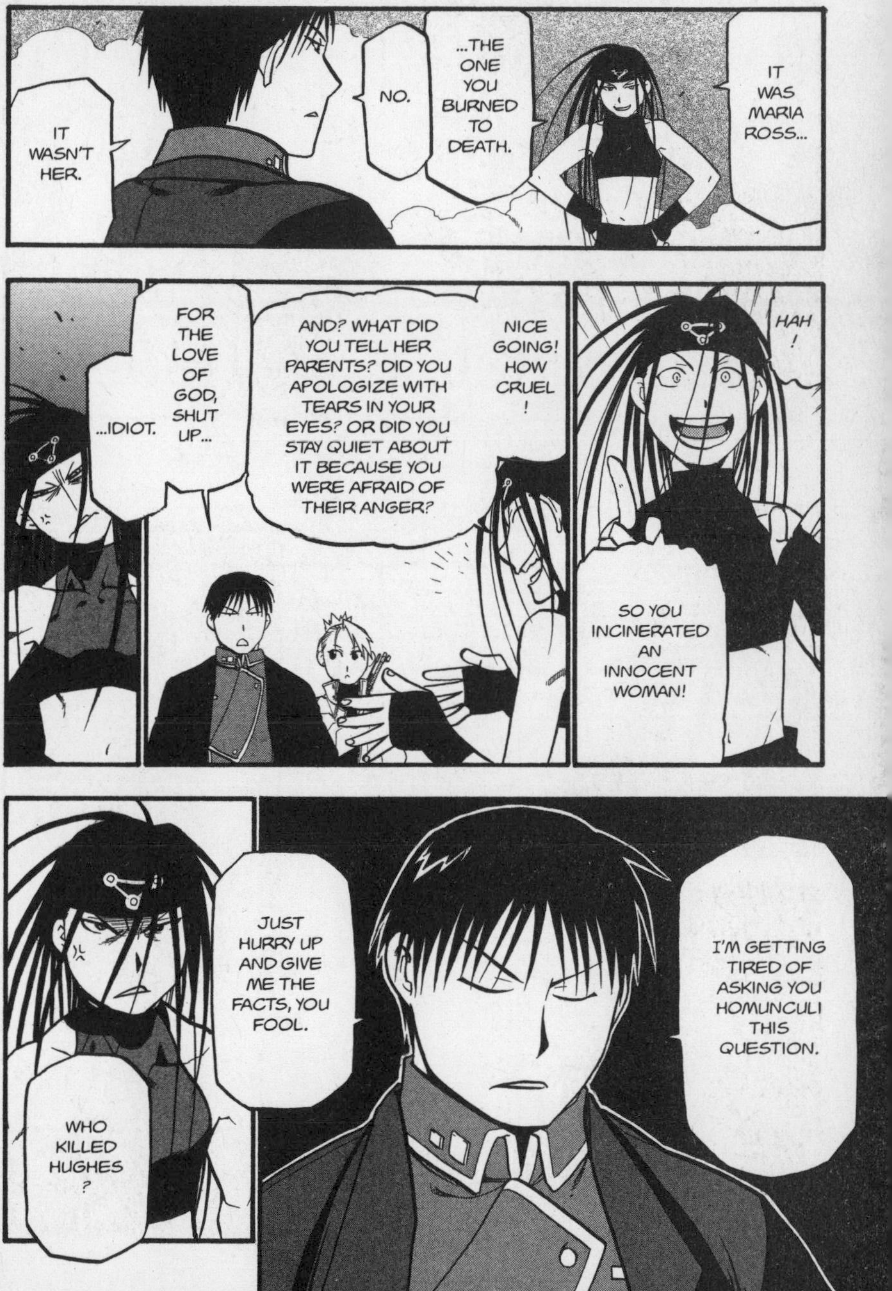
IT WAS MARIA ROSS...
...THE ONE YOU BURNED TO DEATH.
NO.
IT WASN'T HER.
HAH!
SO YOU INCINERATED AN INNOCENT WOMAN!
NICE GOING! HOW CRUEL!
AND? WHAT DID YOU TELL HER PARENTS? DID YOU APOLOGIZE WITH TEARS IN YOUR EYES? OR DID YOU STAY QUIET ABOUT IT BECAUSE YOU WERE AFRAID OF THEIR ANGER?
FOR THE LOVE OF GOD, SHUT UP...
...IDIOT.
I'M GETTING TIRED OF ASKING YOU HOMUNCULI THIS QUESTION.
JUST HURRY UP AND GIVE ME THE FACTS, YOU FOOL.
WHO KILLED HUGHES?

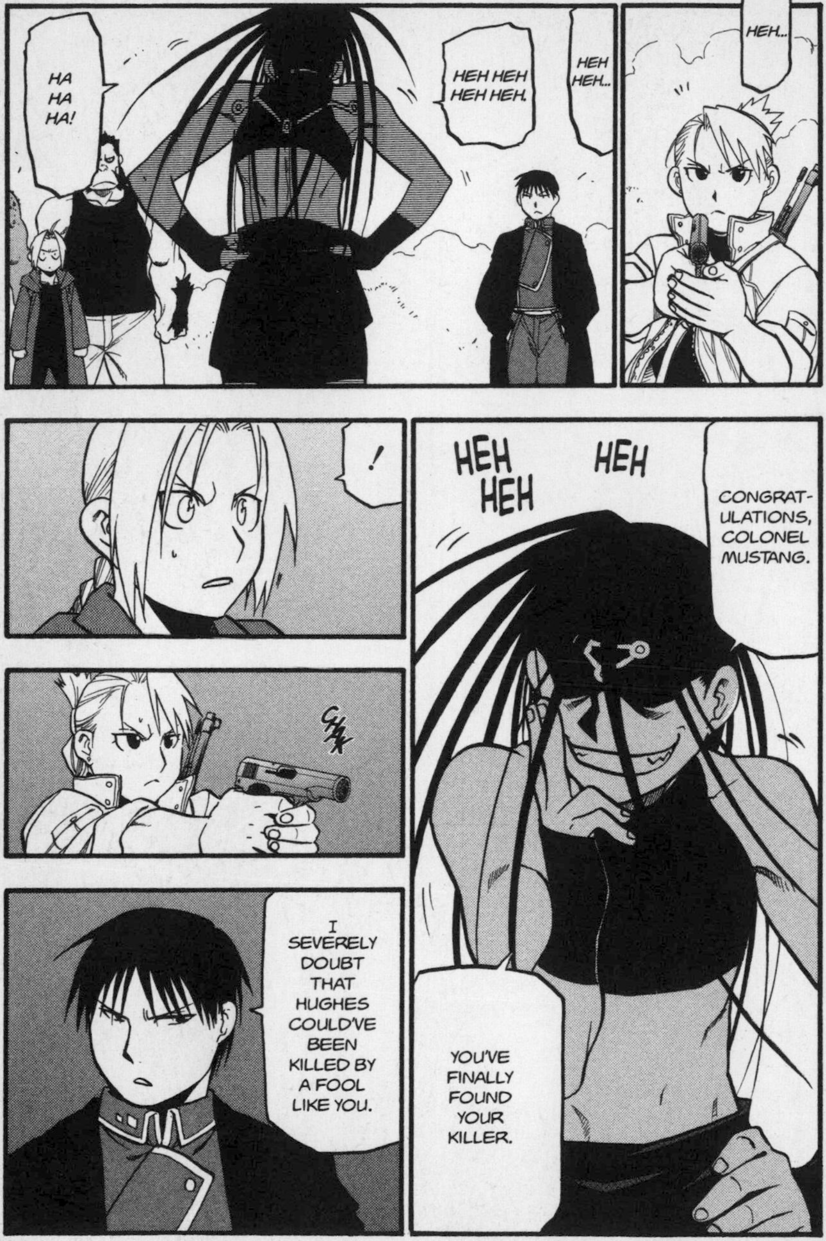
HEH...
HEH HEH...
HEH HEH HEH HEH.
HA HA HA!
HEH HEH HEH
CONGRAT-ULATIONS, COLONEL MUSTANG.
YOU'VE FINALLY FOUND YOUR KILLER.
!
CHAK
I SEVERELY DOUBT THAT HUGHES COULD'VE BEEN KILLED BY A FOOL LIKE YOU.

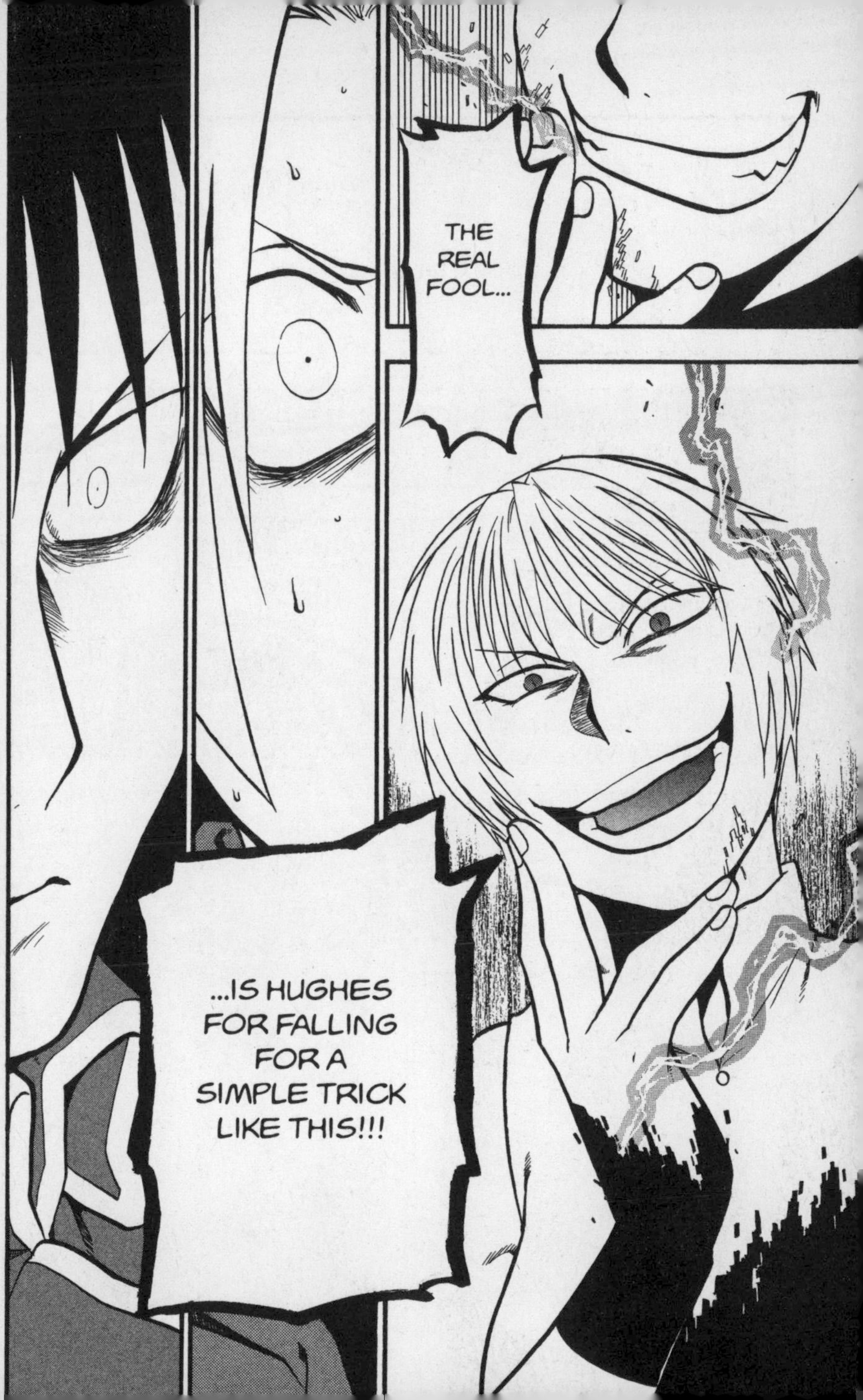
THE REAL FOOL...
...IS HUGHES FOR FALLING FOR A SIMPLE TRICK LIKE THIS!!!

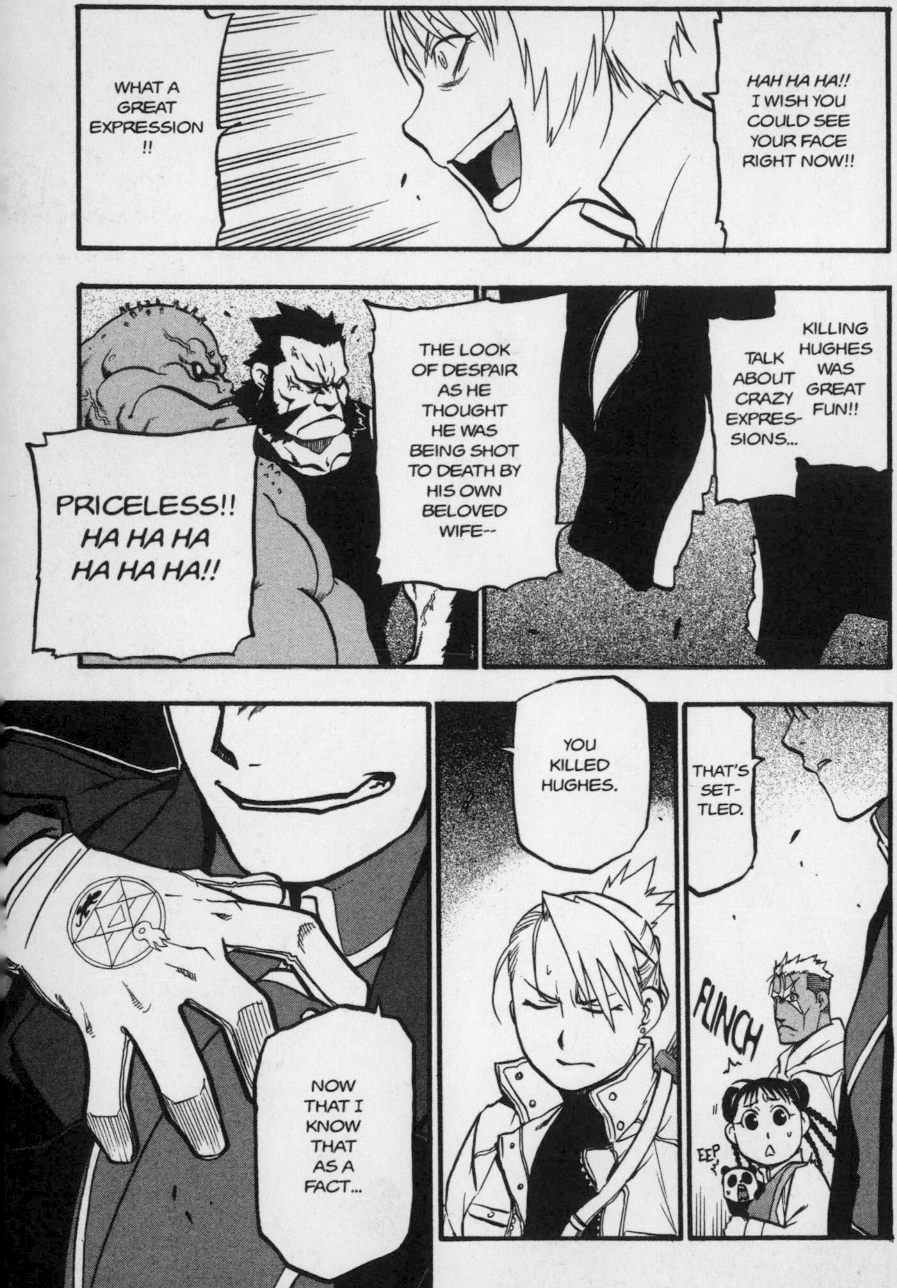
HAH HA HA!! I WISH YOU COULD SEE YOUR FACE RIGHT NOW!!
WHAT A GREAT EXPRESSION !!
KILLING HUGHES WAS GREAT FUN!!
TALK ABOUT CRAZY EXPRES-SIONS...
THE LOOK OF DESPAIR AS HE THOUGHT HE WAS BEING SHOT TO DEATH BY HIS OWN BELOVED WIFE--
PRICELESS!! HA HA HA HA HA HA!!
THAT'S SET-TLED.
FLINCH
EEP
YOU KILLED HUGHES.
NOW THAT I KNOW THAT AS A FACT...

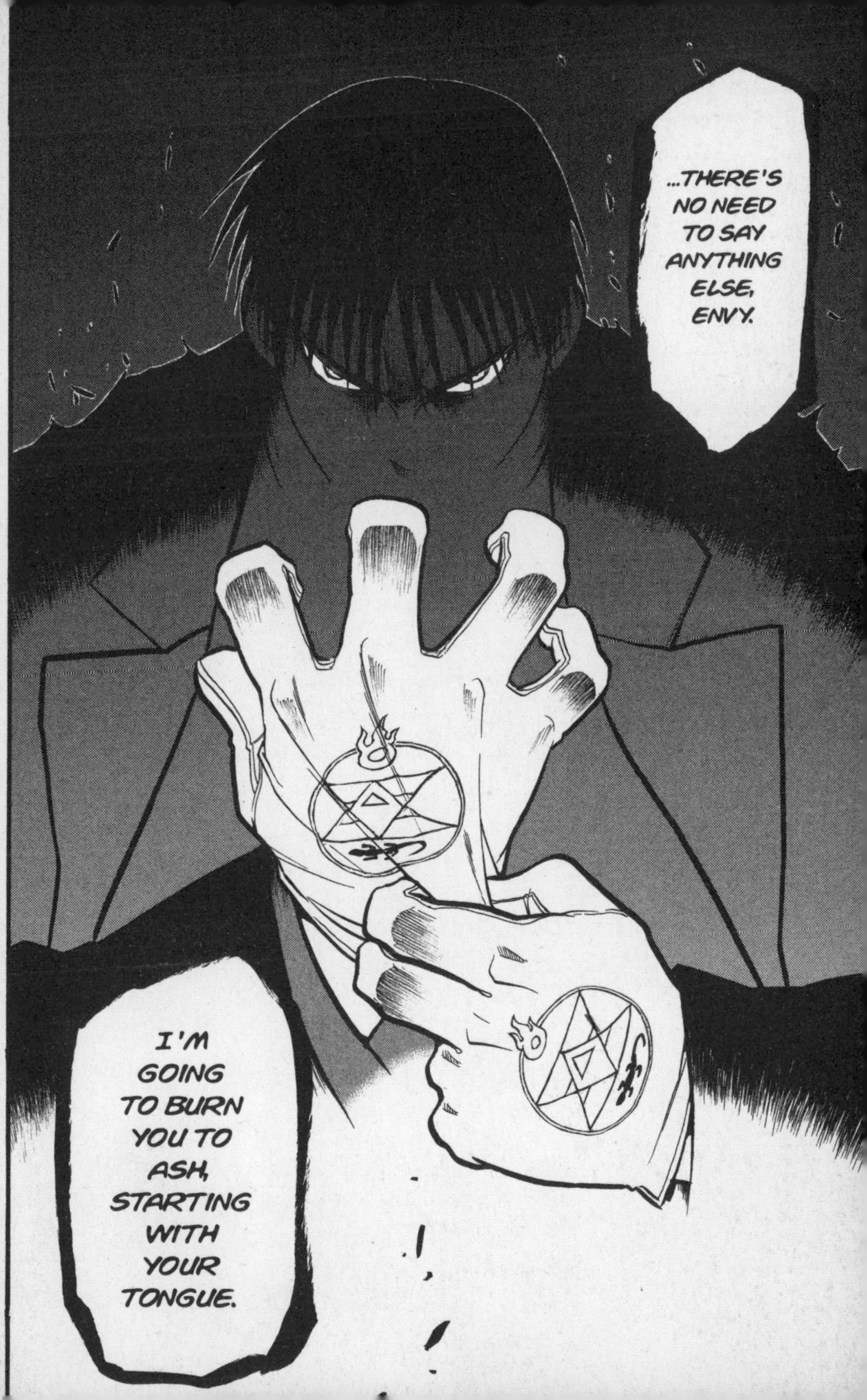
...THERE'S NO NEED TO SAY ANYTHING ELSE, ENVY.
I'M GOING TO BURN YOU TO ASH, STARTING WITH YOUR TONGUE.

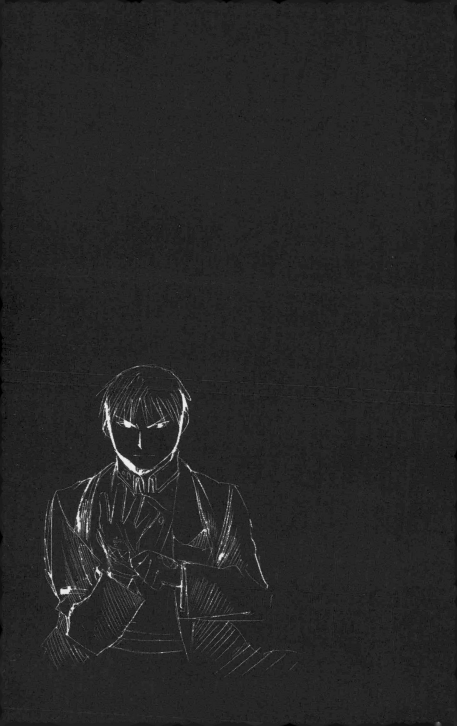

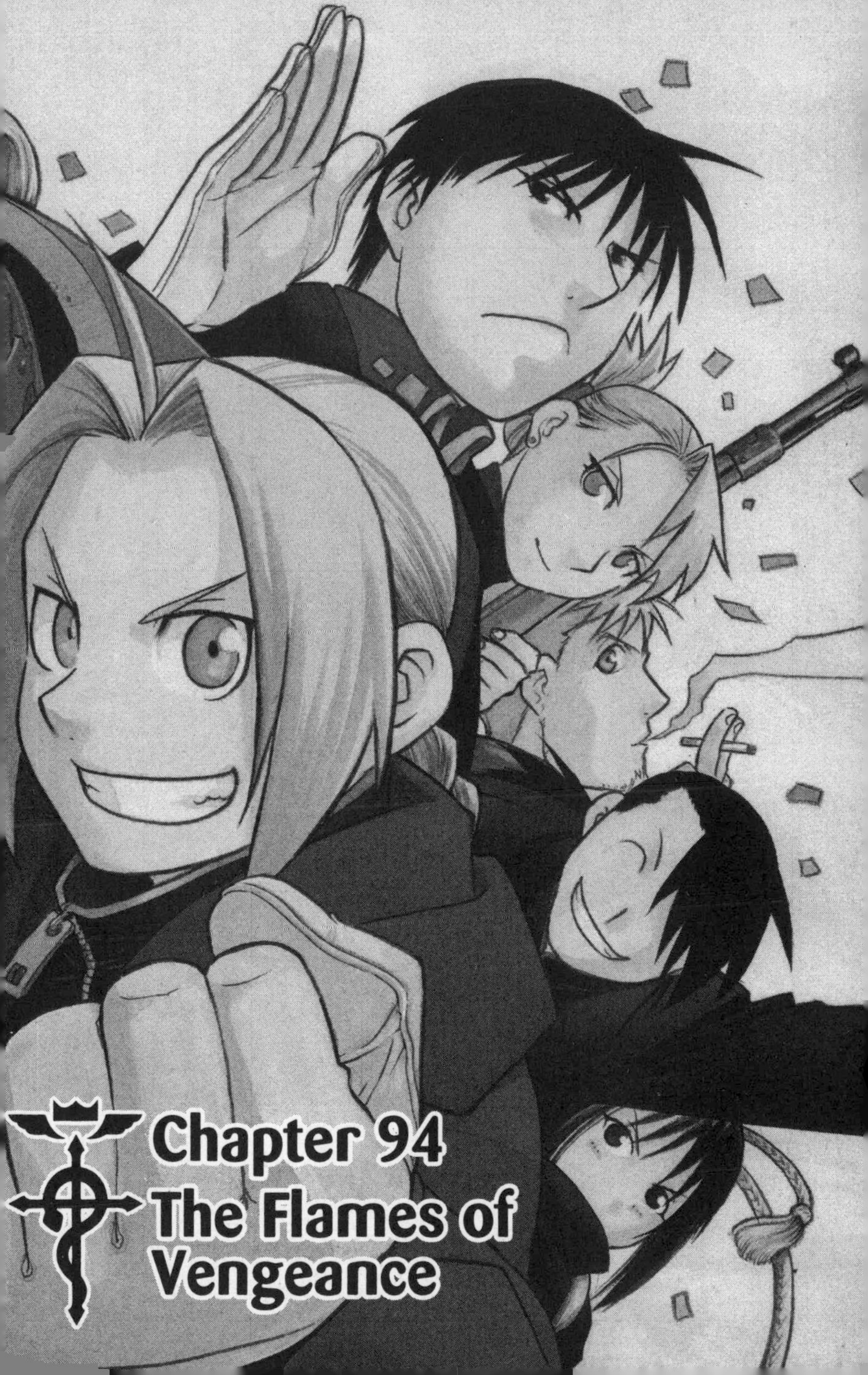
Chapter 94
The Flames of Vengeance

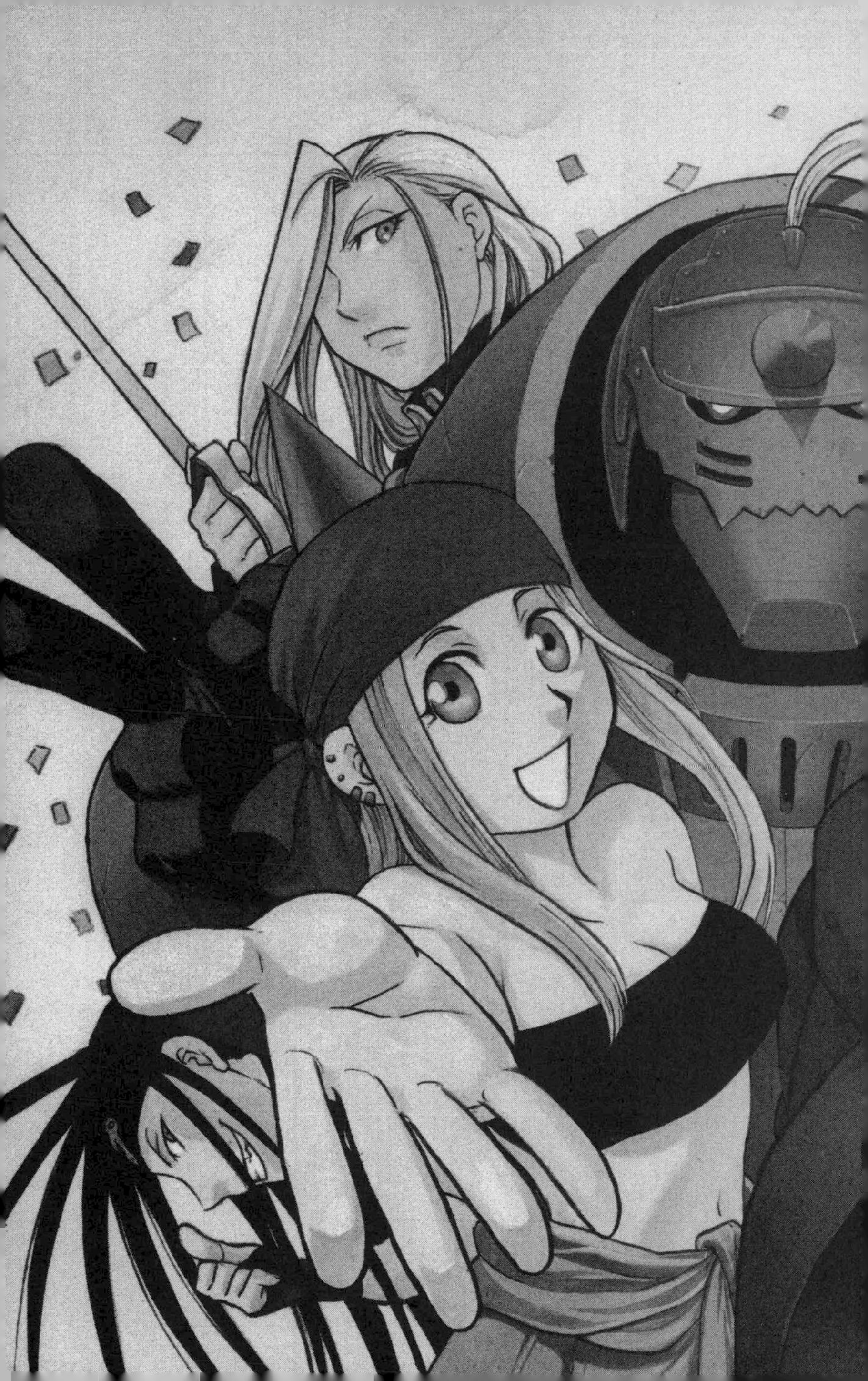

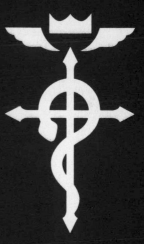

FULLMETAL
ALCHEMIST

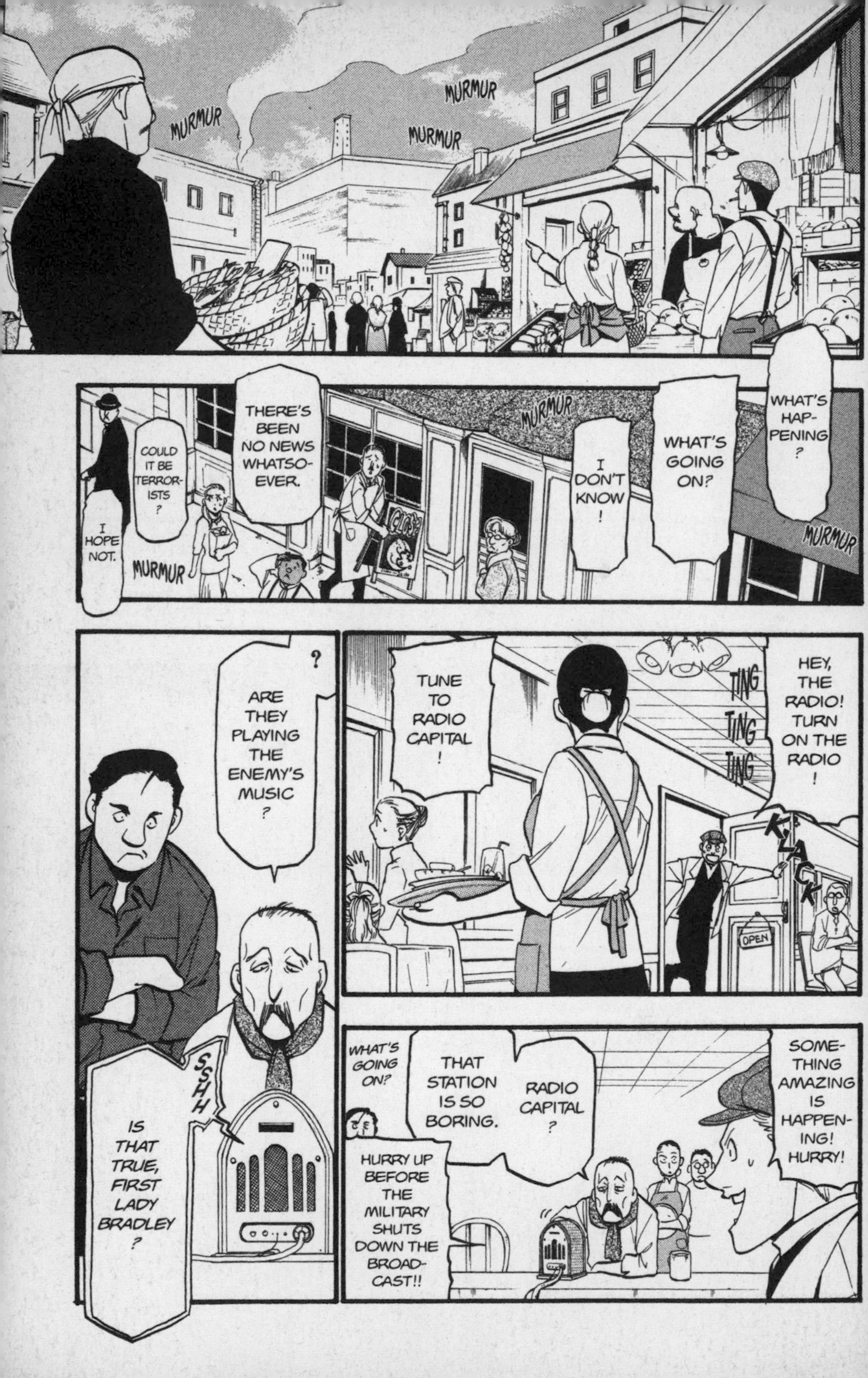
MURMUR
MURMUR
MURMUR
WHAT'S HAP-PENING?
WHAT'S GOING ON?
MURMUR
I DON'T KNOW!
MURMUR
THERE'S BEEN NO NEWS WHATSO-EVER.
COULD IT BE TERROR-ISTS?
I HOPE NOT.
MURMUR
HEY, THE RADIO! TURN ON THE RADIO!
TING TING TING
KLACK
OPEN
TUNE TO RADIO CAPITAL!
SOME-THING AMAZING IS HAPPEN-ING! HURRY!
RADIO CAPITAL?
THAT STATION IS SO BORING.
WHAT'S GOING ON?
HURRY UP BEFORE THE MILITARY SHUTS DOWN THE BROAD-CAST!!
?
ARE THEY PLAYING THE ENEMY'S MUSIC?
SSHH
IS THAT TRUE, FIRST LADY BRADLEY?

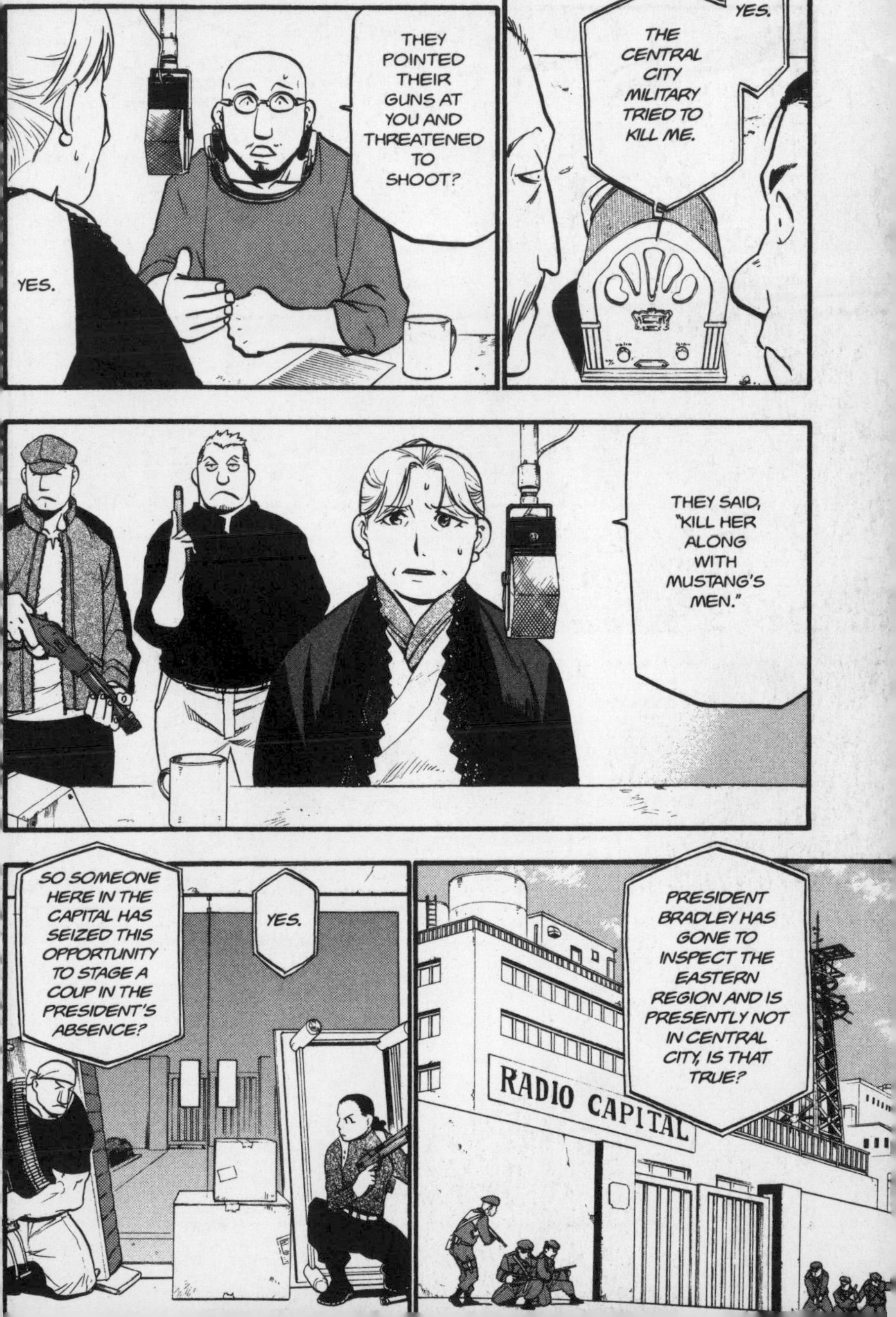
YES.
THE CENTRAL CITY MILITARY TRIED TO KILL ME.
THEY POINTED THEIR GUNS AT YOU AND THREATENED TO SHOOT?
YES.
THEY SAID, "KILL HER ALONG WITH MUSTANG'S MEN."
PRESIDENT BRADLEY HAS GONE TO INSPECT THE EASTERN REGION AND IS PRESENTLY NOT IN CENTRAL CITY, IS THAT TRUE?
RADIO CAPITAL
SO SOMEONE HERE IN THE CAPITAL HAS SEIZED THIS OPPORTUNITY TO STAGE A COUP IN THE PRESIDENT'S ABSENCE?
YES.

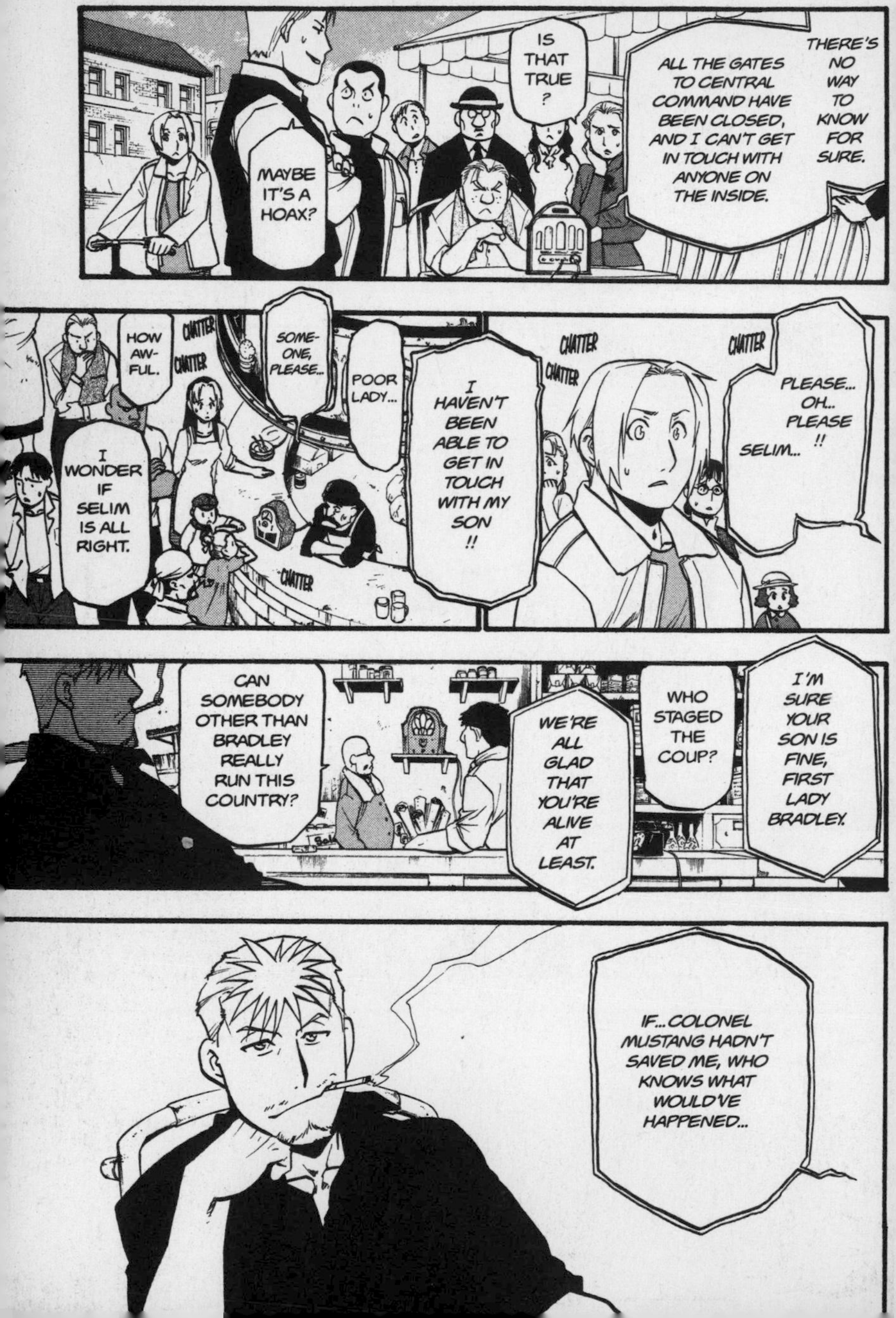
THERE'S NO WAY TO KNOW FOR SURE.
ALL THE GATES TO CENTRAL COMMAND HAVE BEEN CLOSED, AND I CAN'T GET IN TOUCH WITH ANYONE ON THE INSIDE.
IS THAT TRUE?
MAYBE IT'S A HOAX?
CHATTER
CHATTER
CHATTER
PLEASE... OH... PLEASE!!
SELIM...
I HAVEN'T BEEN ABLE TO GET IN TOUCH WITH MY SON!!
POOR LADY...
SOME-ONE, PLEASE...
CHATTER
HOW AW-FUL.
CHATTER
I WONDER IF SELIM IS ALL RIGHT.
CHATTER
I'M SURE YOUR SON IS FINE, FIRST LADY BRADLEY.
WHO STAGED THE COUP?
WE'RE ALL GLAD THAT YOU'RE ALIVE AT LEAST.
CAN SOMEBODY OTHER THAN BRADLEY REALLY RUN THIS COUNTRY?
IF... COLONEL MUSTANG HADN'T SAVED ME, WHO KNOWS WHAT WOULD'VE HAPPENED...

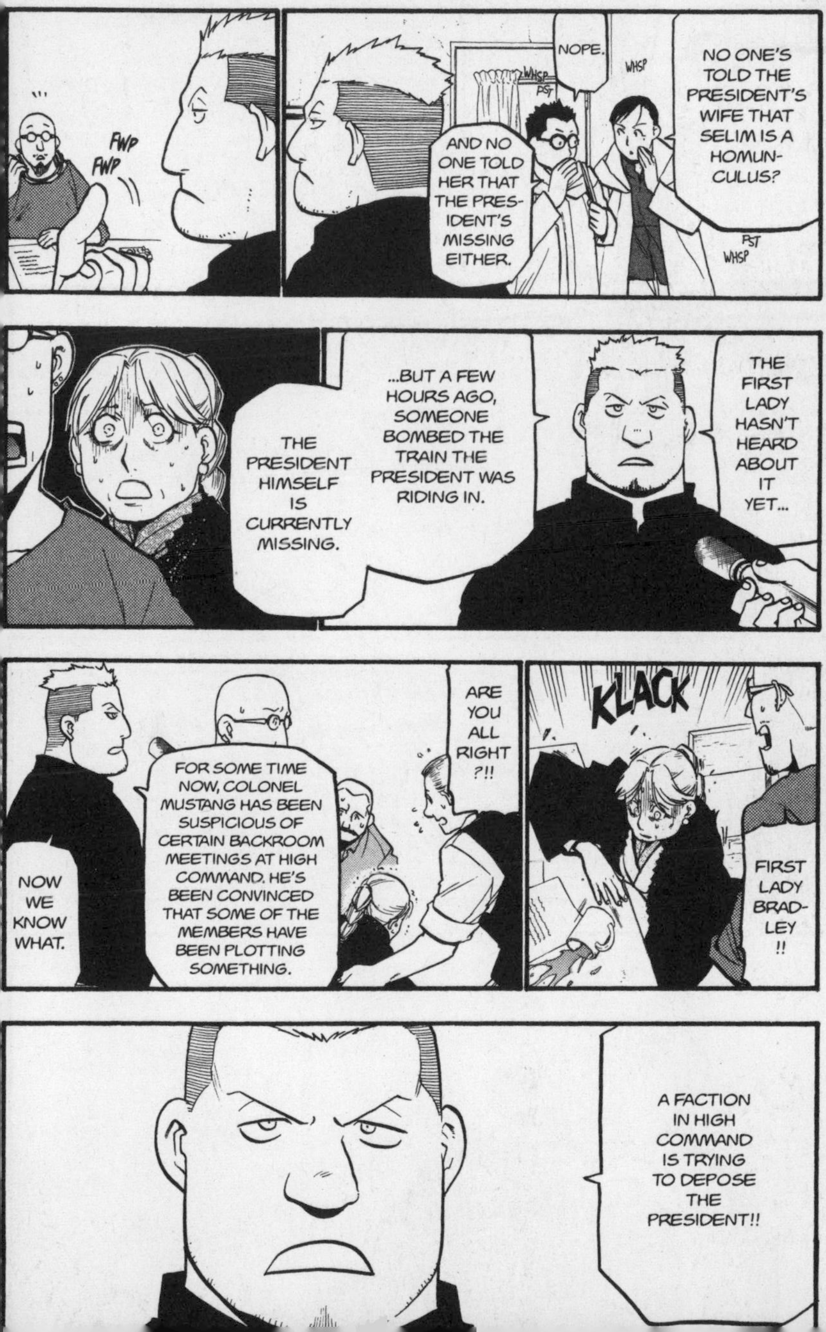
NO ONE'S TOLD THE PRESIDENT'S WIFE THAT SELIM IS A HOMUNCULUS?
WHSP
NOPE.
WHSP PST
AND NO ONE TOLD HER THAT THE PRESIDENT'S MISSING EITHER.
PST WHSP
FWP FWP
THE FIRST LADY HASN'T HEARD ABOUT IT YET...
...BUT A FEW HOURS AGO, SOMEONE BOMBED THE TRAIN THE PRESIDENT WAS RIDING IN.
THE PRESIDENT HIMSELF IS CURRENTLY MISSING.
KLACK
FIRST LADY BRADLEY!!
ARE YOU ALL RIGHT?!!
FOR SOME TIME NOW, COLONEL MUSTANG HAS BEEN SUSPICIOUS OF CERTAIN BACKROOM MEETINGS AT HIGH COMMAND. HE'S BEEN CONVINCED THAT SOME OF THE MEMBERS HAVE BEEN PLOTTING SOMETHING.
NOW WE KNOW WHAT.
A FACTION IN HIGH COMMAND IS TRYING TO DEPOSE THE PRESIDENT!!

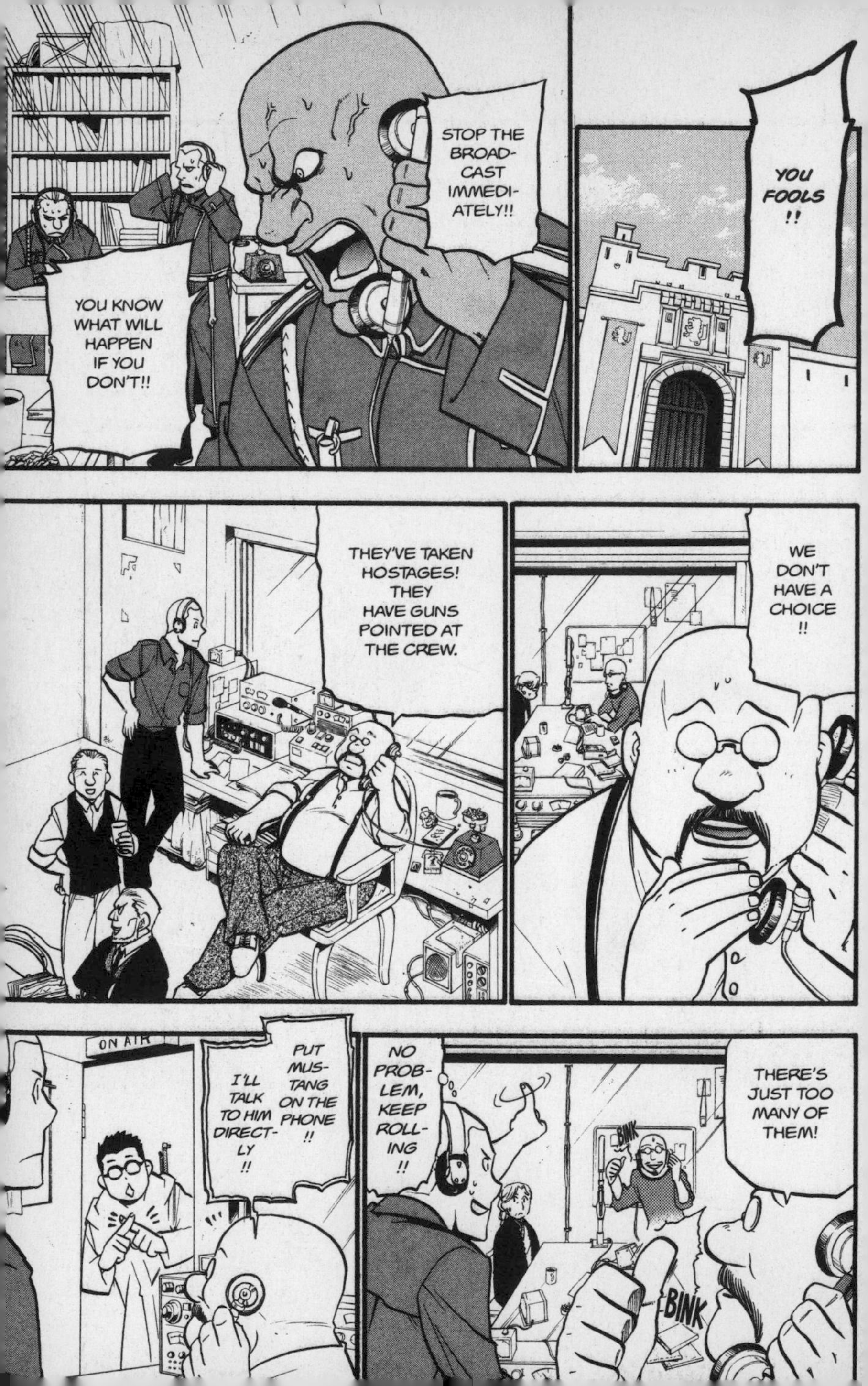
YOU FOOLS !!
STOP THE BROADCAST IMMEDIATELY!!
YOU KNOW WHAT WILL HAPPEN IF YOU DON'T!!
WE DON'T HAVE A CHOICE !!
THEY'VE TAKEN HOSTAGES! THEY HAVE GUNS POINTED AT THE CREW.
THERE'S JUST TOO MANY OF THEM!
NO PROBLEM, KEEP ROLLING !!
BINK
BINK
ON AIR
PUT MUSTANG ON THE PHONE !!
I'LL TALK TO HIM DIRECTLY !!

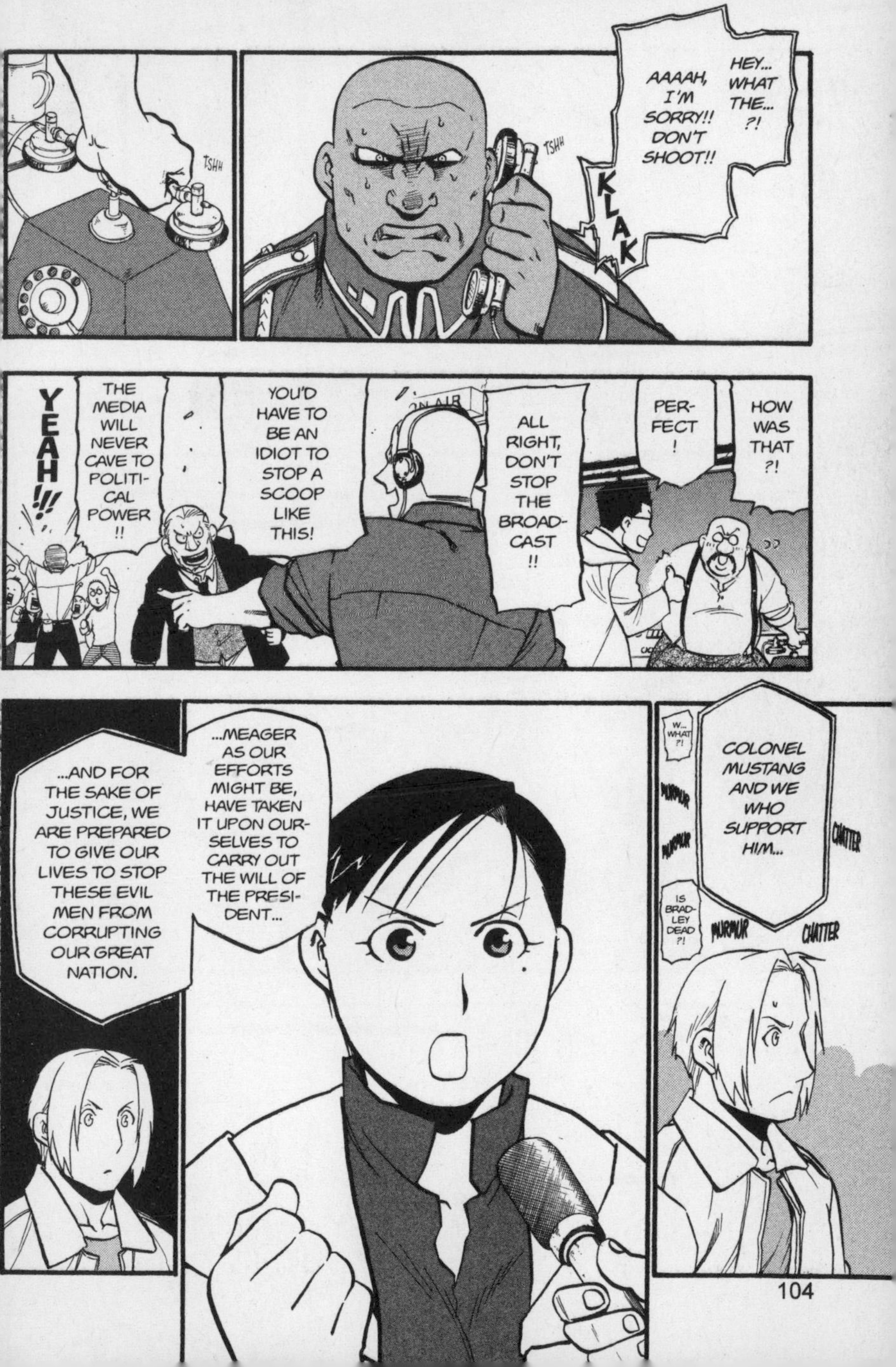
HEY... WHAT THE...?!
AAAAH, I'M SORRY!! DON'T SHOOT!!
KLAK
TSHH
TSHH
HOW WAS THAT?!
PERFECT!
ALL RIGHT, DON'T STOP THE BROADCAST!!
YOU'D HAVE TO BE AN IDIOT TO STOP A SCOOP LIKE THIS!
THE MEDIA WILL NEVER CAVE TO POLITICAL POWER!!
YEAH!!!
COLONEL MUSTANG AND WE WHO SUPPORT HIM...
W... WHAT?!
MURMUR
MURMUR
CHATTER
IS BRADLEY DEAD?!
MURMUR
CHATTER
...MEAGER AS OUR EFFORTS MIGHT BE, HAVE TAKEN IT UPON OURSELVES TO CARRY OUT THE WILL OF THE PRESIDENT...
...AND FOR THE SAKE OF JUSTICE, WE ARE PREPARED TO GIVE OUR LIVES TO STOP THESE EVIL MEN FROM CORRUPTING OUR GREAT NATION.

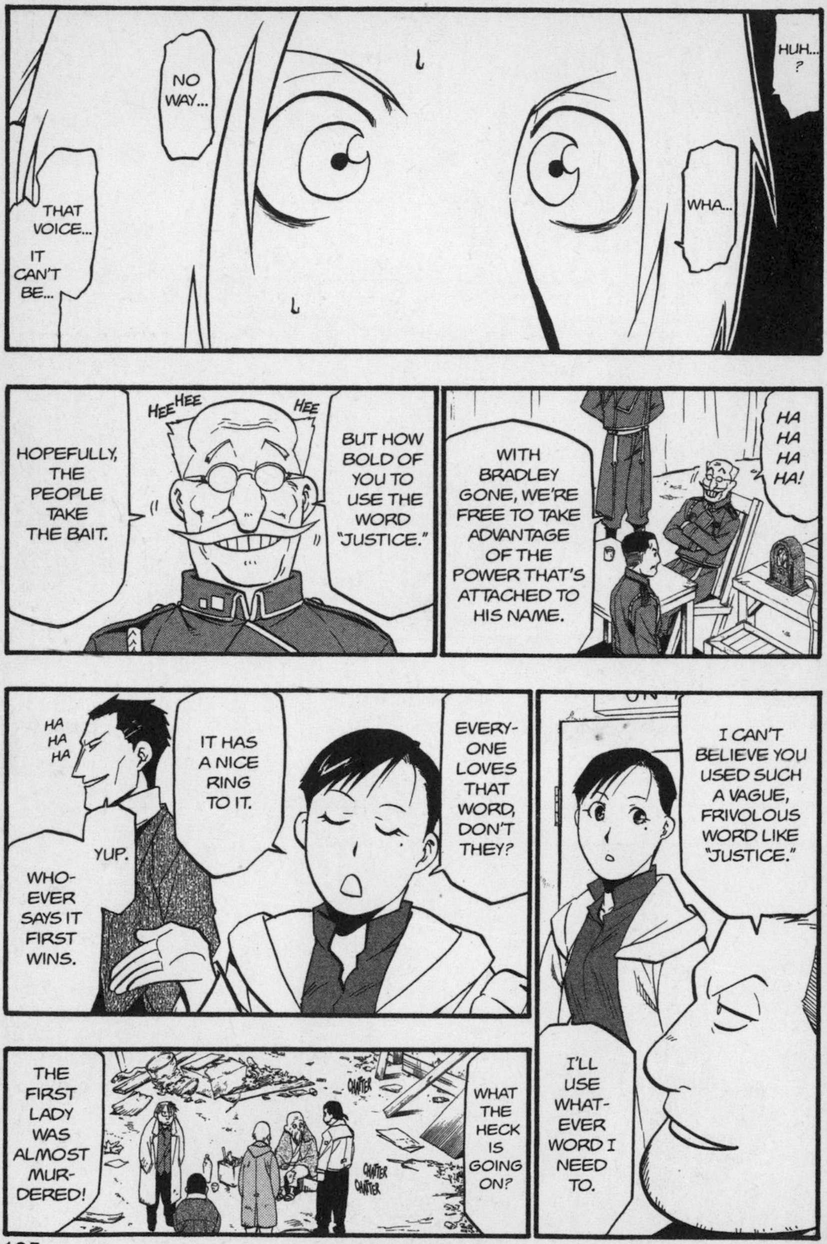
HUH...?
WHA...
NO WAY...
THAT VOICE... IT CAN'T BE...
HA HA HA HA!
WITH BRADLEY GONE, WE'RE FREE TO TAKE ADVANTAGE OF THE POWER THAT'S ATTACHED TO HIS NAME.
HEE HEE HEE
BUT HOW BOLD OF YOU TO USE THE WORD "JUSTICE."
HOPEFULLY, THE PEOPLE TAKE THE BAIT.
I CAN'T BELIEVE YOU USED SUCH A VAGUE, FRIVOLOUS WORD LIKE "JUSTICE."
I'LL USE WHAT-EVER WORD I NEED TO.
EVERY-ONE LOVES THAT WORD, DON'T THEY?
IT HAS A NICE RING TO IT.
HA HA HA
YUP.
WHO-EVER SAYS IT FIRST WINS.
WHAT THE HECK IS GOING ON?
CHATTER
CHATTER CHATTER
THE FIRST LADY WAS ALMOST MUR-DERED!

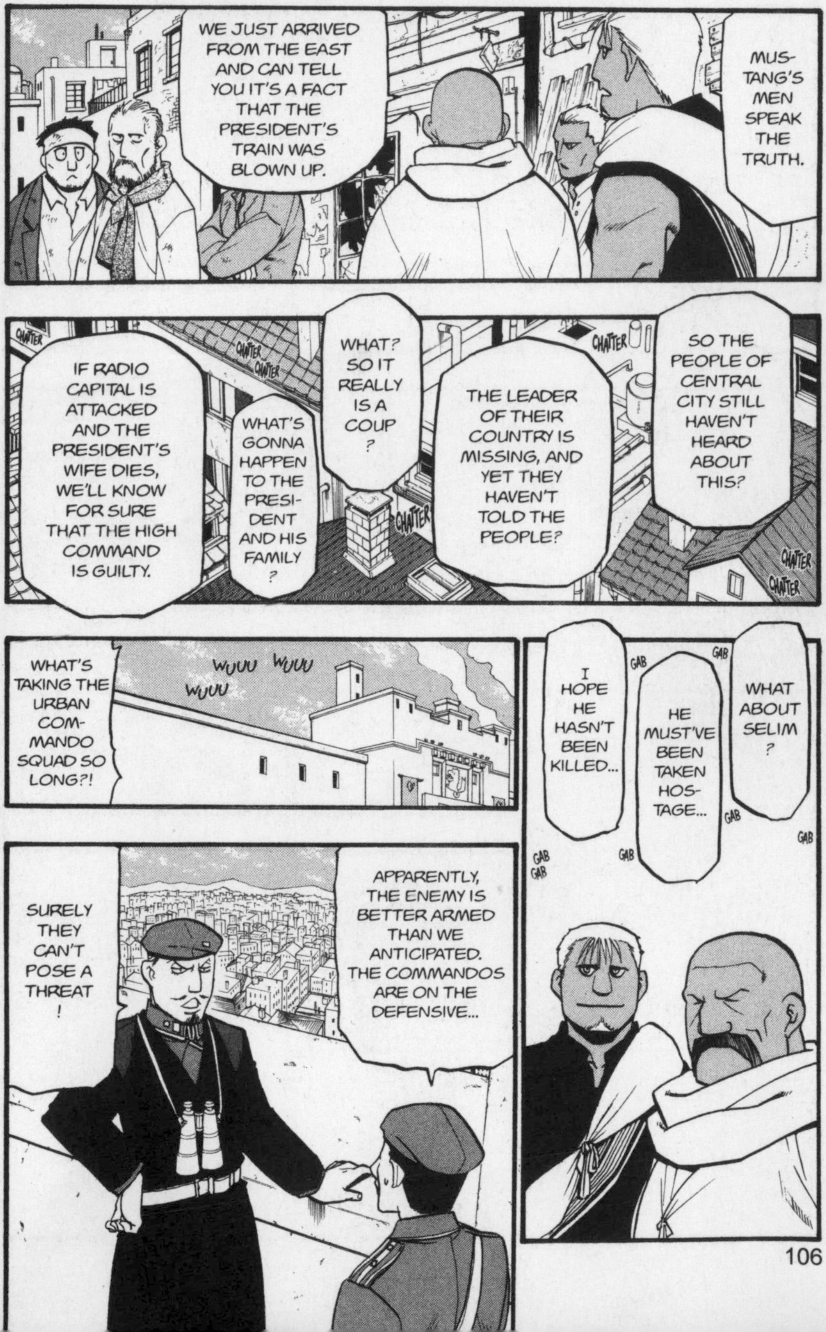
MUSTANG'S MEN SPEAK THE TRUTH.
WE JUST ARRIVED FROM THE EAST AND CAN TELL YOU IT'S A FACT THAT THE PRESIDENT'S TRAIN WAS BLOWN UP.
CHATTER
SO THE PEOPLE OF CENTRAL CITY STILL HAVEN'T HEARD ABOUT THIS?
CHATTER CHATTER
THE LEADER OF THEIR COUNTRY IS MISSING, AND YET THEY HAVEN'T TOLD THE PEOPLE?
WHAT? SO IT REALLY IS A COUP?
CHATTER
CHATTER CHATTER
WHAT'S GONNA HAPPEN TO THE PRESIDENT AND HIS FAMILY?
CHATTER
IF RADIO CAPITAL IS ATTACKED AND THE PRESIDENT'S WIFE DIES, WE'LL KNOW FOR SURE THAT THE HIGH COMMAND IS GUILTY.
GAB
WHAT ABOUT SELIM?
GAB
HE MUST'VE BEEN TAKEN HOSTAGE...
GAB
I HOPE HE HASN'T BEEN KILLED...
GAB
GAB
GAB GAB
WUUU WUUU
WUUU
WHAT'S TAKING THE URBAN COMMANDO SQUAD SO LONG?!
APPARENTLY, THE ENEMY IS BETTER ARMED THAN WE ANTICIPATED. THE COMMANDOS ARE ON THE DEFENSIVE...
SURELY THEY CAN'T POSE A THREAT!

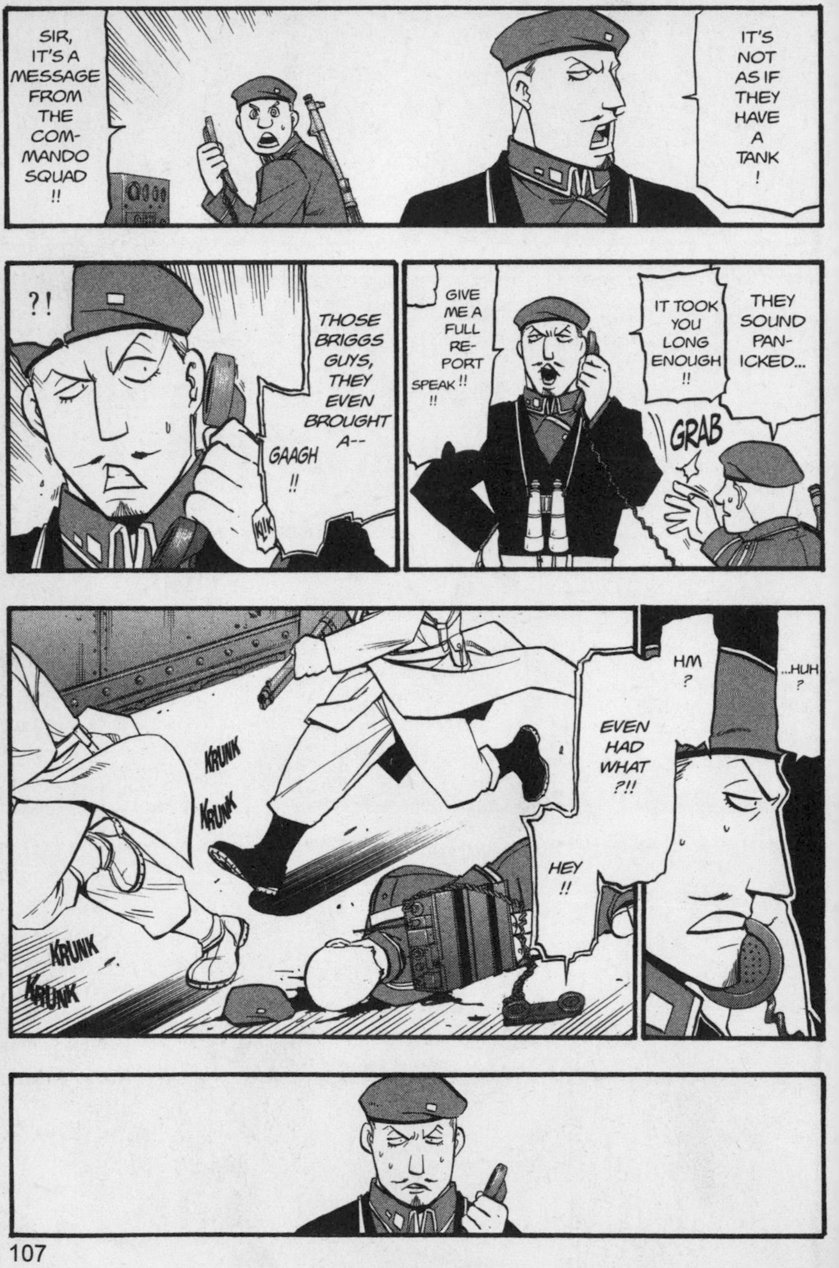
IT'S NOT AS IF THEY HAVE A TANK!
SIR, IT'S A MESSAGE FROM THE COMMANDO SQUAD!!
THEY SOUND PANICKED...
IT TOOK YOU LONG ENOUGH!!
GRAB
GIVE ME A FULL REPORT!!
SPEAK!!
?!
THOSE BRIGGS GUYS, THEY EVEN BROUGHT A--
GAAGH!!
KLIK
...HUH?
HM?
EVEN HAD WHAT?!!
HEY!!
KRUNK
KRUNK
KRUNK
KRUNK

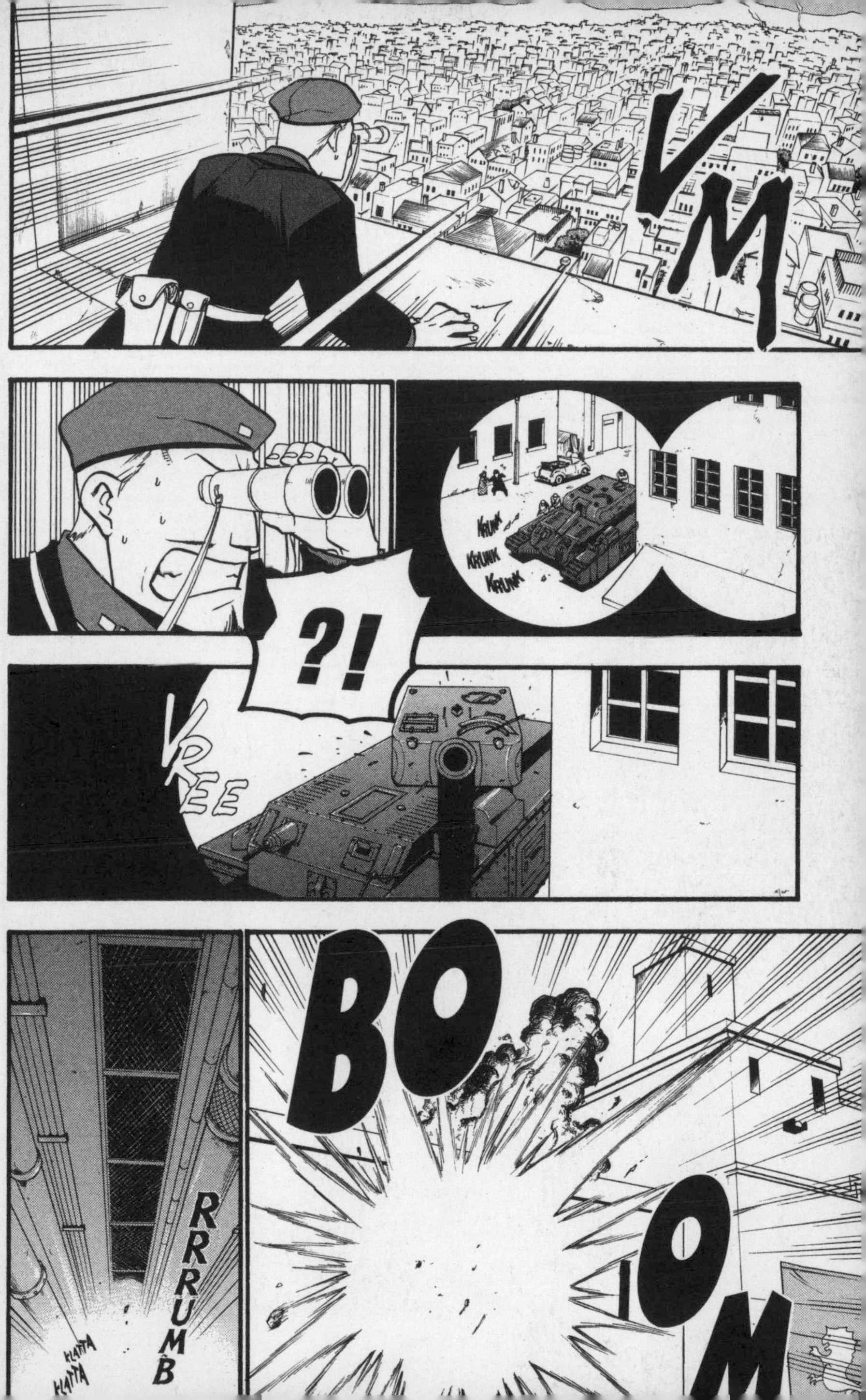
VM
KRUNK
KRUNK
KRUNK
?!
VREE
BOOM
RRRUMB
KLATTA
KLATTA

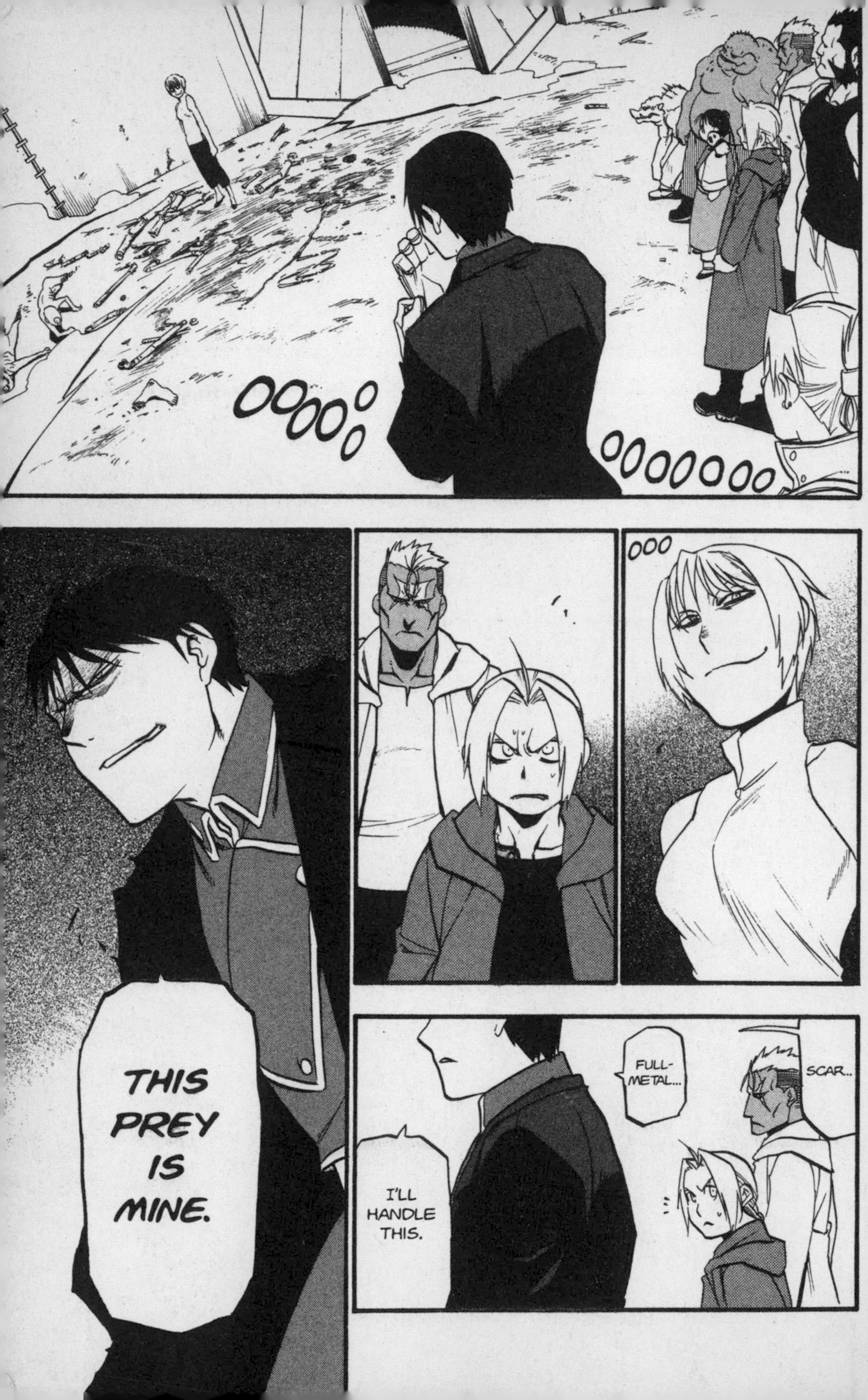
OOOOOOOO
OOOOOOO
OOO
SCAR...
FULL-METAL...
I'LL HANDLE THIS.
THIS PREY IS MINE.

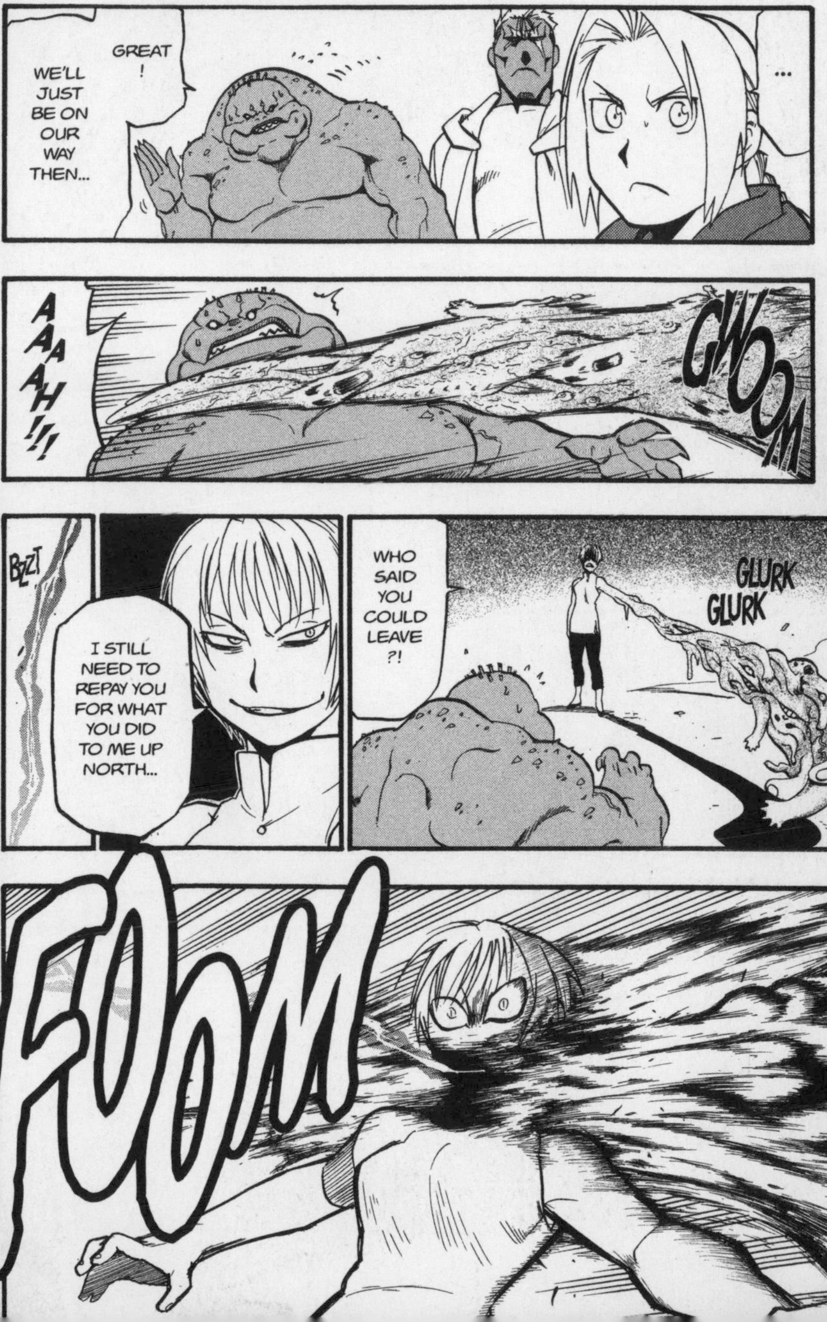
...
GREAT!
WE'LL JUST BE ON OUR WAY THEN...
GWOOM
AAAAH!!!
GLURK GLURK
WHO SAID YOU COULD LEAVE?!
I STILL NEED TO REPAY YOU FOR WHAT YOU DID TO ME UP NORTH...
BZZT
FOOM

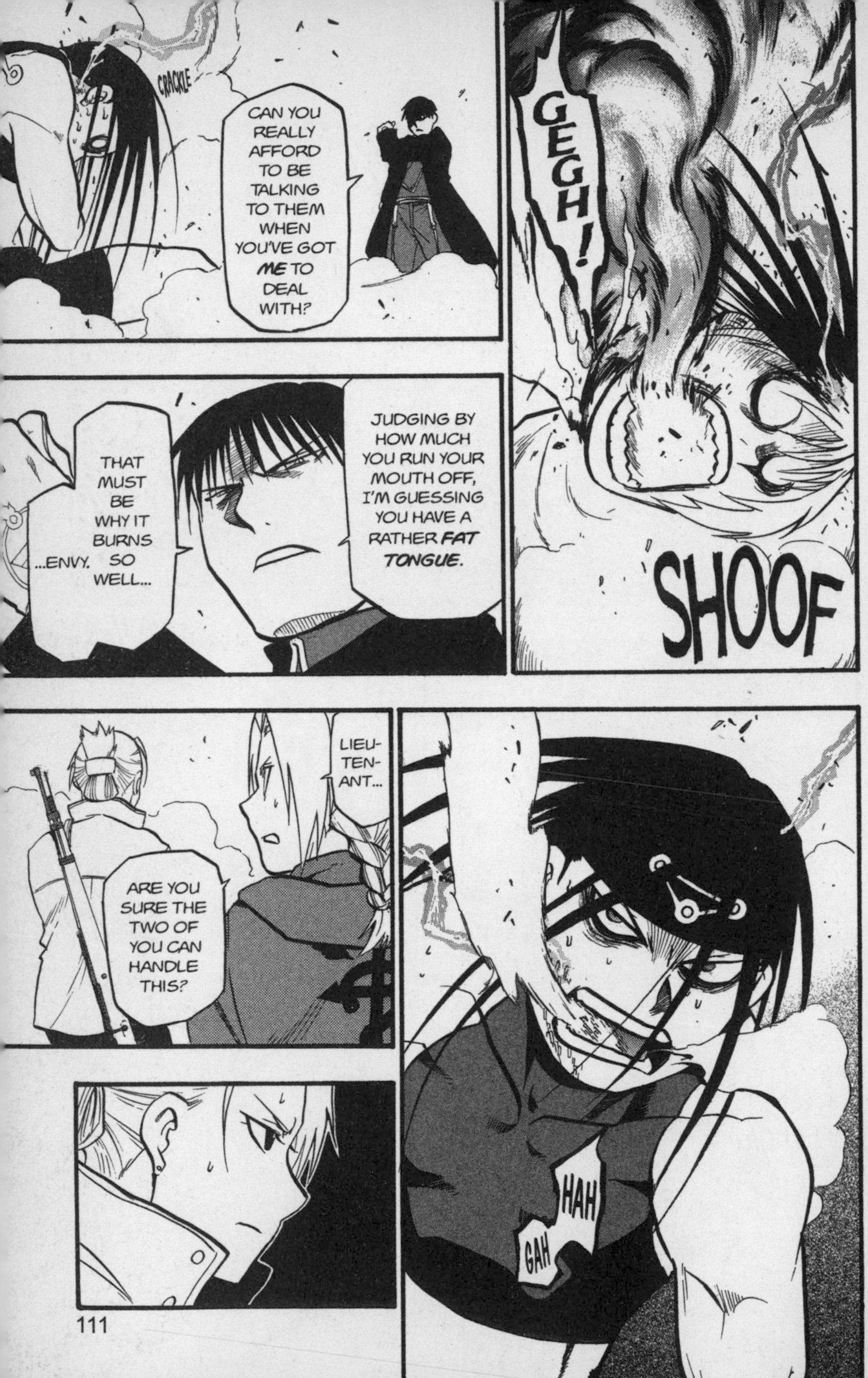
GEGH!
SHOOF
CRACKLE
CAN YOU REALLY AFFORD TO BE TALKING TO THEM WHEN YOU'VE GOT ME TO DEAL WITH?
JUDGING BY HOW MUCH YOU RUN YOUR MOUTH OFF, I'M GUESSING YOU HAVE A RATHER FAT TONGUE.
THAT MUST BE WHY IT BURNS SO WELL...
...ENVY.
HAH
GAH
LIEU-TEN-ANT...
ARE YOU SURE THE TWO OF YOU CAN HANDLE THIS?

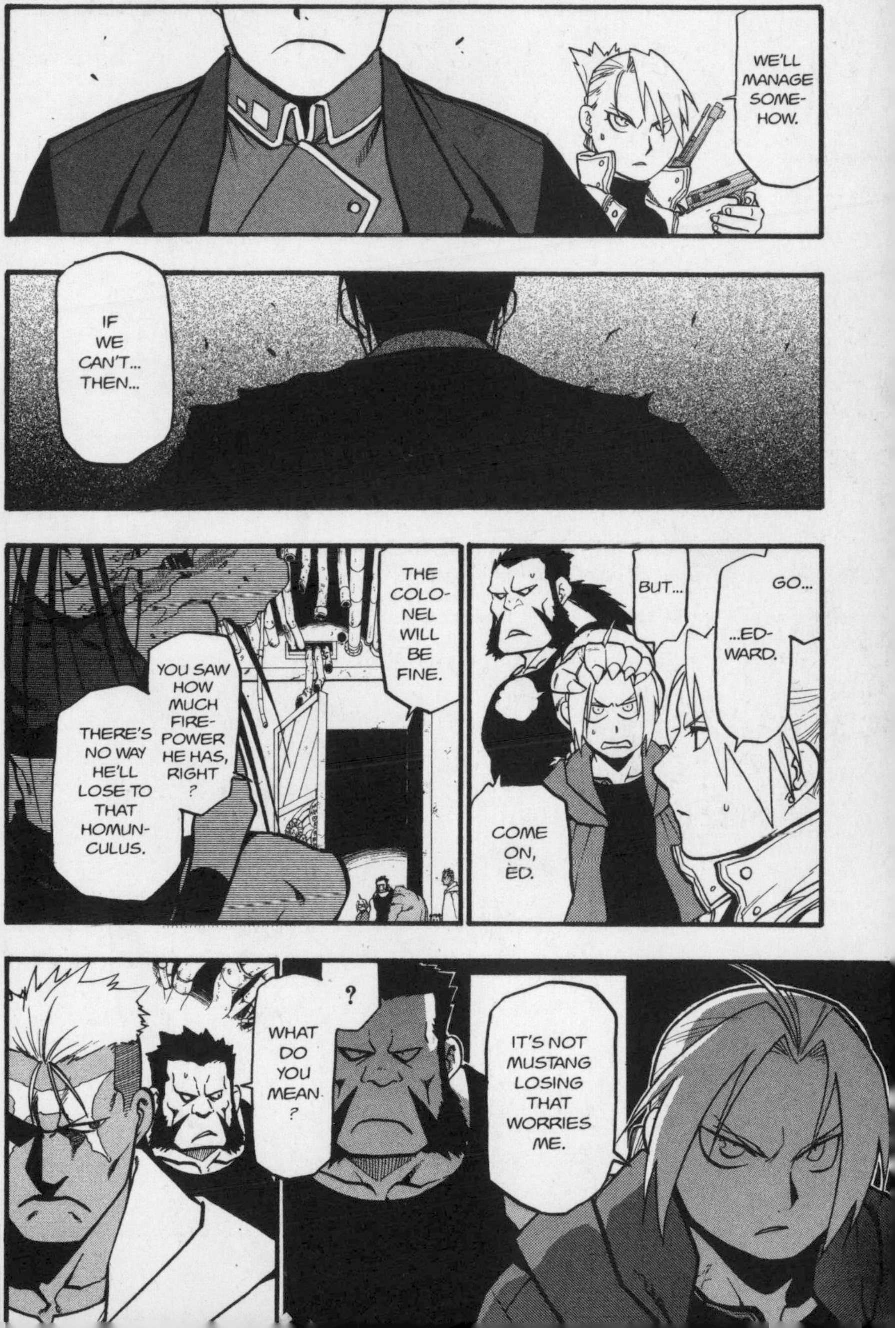
WE'LL MANAGE SOMEHOW.
IF WE CAN'T... THEN...
GO...
...EDWARD.
BUT...
COME ON, ED.
THE COLONEL WILL BE FINE.
YOU SAW HOW MUCH FIREPOWER HE HAS, RIGHT?
THERE'S NO WAY HE'LL LOSE TO THAT HOMUNCULUS.
IT'S NOT MUSTANG LOSING THAT WORRIES ME.
?
WHAT DO YOU MEAN?

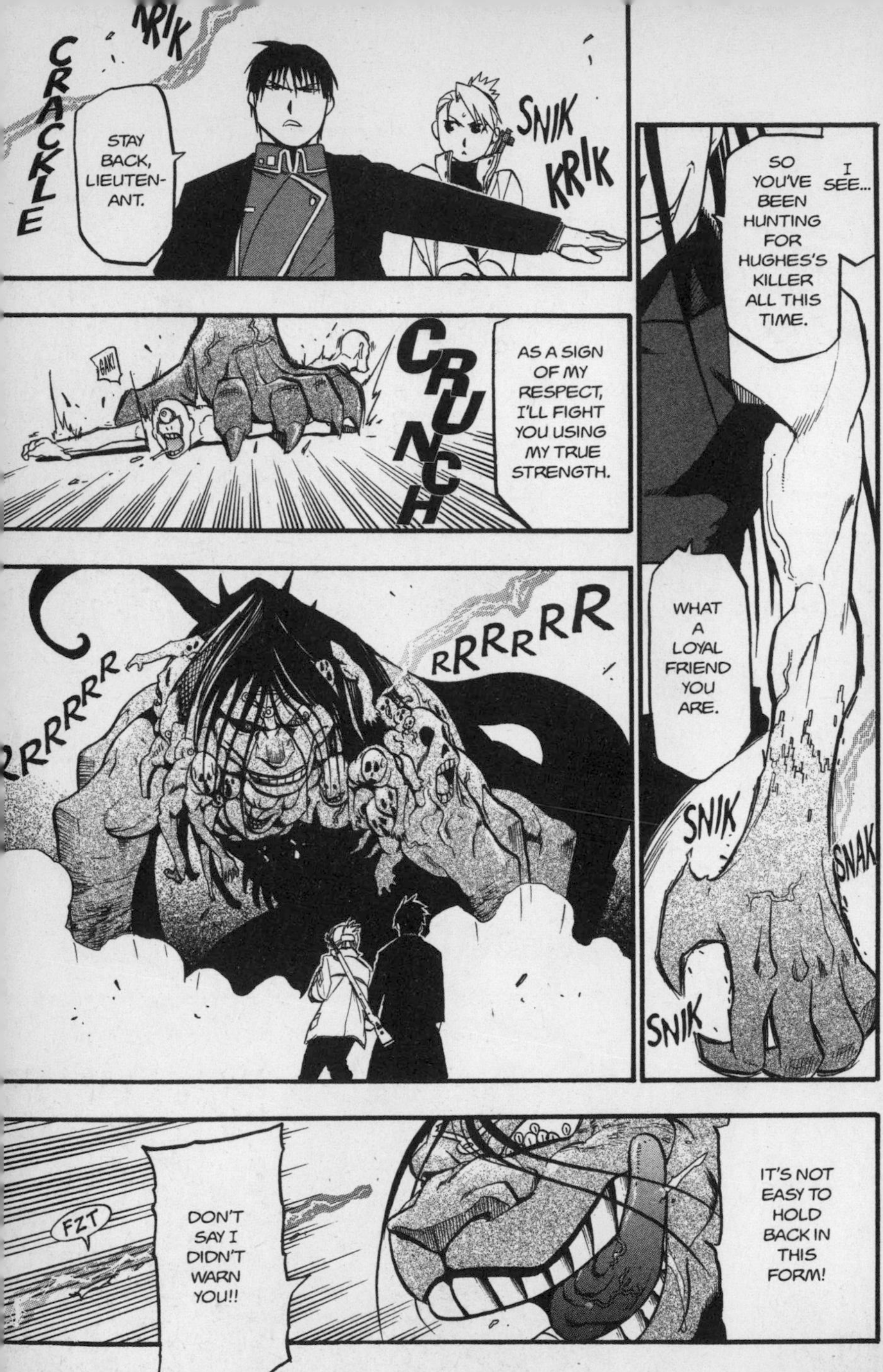
I SEE...
SO YOU'VE BEEN HUNTING FOR HUGHES'S KILLER ALL THIS TIME.
WHAT A LOYAL FRIEND YOU ARE.
SNIK
SNAK
SNIK
KRIK
SNIK
STAY BACK, LIEUTEN-ANT.
NRIK
CRACKLE
AS A SIGN OF MY RESPECT, I'LL FIGHT YOU USING MY TRUE STRENGTH.
CRUNCH
GAK!
RRRRRRR
RRRRRR
IT'S NOT EASY TO HOLD BACK IN THIS FORM!
DON'T SAY I DIDN'T WARN YOU!!
FZT

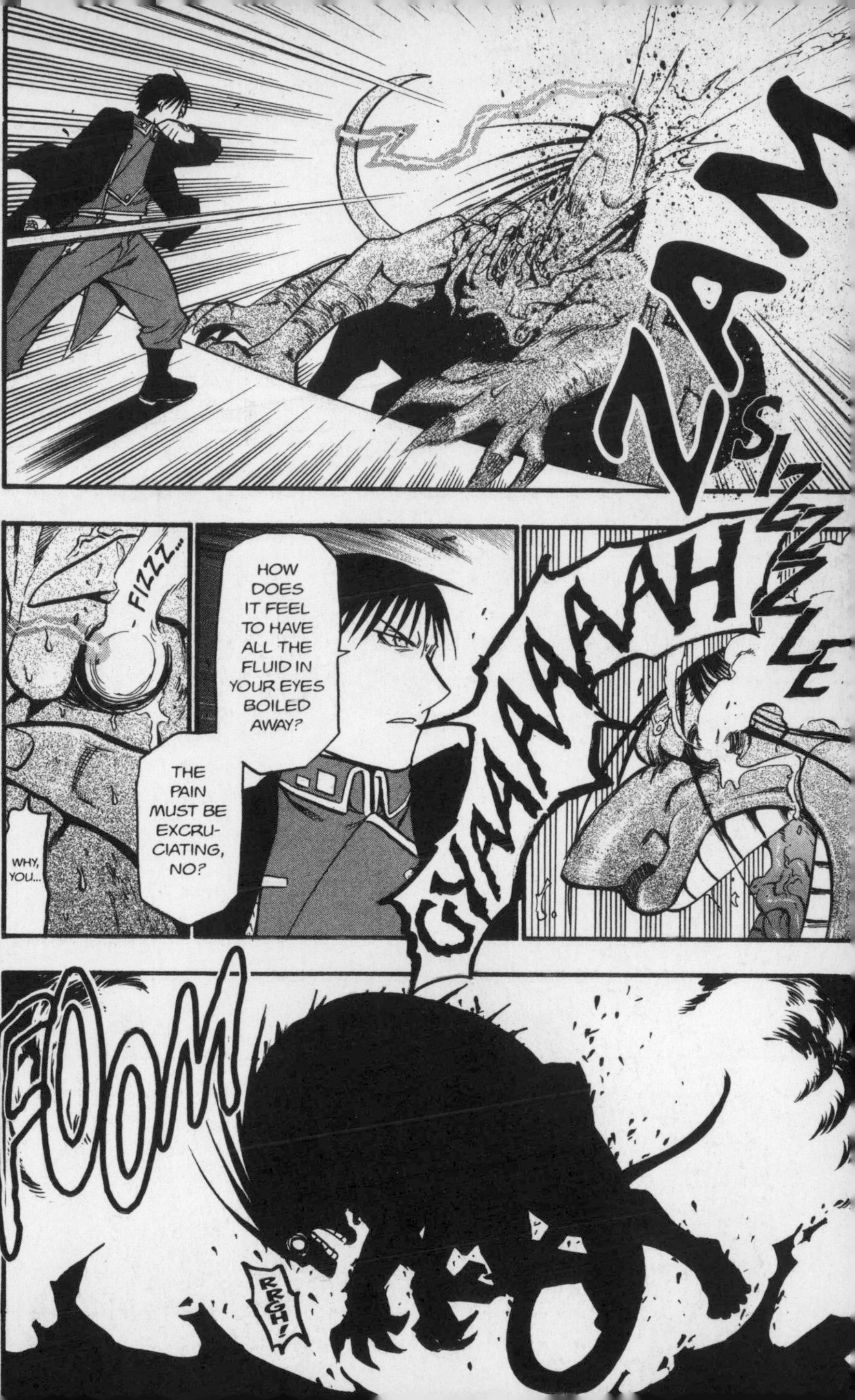
ZAM
SIZZZZLE
GYAAAAAH
HOW DOES IT FEEL TO HAVE ALL THE FLUID IN YOUR EYES BOILED AWAY?
THE PAIN MUST BE EXCRUCIATING, NO?
FIZZZ...
WHY, YOU...
FOOM
RRGH!

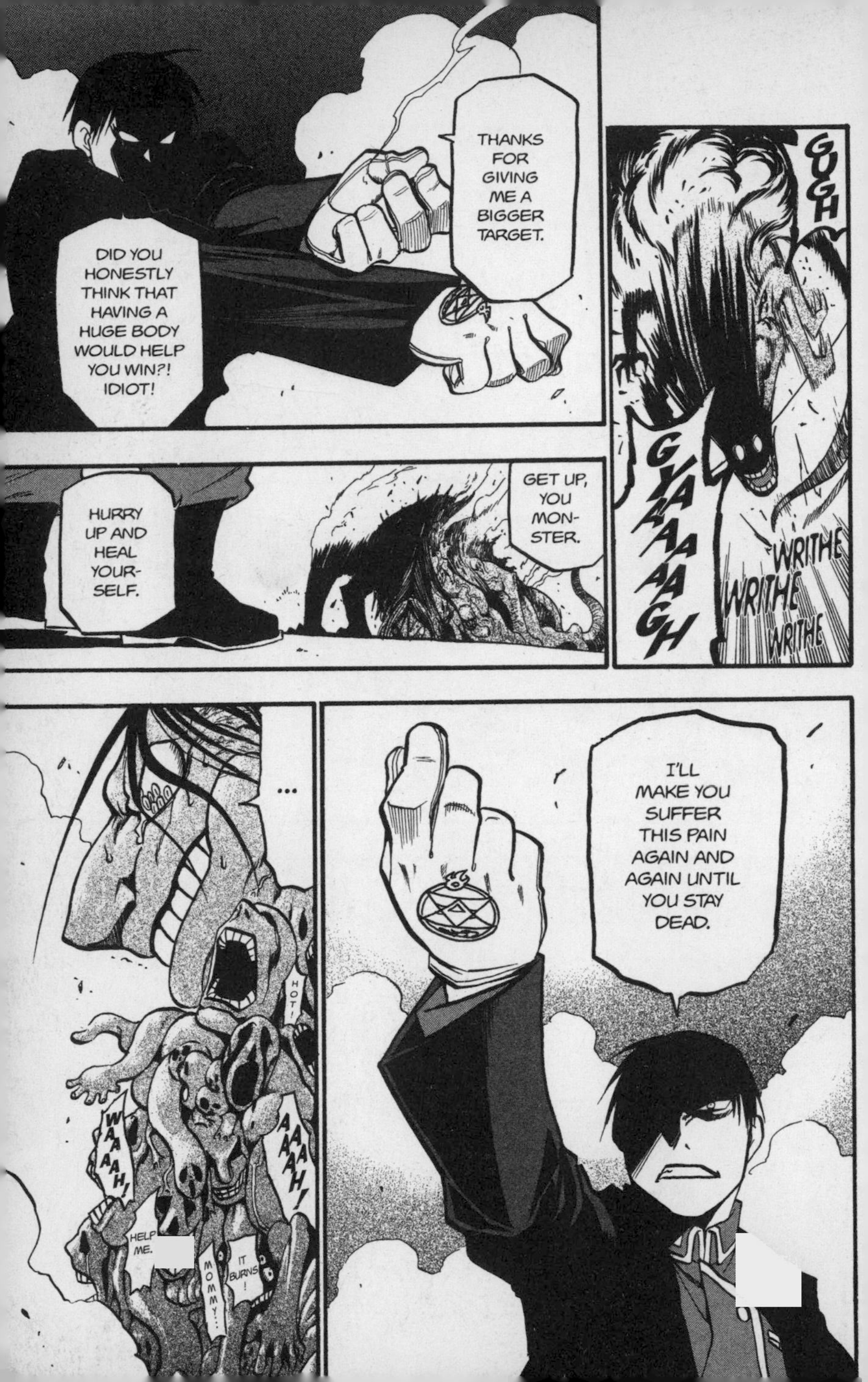
GUGH
GYAAAAAAGH
WRITHE
WRITHE
WRITHE
THANKS FOR GIVING ME A BIGGER TARGET.
DID YOU HONESTLY THINK THAT HAVING A HUGE BODY WOULD HELP YOU WIN?! IDIOT!
GET UP, YOU MON-STER.
HURRY UP AND HEAL YOUR-SELF.
I'LL MAKE YOU SUFFER THIS PAIN AGAIN AND AGAIN UNTIL YOU STAY DEAD.
...
HOT!
AAAAH!
WAAAAH!
IT BURNS!
MOMMY...
HELP ME.

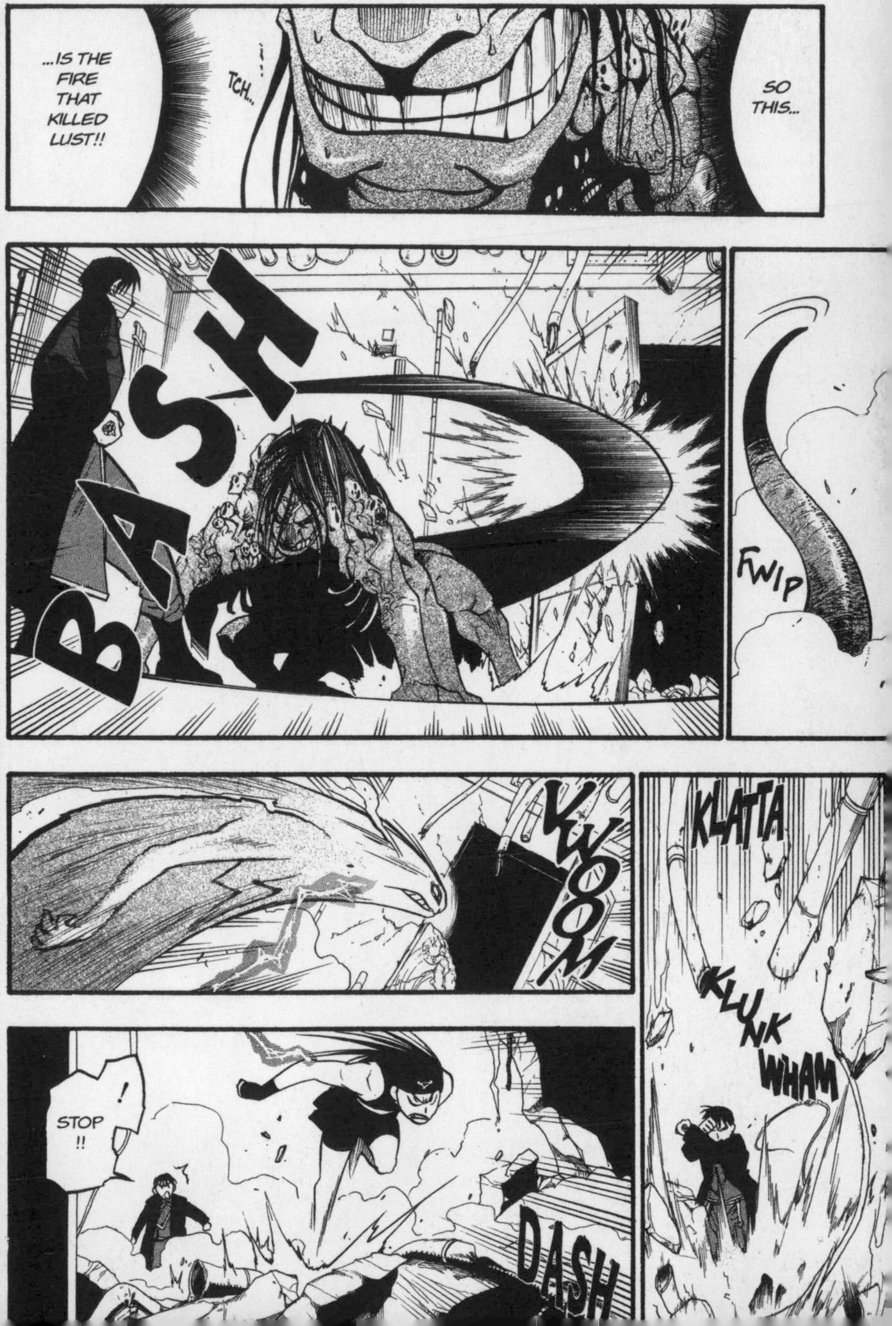
SO THIS...
TCH...
...IS THE FIRE THAT KILLED LUST!!
FWIP
BASH
KLATTA
KLUNK
WHAM
VWOOOM
STOP !!
DASH

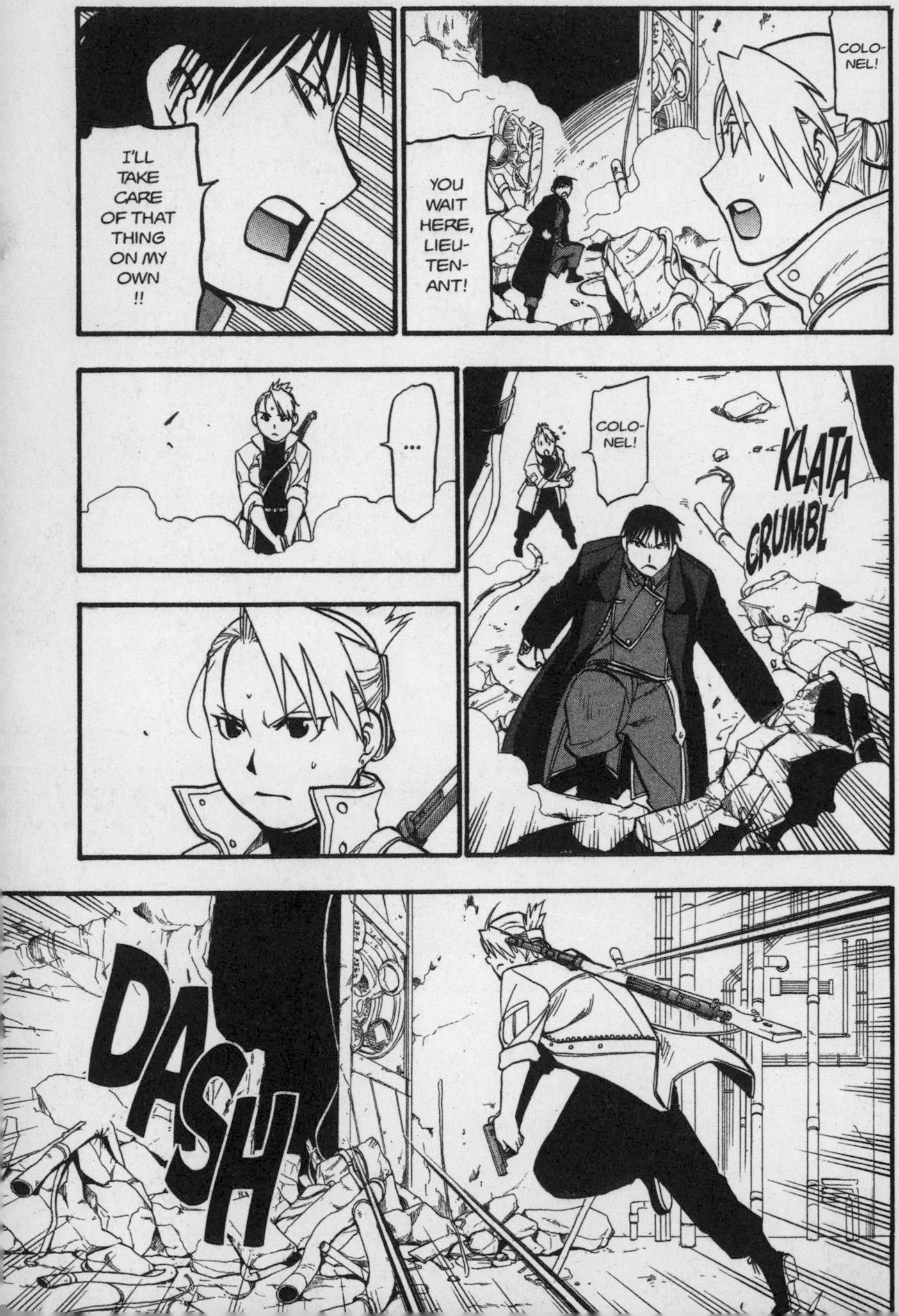
COLO-NEL!
YOU WAIT HERE, LIEU-TEN-ANT!
I'LL TAKE CARE OF THAT THING ON MY OWN !!
COLO-NEL!
KLATA
CRUMBL
...
DASH

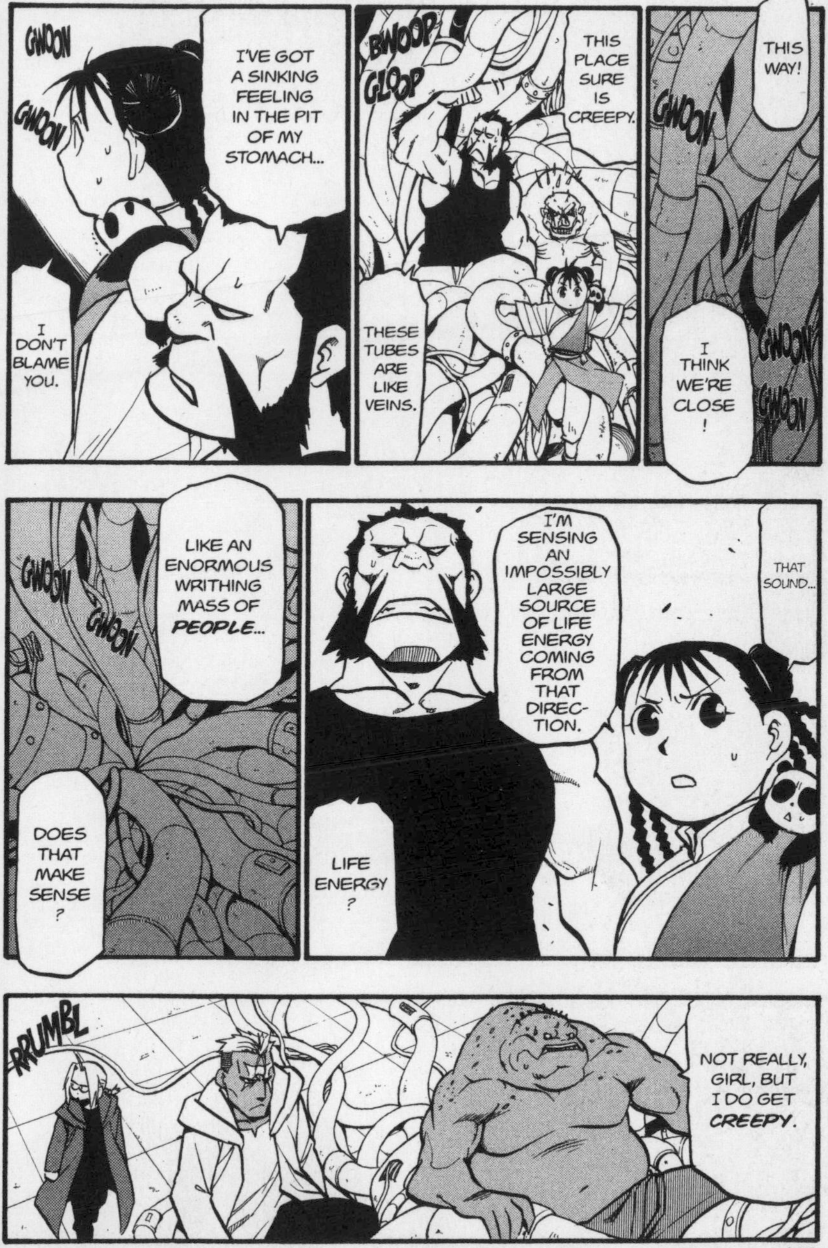
THIS WAY!
GWOON
I THINK WE'RE CLOSE!
GWOON
GWOON
THIS PLACE SURE IS CREEPY.
BWOOP
GLOOP
THESE TUBES ARE LIKE VEINS.
I'VE GOT A SINKING FEELING IN THE PIT OF MY STOMACH...
GWOON
GWOON
I DON'T BLAME YOU.
THAT SOUND...
I'M SENSING AN IMPOSSIBLY LARGE SOURCE OF LIFE ENERGY COMING FROM THAT DIRECTION.
LIFE ENERGY?
LIKE AN ENORMOUS WRITHING MASS OF *PEOPLE*...
GWOON
GWOON
DOES THAT MAKE SENSE?
NOT REALLY, GIRL, BUT I DO GET *CREEPY*.
RRUMBL

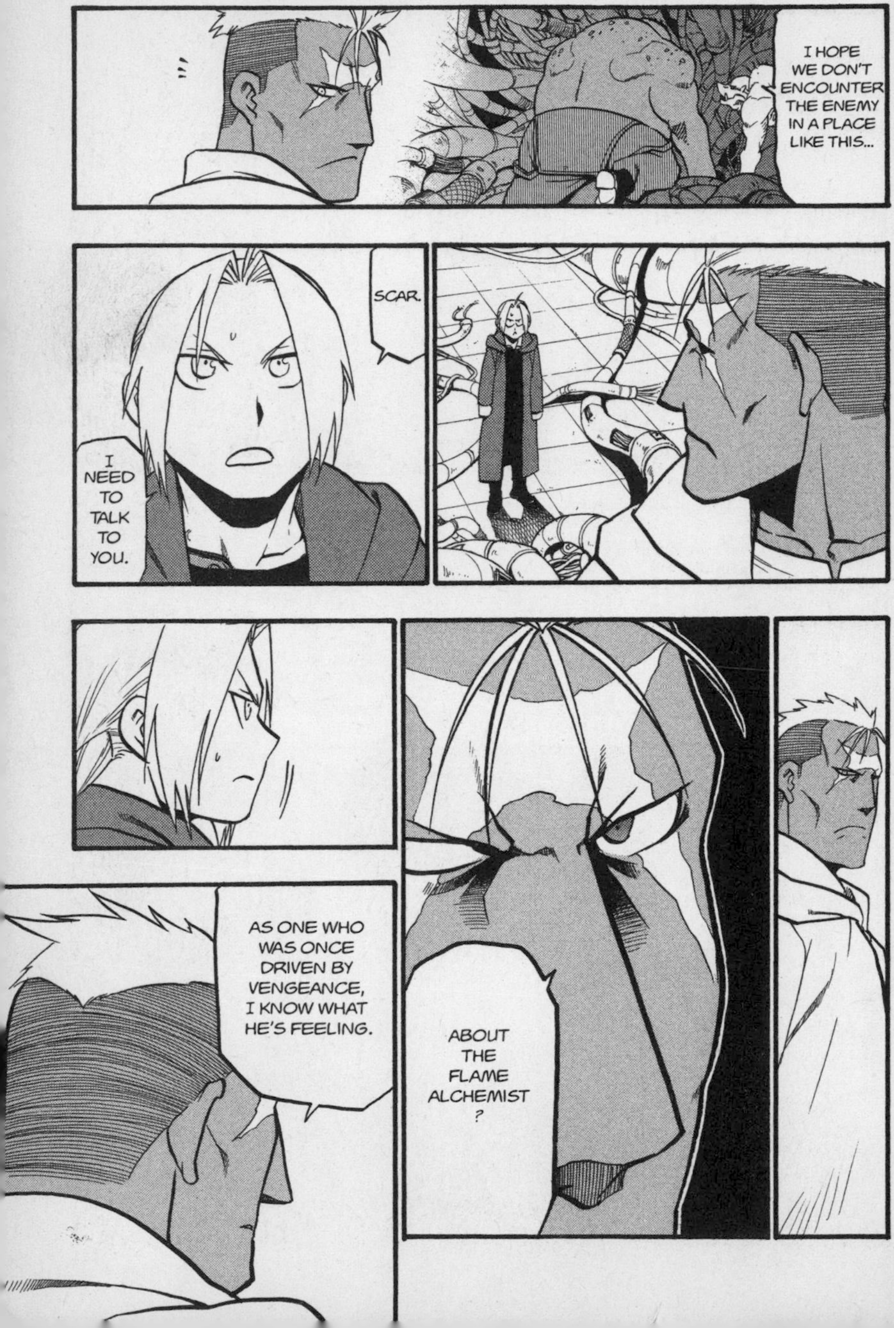
I HOPE WE DON'T ENCOUNTER THE ENEMY IN A PLACE LIKE THIS...
SCAR.
I NEED TO TALK TO YOU.
ABOUT THE FLAME ALCHEMIST?
AS ONE WHO WAS ONCE DRIVEN BY VENGEANCE, I KNOW WHAT HE'S FEELING.

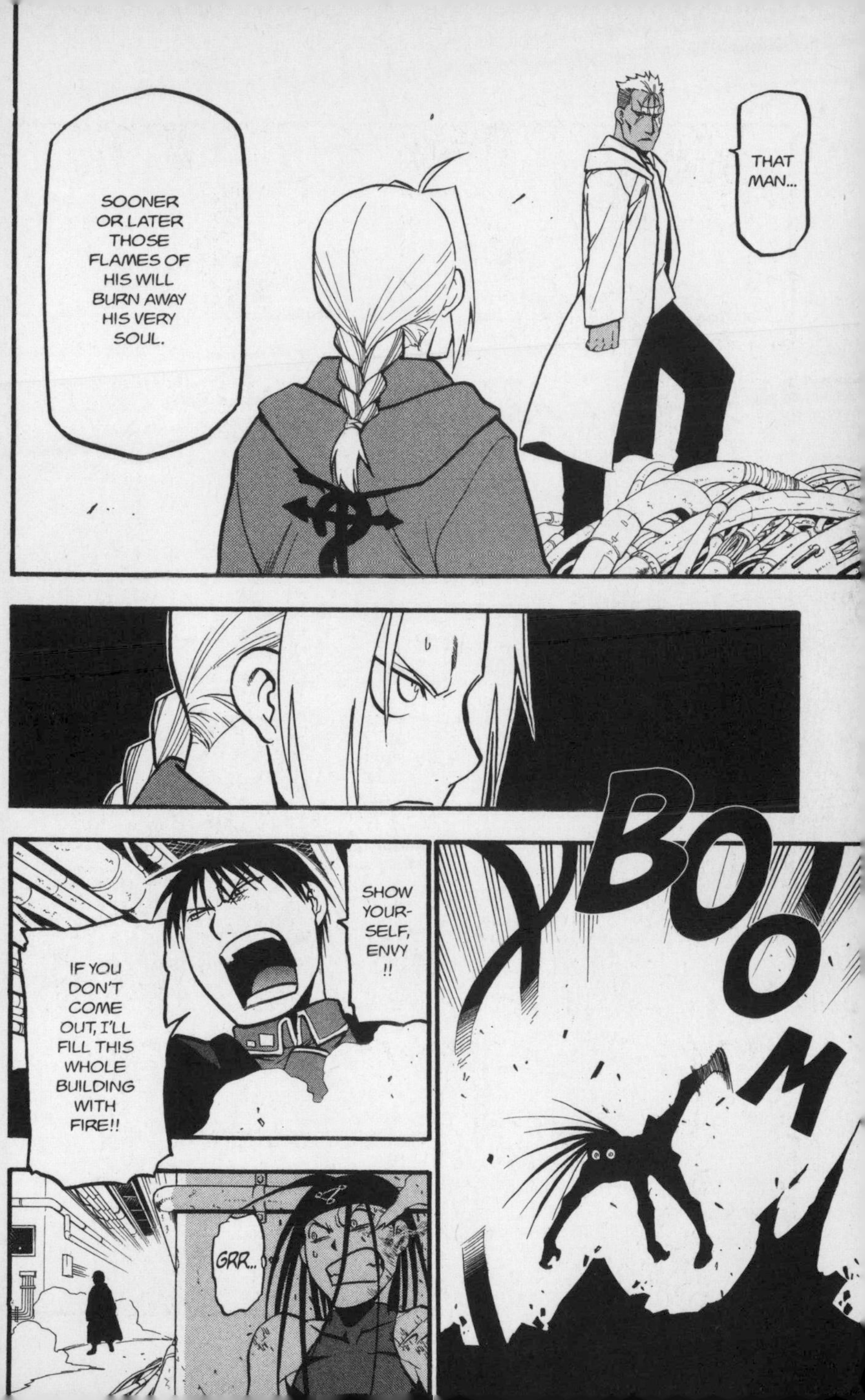
THAT MAN...
SOONER OR LATER THOSE FLAMES OF HIS WILL BURN AWAY HIS VERY SOUL.
BOOOM
SHOW YOURSELF, ENVY!!
IF YOU DON'T COME OUT, I'LL FILL THIS WHOLE BUILDING WITH FIRE!!
GRR..

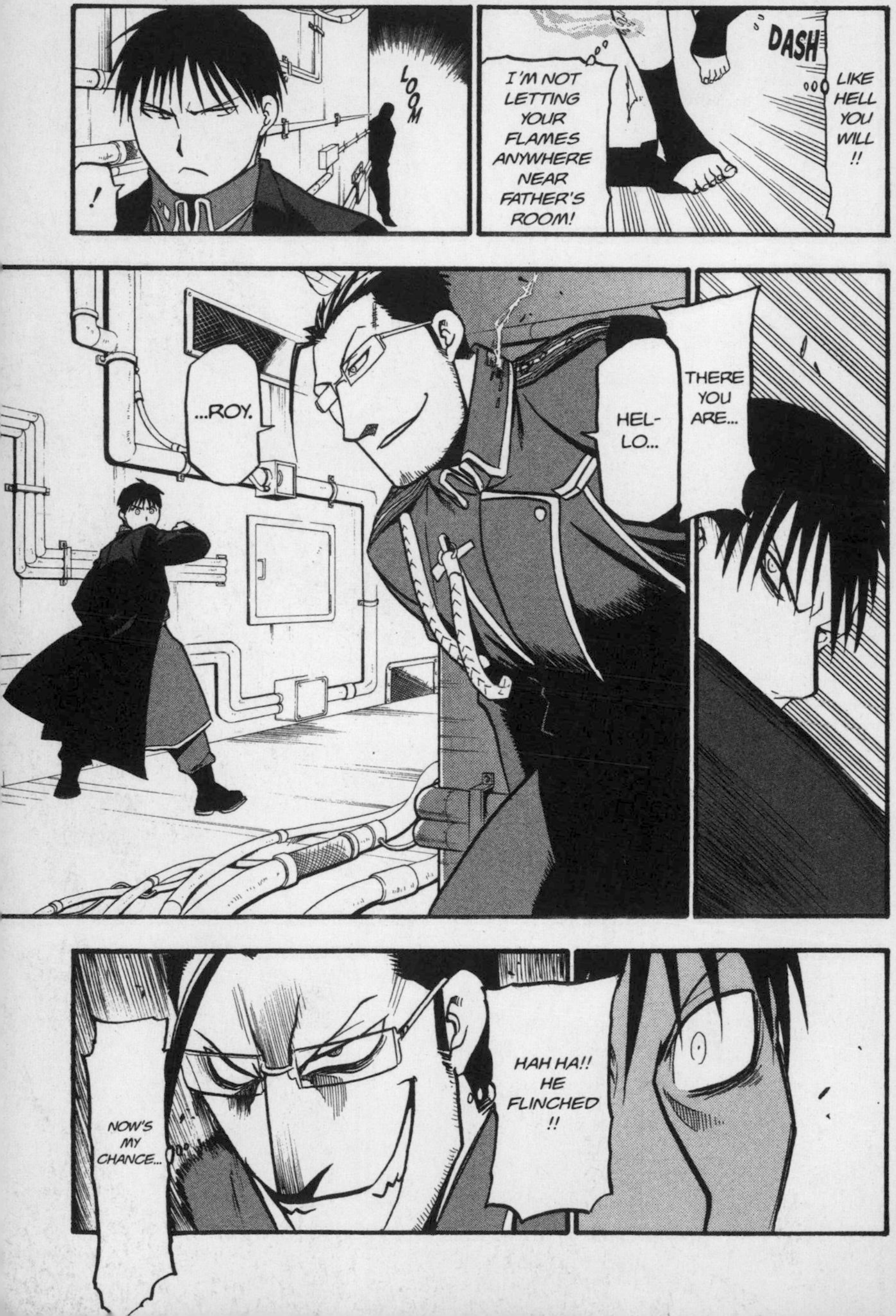
DASH
LIKE HELL YOU WILL !!
I'M NOT LETTING YOUR FLAMES ANYWHERE NEAR FATHER'S ROOM!
LOOM
!
THERE YOU ARE...
HEL-LO...
...ROY.
HAH HA!! HE FLINCHED !!
NOW'S MY CHANCE...

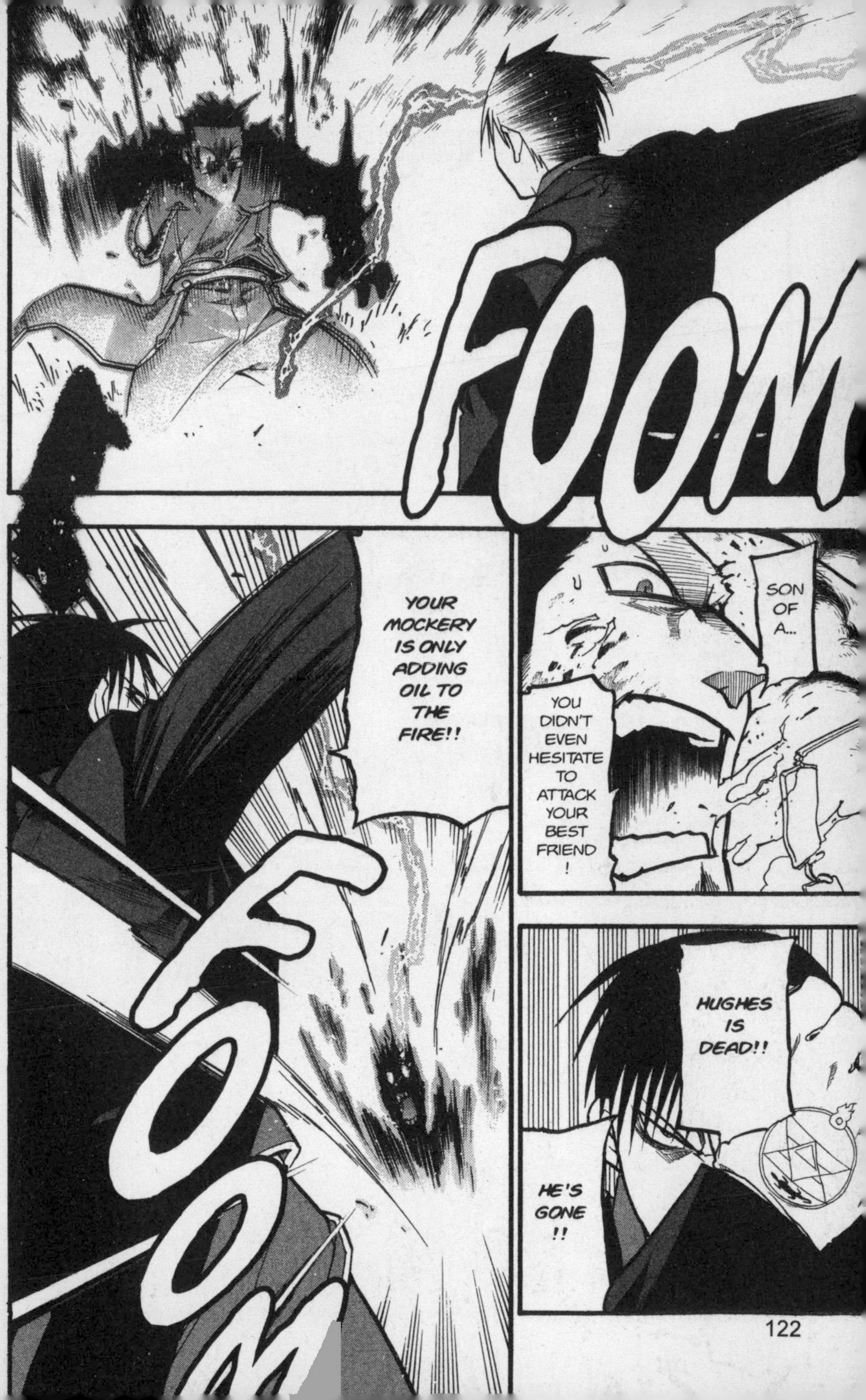
FOOM
SON OF A...
YOU DIDN'T EVEN HESITATE TO ATTACK YOUR BEST FRIEND!
YOUR MOCKERY IS ONLY ADDING OIL TO THE FIRE!!
HUGHES IS DEAD!!
HE'S GONE!!
FOOOM

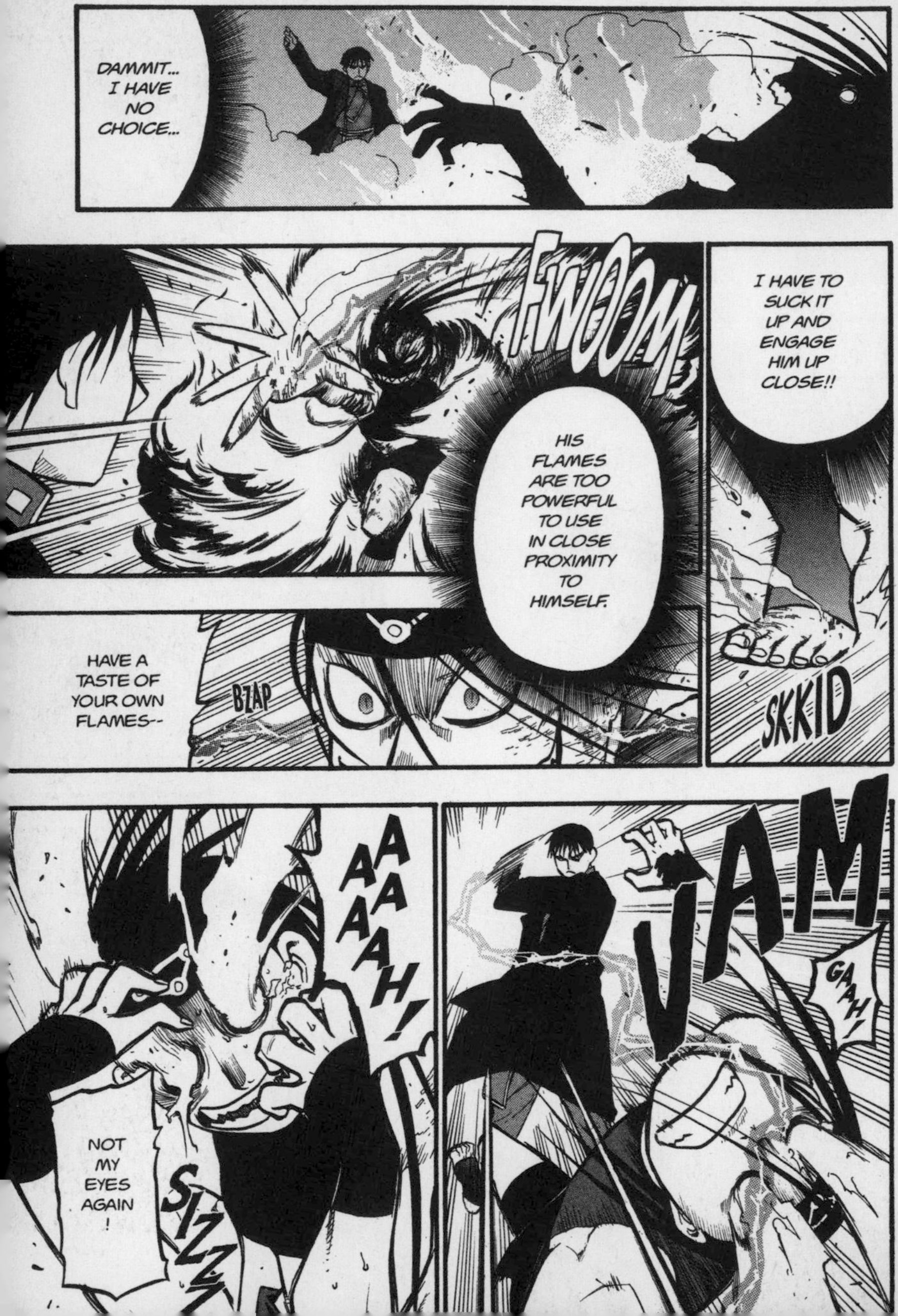
DAMMIT... I HAVE NO CHOICE...
I HAVE TO SUCK IT UP AND ENGAGE HIM UP CLOSE!!
SKKID
FWOOM
HIS FLAMES ARE TOO POWERFUL TO USE IN CLOSE PROXIMITY TO HIMSELF.
BZAP
HAVE A TASTE OF YOUR OWN FLAMES--
JAM
GAAAH!
AAAAAAH!
SIZZZ
NOT MY EYES AGAIN!

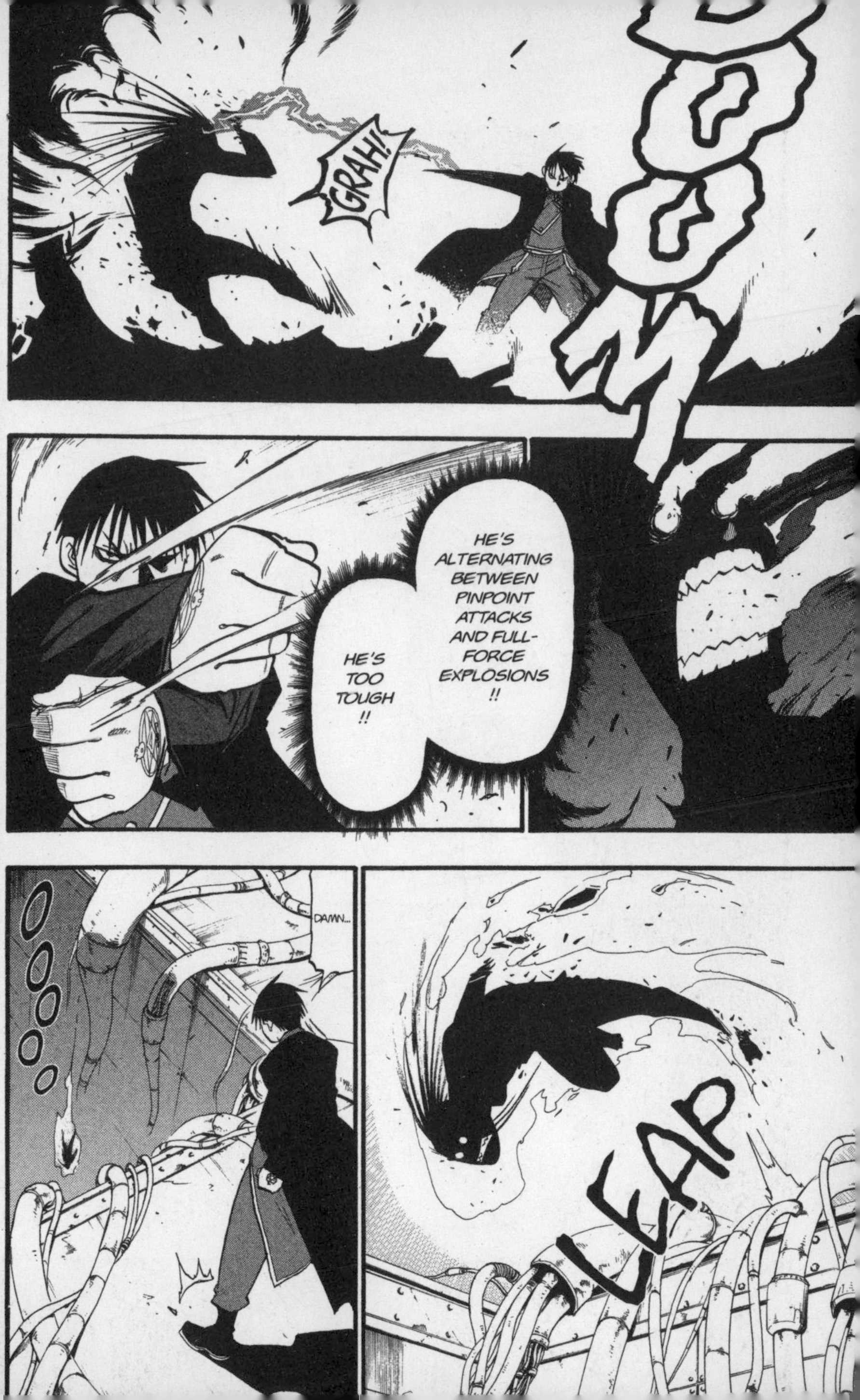
OOM
GRAH!
HE'S ALTERNATING BETWEEN PINPOINT ATTACKS AND FULL-FORCE EXPLOSIONS !!
HE'S TOO TOUGH !!
LEAP
DAMN...
OOOOOO

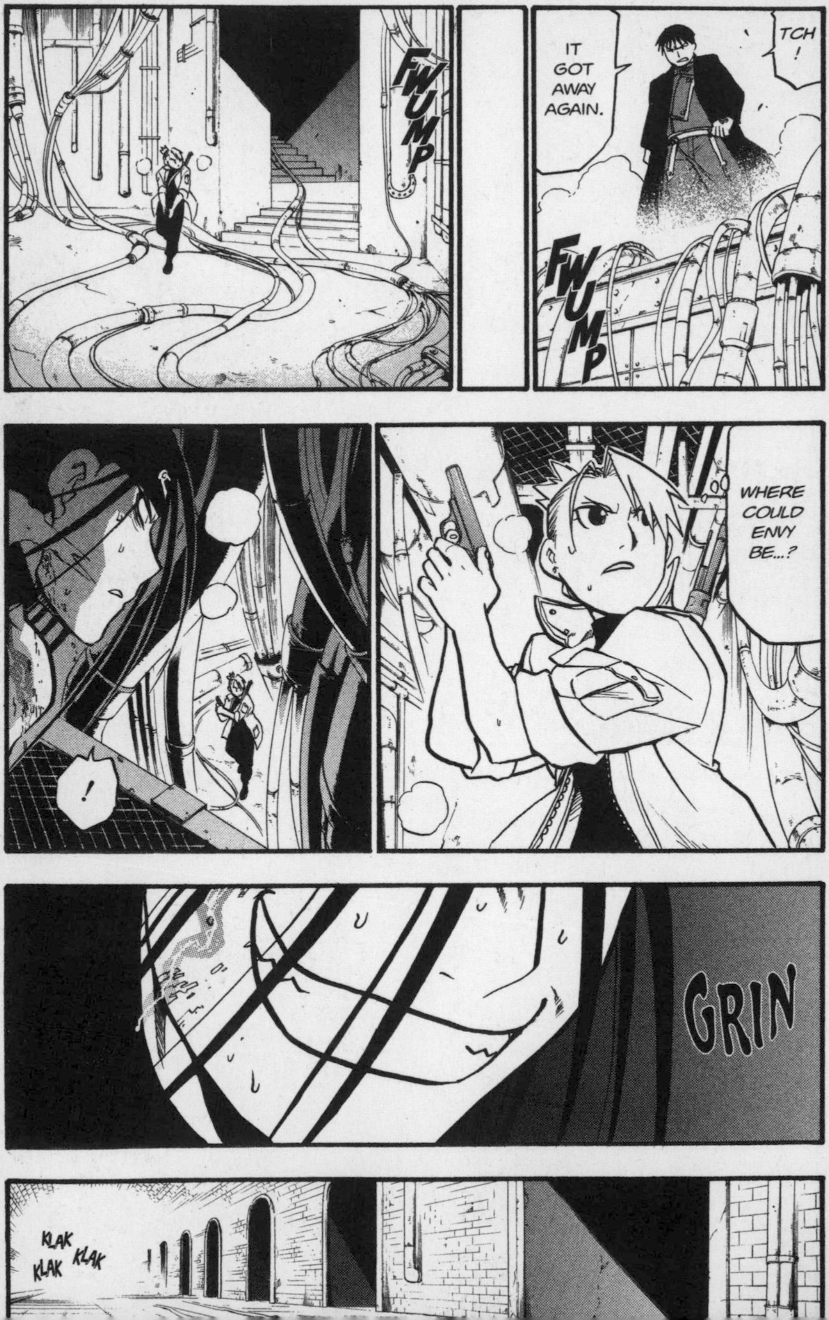
TCH!
IT GOT AWAY AGAIN.
FWUMP
FWUMP
WHERE COULD ENVY BE...?
!
GRIN
KLAK KLAK KLAK

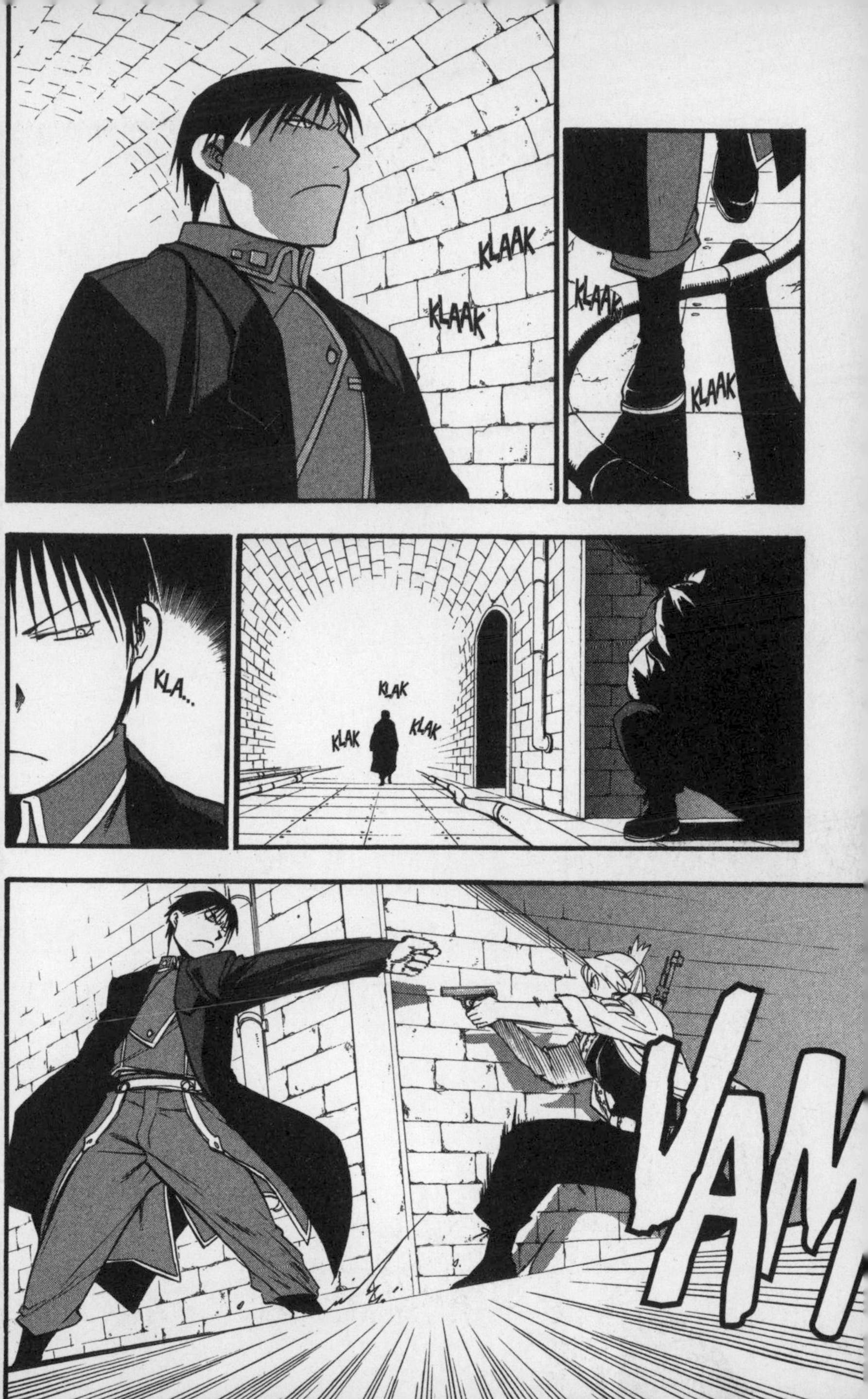
KLAAK
KLAAK
KLAAK
KLAAK
KLAK
KLAK
KLAK
KLA...
VAM

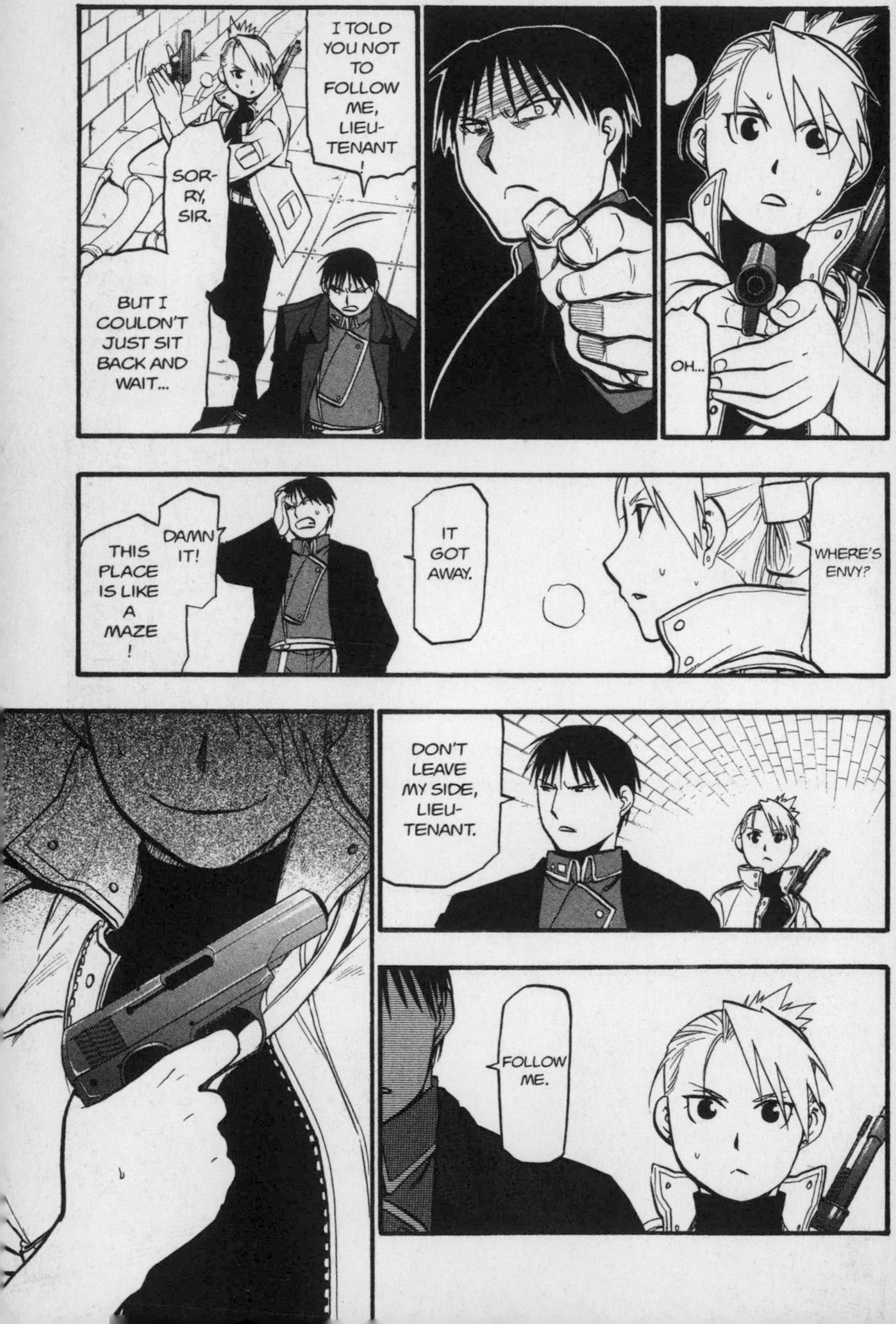
OH...
I TOLD YOU NOT TO FOLLOW ME, LIEUTENANT!
SORRY, SIR.
BUT I COULDN'T JUST SIT BACK AND WAIT...
WHERE'S ENVY?
IT GOT AWAY.
DAMN IT!
THIS PLACE IS LIKE A MAZE!
DON'T LEAVE MY SIDE, LIEUTENANT.
FOLLOW ME.

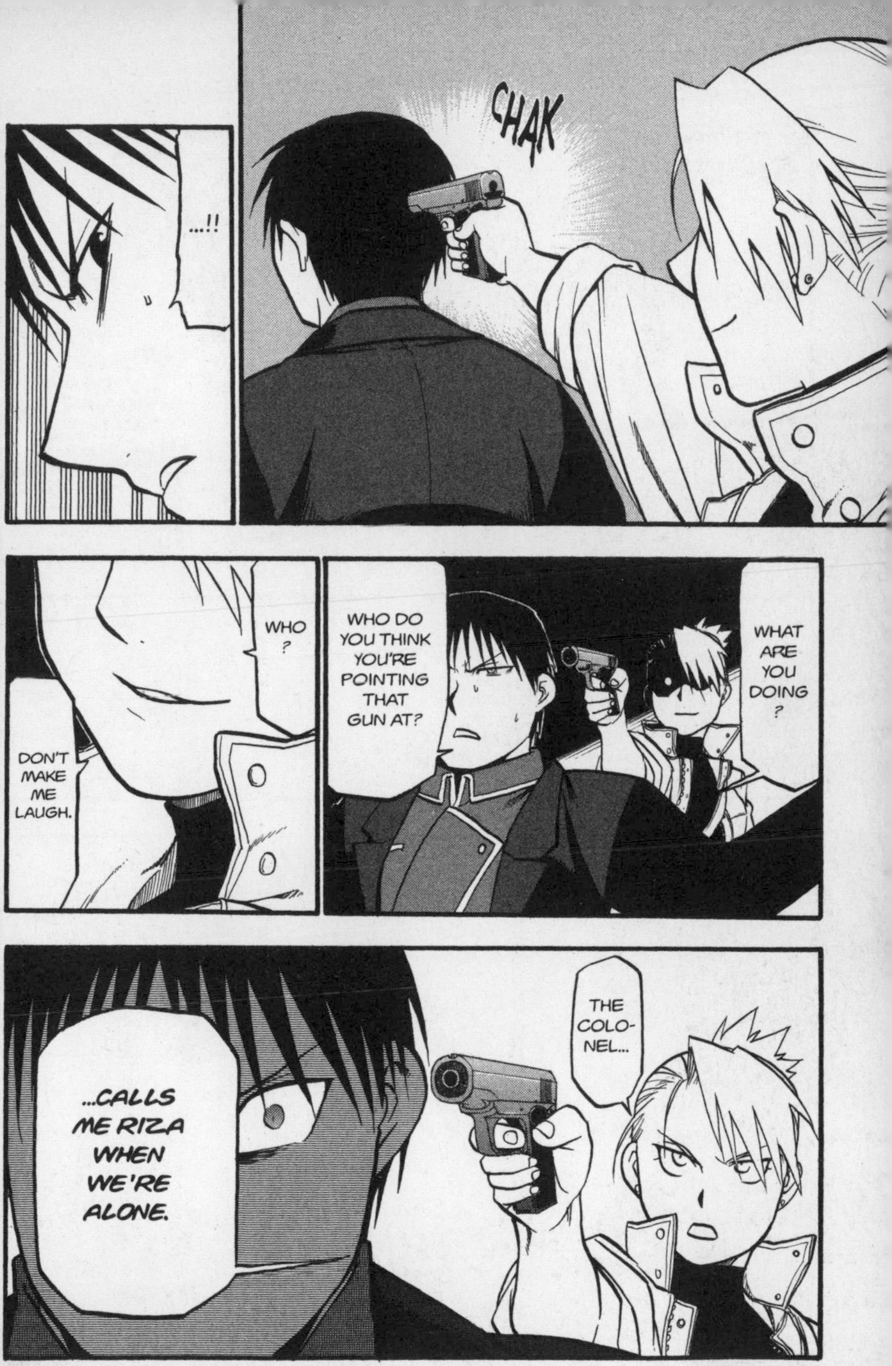
CHAK
...!!
WHAT ARE YOU DOING?
WHO DO YOU THINK YOU'RE POINTING THAT GUN AT?
WHO?
DON'T MAKE ME LAUGH.
THE COLONEL...
...CALLS ME RIZA WHEN WE'RE ALONE.

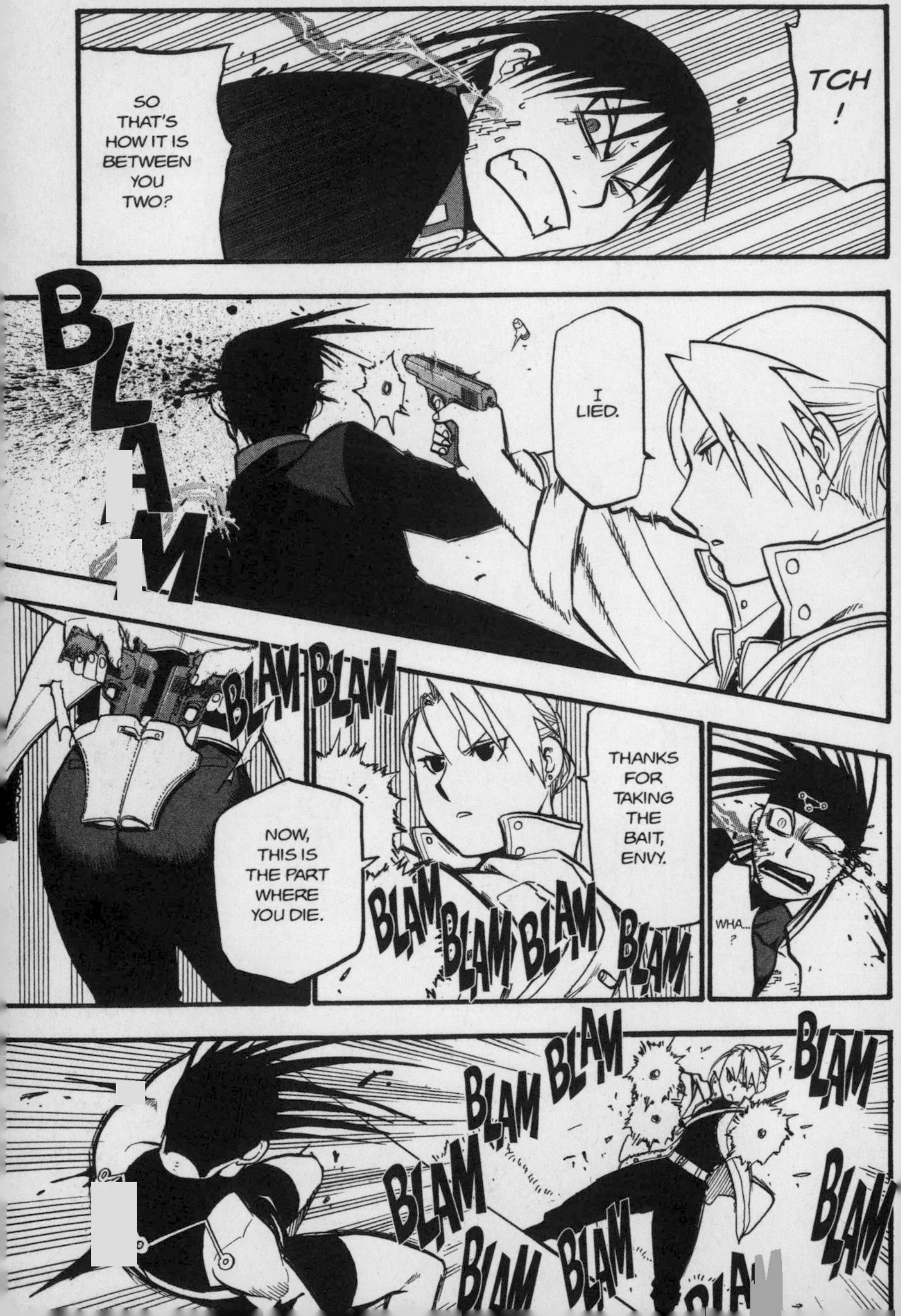
TCH !
SO THAT'S HOW IT IS BETWEEN YOU TWO?
I LIED.
BLAM
WHA... ?
THANKS FOR TAKING THE BAIT, ENVY.
BLAM BLAM BLAM BLAM
NOW, THIS IS THE PART WHERE YOU DIE.
BLAM BLAM
BLAM
BLAM
BLAM
BLAM
BLAM
BLAM
BLAM
BLAM

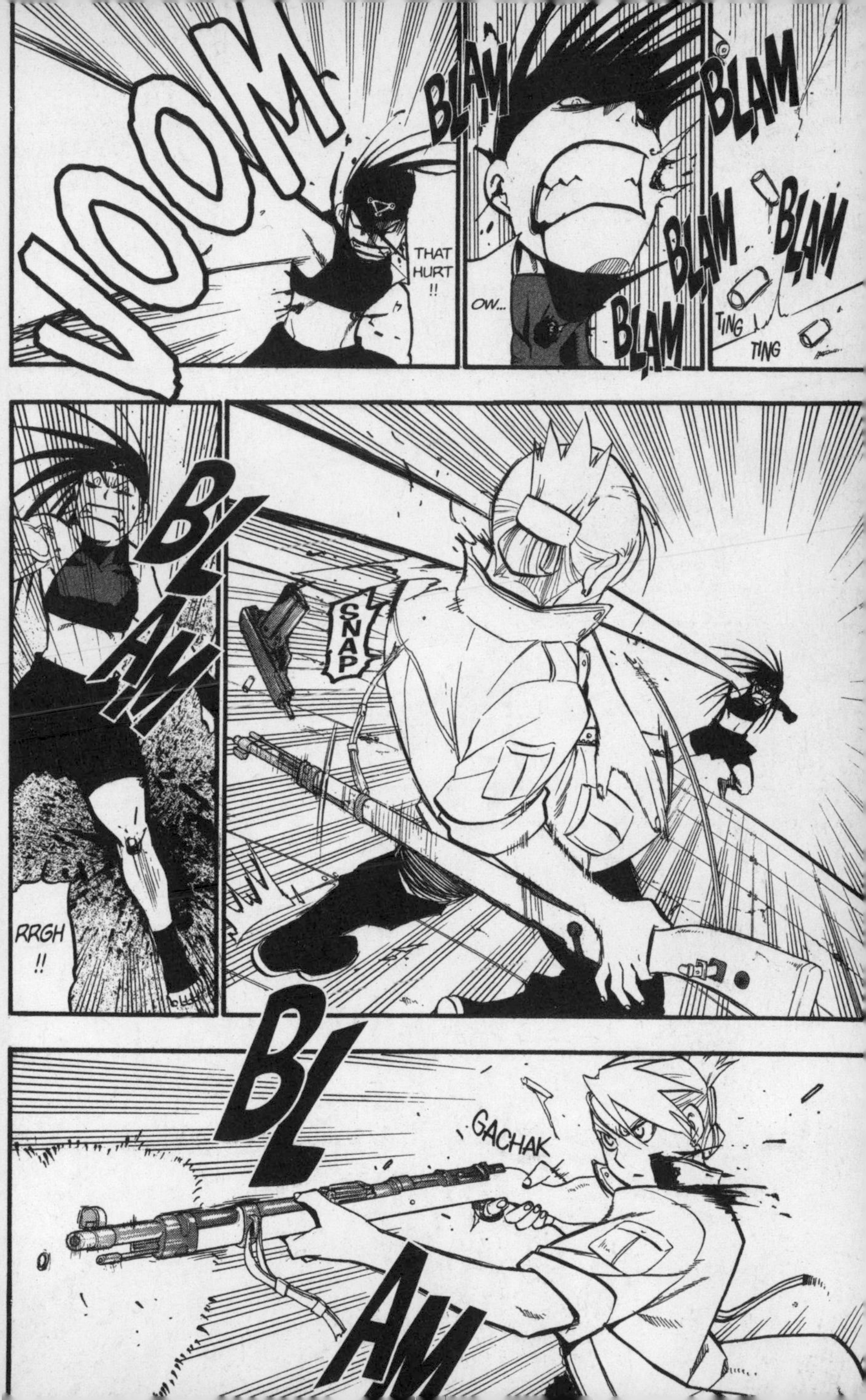

BLAM
BLAM
BLAM
BLAM
TING
TING
BLAM
OW...
BLAM
VOOOM
THAT HURT!!
SNAP
BLAM
RRGH!!
GACHAK
BLAM

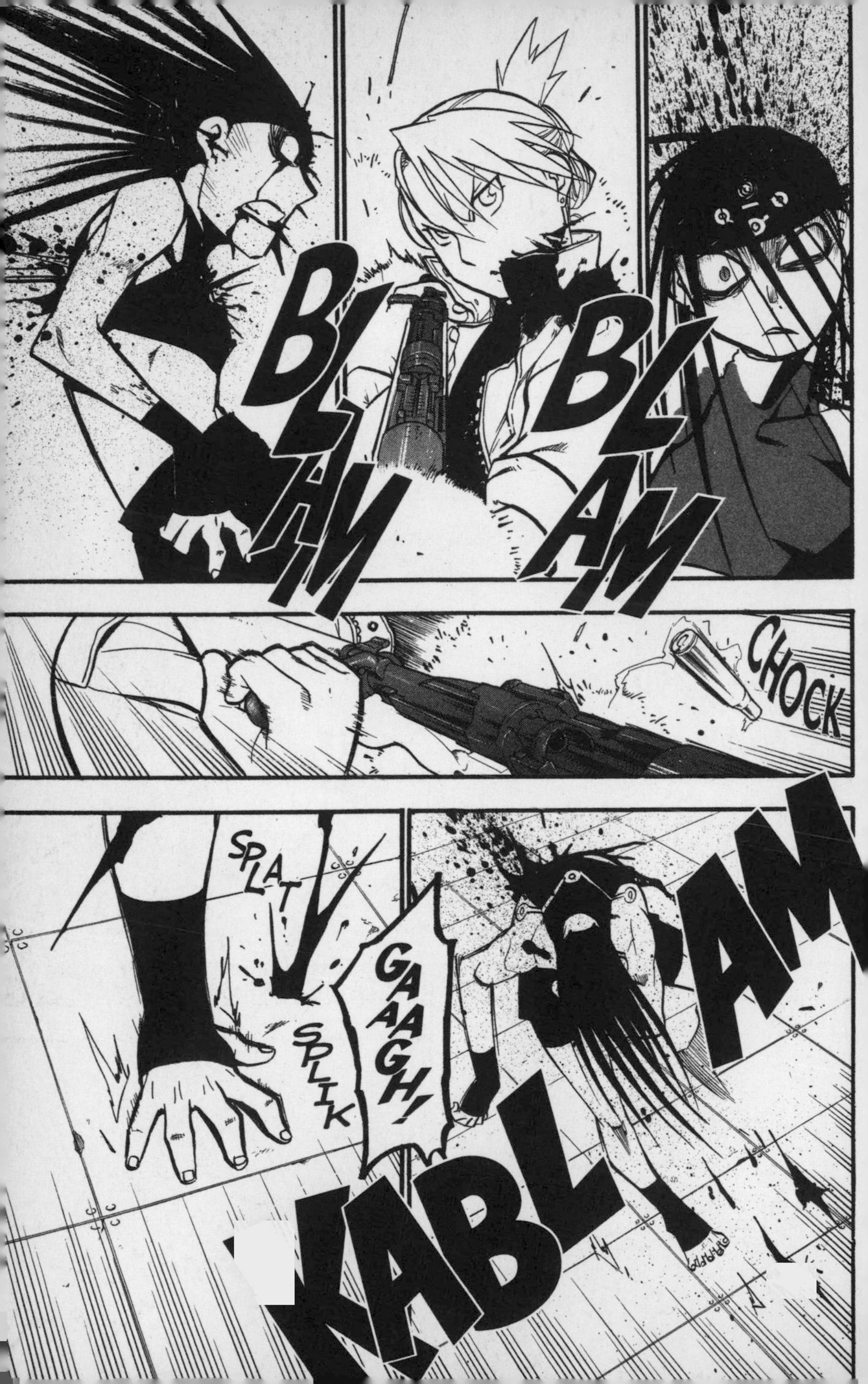
BLAM
BLAM
CHOCK
KABLAM
GAAAGH!
SPLAT
SPLIK

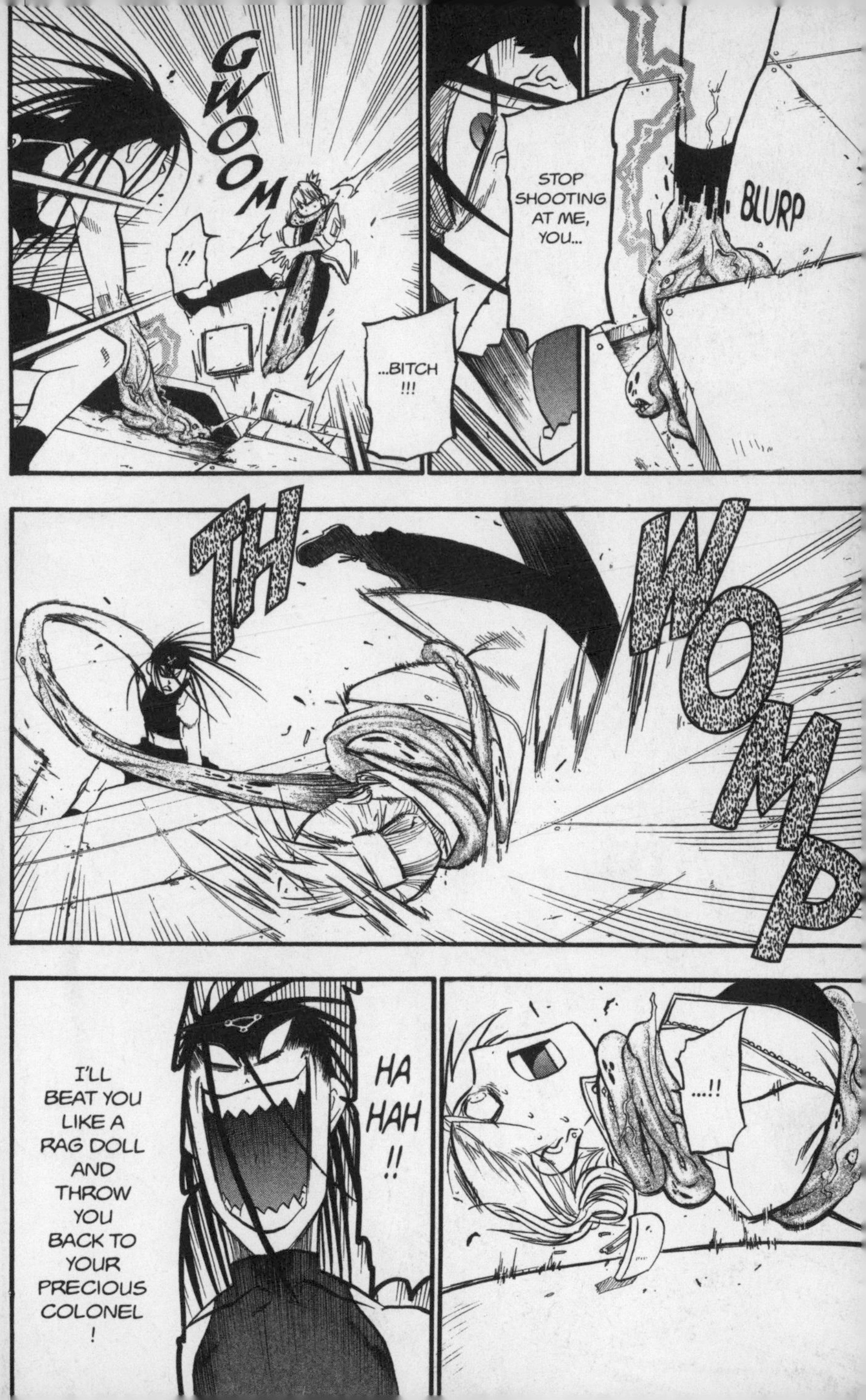
BLURP
STOP SHOOTING AT ME, YOU...
GWOOM
!!
...BITCH !!!
THWOMP
...!!
HA HAH !!
I'LL BEAT YOU LIKE A RAG DOLL AND THROW YOU BACK TO YOUR PRECIOUS COLONEL !

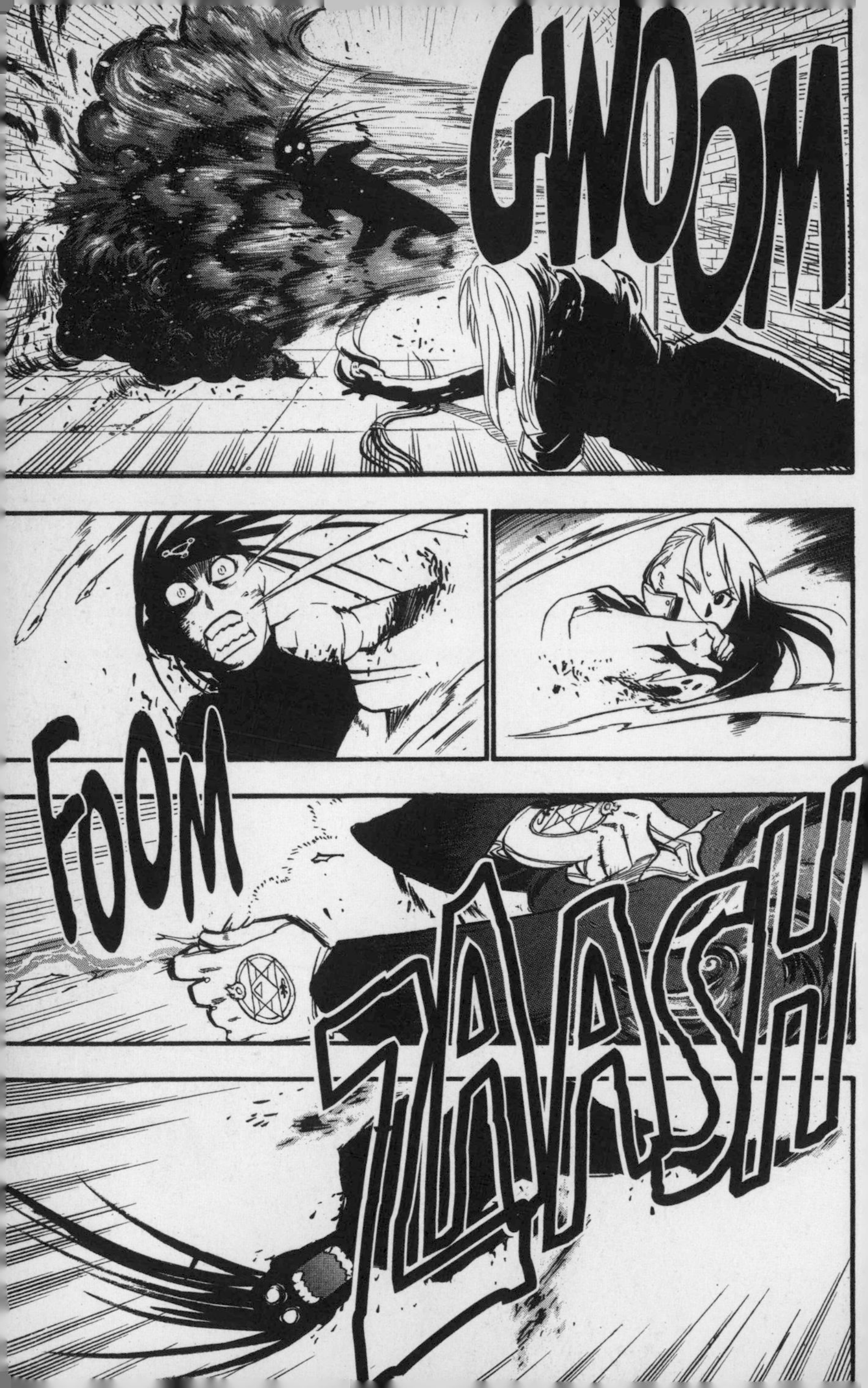
GWOOM
FOOM
ZAASH

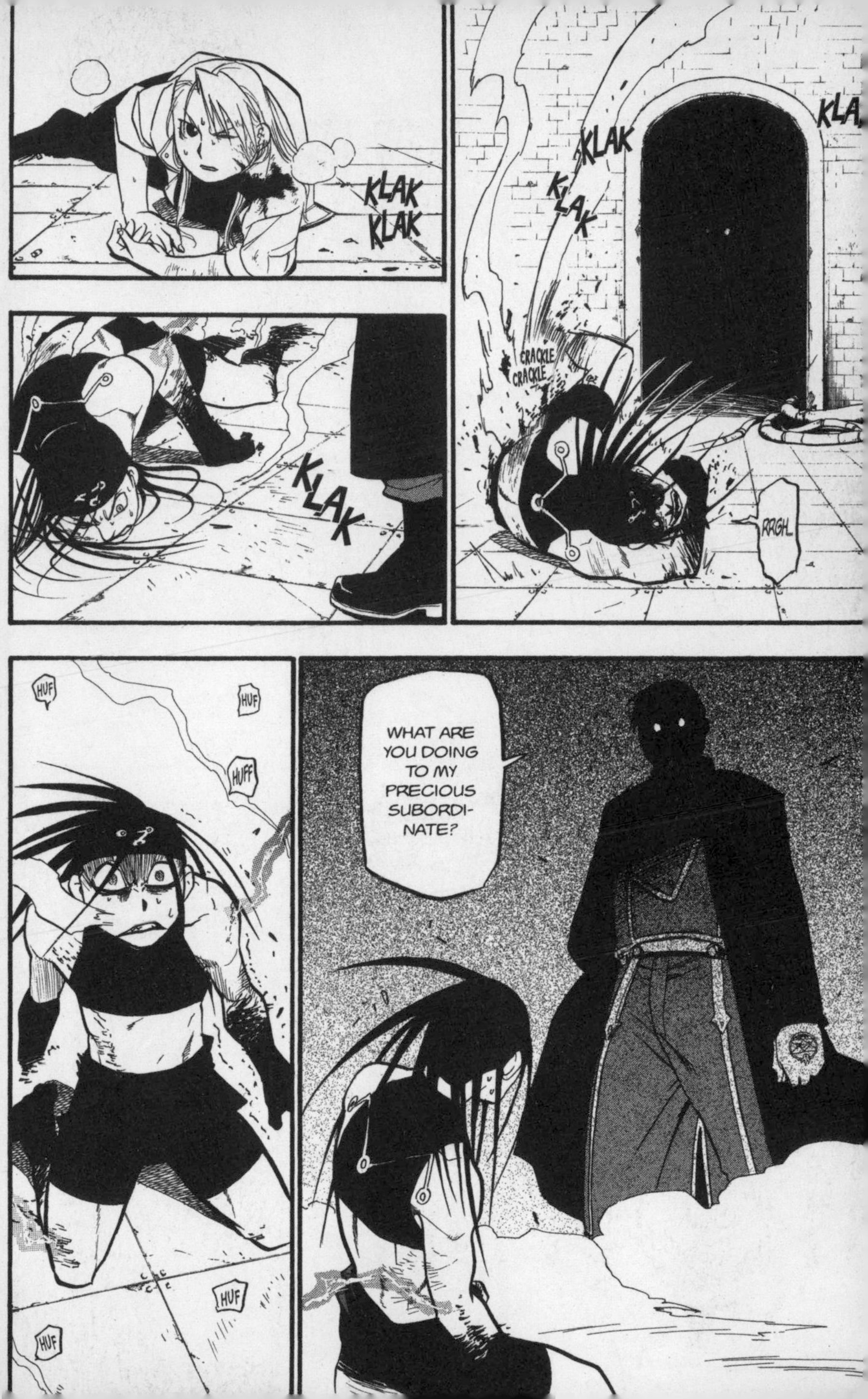
KLA
KLAK
KLAK
CRACKLE
CRACKLE
RRGH...
KLAK
KLAK
KLAK
WHAT ARE YOU DOING TO MY PRECIOUS SUBORDI-NATE?
HUF
HUF
HUFF
HUF
HUF

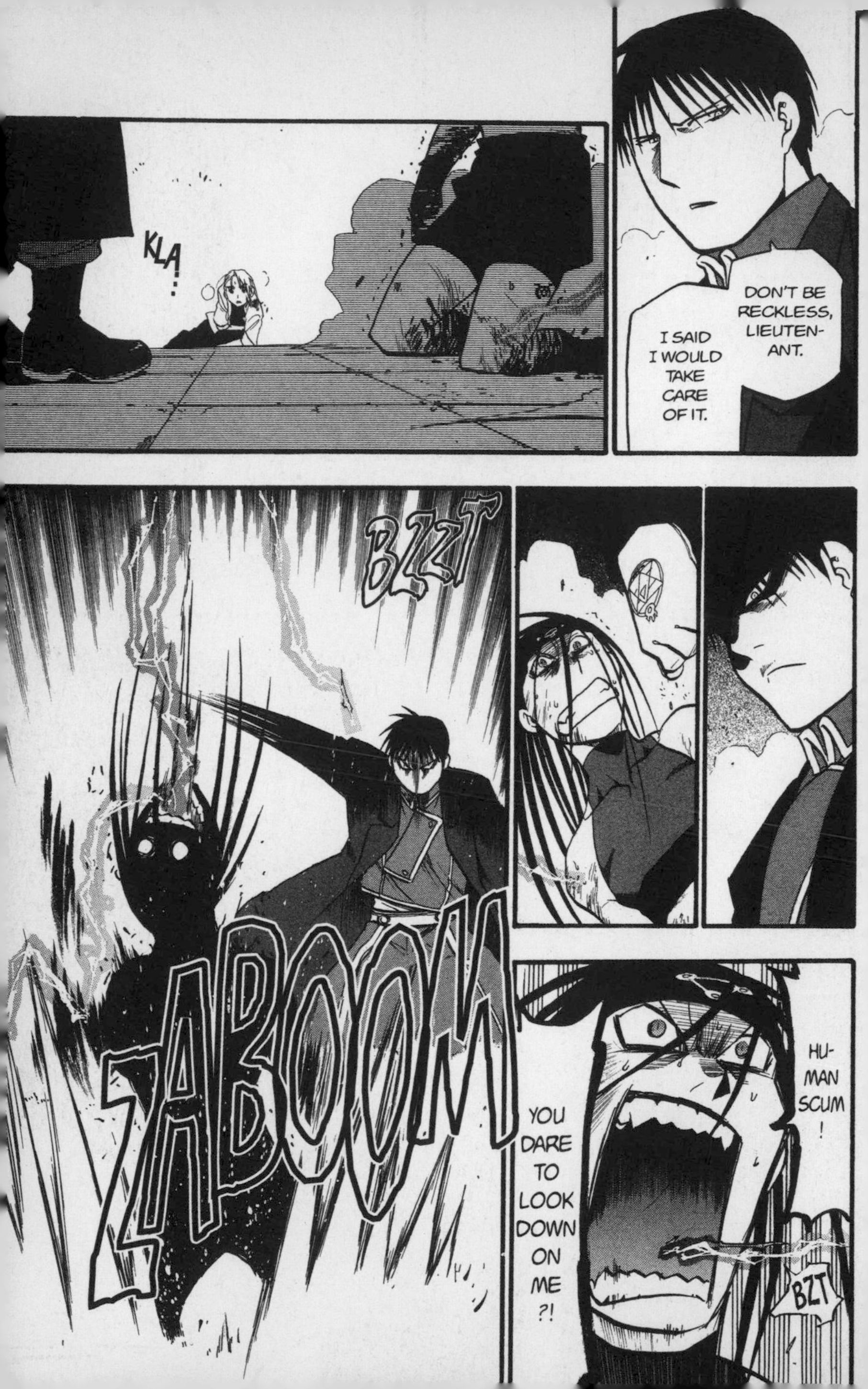

DON'T BE RECKLESS, LIEUTEN-ANT.
I SAID I WOULD TAKE CARE OF IT.
KLA
BZZT
ZABOOM
HU-MAN SCUM!
YOU DARE TO LOOK DOWN ON ME?!
BZT

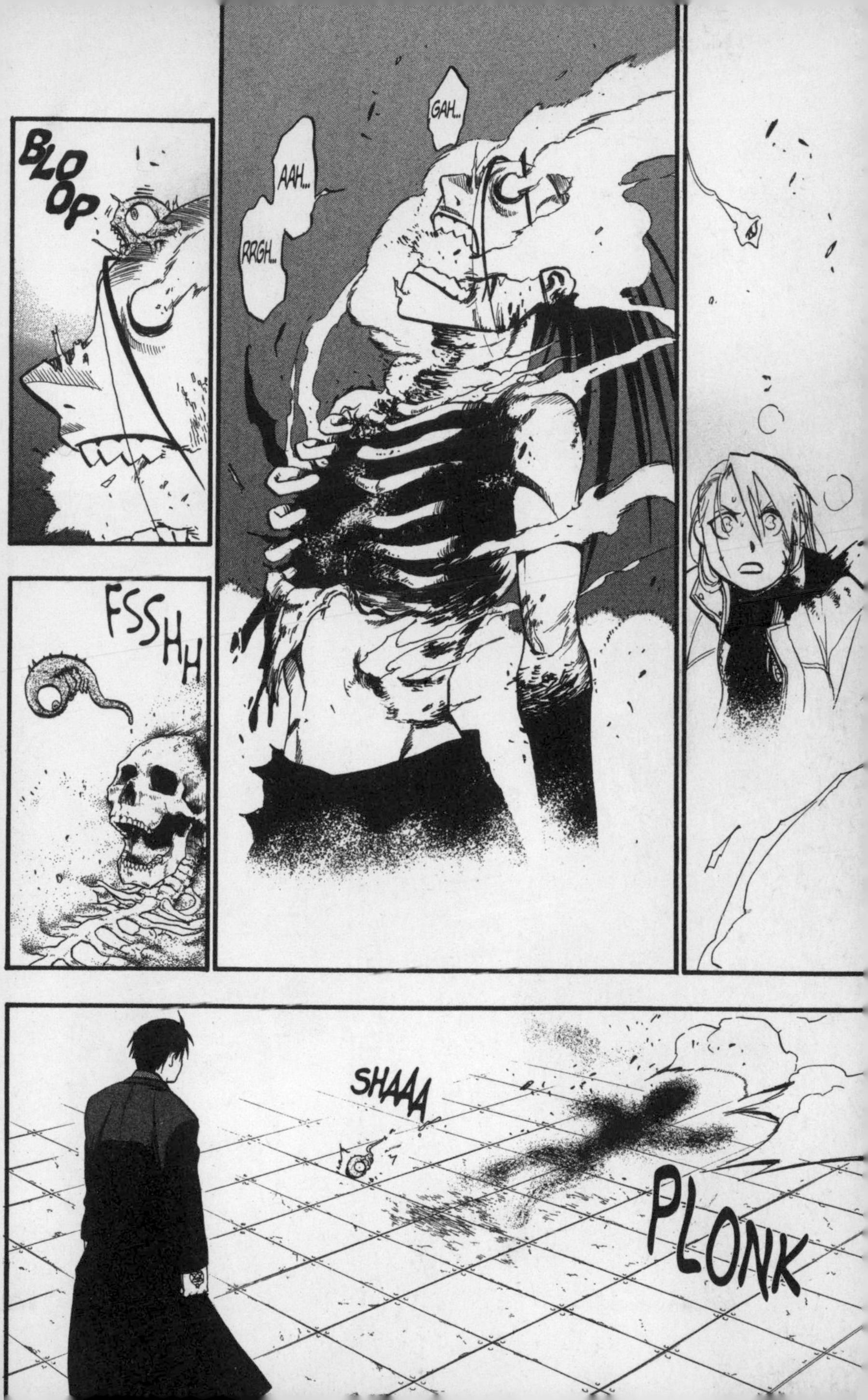
GAH...
AAH...
RRGH...
BLOOP
FSSHH
SHAAA
PLONK

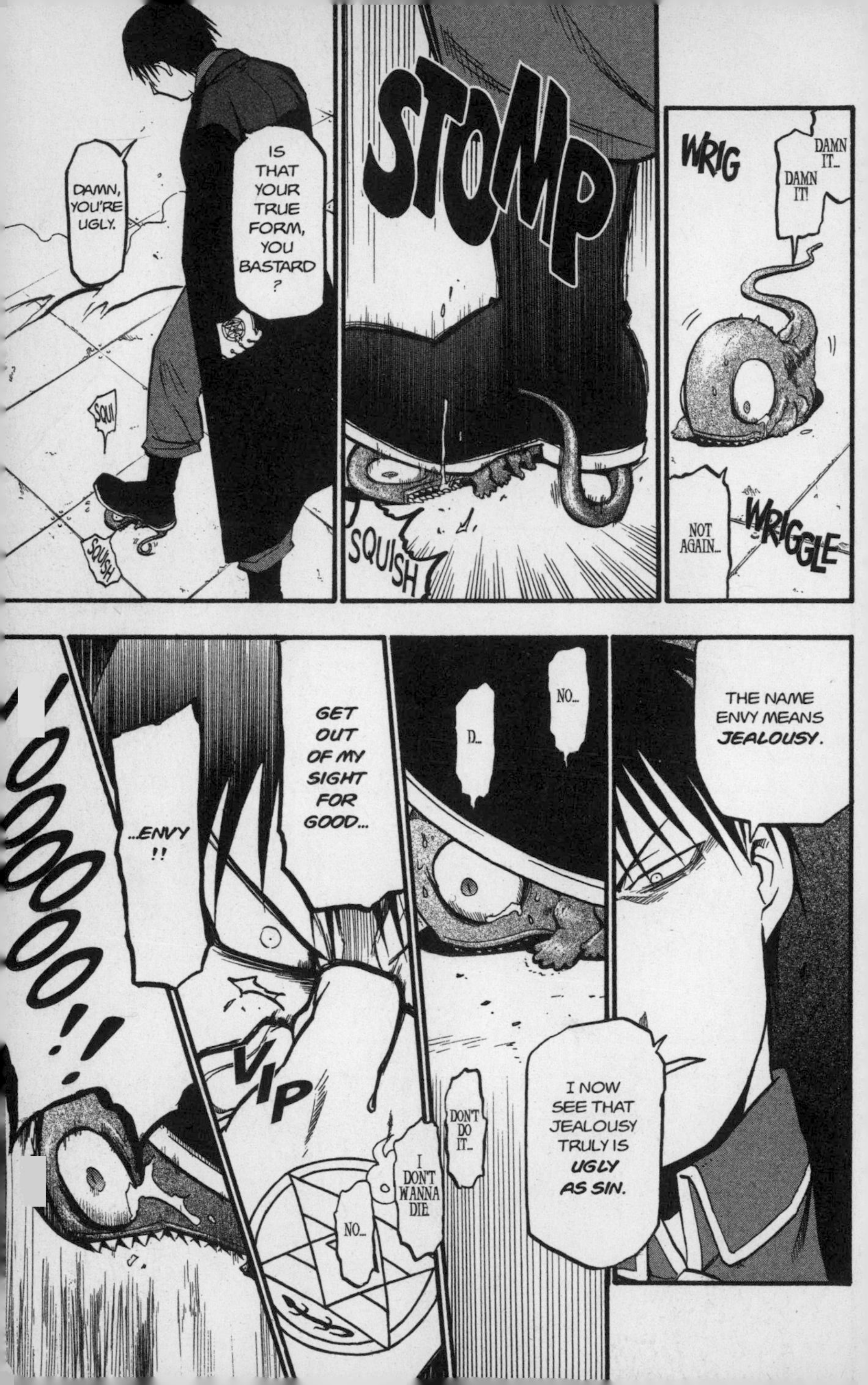
WRIG
DAMN IT... DAMN IT!
NOT AGAIN...
WRIGGLE
STOMP
SQUISH
IS THAT YOUR TRUE FORM, YOU BASTARD?
DAMN, YOU'RE UGLY.
SQUI
SQUISH
THE NAME ENVY MEANS JEALOUSY.
I NOW SEE THAT JEALOUSY TRULY IS UGLY AS SIN.
NO...
D...
DON'T DO IT...
GET OUT OF MY SIGHT FOR GOOD...
...ENVY!!
VIP
I DON'T WANNA DIE
NO...
OOOOOOO!!

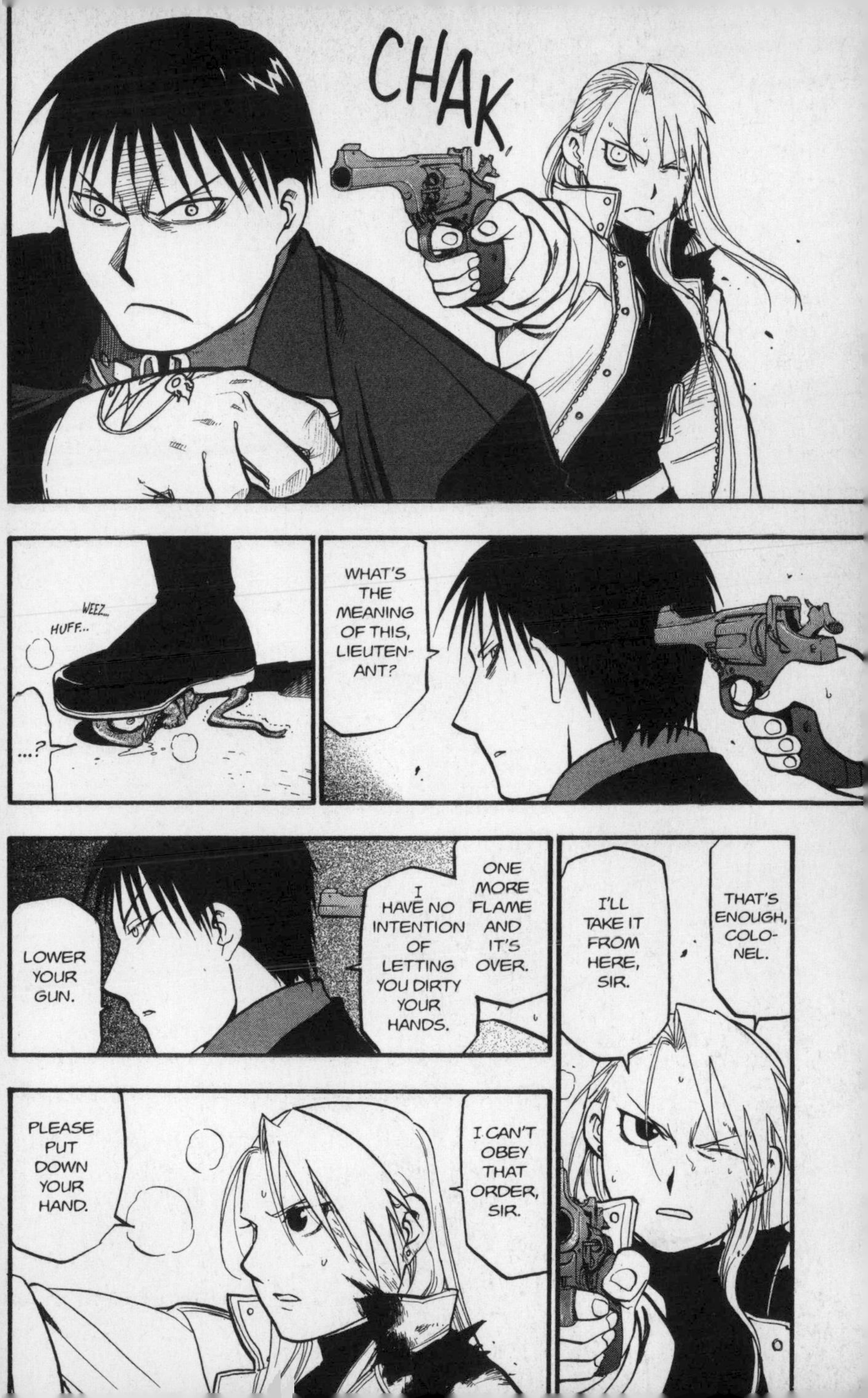
CHAK
WHAT'S THE MEANING OF THIS, LIEUTENANT?
WEEZ... HUFF...
...?
THAT'S ENOUGH, COLONEL.
I'LL TAKE IT FROM HERE, SIR.
ONE MORE FLAME AND IT'S OVER.
I HAVE NO INTENTION OF LETTING YOU DIRTY YOUR HANDS.
LOWER YOUR GUN.
I CAN'T OBEY THAT ORDER, SIR.
PLEASE PUT DOWN YOUR HAND.

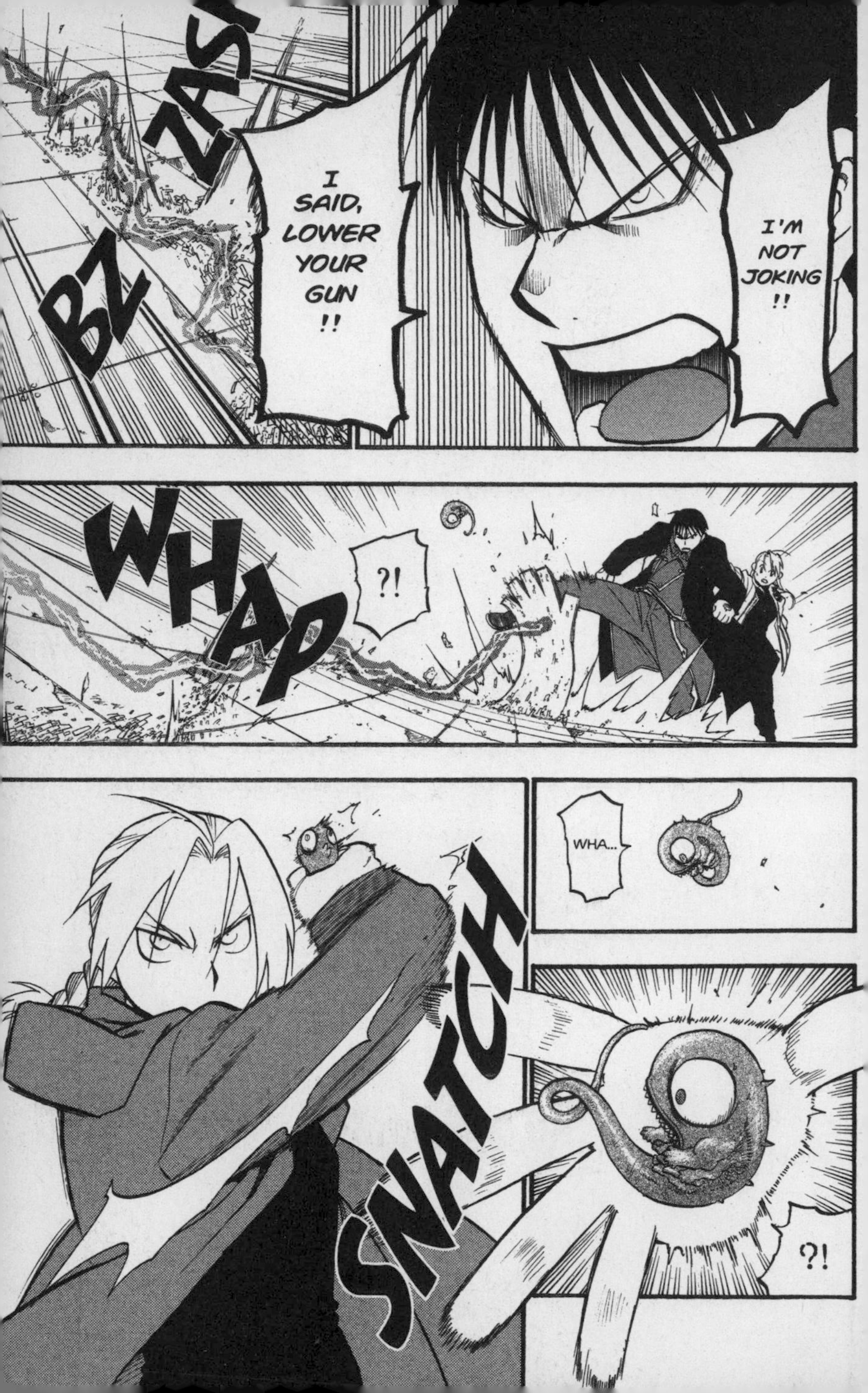
I SAID, LOWER YOUR GUN !!
I'M NOT JOKING !!
BZZASH
?!
WHAP
WHA...
?!
SNATCH

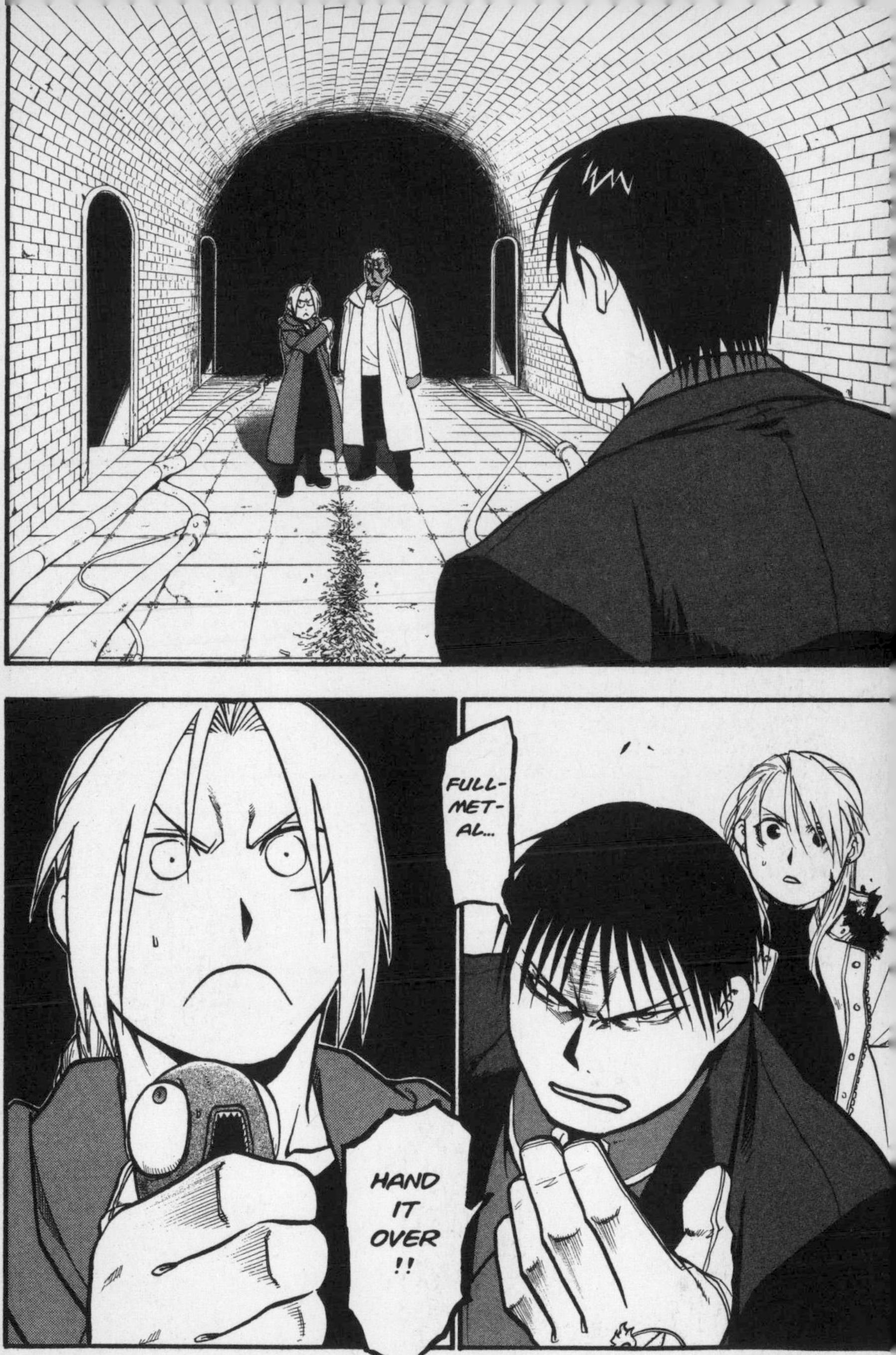
FULL-
MET-
AL...
HAND
IT
OVER
!!

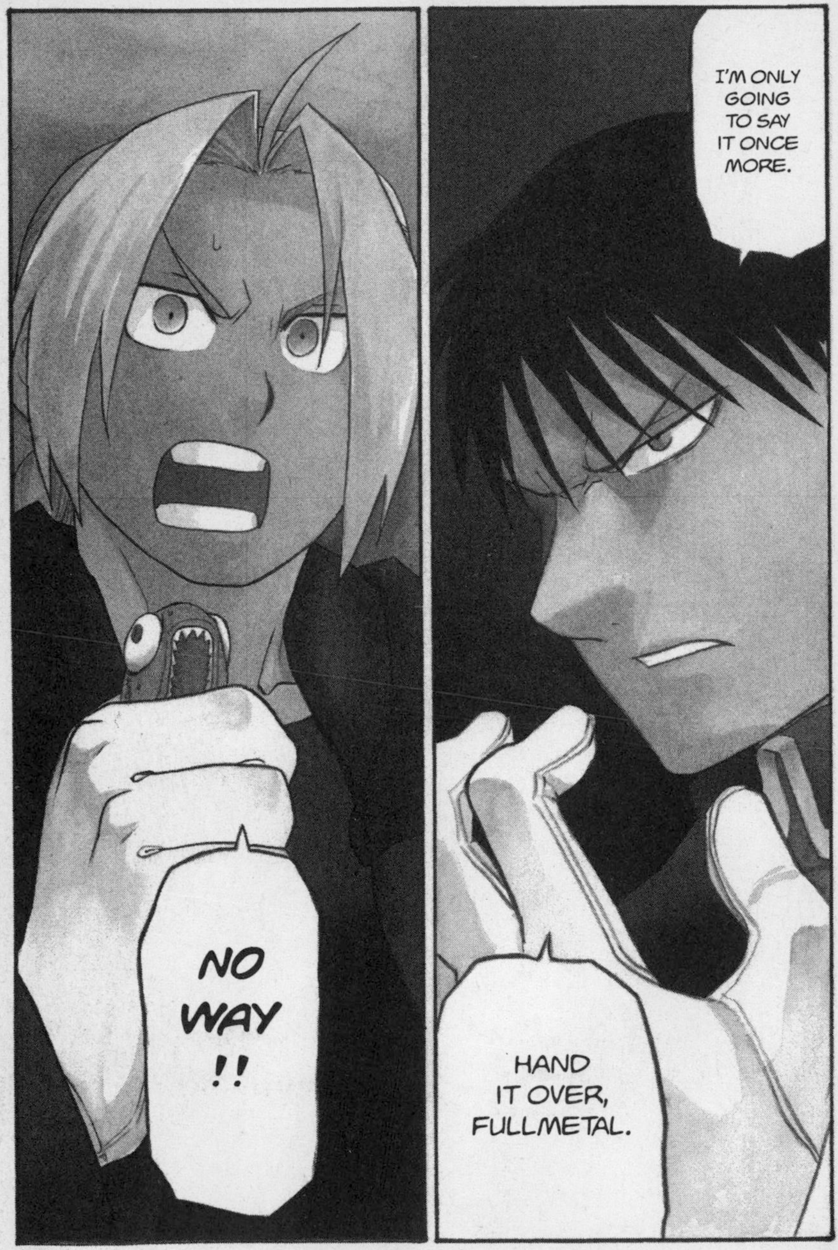
I'M ONLY GOING TO SAY IT ONCE MORE.
HAND IT OVER, FULLMETAL.
NO WAY!!

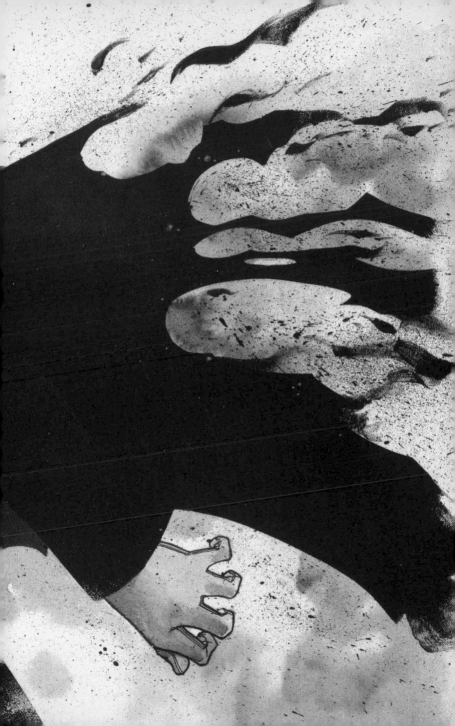

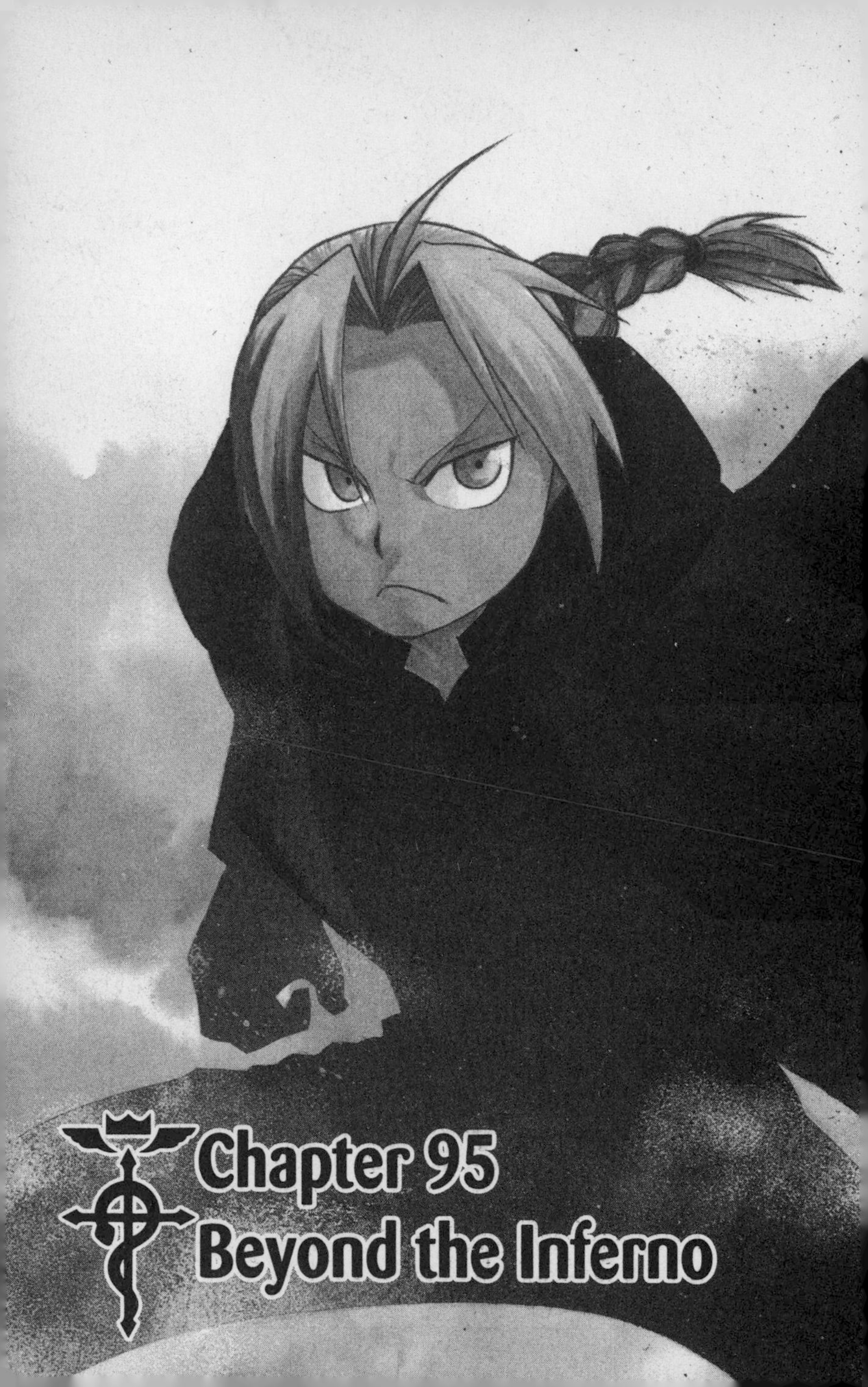
Chapter 95
Beyond the Inferno

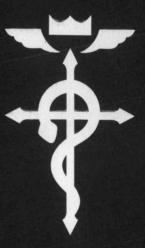

FULLMETAL
ALCHEMIST

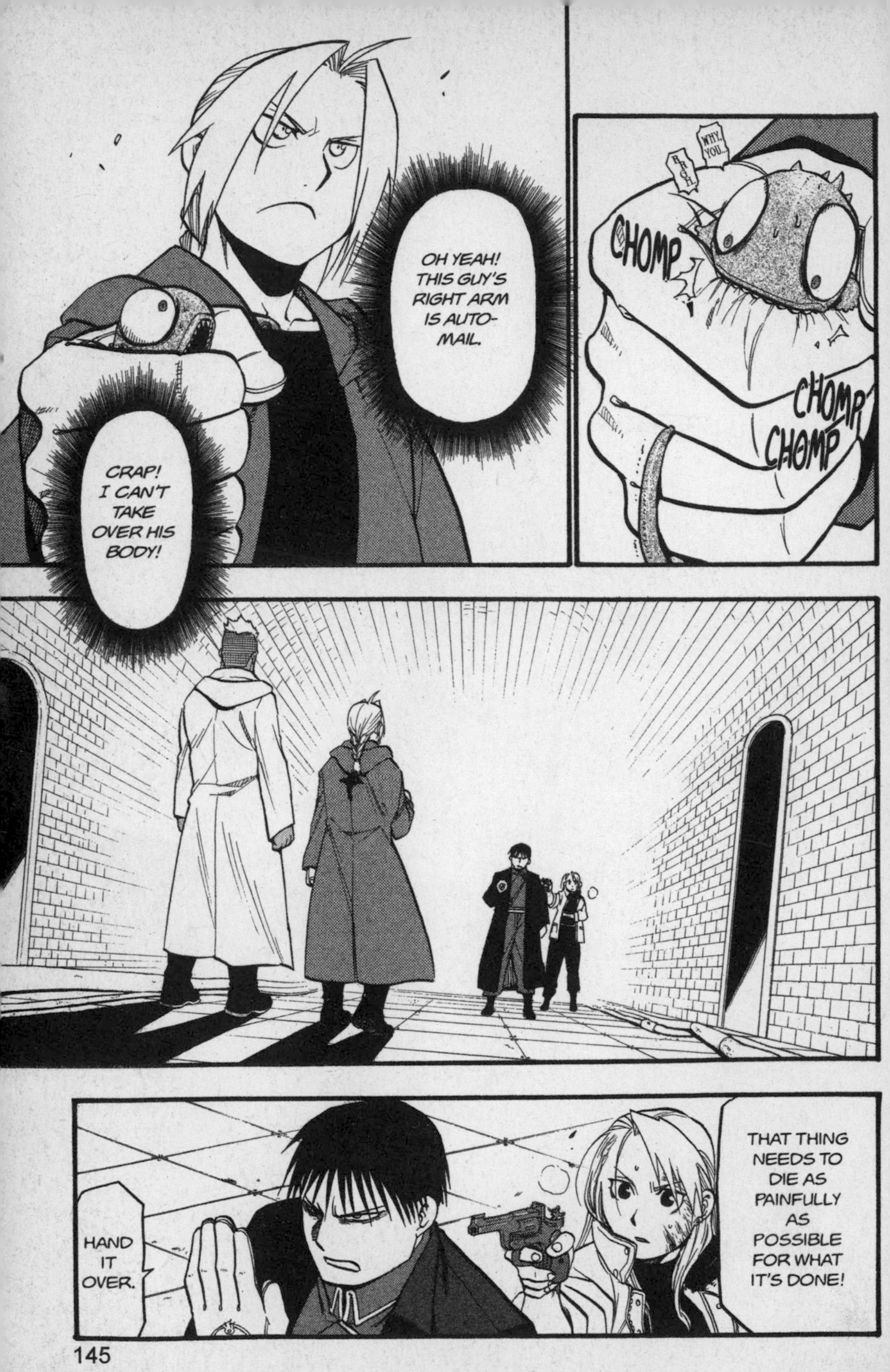
WHY, YOU...
RRGH.
CHOMP
CHOMP
CHOMP
OH YEAH! THIS GUY'S RIGHT ARM IS AUTO-MAIL.
CRAP! I CAN'T TAKE OVER HIS BODY!
THAT THING NEEDS TO DIE AS PAINFULLY AS POSSIBLE FOR WHAT IT'S DONE!
HAND IT OVER.

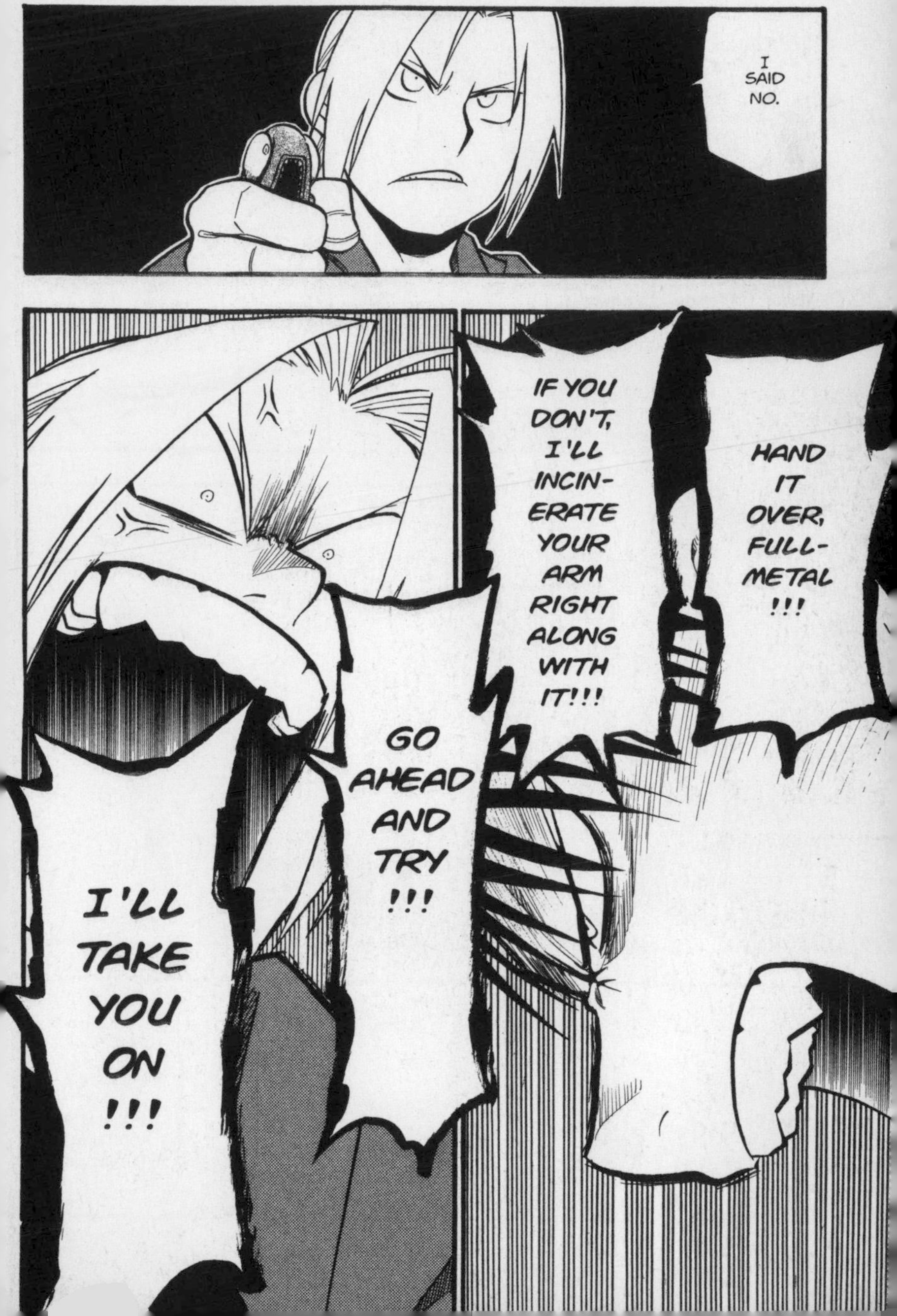
I SAID NO.
HAND IT OVER, FULL-METAL!!!
IF YOU DON'T, I'LL INCIN-ERATE YOUR ARM RIGHT ALONG WITH IT!!!
GO AHEAD AND TRY!!!
I'LL TAKE YOU ON!!!

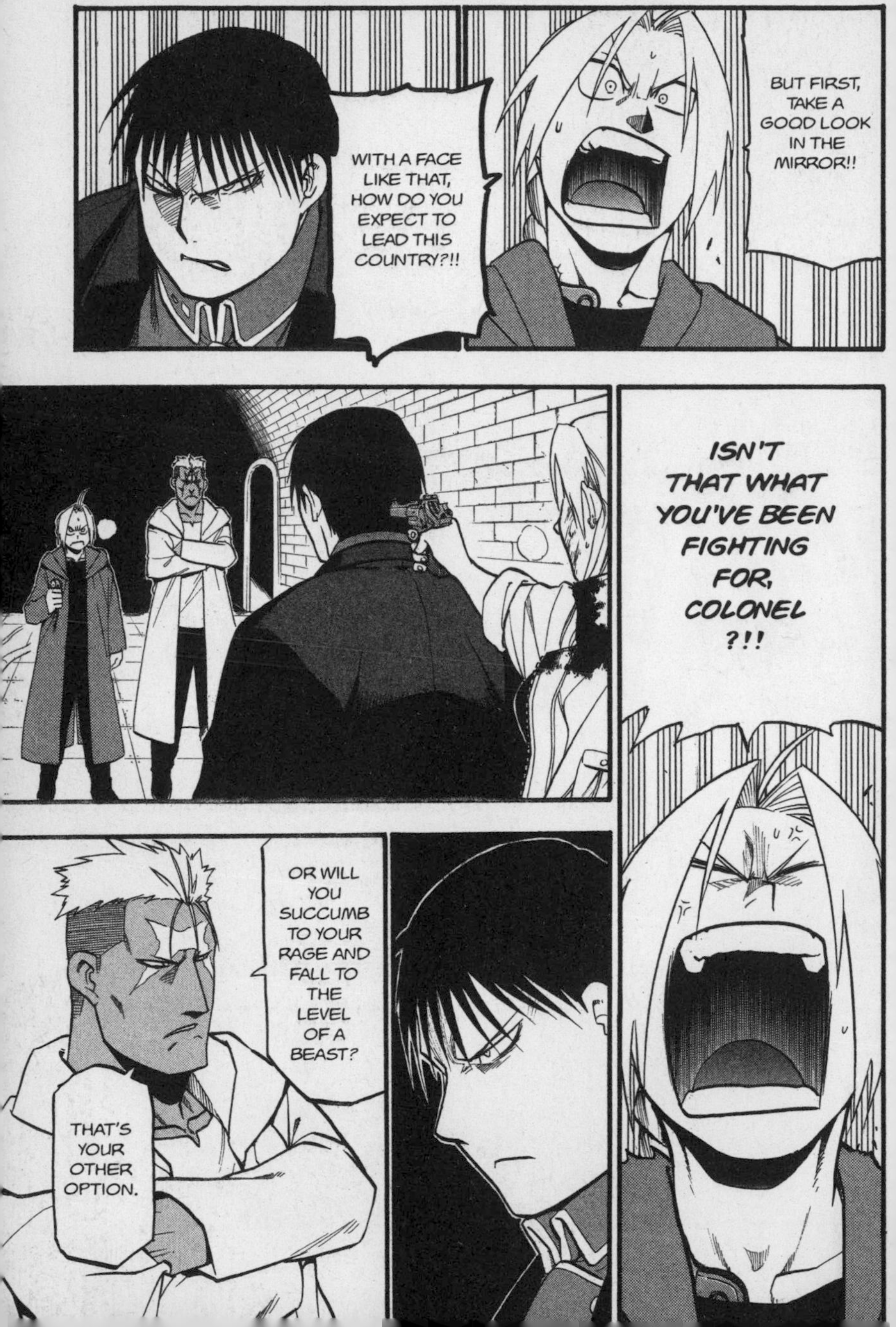
BUT FIRST, TAKE A GOOD LOOK IN THE MIRROR!!
WITH A FACE LIKE THAT, HOW DO YOU EXPECT TO LEAD THIS COUNTRY?!!
ISN'T THAT WHAT YOU'VE BEEN FIGHTING FOR, COLONEL ?!!
OR WILL YOU SUCCUMB TO YOUR RAGE AND FALL TO THE LEVEL OF A BEAST?
THAT'S YOUR OTHER OPTION.

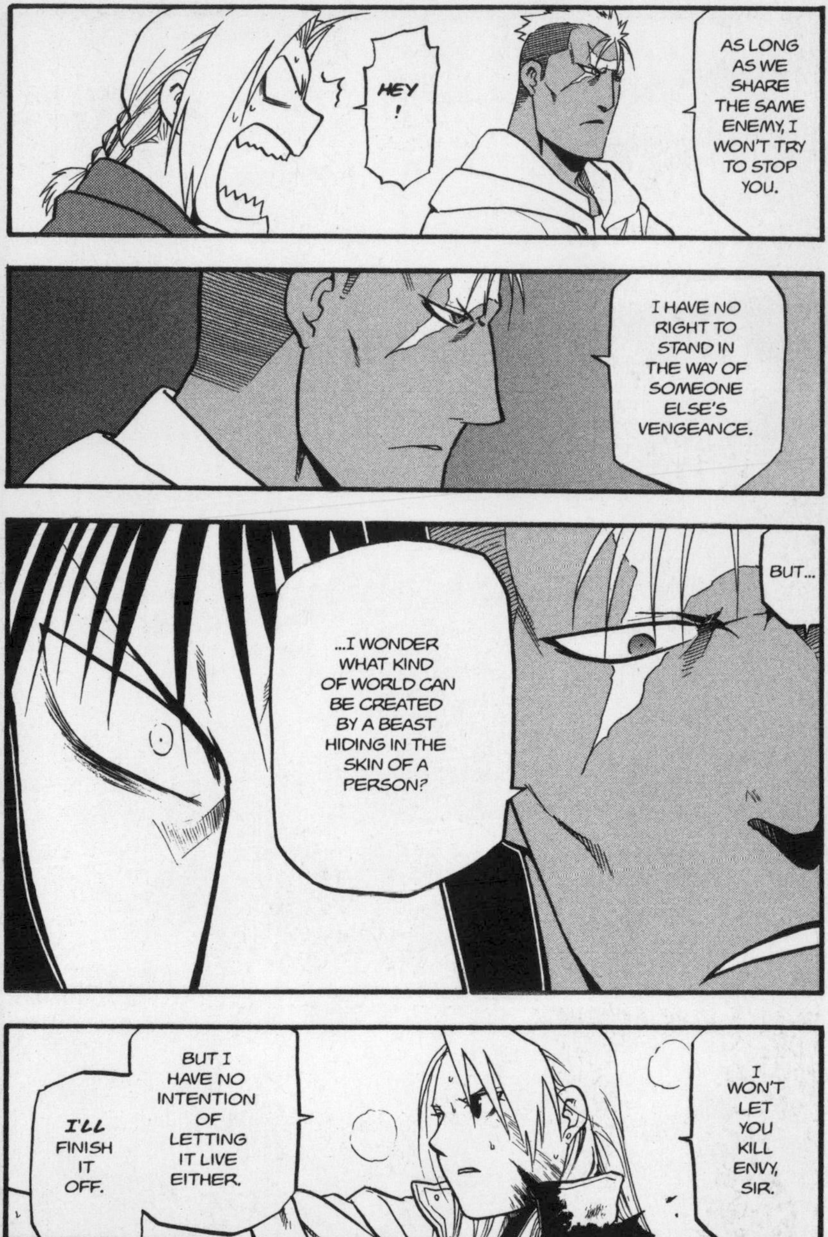
AS LONG AS WE SHARE THE SAME ENEMY, I WON'T TRY TO STOP YOU.
HEY!
I HAVE NO RIGHT TO STAND IN THE WAY OF SOMEONE ELSE'S VENGEANCE.
BUT...
...I WONDER WHAT KIND OF WORLD CAN BE CREATED BY A BEAST HIDING IN THE SKIN OF A PERSON?
I WON'T LET YOU KILL ENVY, SIR.
BUT I HAVE NO INTENTION OF LETTING IT LIVE EITHER.
I'LL FINISH IT OFF.

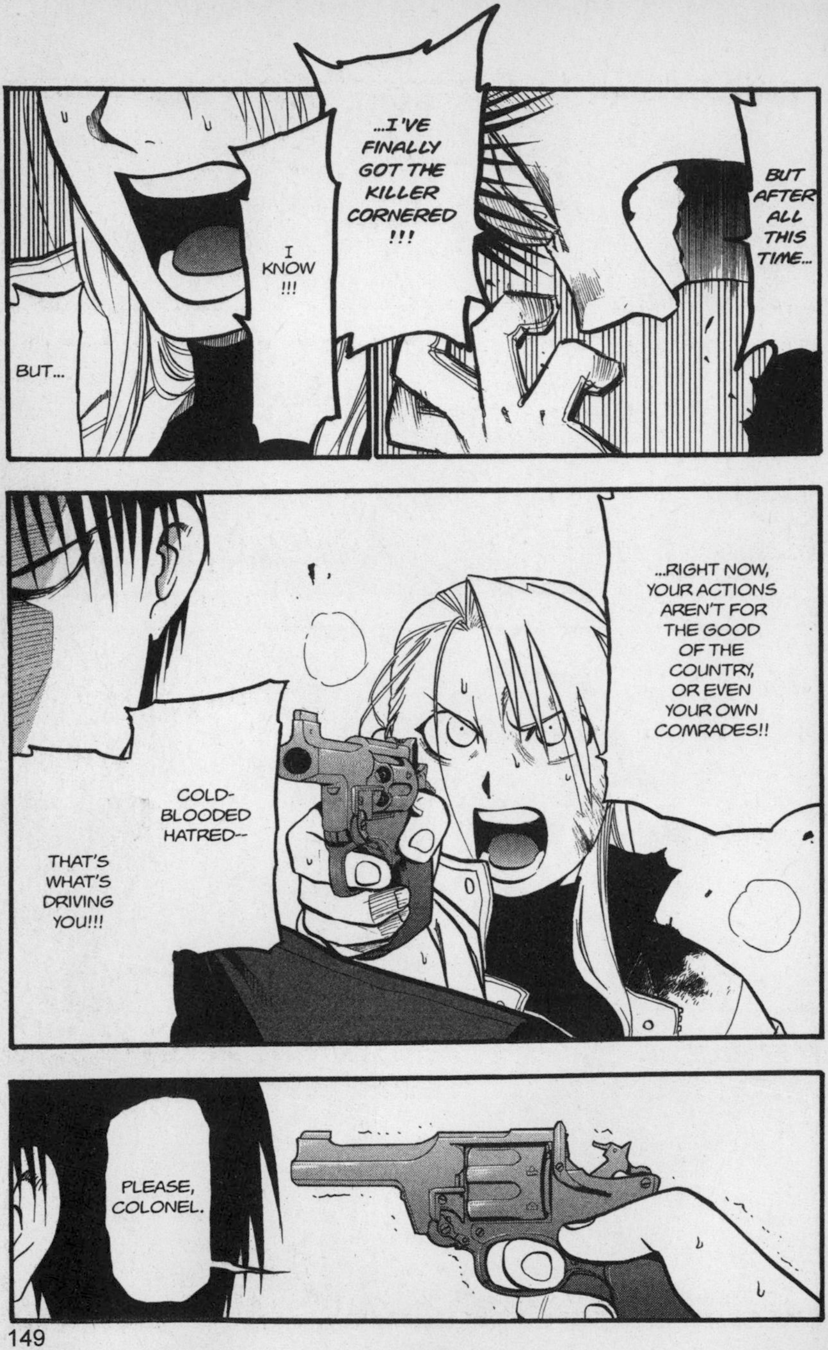
BUT AFTER ALL THIS TIME...
...I'VE FINALLY GOT THE KILLER CORNERED!!!
I KNOW!!!
BUT...
...RIGHT NOW, YOUR ACTIONS AREN'T FOR THE GOOD OF THE COUNTRY, OR EVEN YOUR OWN COMRADES!!
COLD-BLOODED HATRED--
THAT'S WHAT'S DRIVING YOU!!!
PLEASE, COLONEL.

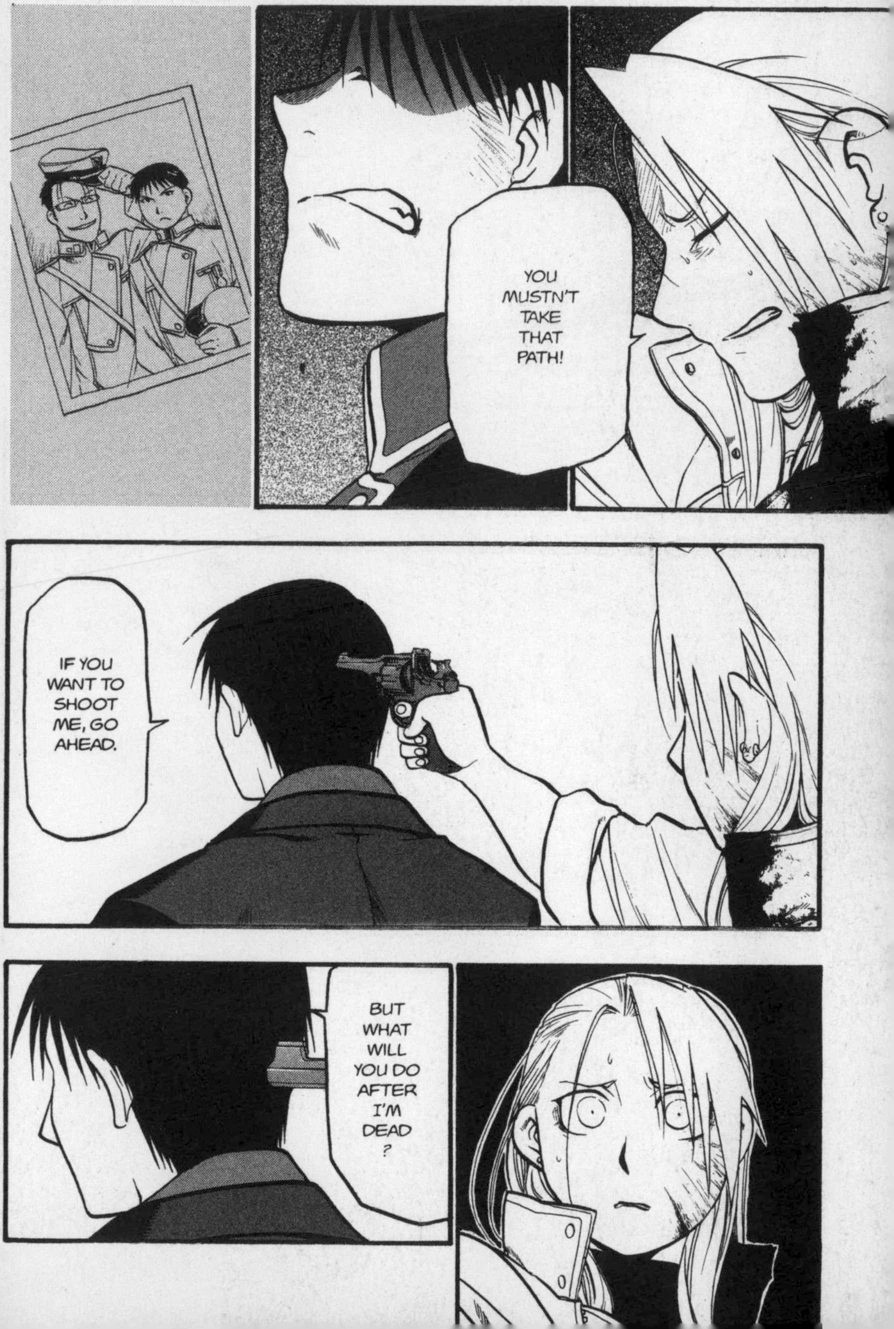
YOU MUSTN'T TAKE THAT PATH!
IF YOU WANT TO SHOOT ME, GO AHEAD.
BUT WHAT WILL YOU DO AFTER I'M DEAD?

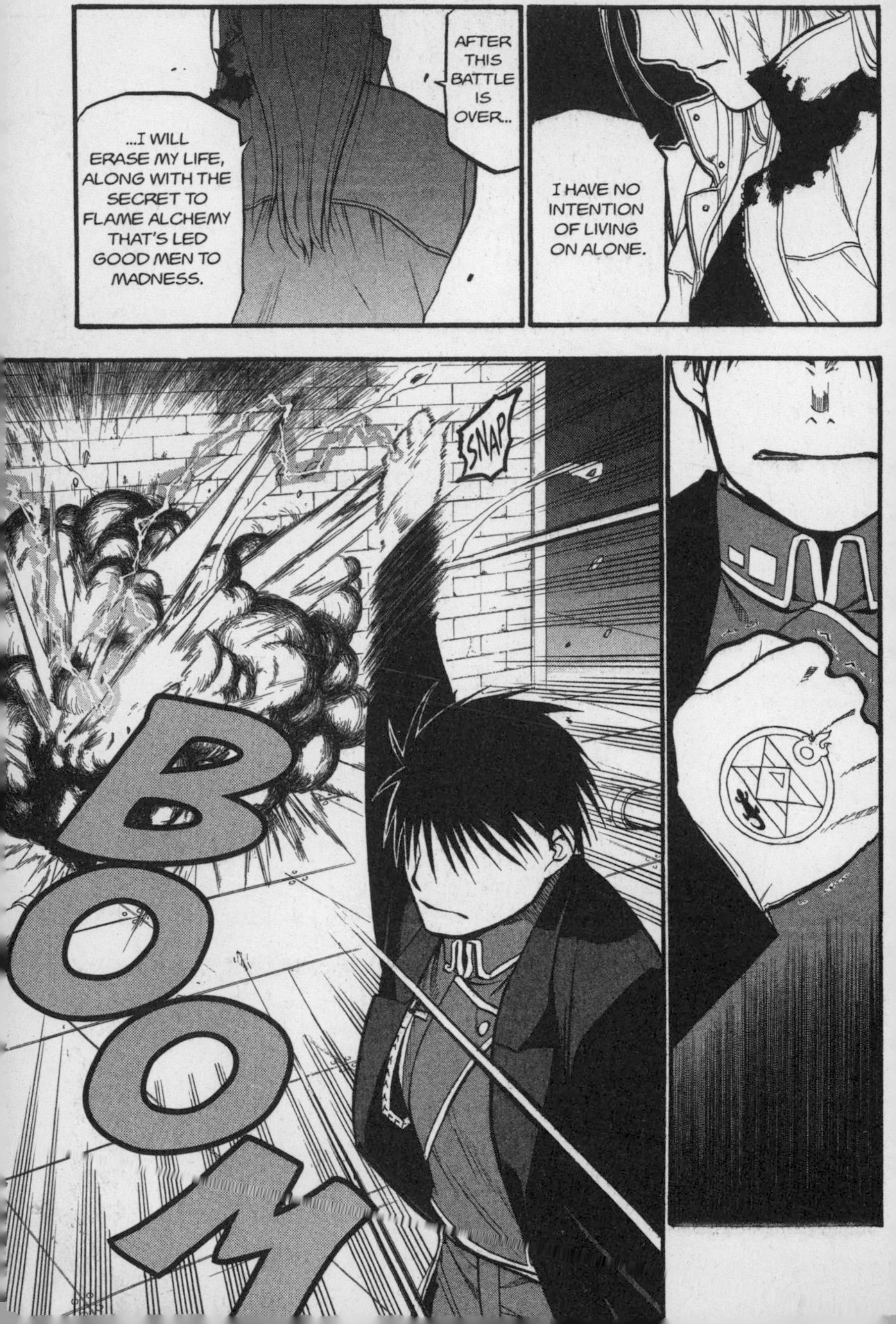
I HAVE NO INTENTION OF LIVING ON ALONE.
AFTER THIS BATTLE IS OVER...
...I WILL ERASE MY LIFE, ALONG WITH THE SECRET TO FLAME ALCHEMY THAT'S LED GOOD MEN TO MADNESS.
SNAP
BOOM

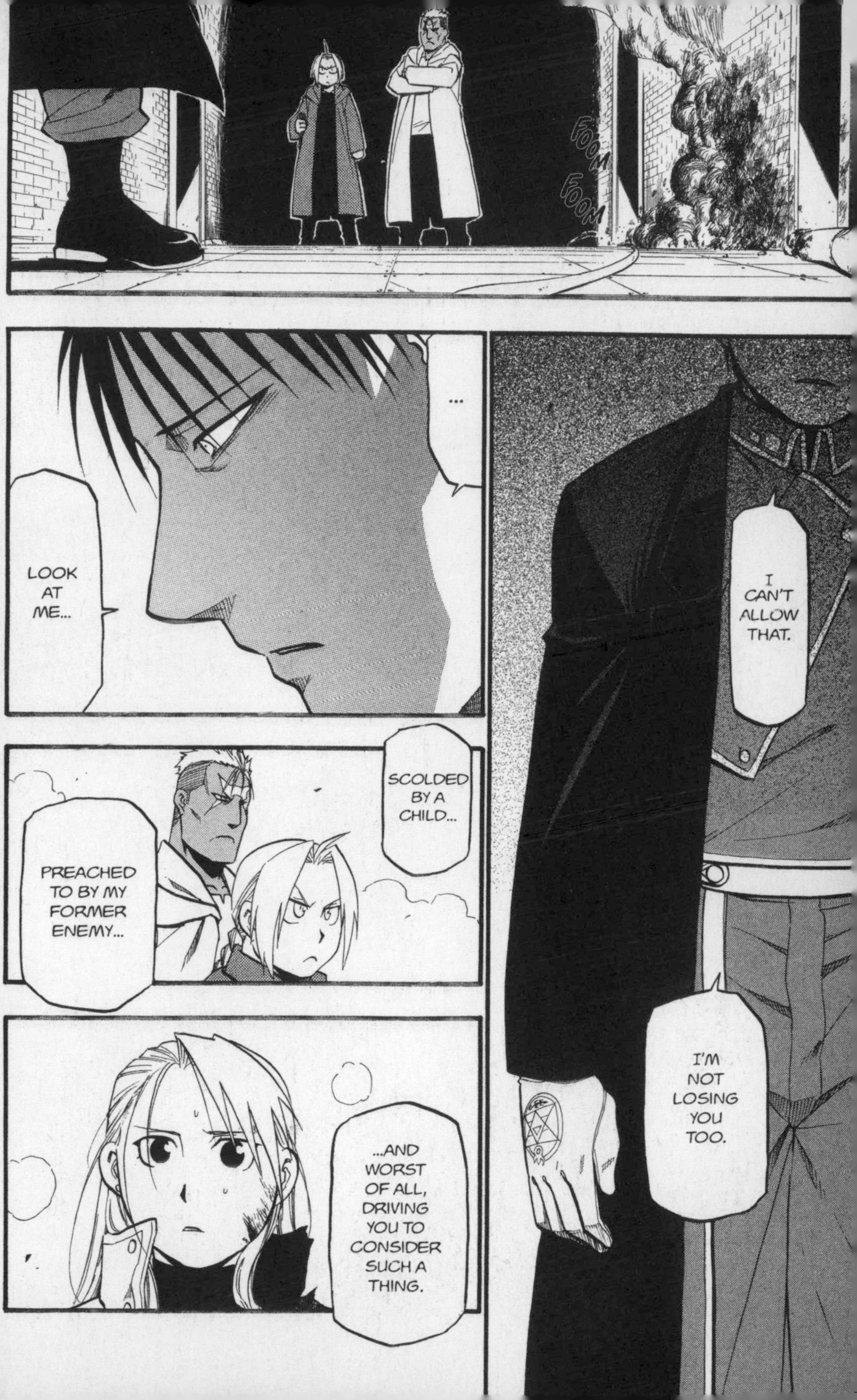
FOOM
FOOM
I CAN'T ALLOW THAT.
I'M NOT LOSING YOU TOO.
...
LOOK AT ME...
SCOLDED BY A CHILD...
PREACHED TO BY MY FORMER ENEMY...
...AND WORST OF ALL, DRIVING YOU TO CONSIDER SUCH A THING.

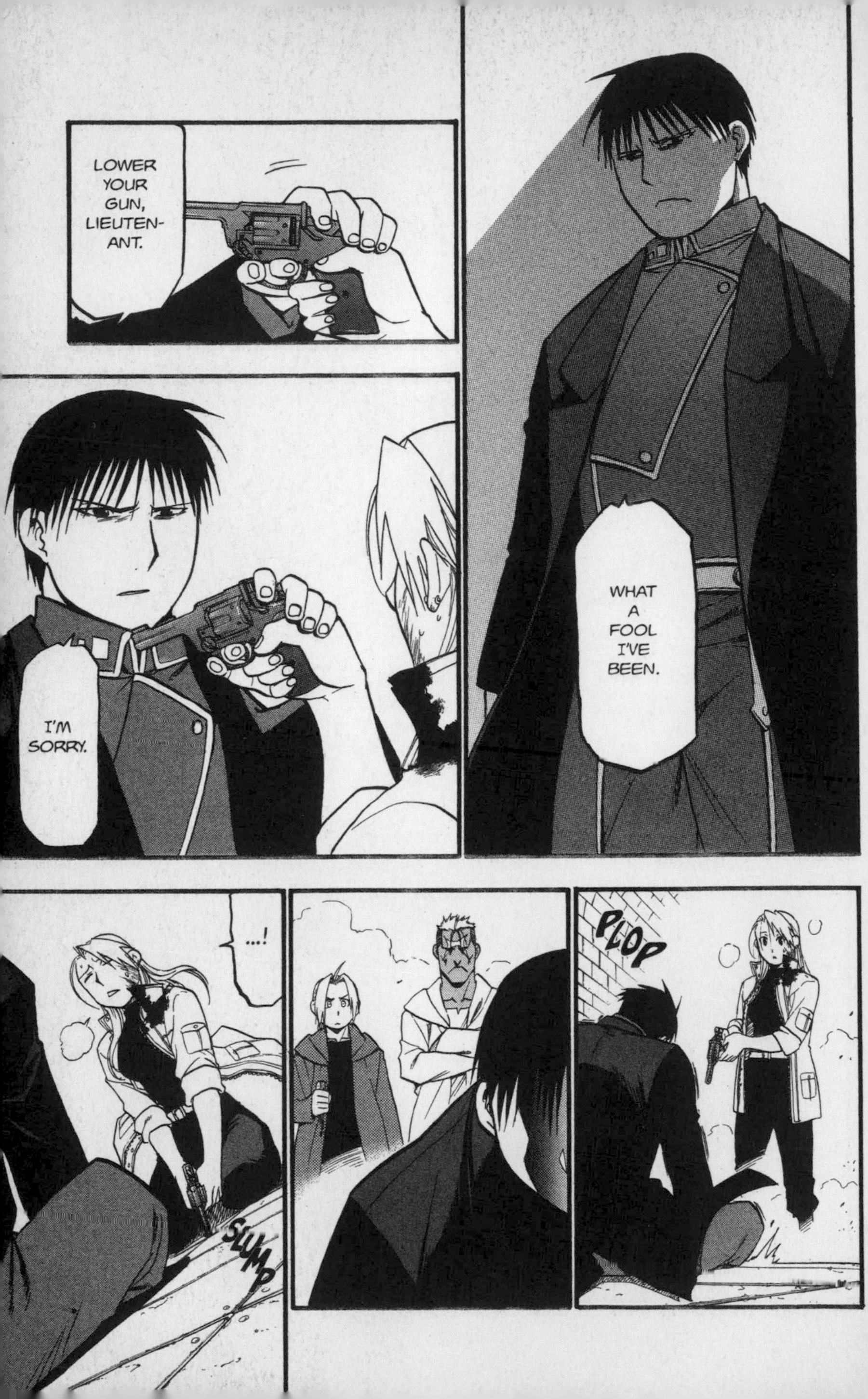
WHAT A FOOL I'VE BEEN.
LOWER YOUR GUN, LIEUTENANT.
I'M SORRY.
PLOP
...!
SLUMP

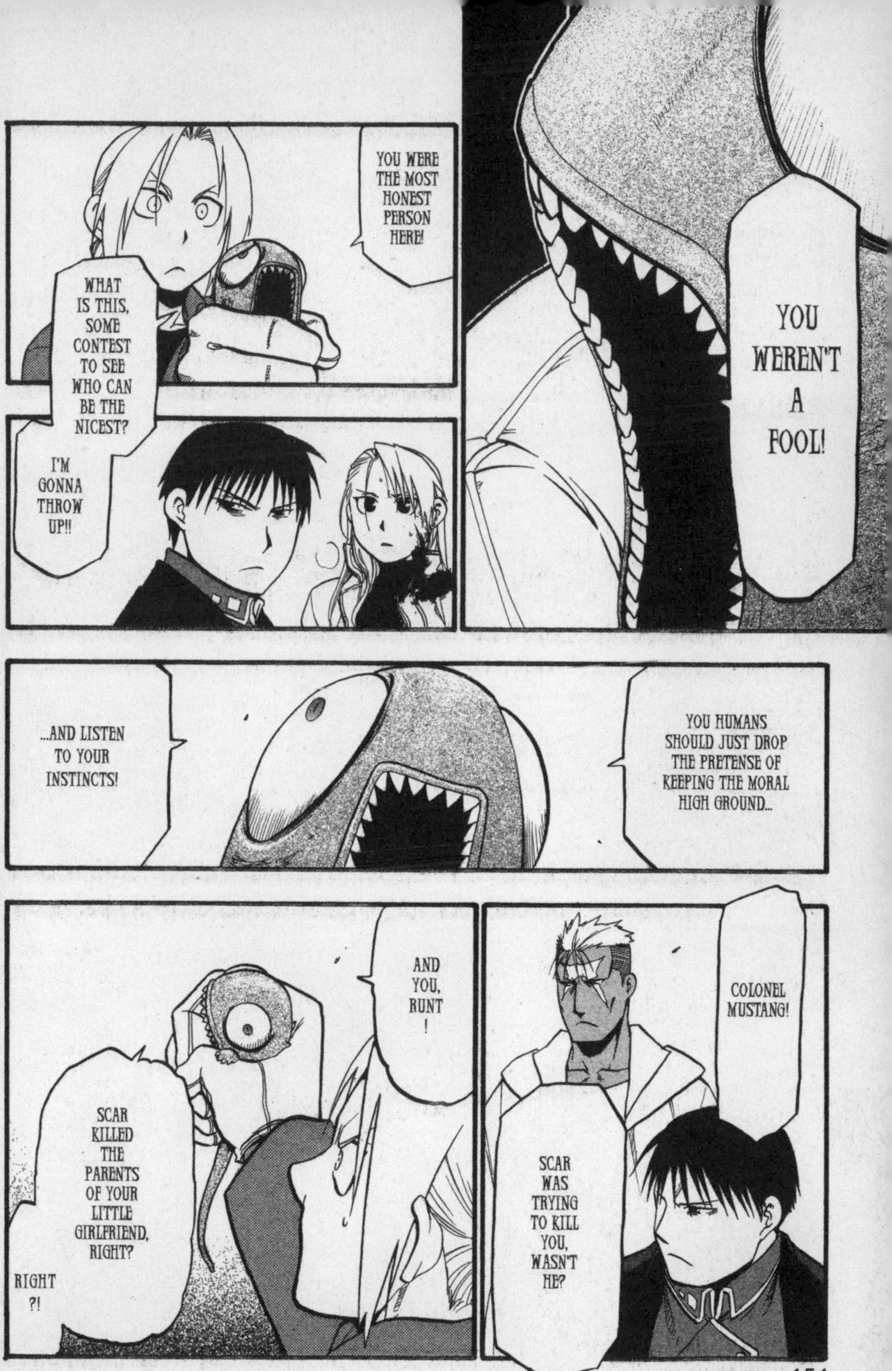
YOU WEREN'T A FOOL!
YOU WERE THE MOST HONEST PERSON HERE!
WHAT IS THIS, SOME CONTEST TO SEE WHO CAN BE THE NICEST?
I'M GONNA THROW UP!!
YOU HUMANS SHOULD JUST DROP THE PRETENSE OF KEEPING THE MORAL HIGH GROUND...
...AND LISTEN TO YOUR INSTINCTS!
COLONEL MUSTANG!
SCAR WAS TRYING TO KILL YOU, WASN'T HE?
AND YOU, RUNT!
SCAR KILLED THE PARENTS OF YOUR LITTLE GIRLFRIEND, RIGHT?
RIGHT?!

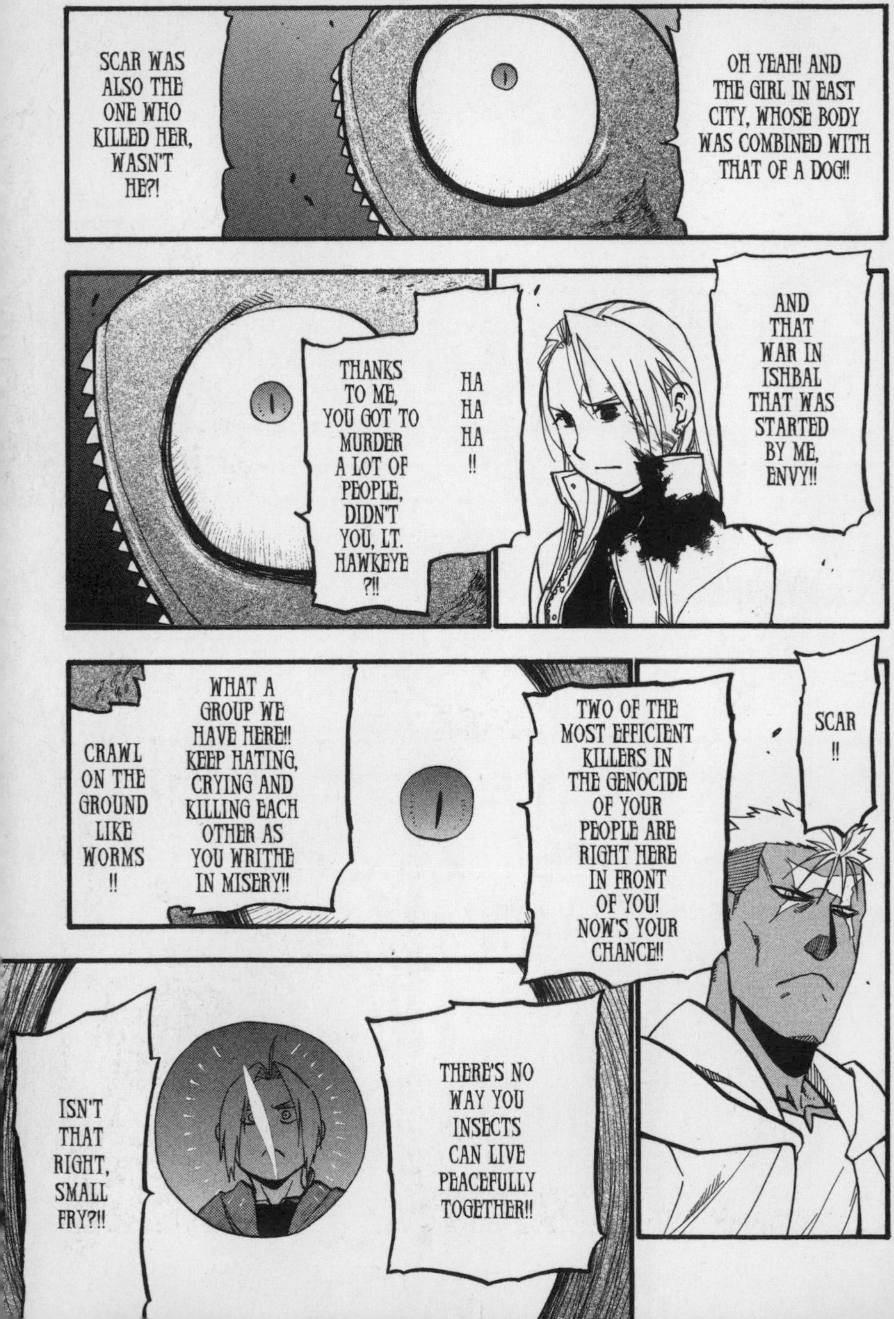
OH YEAH! AND THE GIRL IN EAST CITY, WHOSE BODY WAS COMBINED WITH THAT OF A DOG!!
SCAR WAS ALSO THE ONE WHO KILLED HER, WASN'T HE?!
AND THAT WAR IN ISHBAL THAT WAS STARTED BY ME, ENVY!!
HA HA HA !!
THANKS TO ME, YOU GOT TO MURDER A LOT OF PEOPLE, DIDN'T YOU, LT. HAWKEYE ?!!
SCAR !!
TWO OF THE MOST EFFICIENT KILLERS IN THE GENOCIDE OF YOUR PEOPLE ARE RIGHT HERE IN FRONT OF YOU! NOW'S YOUR CHANCE!!
WHAT A GROUP WE HAVE HERE!! KEEP HATING, CRYING AND KILLING EACH OTHER AS YOU WRITHE IN MISERY!!
CRAWL ON THE GROUND LIKE WORMS !!
THERE'S NO WAY YOU INSECTS CAN LIVE PEACEFULLY TOGETHER!!
ISN'T THAT RIGHT, SMALL FRY?!!

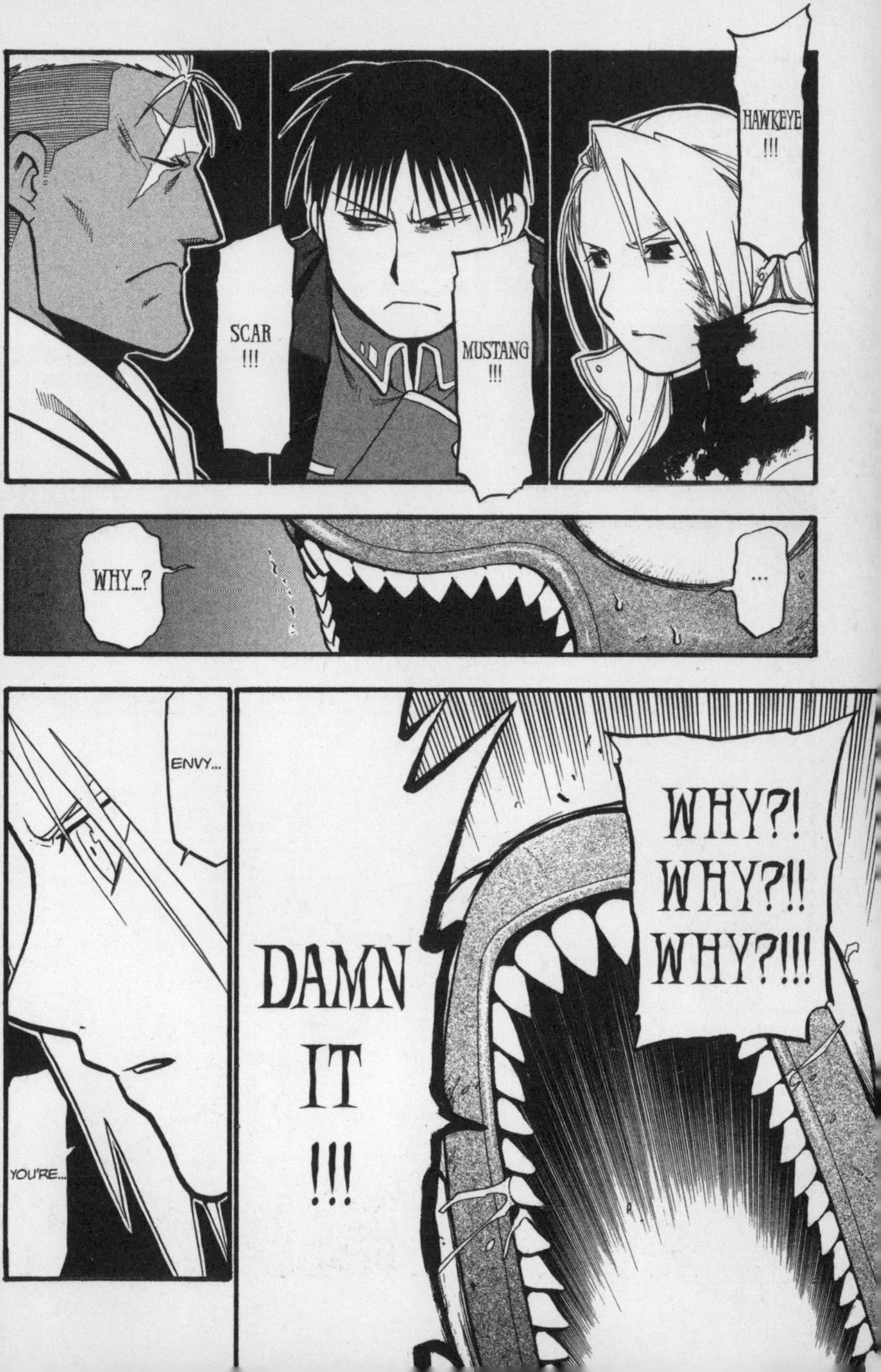
HAWKEYE !!!
MUSTANG !!!
SCAR !!!
...
WHY...?
WHY?! WHY?!! WHY?!!!
DAMN IT !!!
ENVY...
YOU'RE...

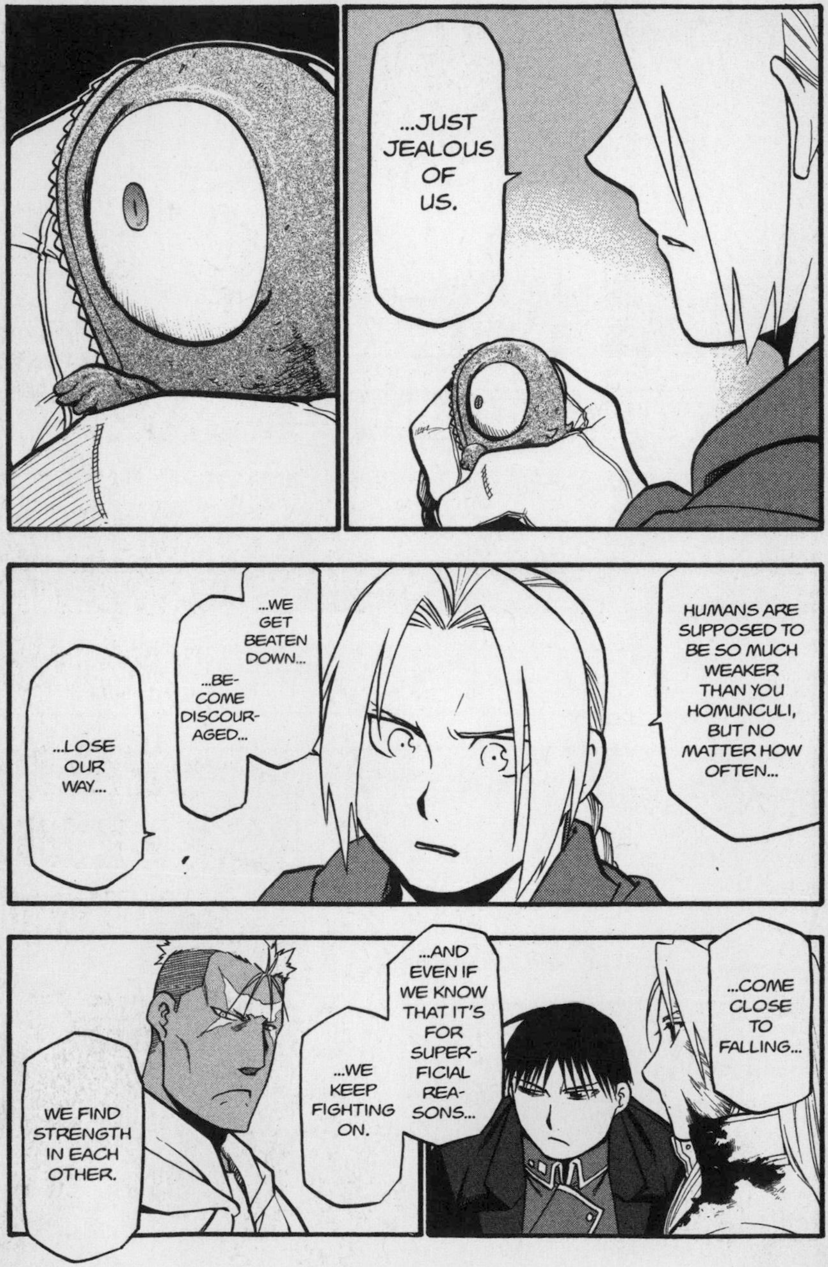
...JUST JEALOUS OF US.
HUMANS ARE SUPPOSED TO BE SO MUCH WEAKER THAN YOU HOMUNCULI, BUT NO MATTER HOW OFTEN...
...WE GET BEATEN DOWN... ...BECOME DISCOURAGED...
...LOSE OUR WAY...
...COME CLOSE TO FALLING...
...AND EVEN IF WE KNOW THAT IT'S FOR SUPERFICIAL REASONS...
...WE KEEP FIGHTING ON.
WE FIND STRENGTH IN EACH OTHER.

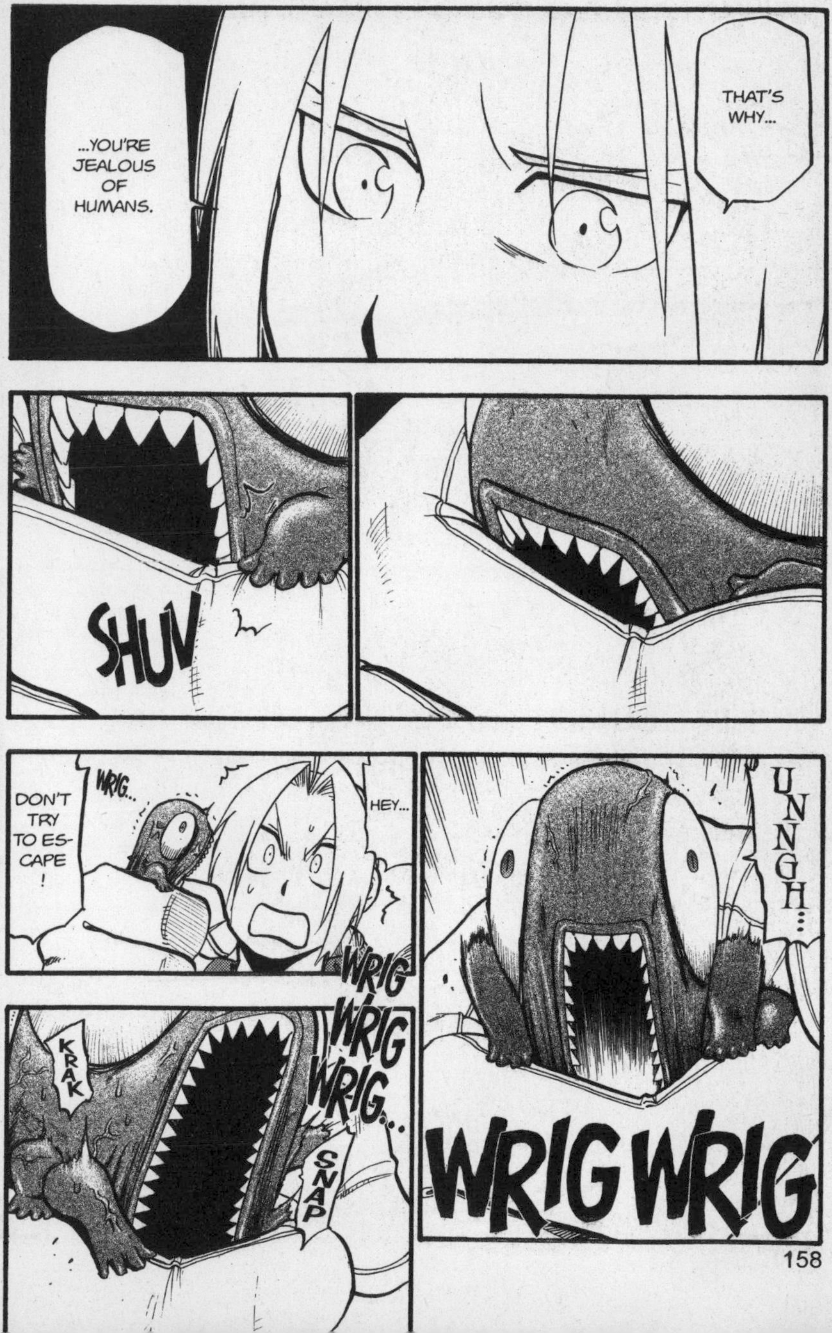
THAT'S WHY...
...YOU'RE JEALOUS OF HUMANS.
SHUV
UNNGH...
WRIG WRIG
HEY...
WRIG...
DON'T TRY TO ES-CAPE!
WRIG WRIG WRIG...
SNAP
KRAK

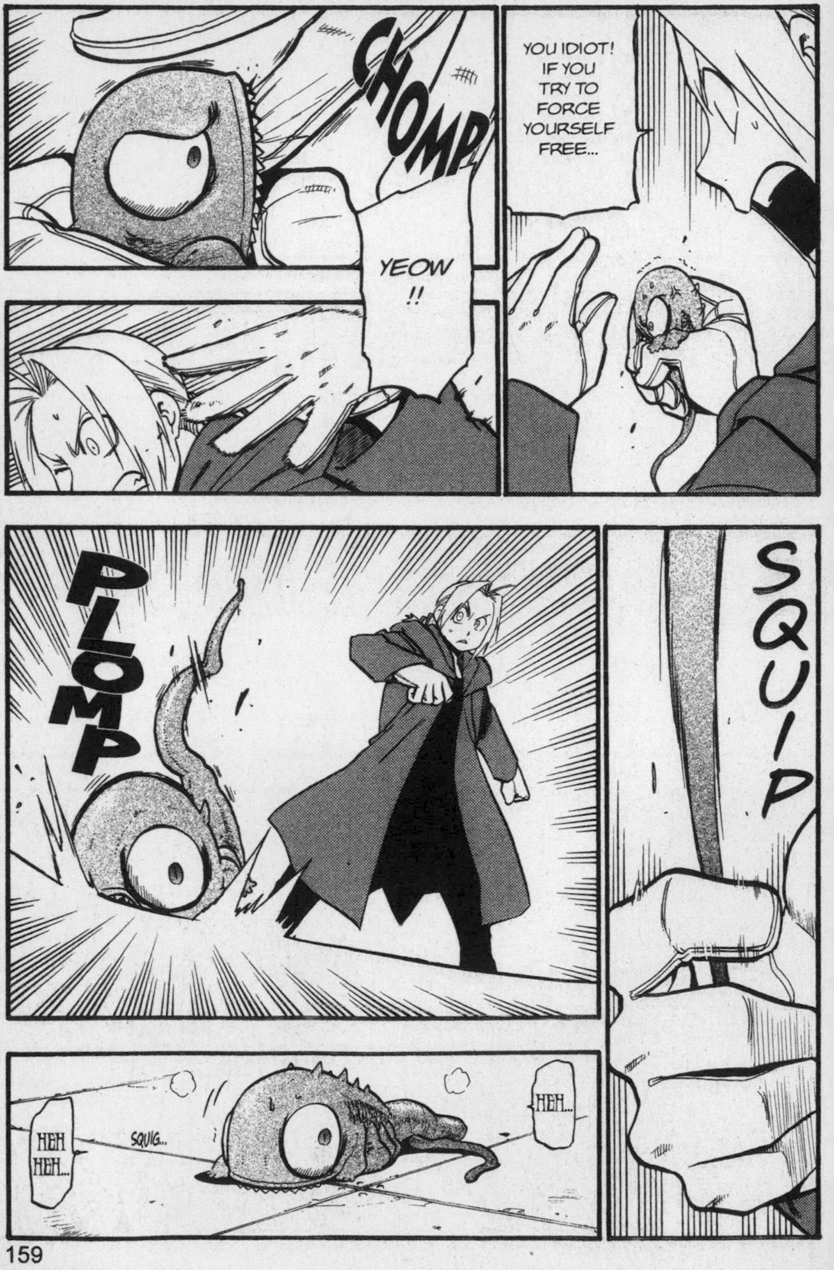
YOU IDIOT! IF YOU TRY TO FORCE YOURSELF FREE...
CHOMP
YEOW !!
SQUIP
PLOMP
HEH...
SQUIG...
HEH HEH...

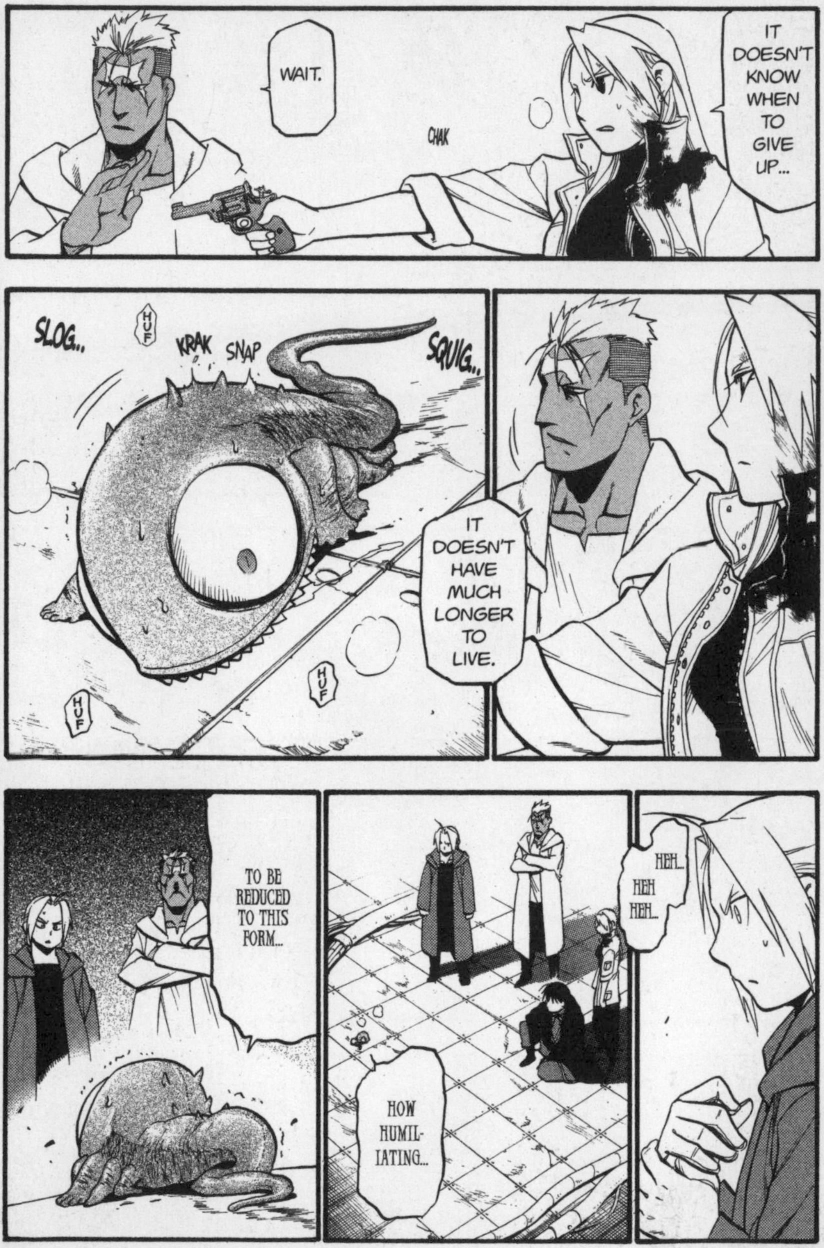

IT DOESN'T KNOW WHEN TO GIVE UP...
WAIT.
CHAK
IT DOESN'T HAVE MUCH LONGER TO LIVE.
SQUIG...
SNAP
KRAK
HUF
SLOG...
HUF
HUF
HEH... HEH HEH...
HOW HUMIL-IATING...
TO BE REDUCED TO THIS FORM...

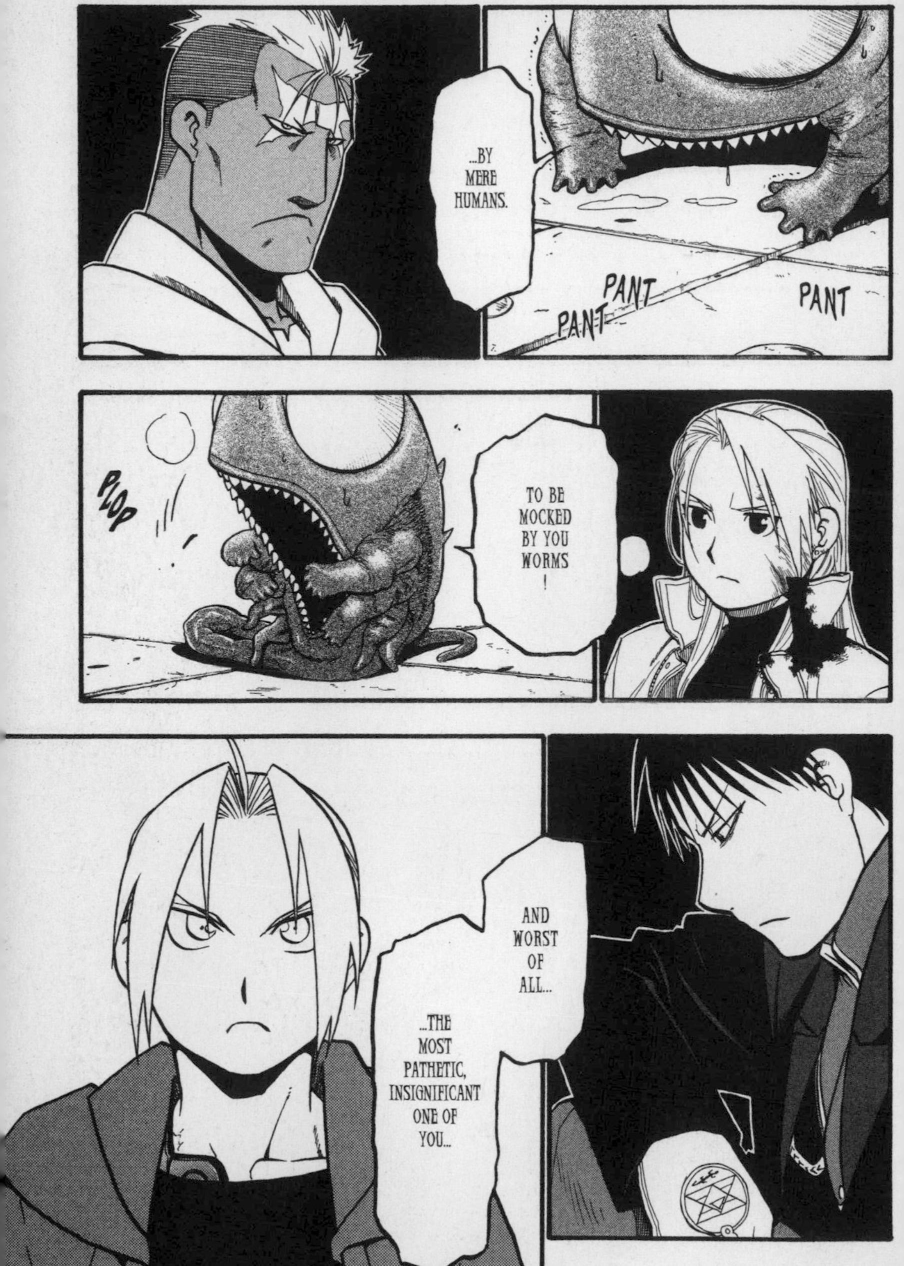
...BY MERE HUMANS.
PANT
PANT
PANT
TO BE MOCKED BY YOU WORMS!
PLOP
AND WORST OF ALL...
...THE MOST PATHETIC, INSIGNIFICANT ONE OF YOU...

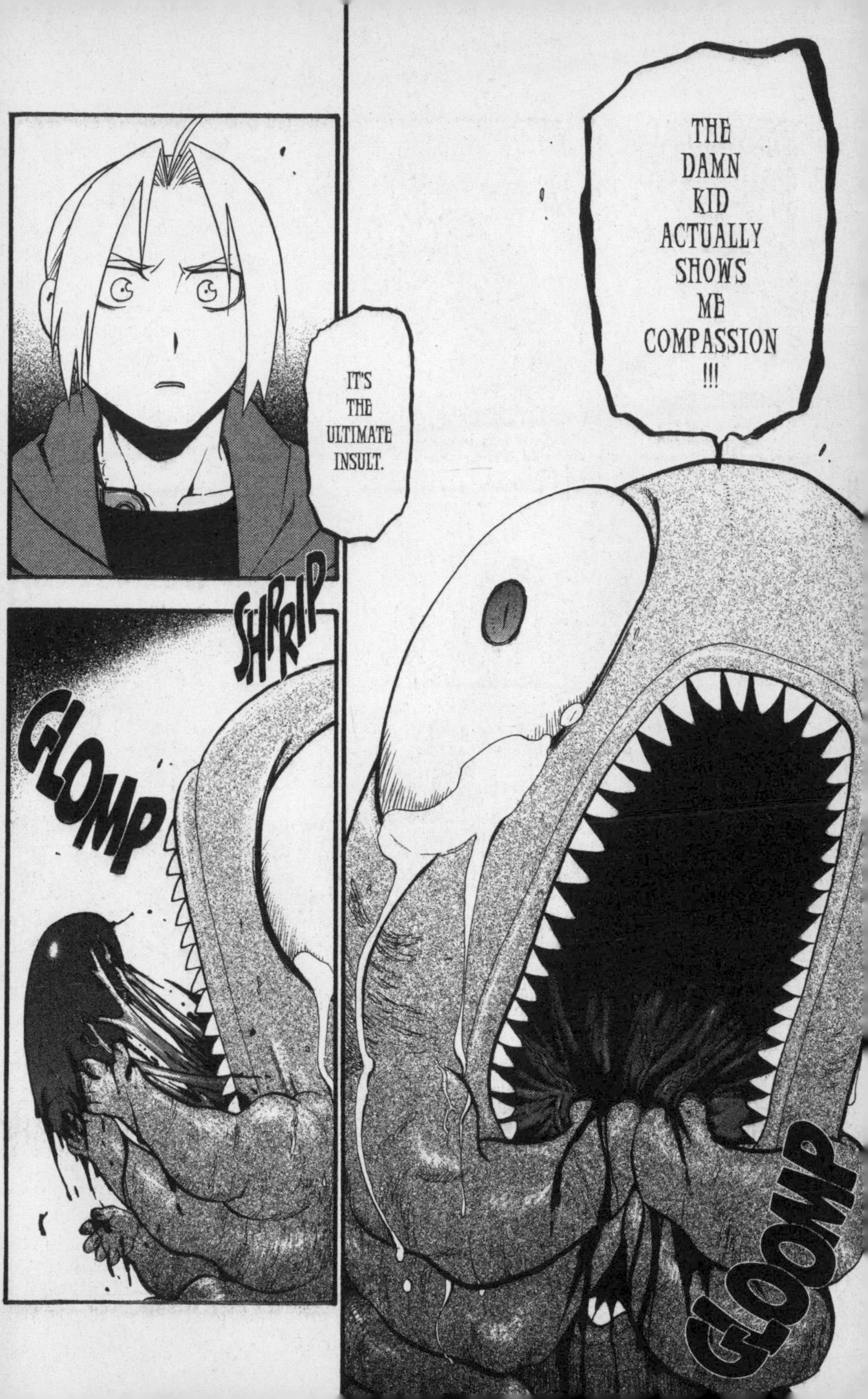
THE DAMN KID ACTUALLY SHOWS ME COMPASSION!!!
IT'S THE ULTIMATE INSULT.
GLOOMP
SHRIP
GLOMP

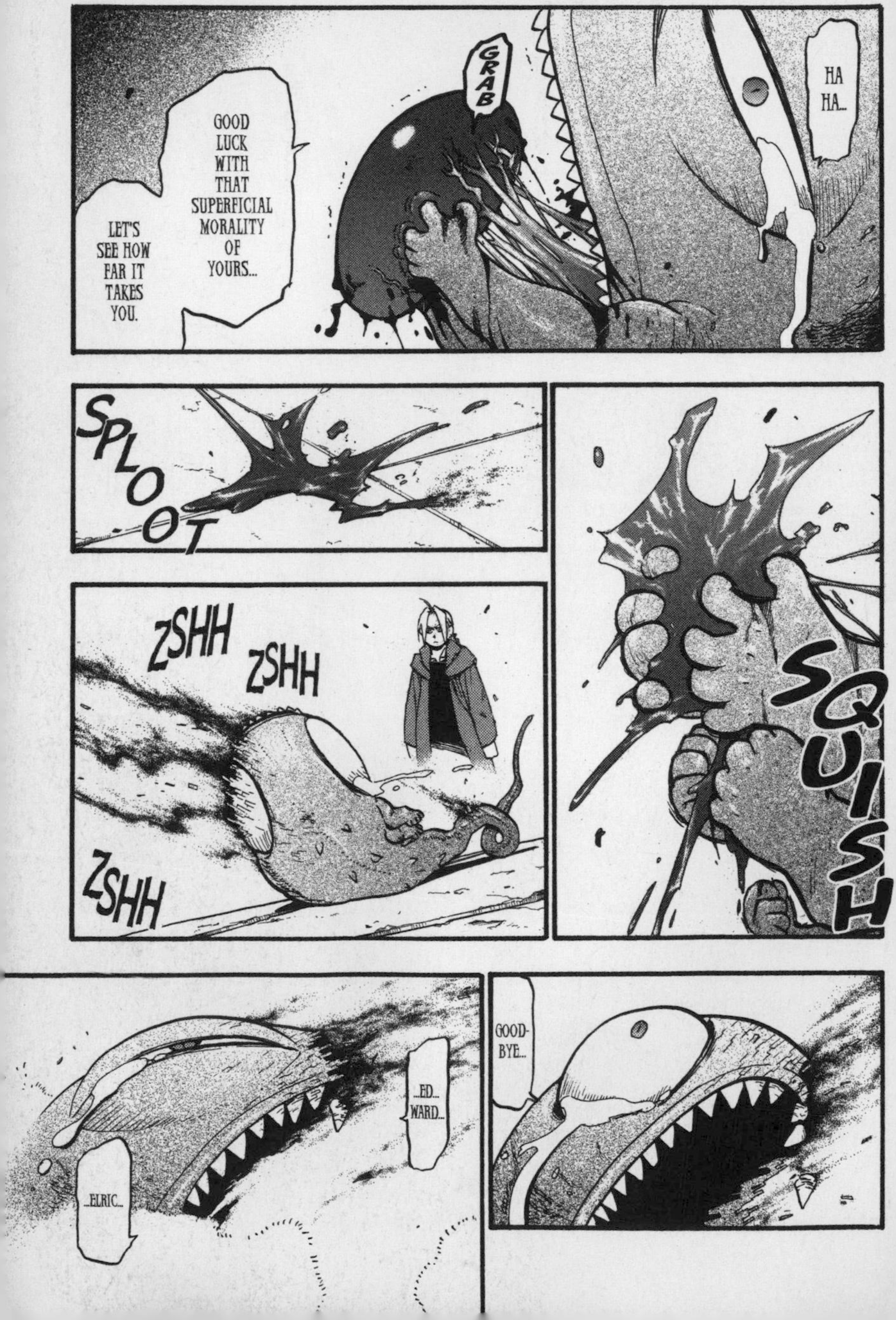
HA HA...
GRAB
GOOD LUCK WITH THAT SUPERFICIAL MORALITY OF YOURS...
LET'S SEE HOW FAR IT TAKES YOU.
SQUISH
SPLOOT
ZSHH
ZSHH
ZSHH
GOOD-BYE...
...ED... WARD...
...ELRIC...

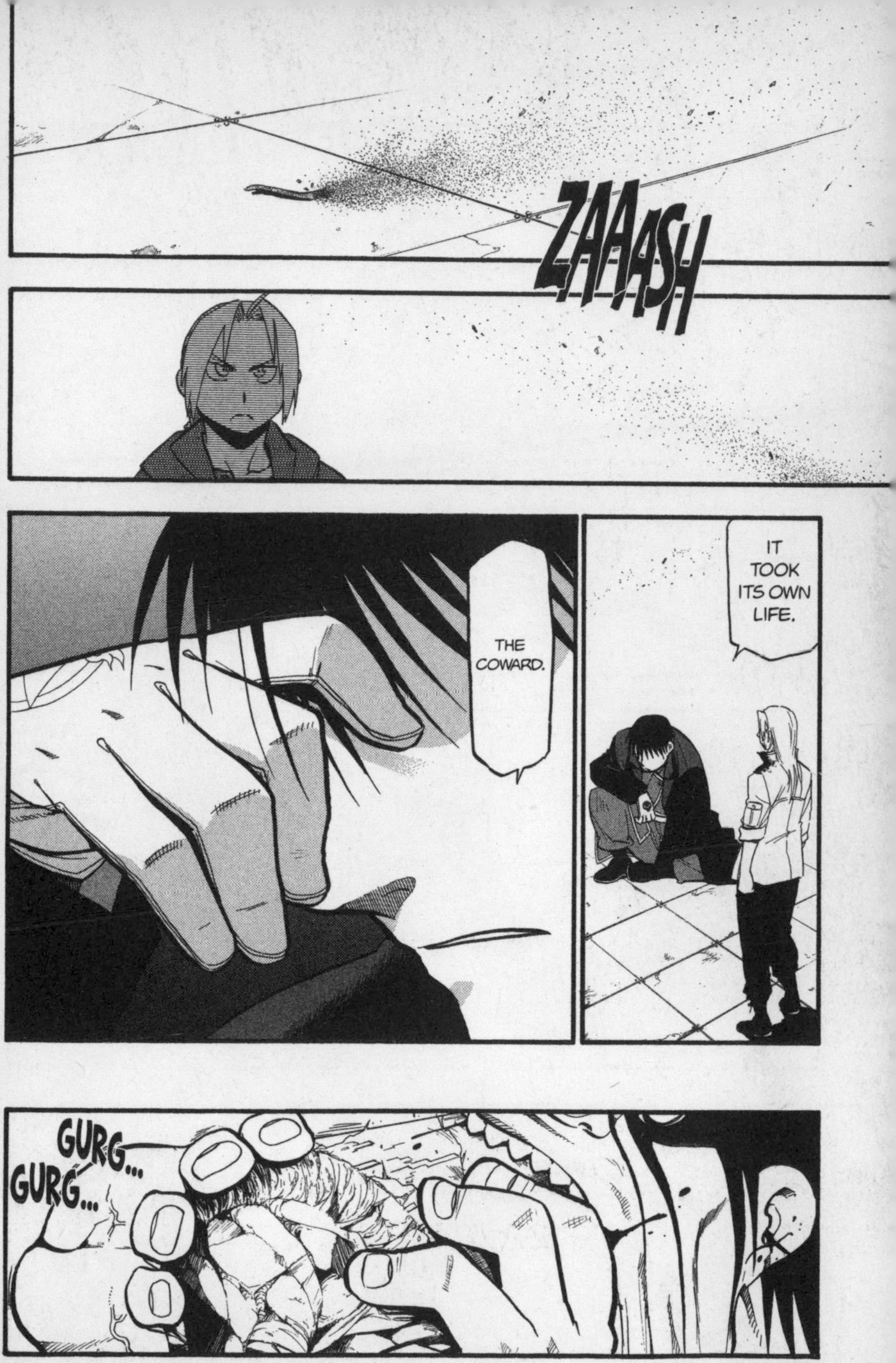
ZAAASH
IT TOOK ITS OWN LIFE.
THE COWARD.
GURG... GURG...

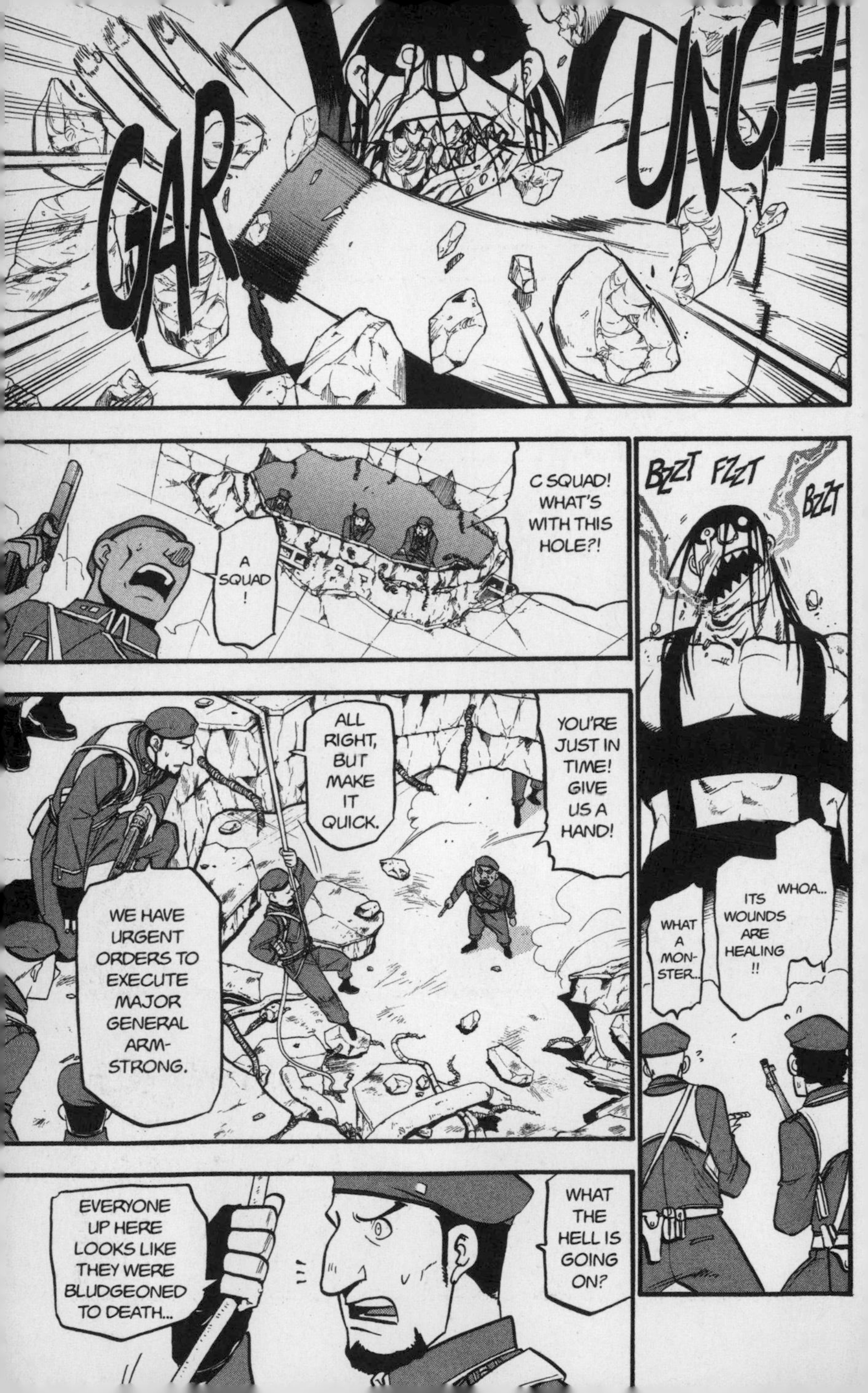
GAR
UNCH
BZZT FZZT
BZZT
WHOA...
ITS WOUNDS ARE HEALING!!
WHAT A MON-STER...
C SQUAD! WHAT'S WITH THIS HOLE?!
A SQUAD!
YOU'RE JUST IN TIME! GIVE US A HAND!
ALL RIGHT, BUT MAKE IT QUICK.
WE HAVE URGENT ORDERS TO EXECUTE MAJOR GENERAL ARM-STRONG.
WHAT THE HELL IS GOING ON?
EVERYONE UP HERE LOOKS LIKE THEY WERE BLUDGEONED TO DEATH...

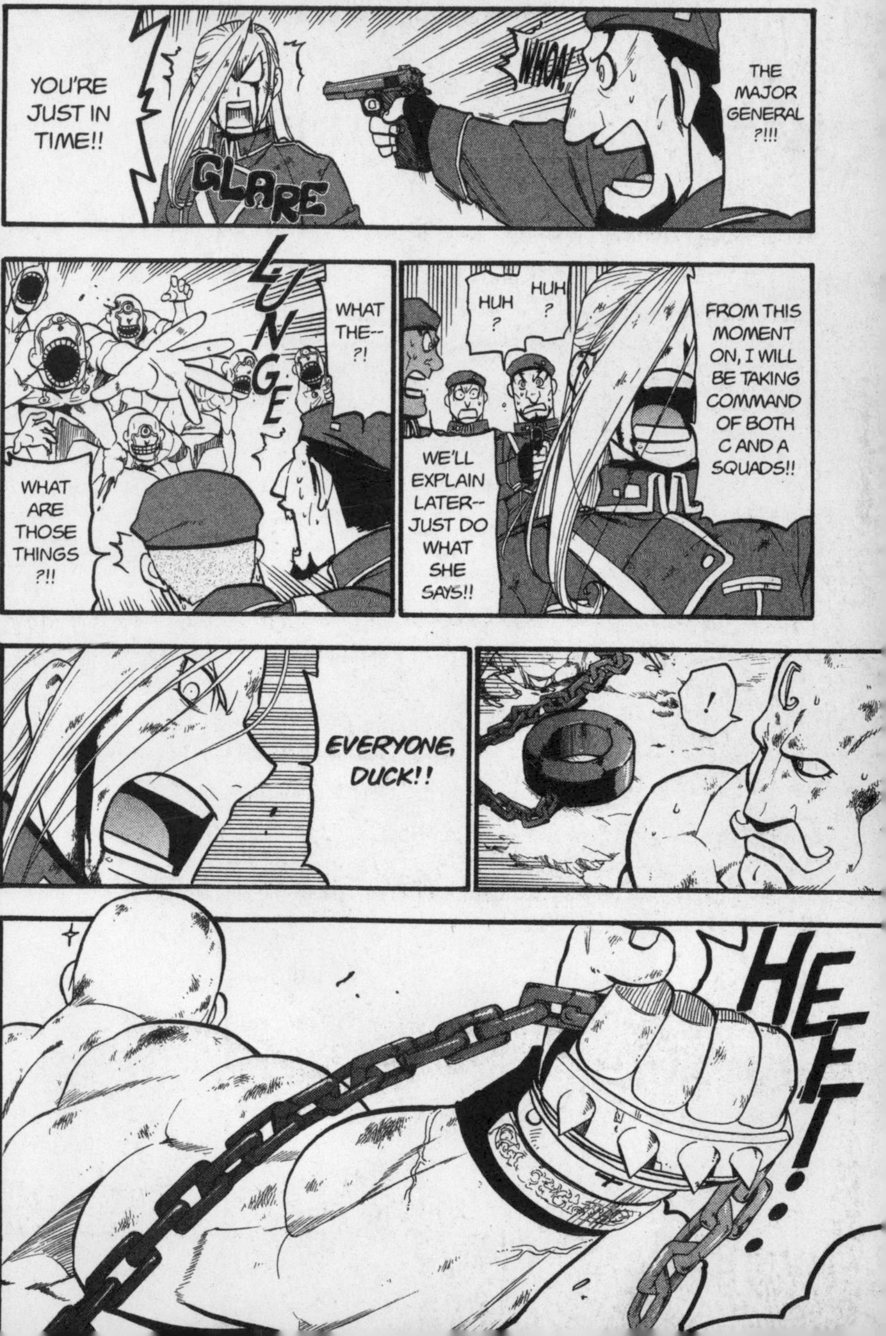
WHOA!
THE MAJOR GENERAL ?!!!
YOU'RE JUST IN TIME!!
GLARE
FROM THIS MOMENT ON, I WILL BE TAKING COMMAND OF BOTH C AND A SQUADS!!
HUH ?
HUH ?
WE'LL EXPLAIN LATER-- JUST DO WHAT SHE SAYS!!
WHAT THE-- ?!
LUNGE
WHAT ARE THOSE THINGS ?!!
!
EVERYONE, DUCK!!
HEFT!!

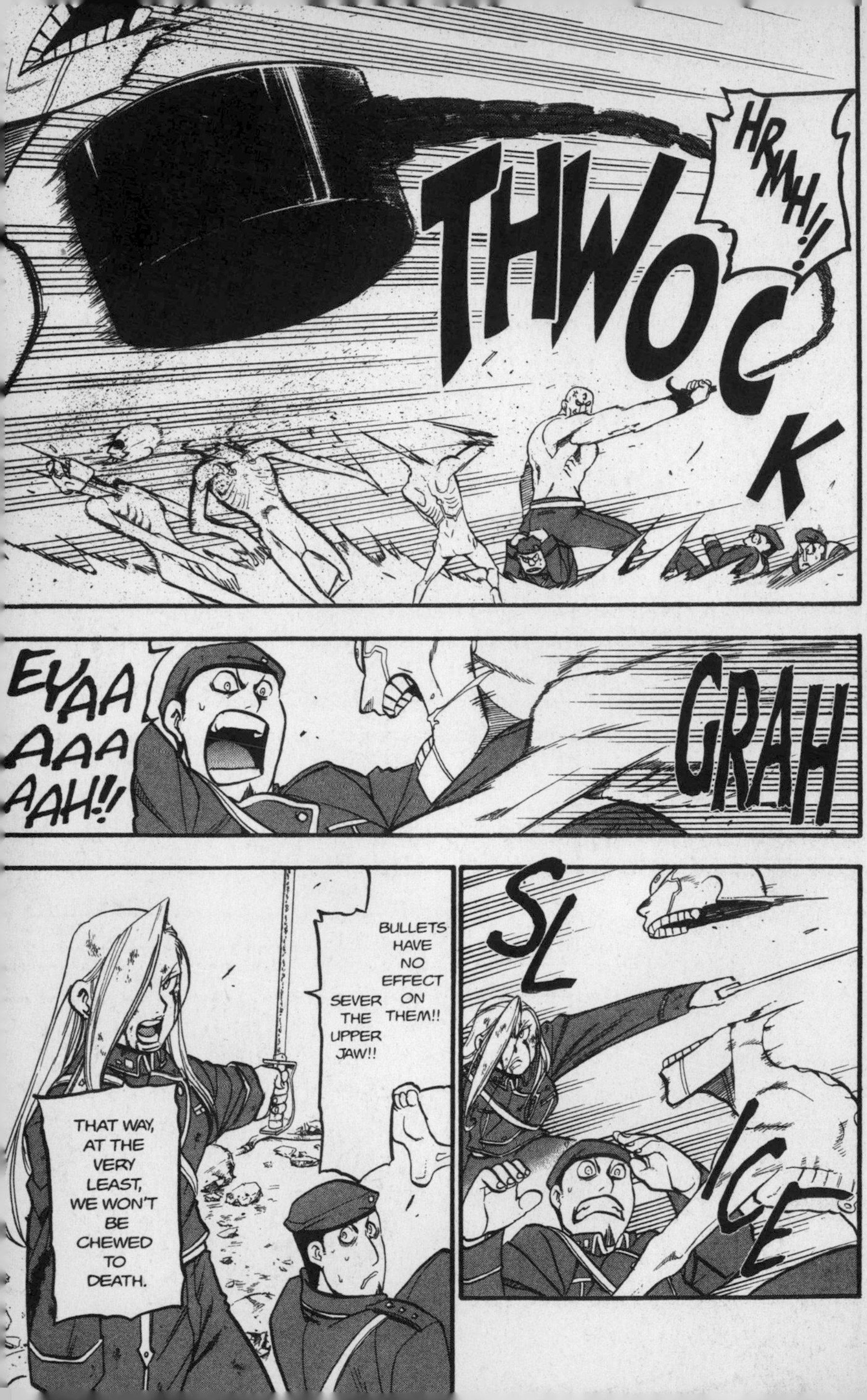
HRAAH!!
THWOCK
GRAH
EYAAAAAAAH!!
SLICE
BULLETS HAVE NO EFFECT ON THEM!! SEVER THE UPPER JAW!!
THAT WAY, AT THE VERY LEAST, WE WON'T BE CHEWED TO DEATH.

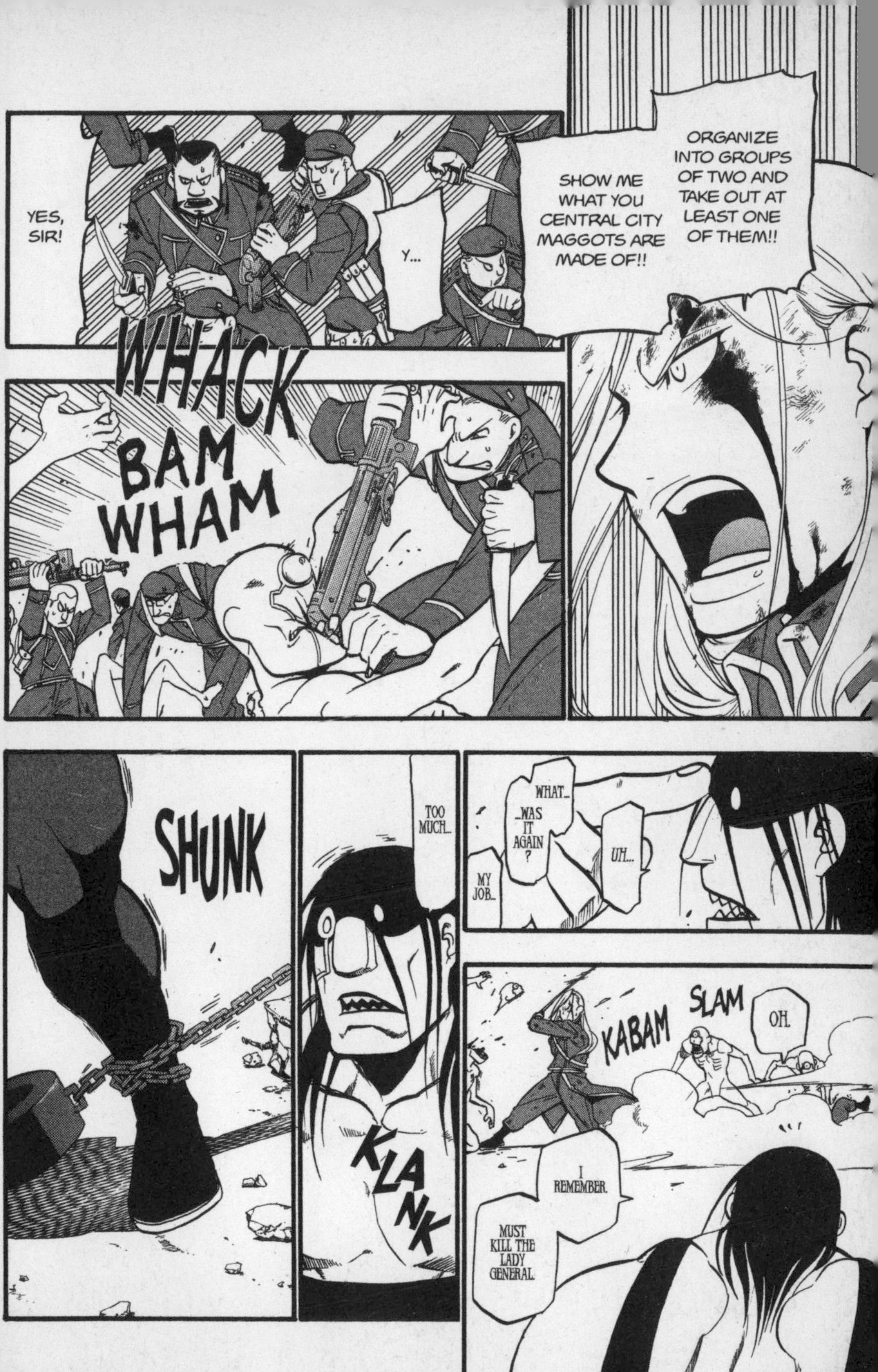
ORGANIZE INTO GROUPS OF TWO AND TAKE OUT AT LEAST ONE OF THEM!!
SHOW ME WHAT YOU CENTRAL CITY MAGGOTS ARE MADE OF!!
Y...
YES, SIR!
WHACK
BAM
WHAM
UH...
WHAT...
...WAS IT AGAIN?
MY JOB...
OH.
SLAM
KABAM
I REMEMBER.
MUST KILL THE LADY GENERAL.
TOO MUCH...
KLANK
SHUNK

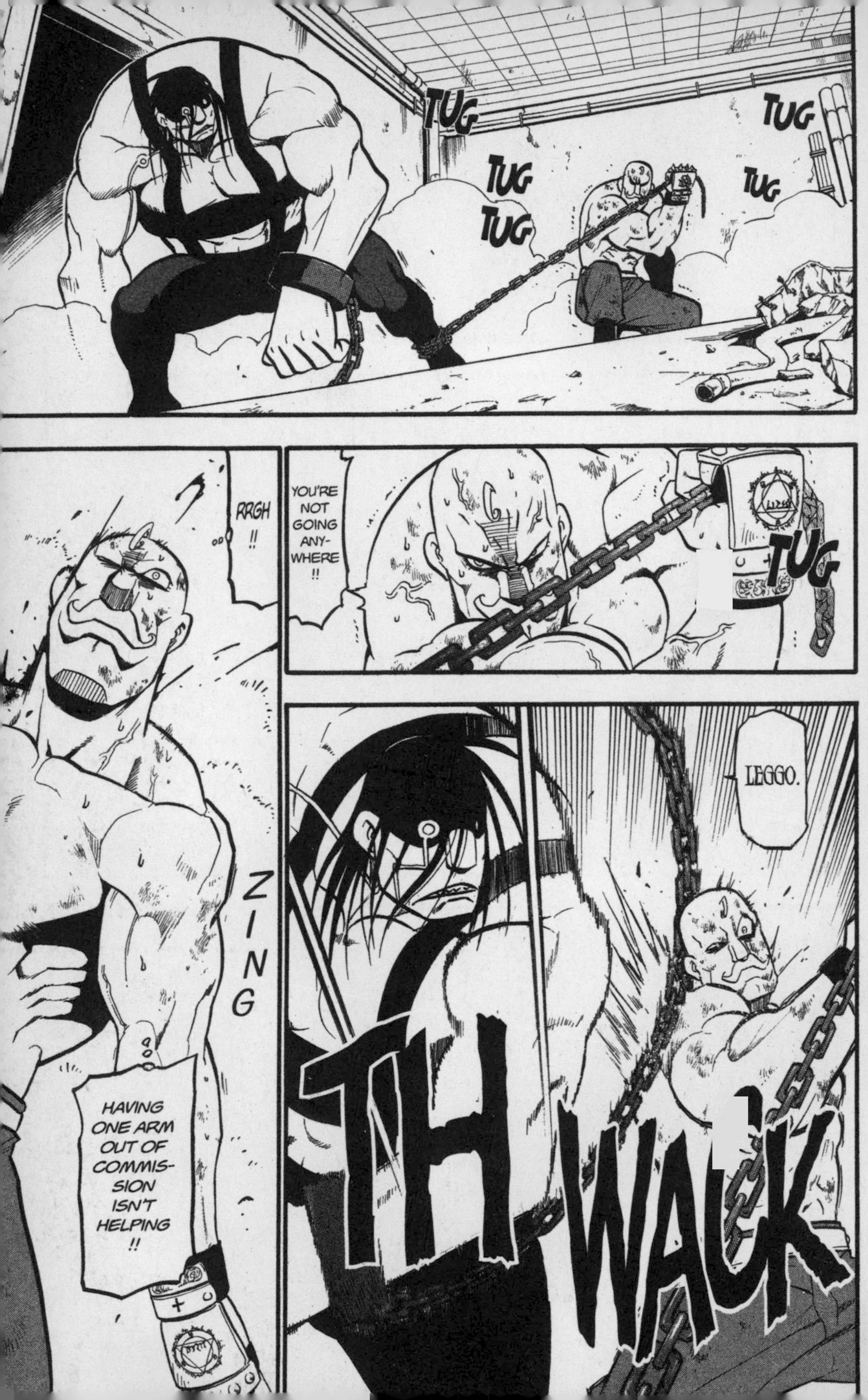
TUG
TUG
TUG
TUG
TUG
YOU'RE NOT GOING ANYWHERE!!
TUG
LEGGO.
THWACK
RRGH!!
ZING
HAVING ONE ARM OUT OF COMMISSION ISN'T HELPING!!

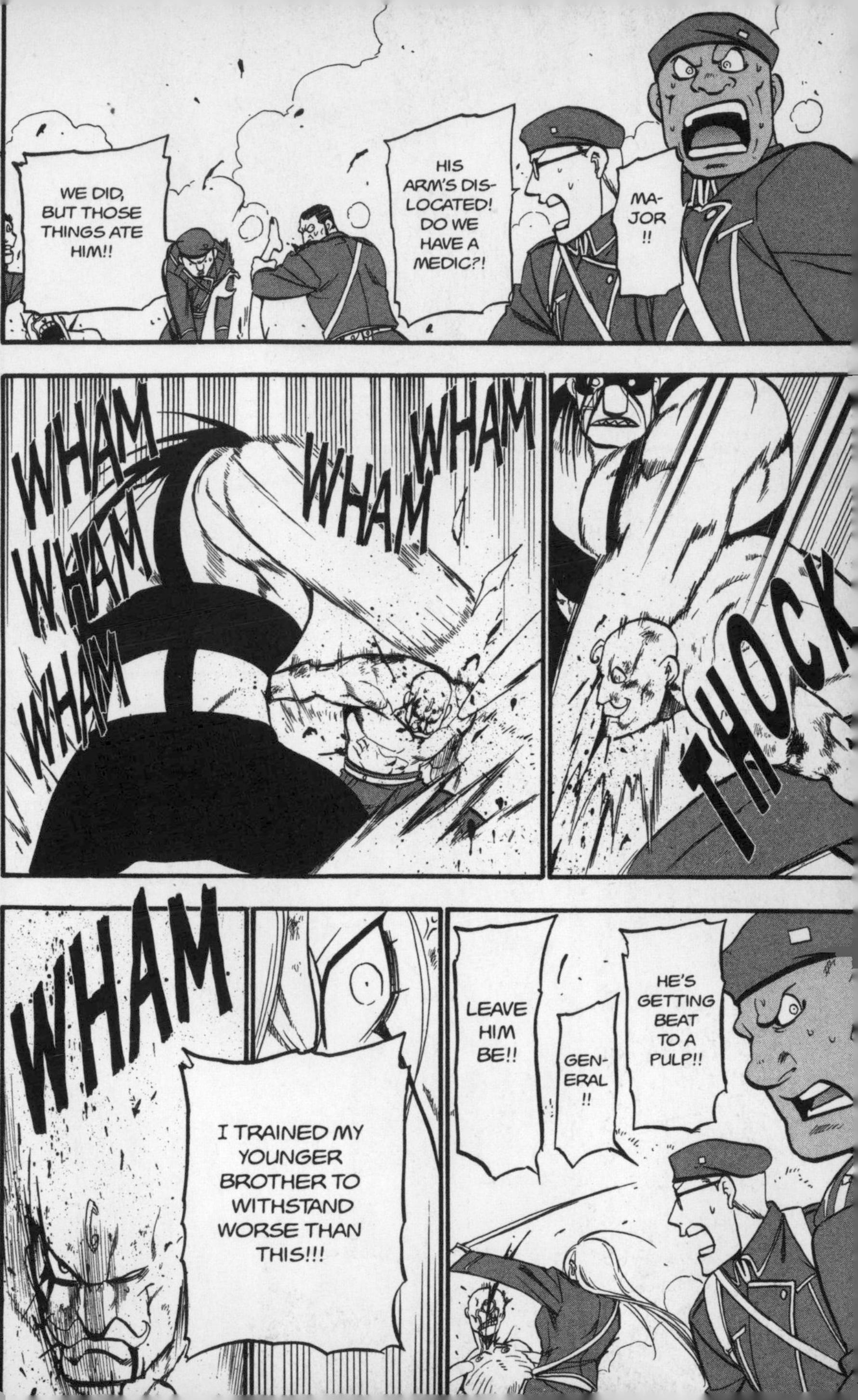
MAJOR !!
HIS ARM'S DISLOCATED! DO WE HAVE A MEDIC?!
WE DID, BUT THOSE THINGS ATE HIM!!
THOCK
WHAM WHAM
WHAM WHAM WHAM WHAM
HE'S GETTING BEAT TO A PULP!!
GENERAL !!
LEAVE HIM BE!!
I TRAINED MY YOUNGER BROTHER TO WITHSTAND WORSE THAN THIS!!!
WHAM

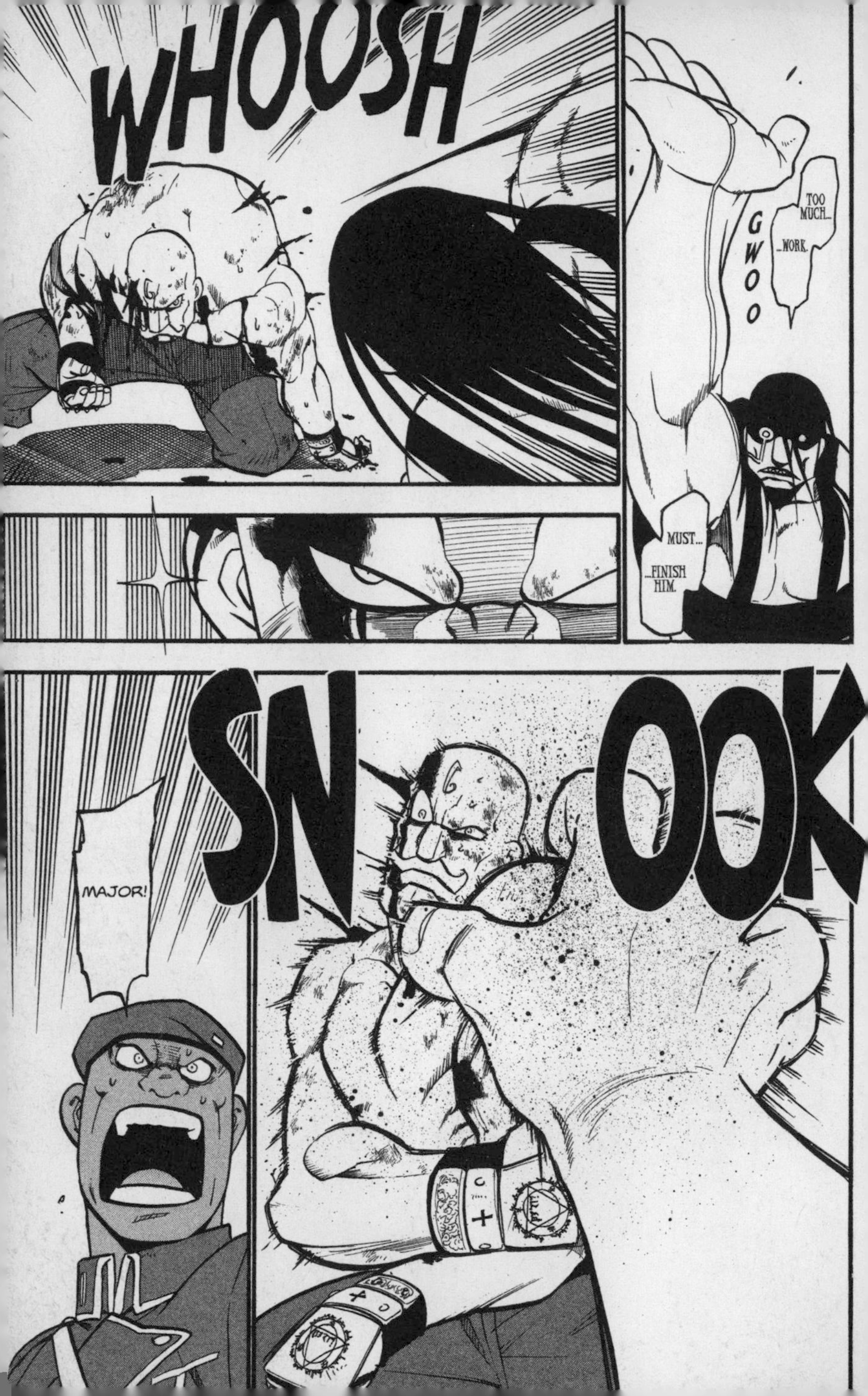
TOO MUCH...
...WORK.
GWOO
MUST...
...FINISH HIM.
WHOOSH
SNOOK
MAJOR!

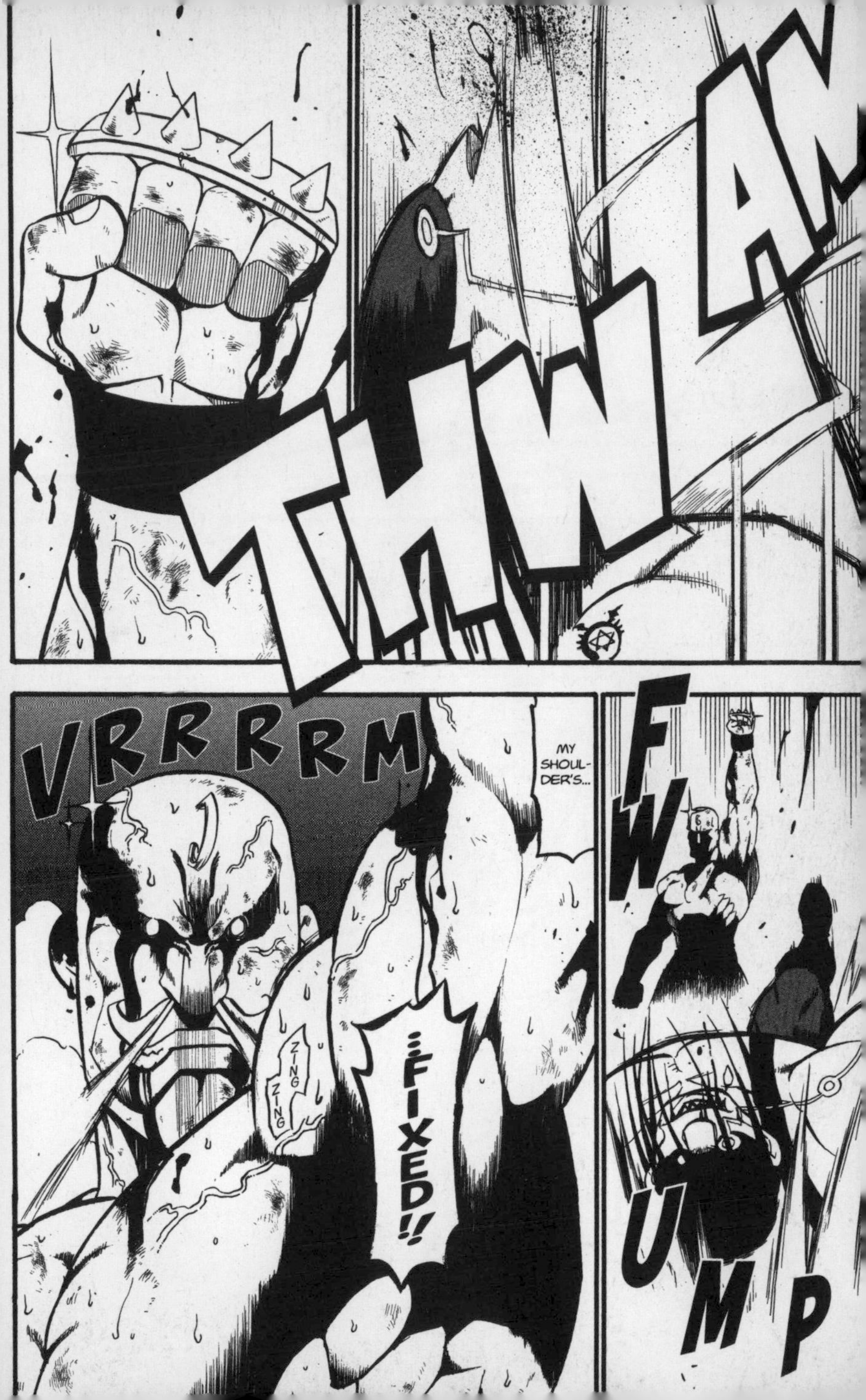
THWAM
FWUMP
MY SHOUL-DER'S...
...FIXED!!
VRRRRM
ZING ZING

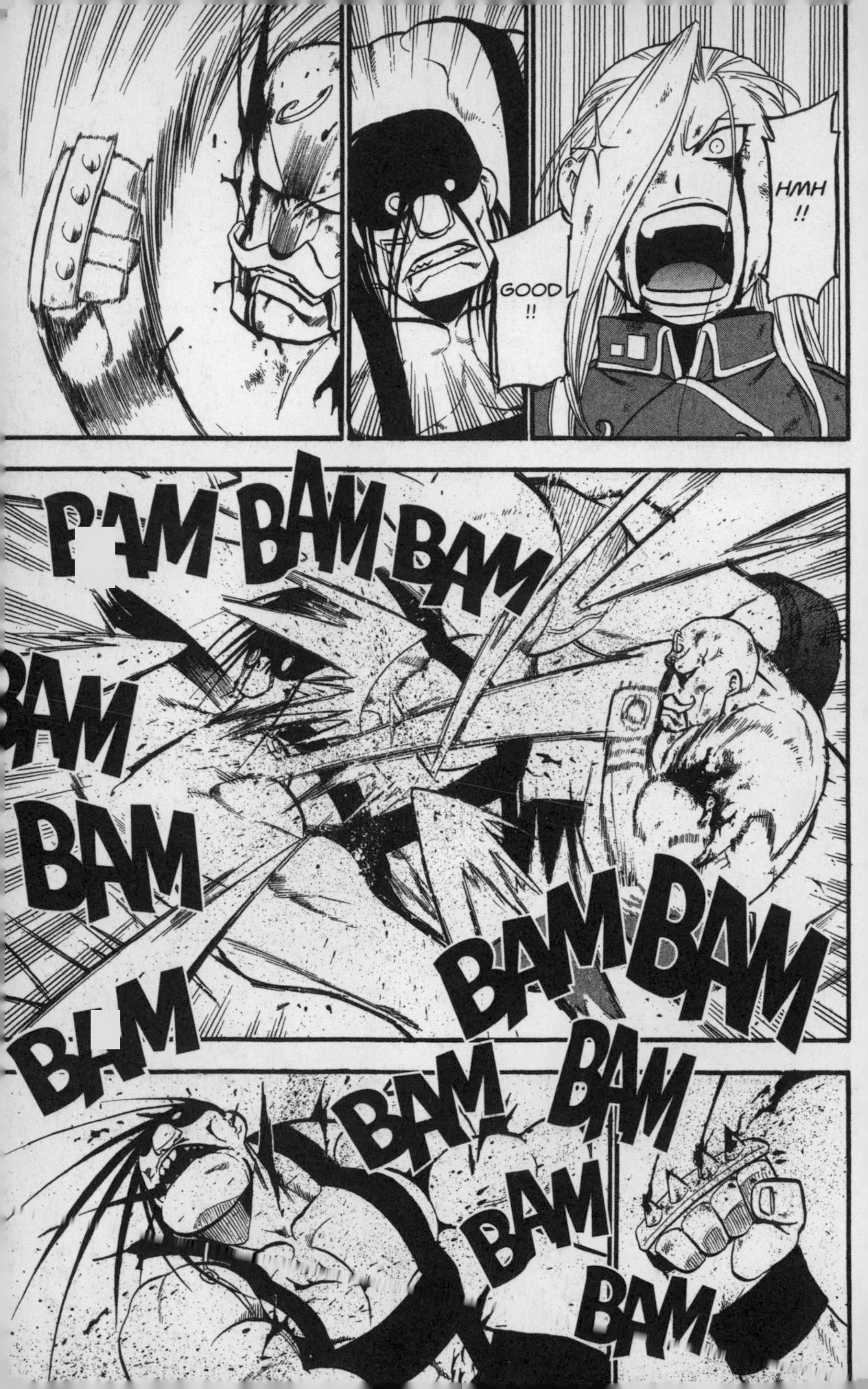
HMH !!
GOOD !!
BAM BAM BAM
BAM
BAM
BAM BAM
BAM
BAM
BAM
BAM
BAM
BAM

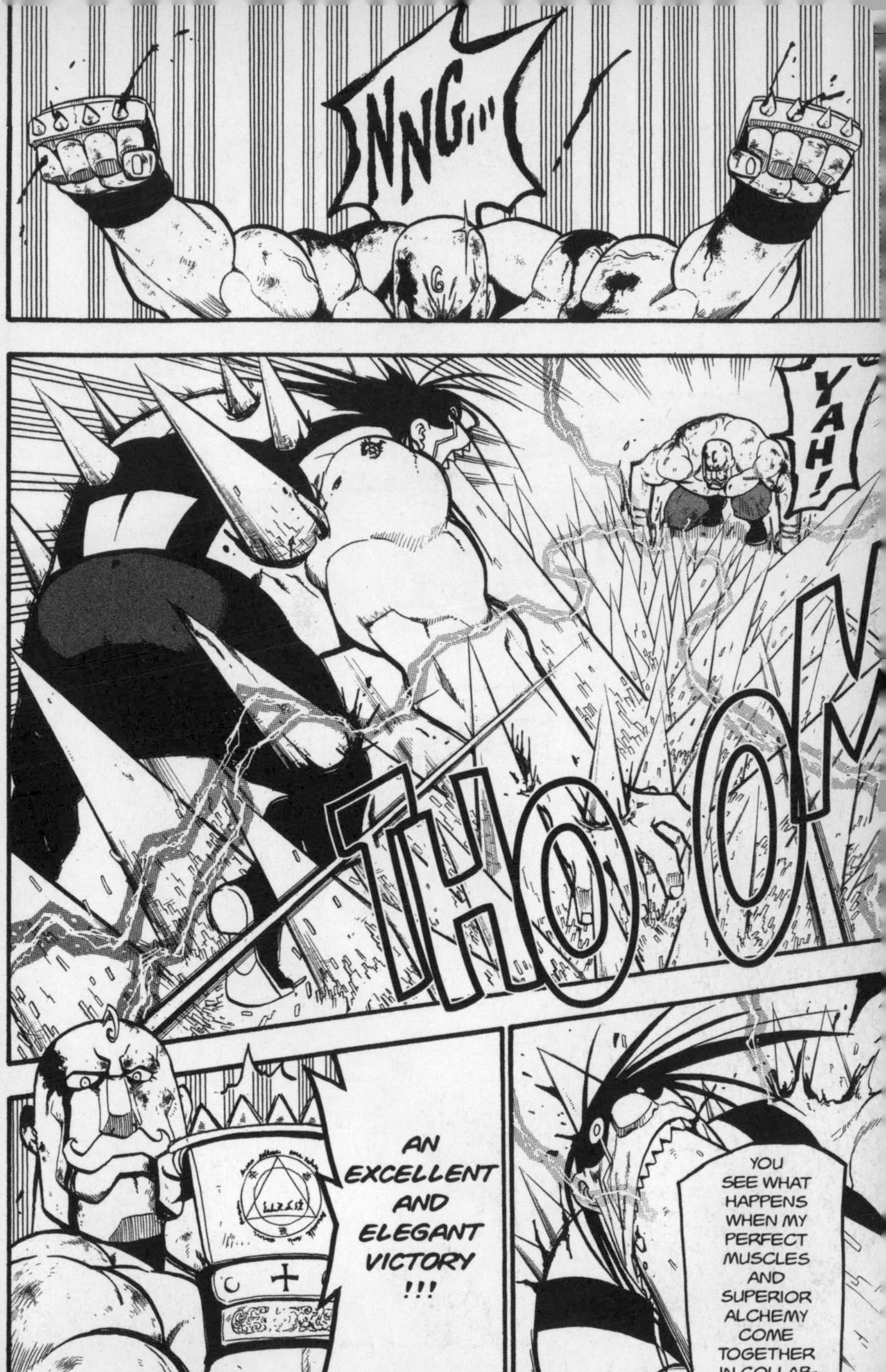
NNG!!
YAH!
THO-OM
YOU SEE WHAT HAPPENS WHEN MY PERFECT MUSCLES AND SUPERIOR ALCHEMY COME TOGETHER IN COLLAB-ORATION?!
AN EXCELLENT AND ELEGANT VICTORY!!!

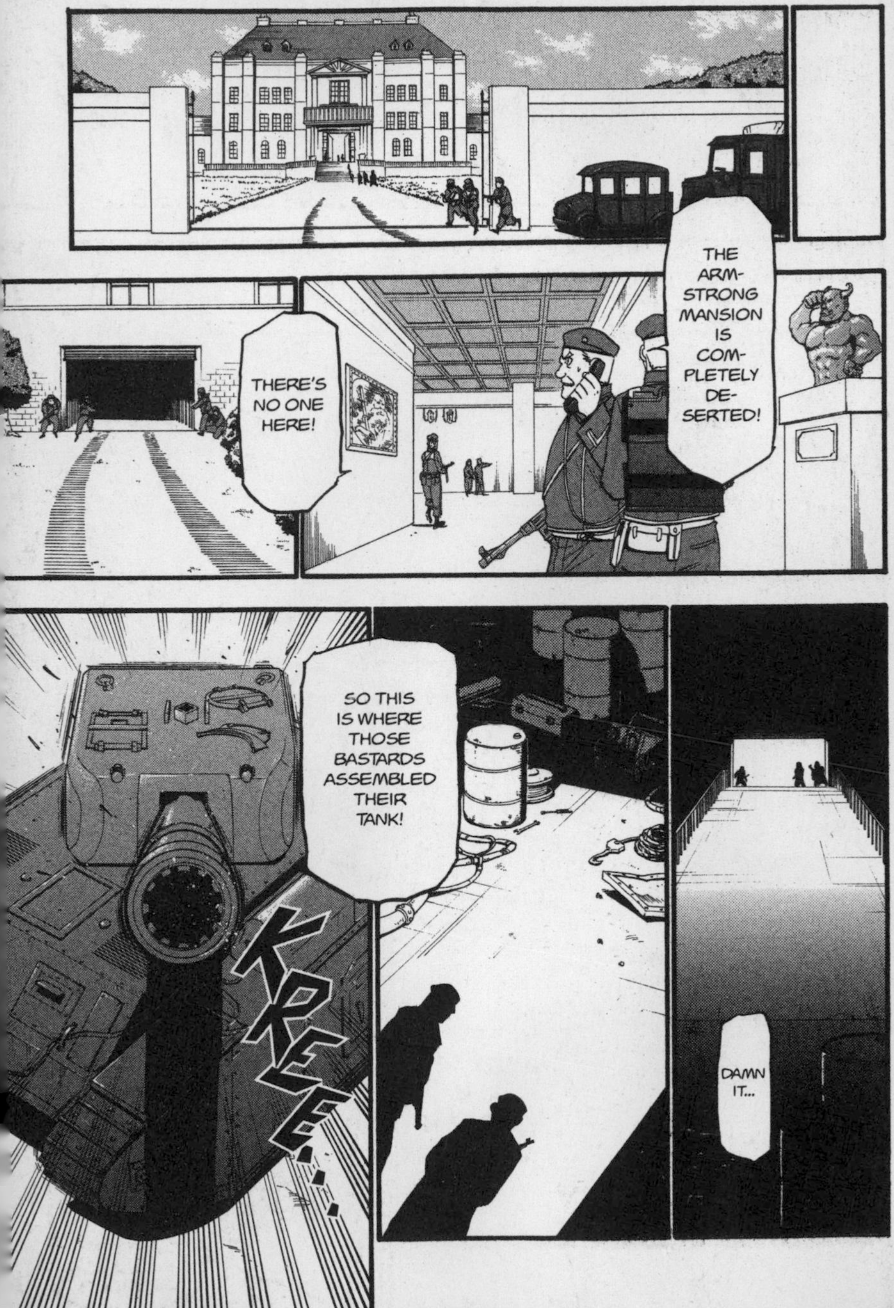
THE ARMSTRONG MANSION IS COMPLETELY DESERTED!
THERE'S NO ONE HERE!
DAMN IT...
SO THIS IS WHERE THOSE BASTARDS ASSEMBLED THEIR TANK!
KREE...

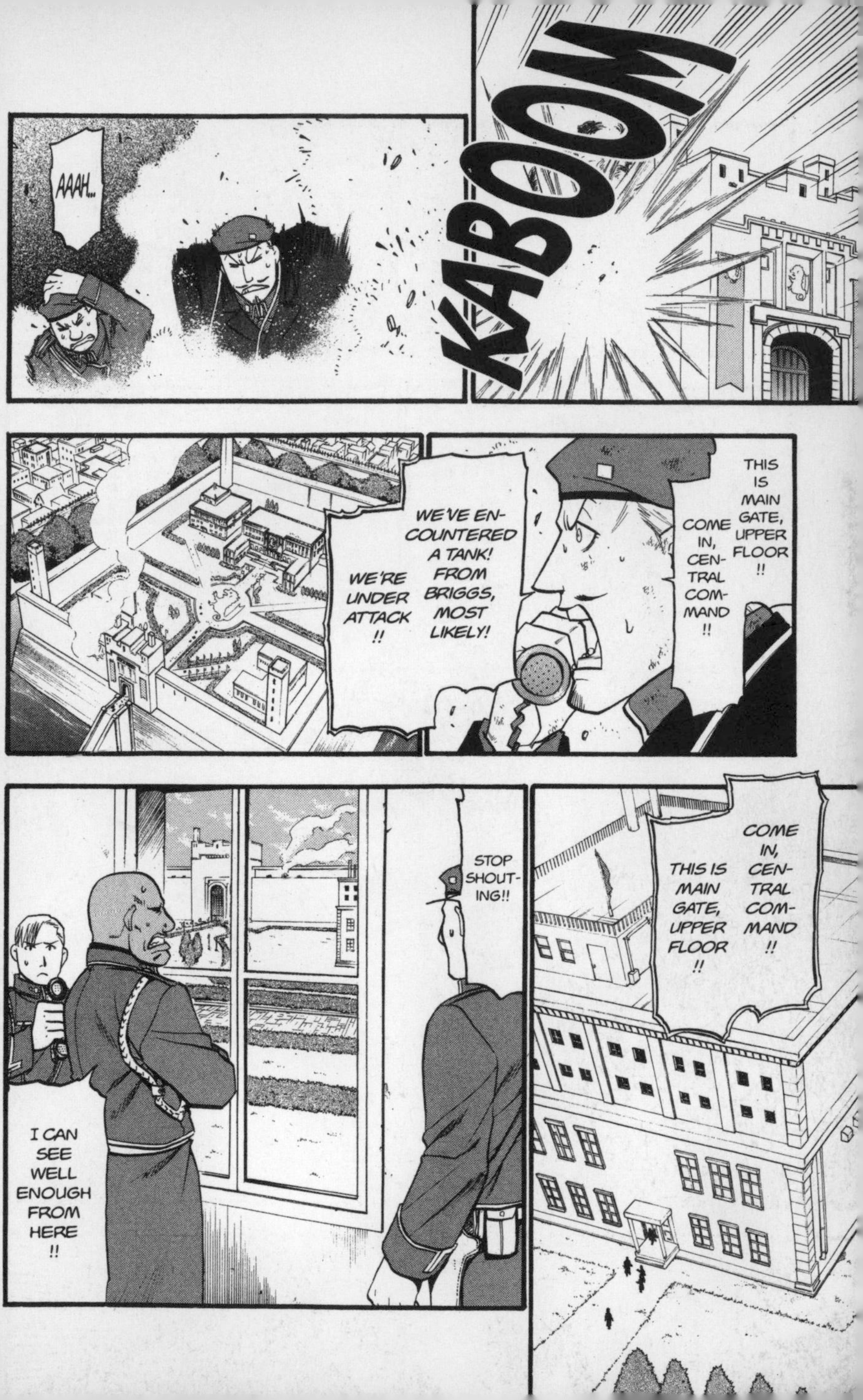
KABOOM
AAAH...
THIS IS MAIN GATE, UPPER FLOOR!!
COME IN, CENTRAL COMMAND!!
WE'VE ENCOUNTERED A TANK! FROM BRIGGS, MOST LIKELY!
WE'RE UNDER ATTACK!!
COME IN, CENTRAL COMMAND!!
THIS IS MAIN GATE, UPPER FLOOR!!
STOP SHOUTING!!
I CAN SEE WELL ENOUGH FROM HERE!!

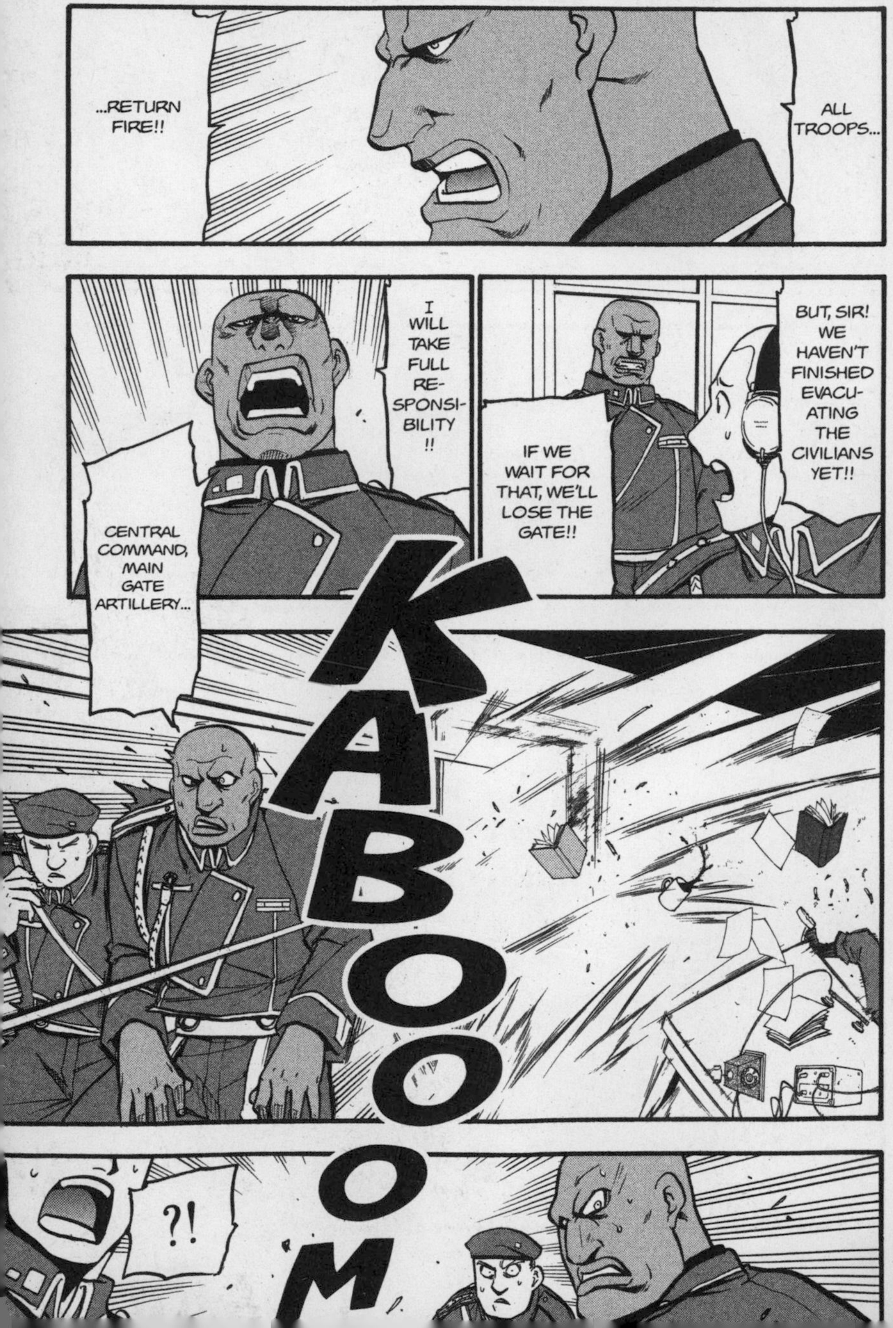
ALL TROOPS...
...RETURN FIRE!!
BUT, SIR! WE HAVEN'T FINISHED EVACUATING THE CIVILIANS YET!!
IF WE WAIT FOR THAT, WE'LL LOSE THE GATE!!
I WILL TAKE FULL RESPONSIBILITY!!
CENTRAL COMMAND, MAIN GATE ARTILLERY...
KABOOOOM
?!

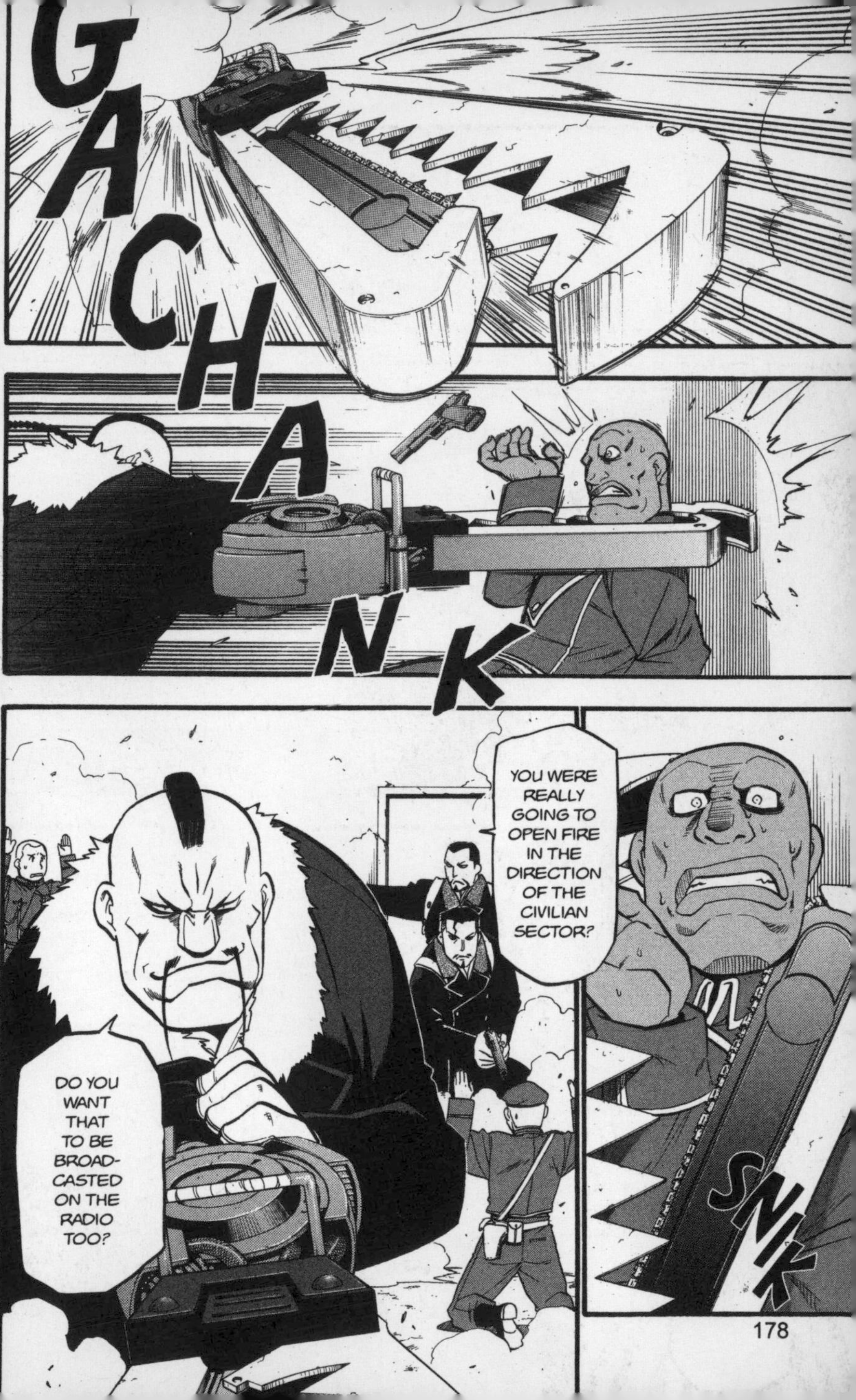
GACHANK
SNIK
YOU WERE REALLY GOING TO OPEN FIRE IN THE DIRECTION OF THE CIVILIAN SECTOR?
DO YOU WANT THAT TO BE BROAD-CASTED ON THE RADIO TOO?

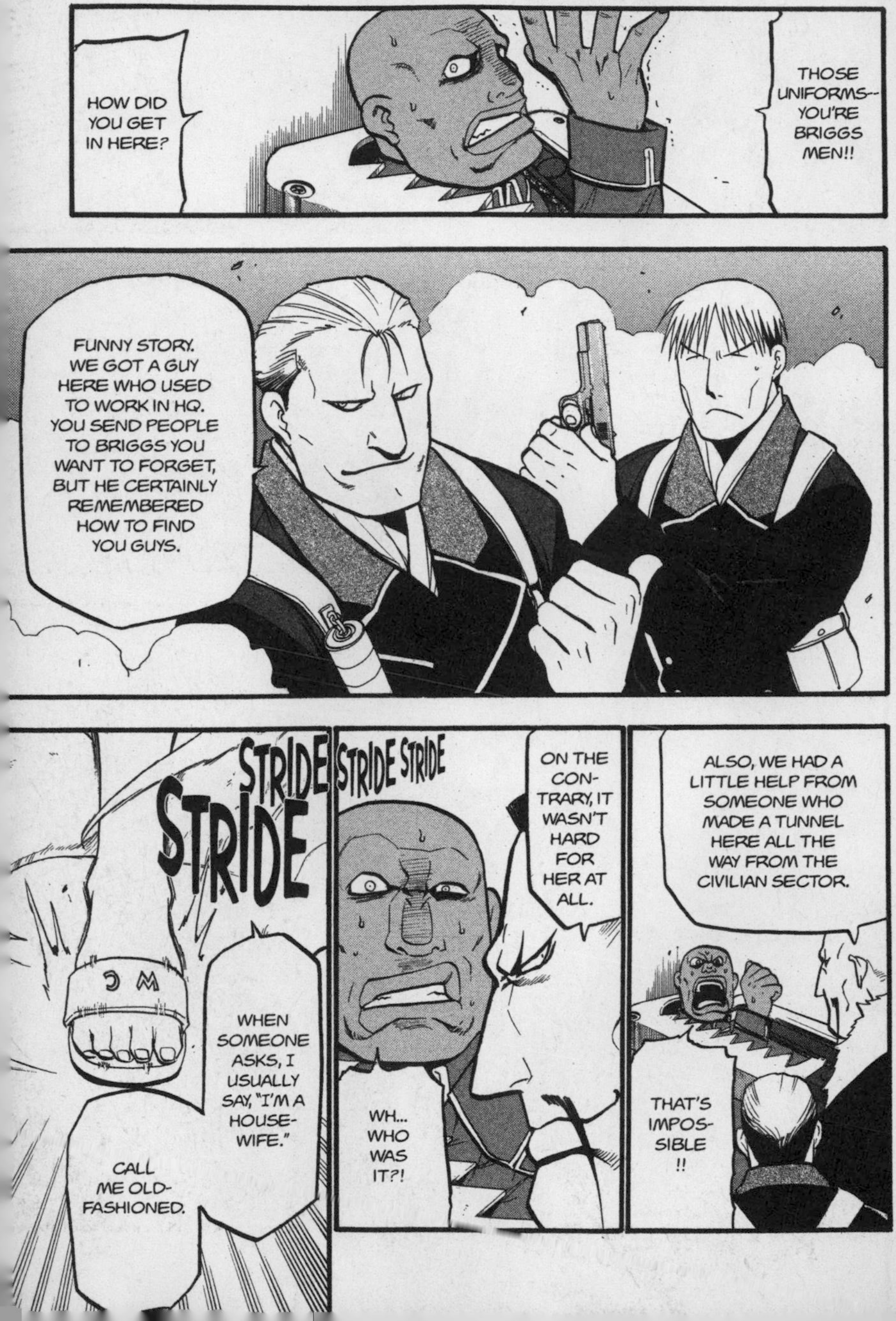
THOSE UNIFORMS-- YOU'RE BRIGGS MEN!!
HOW DID YOU GET IN HERE?
FUNNY STORY. WE GOT A GUY HERE WHO USED TO WORK IN HQ. YOU SEND PEOPLE TO BRIGGS YOU WANT TO FORGET, BUT HE CERTAINLY REMEMBERED HOW TO FIND YOU GUYS.
ALSO, WE HAD A LITTLE HELP FROM SOMEONE WHO MADE A TUNNEL HERE ALL THE WAY FROM THE CIVILIAN SECTOR.
THAT'S IMPOSSIBLE!!
ON THE CONTRARY, IT WASN'T HARD FOR HER AT ALL.
WH... WHO WAS IT?!
STRIDE STRIDE
STRIDE
STRIDE
WHEN SOMEONE ASKS, I USUALLY SAY, "I'M A HOUSEWIFE."
CALL ME OLD-FASHIONED.

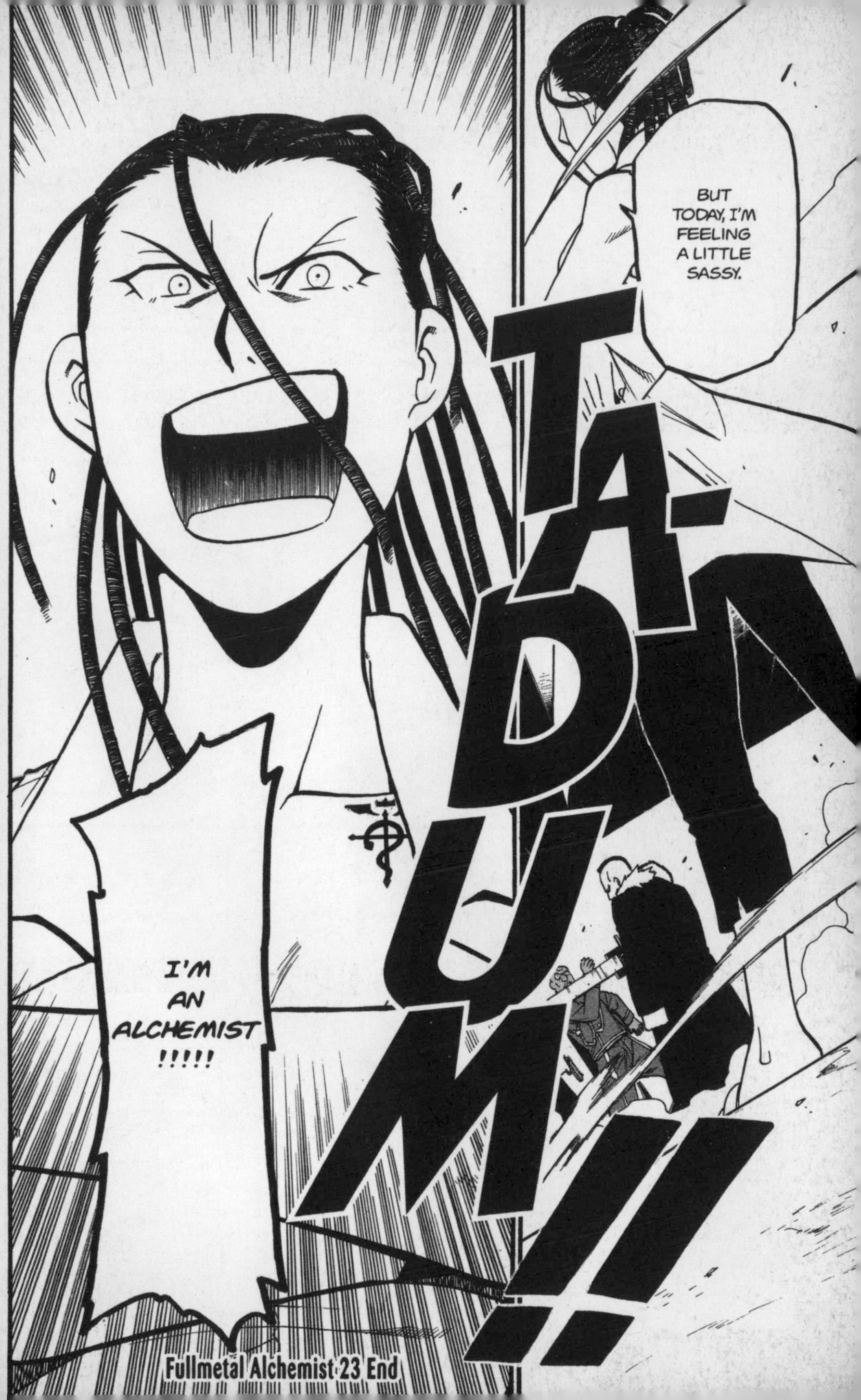
BUT TODAY, I'M FEELING A LITTLE SASSY.
TA-DA-UM!!
I'M AN ALCHEMIST!!!!!

Fullmetal Alchemist 23 End

Special Episode: Fullmetal Alchemist, Wii: Prince of Dawn

Prologue

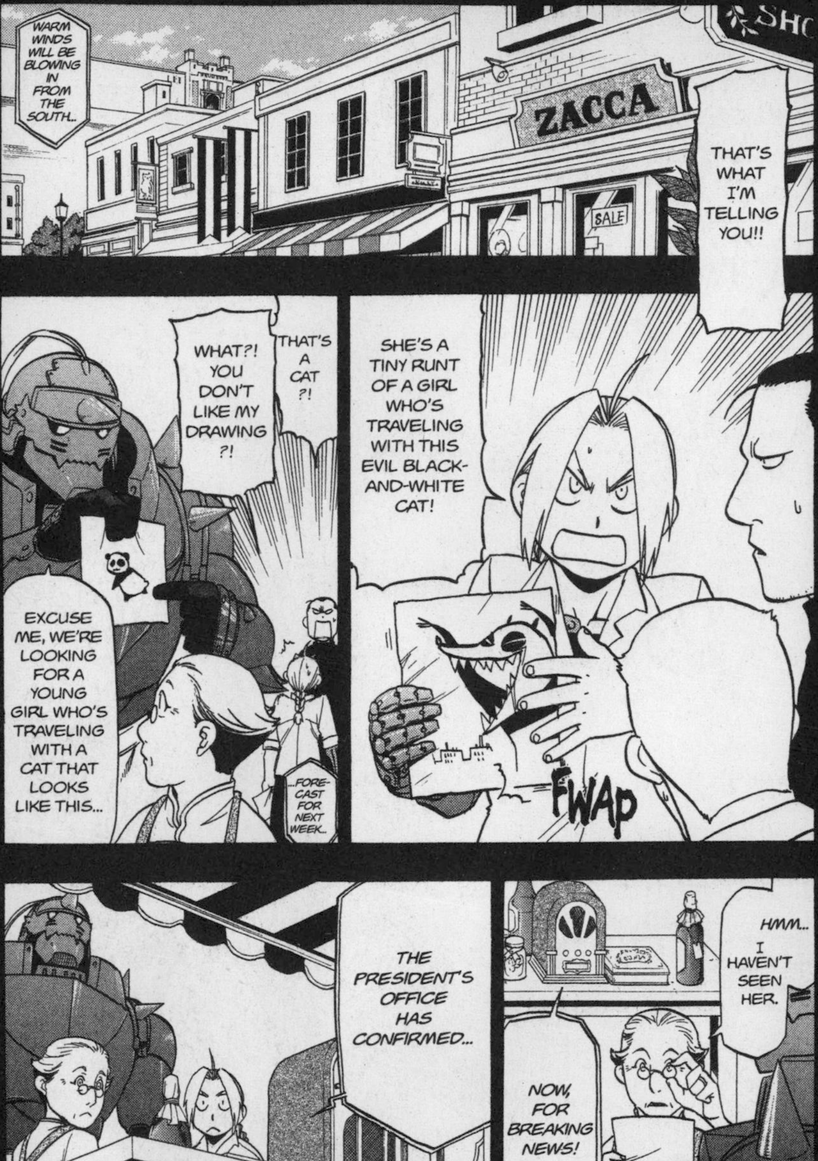

WARM WINDS WILL BE BLOWING IN FROM THE SOUTH...
ZACCA
SALE
THAT'S WHAT I'M TELLING YOU!!
SHE'S A TINY RUNT OF A GIRL WHO'S TRAVELING WITH THIS EVIL BLACK-AND-WHITE CAT!
FWAP
THAT'S A CAT?!
WHAT?! YOU DON'T LIKE MY DRAWING?!
EXCUSE ME, WE'RE LOOKING FOR A YOUNG GIRL WHO'S TRAVELING WITH A CAT THAT LOOKS LIKE THIS...
...FORECAST FOR NEXT WEEK...
HMM... I HAVEN'T SEEN HER.
NOW, FOR BREAKING NEWS!
THE PRESIDENT'S OFFICE HAS CONFIRMED...

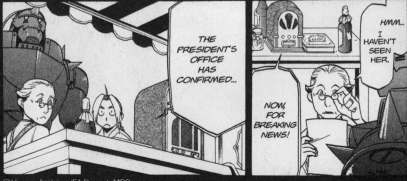

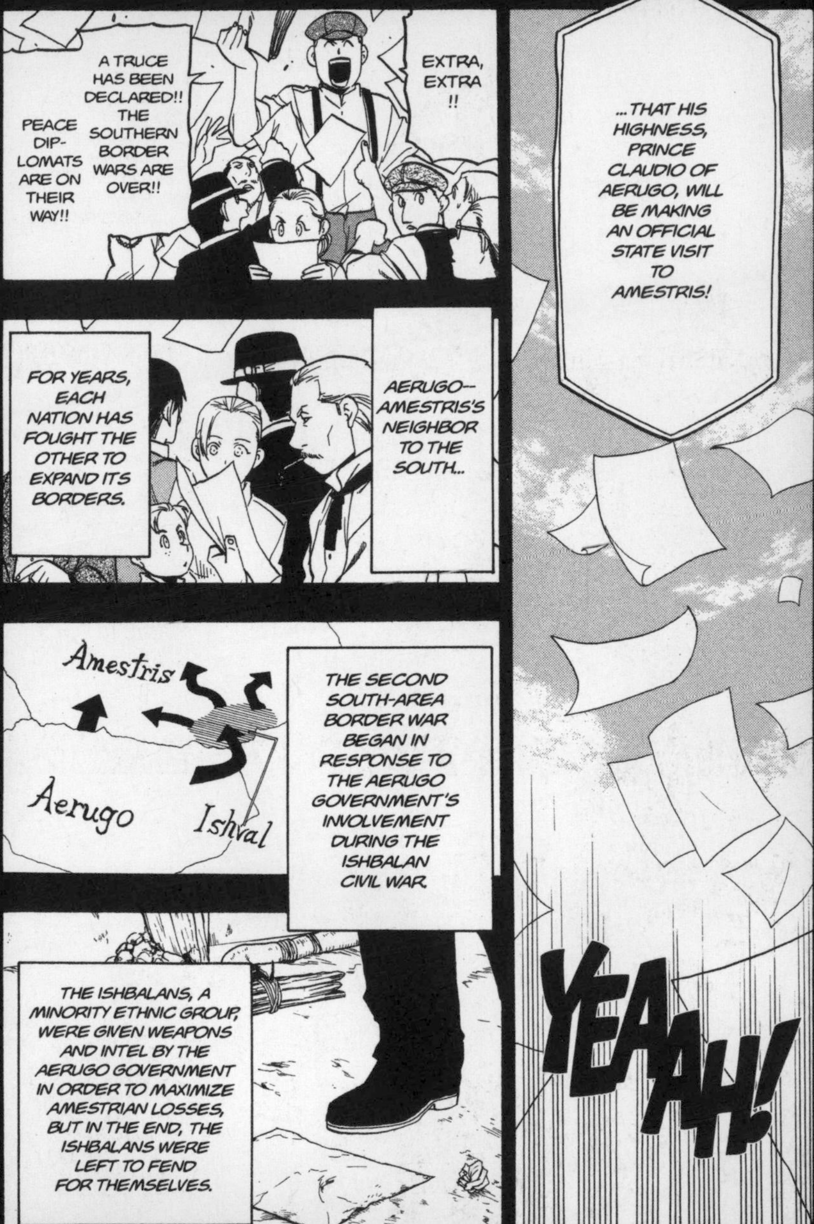
...THAT HIS HIGHNESS, PRINCE CLAUDIO OF AERUGO, WILL BE MAKING AN OFFICIAL STATE VISIT TO AMESTRIS!
YEAAH!
EXTRA, EXTRA!!
A TRUCE HAS BEEN DECLARED!! THE SOUTHERN BORDER WARS ARE OVER!!
PEACE DIPLOMATS ARE ON THEIR WAY!!
AERUGO—AMESTRIS'S NEIGHBOR TO THE SOUTH...
FOR YEARS, EACH NATION HAS FOUGHT THE OTHER TO EXPAND ITS BORDERS.
THE SECOND SOUTH-AREA BORDER WAR BEGAN IN RESPONSE TO THE AERUGO GOVERNMENT'S INVOLVEMENT DURING THE ISHBALAN CIVIL WAR.
Amestris
Aerugo
Ishval
THE ISHBALANS, A MINORITY ETHNIC GROUP, WERE GIVEN WEAPONS AND INTEL BY THE AERUGO GOVERNMENT IN ORDER TO MAXIMIZE AMESTRIAN LOSSES, BUT IN THE END, THE ISHBALANS WERE LEFT TO FEND FOR THEMSELVES.

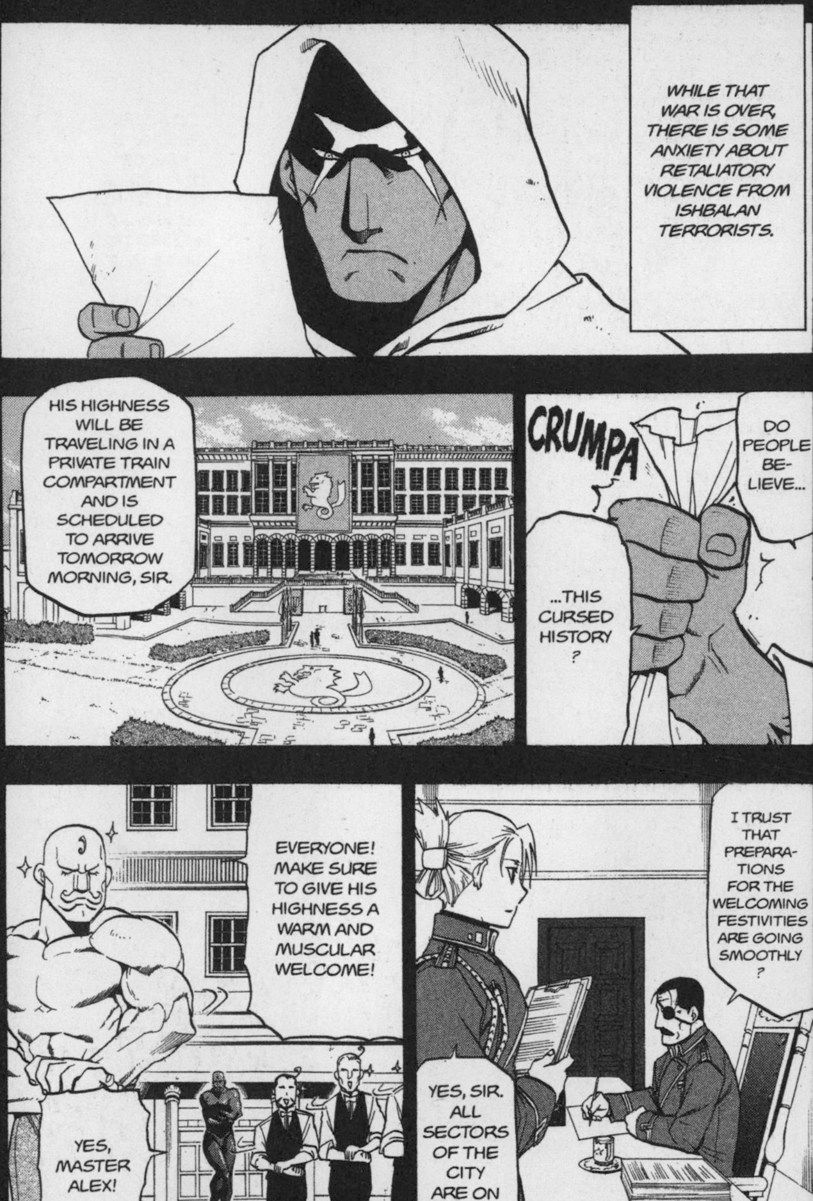
WHILE THAT WAR IS OVER, THERE IS SOME ANXIETY ABOUT RETALIATORY VIOLENCE FROM ISHBALAN TERRORISTS.
DO PEOPLE BE-LIEVE...
CRUMPA
...THIS CURSED HISTORY?
HIS HIGHNESS WILL BE TRAVELING IN A PRIVATE TRAIN COMPARTMENT AND IS SCHEDULED TO ARRIVE TOMORROW MORNING, SIR.
I TRUST THAT PREPARA-TIONS FOR THE WELCOMING FESTIVITIES ARE GOING SMOOTHLY?
YES, SIR. ALL SECTORS OF THE CITY ARE ON TRACK.
EVERYONE! MAKE SURE TO GIVE HIS HIGHNESS A WARM AND MUSCULAR WELCOME!
YES, MASTER ALEX!

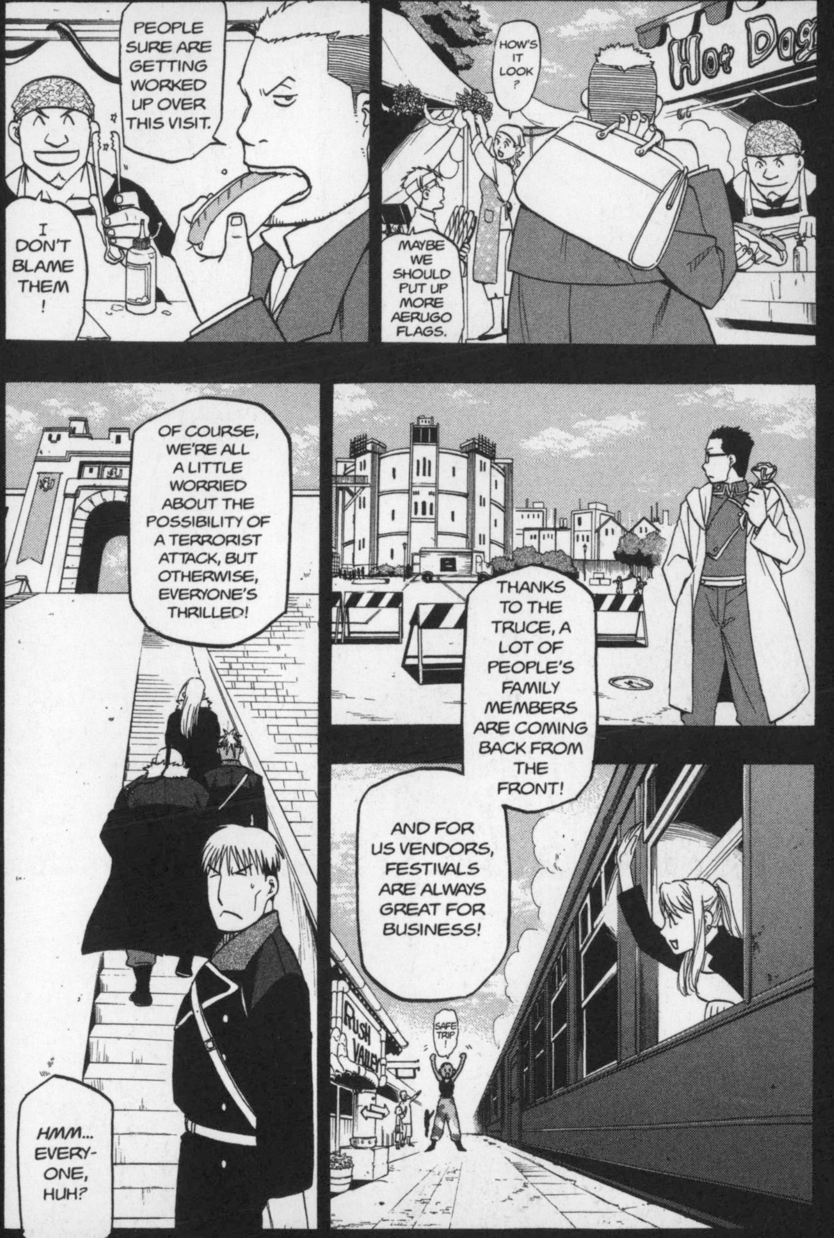
HOW'S IT LOOK?
MAYBE WE SHOULD PUT UP MORE AERUGO FLAGS.
PEOPLE SURE ARE GETTING WORKED UP OVER THIS VISIT.
I DON'T BLAME THEM!
THANKS TO THE TRUCE, A LOT OF PEOPLE'S FAMILY MEMBERS ARE COMING BACK FROM THE FRONT!
AND FOR US VENDORS, FESTIVALS ARE ALWAYS GREAT FOR BUSINESS!
SAFE TRIP!
RUSH VALLEY
OF COURSE, WE'RE ALL A LITTLE WORRIED ABOUT THE POSSIBILITY OF A TERRORIST ATTACK, BUT OTHERWISE, EVERYONE'S THRILLED!
HMM... EVERY-ONE, HUH?

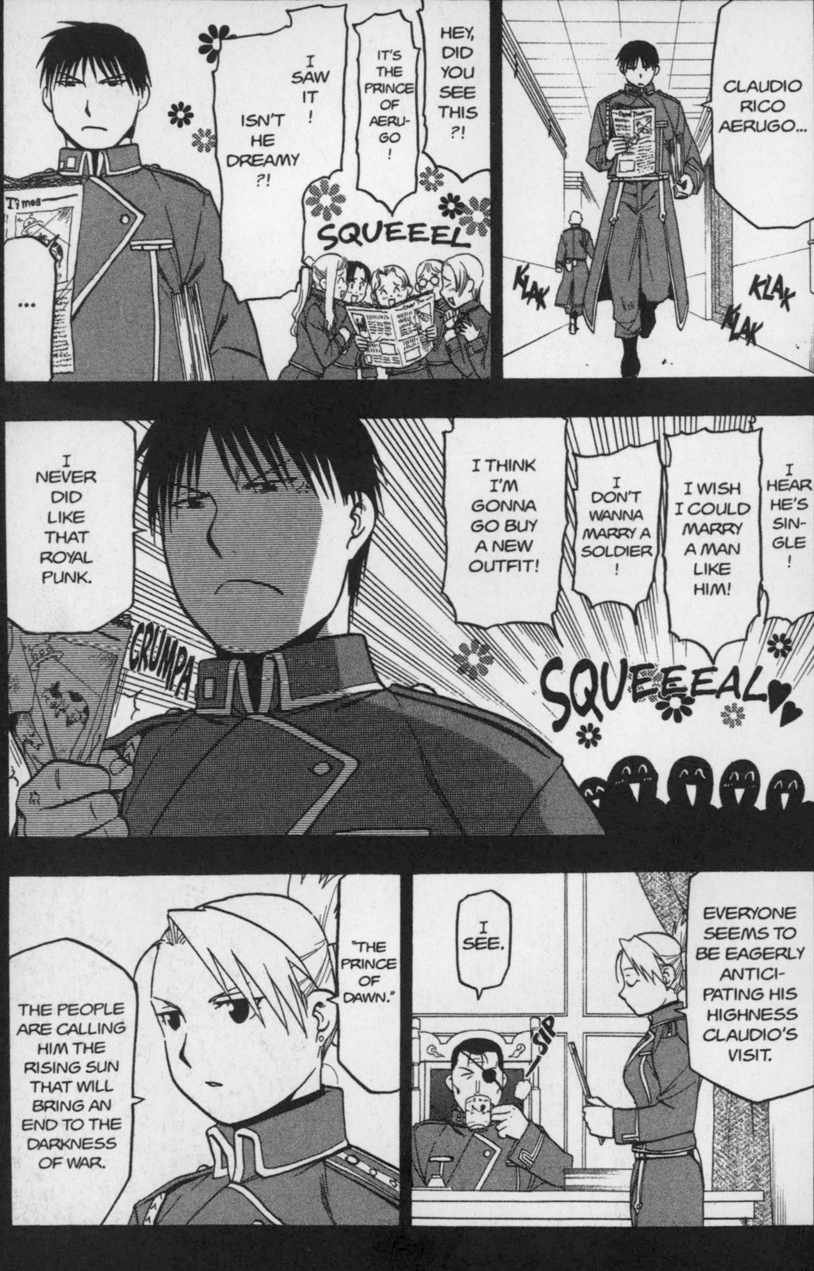
CLAUDIO RICO AERUGO...
KLAK
KLAK
KLAK
HEY, DID YOU SEE THIS?!
IT'S THE PRINCE OF AERU-GO!
I SAW IT!
ISN'T HE DREAMY?!
SQUEEEL
...
I HEAR HE'S SIN-GLE!
I WISH I COULD MARRY A MAN LIKE HIM!
I DON'T WANNA MARRY A SOLDIER!
I THINK I'M GONNA GO BUY A NEW OUTFIT!
SQUEEEAL
CRUMPA
I NEVER DID LIKE THAT ROYAL PUNK.
EVERYONE SEEMS TO BE EAGERLY ANTICI-PATING HIS HIGHNESS CLAUDIO'S VISIT.
SIP
I SEE.
"THE PRINCE OF DAWN."
THE PEOPLE ARE CALLING HIM THE RISING SUN THAT WILL BRING AN END TO THE DARKNESS OF WAR.

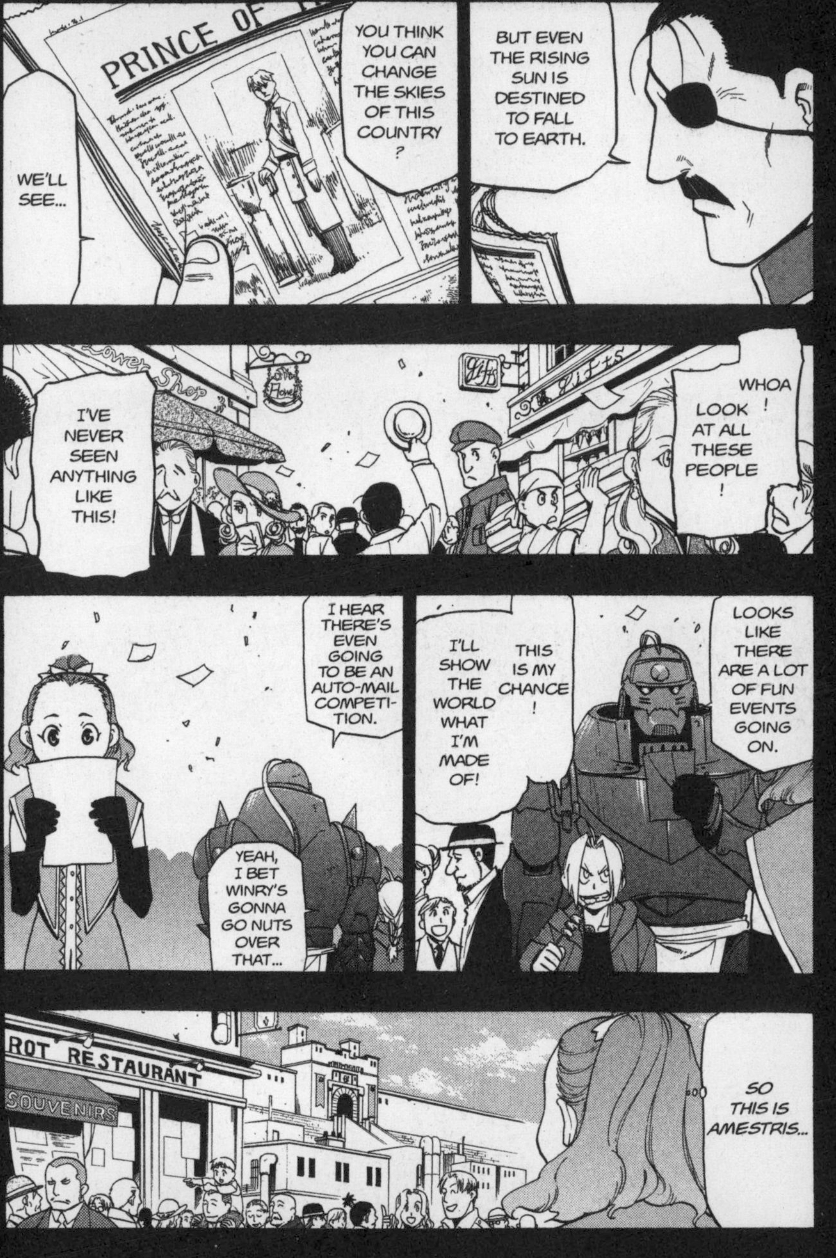
BUT EVEN THE RISING SUN IS DESTINED TO FALL TO EARTH.
PRINCE OF
YOU THINK YOU CAN CHANGE THE SKIES OF THIS COUNTRY?
WE'LL SEE...
WHOA! LOOK AT ALL THESE PEOPLE!
Gifts
I'VE NEVER SEEN ANYTHING LIKE THIS!
LOOKS LIKE THERE ARE A LOT OF FUN EVENTS GOING ON.
THIS IS MY CHANCE!
I'LL SHOW THE WORLD WHAT I'M MADE OF!
I HEAR THERE'S EVEN GOING TO BE AN AUTO-MAIL COMPETITION.
YEAH, I BET WINRY'S GONNA GO NUTS OVER THAT...
SO THIS IS AMESTRIS...
ROT RESTAURANT
SOUVENIRS

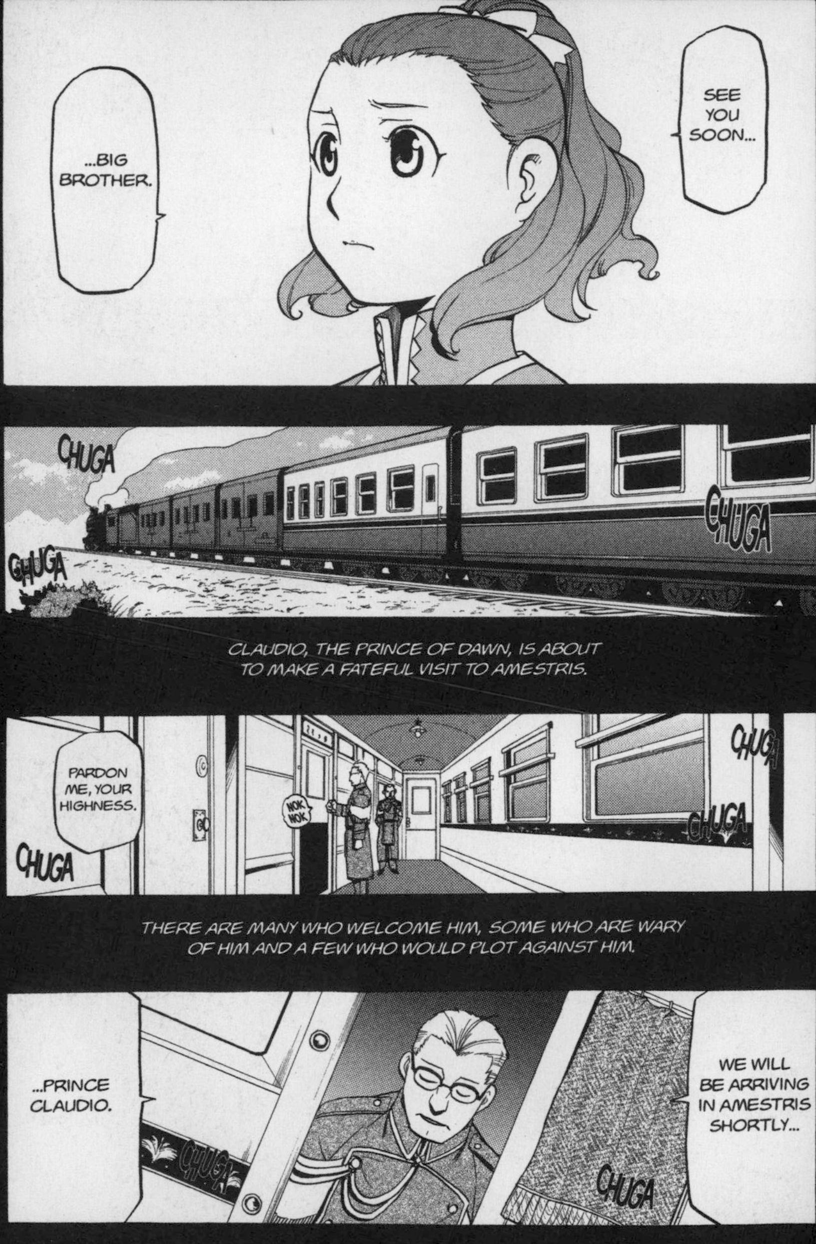
SEE YOU SOON...
...BIG BROTHER.
CHUGA
CHUGA
CHUGA
CLAUDIO, THE PRINCE OF DAWN, IS ABOUT TO MAKE A FATEFUL VISIT TO AMESTRIS.
CHUGA
CHUGA
NOK NOK
PARDON ME, YOUR HIGHNESS.
CHUGA
THERE ARE MANY WHO WELCOME HIM, SOME WHO ARE WARY OF HIM AND A FEW WHO WOULD PLOT AGAINST HIM.
WE WILL BE ARRIVING IN AMESTRIS SHORTLY...
CHUGA
CHUGA
...PRINCE CLAUDIO.

IN CENTRAL CITY, IN THE MIDST OF CELEBRATION, EACH OF THESE VIEWPOINTS IS ABOUT TO COLLIDE!

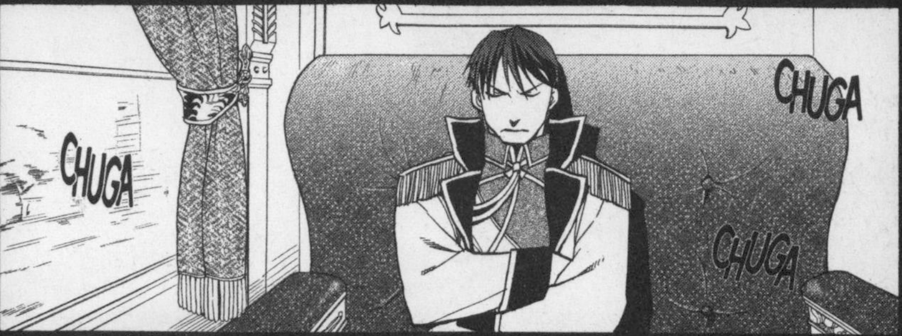
CHUGA
CHUGA
CHUGA

FULLMETAL ALCHEMIST
PRINCE OF DAWN

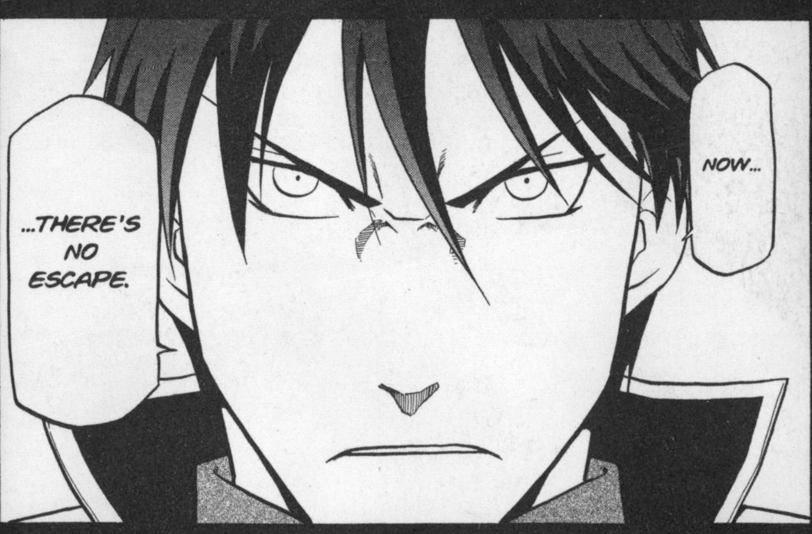
NOW...
...THERE'S NO ESCAPE.

HOW WILL IT GO DOWN?!

FIND OUT...ONLY ON NINTENDO WII!!

STRONG!!

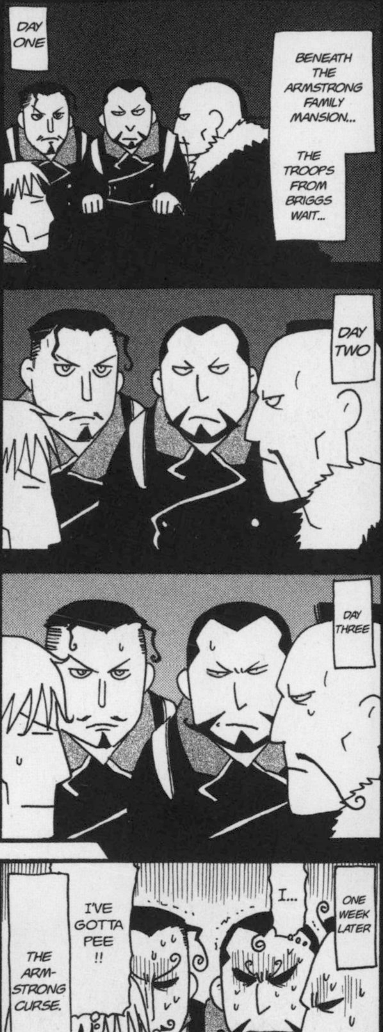

BENEATH THE ARMSTRONG FAMILY MANSION... THE TROOPS FROM BRIGGS WAIT...
DAY ONE
DAY TWO
DAY THREE
ONE WEEK LATER
I...
I'VE GOTTA PEE !!
THE ARM-STRONG CURSE.

FULLMETAL ALCHEMIST 23

SPECIAL THANKS to:

Jun Tohko
Noriko Tsubota
Kori Sakano
Masashi Mizutani
Haruhi Nakamura
Manatsu Sakura
Mr. Coupon
Kazufumi Kaneko
Teru Miyoshi
Yota Arao

My Editor, Yuichi Shimomura

AND YOU!!

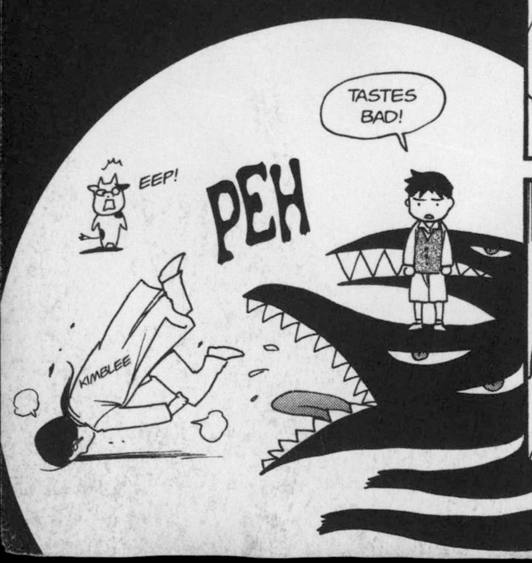

TASTES BAD!
EEP!
PEH
KIMBLEE

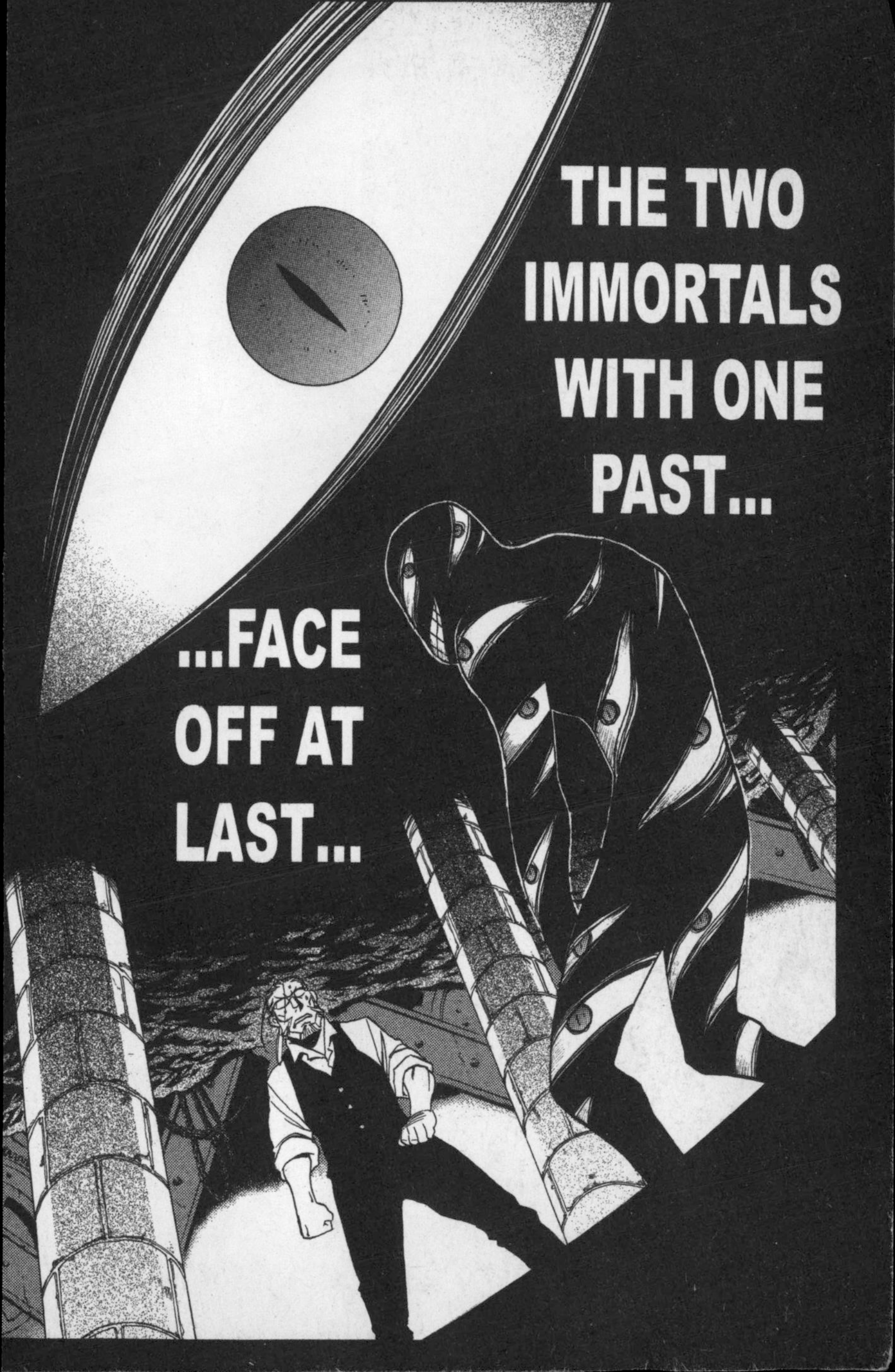
THE TWO IMMORTALS WITH ONE PAST...
...FACE OFF AT LAST...

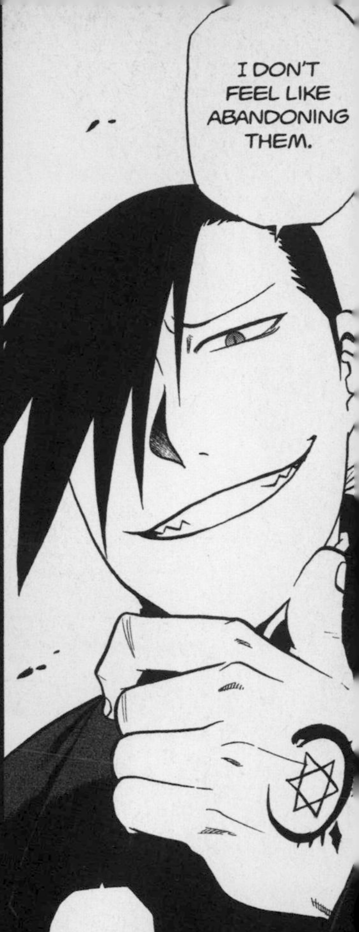

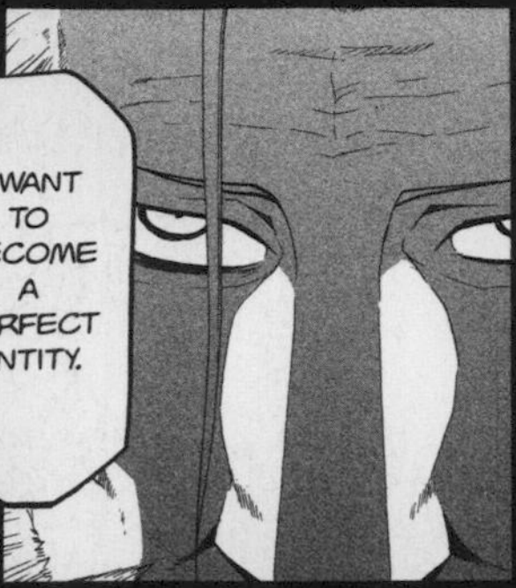

...AND THE WORLD IS IN THE BALANCE!

A battle beyond human comprehension ensues with Hohenheim's clone, the Dwarf in the Flask. As the battle switches back and forth from offense to defense, who will strike the final blow?!! In the world's best-selling dark fantasy manga, events take a turn for the darker!!

THE EAGERLY ANTICIPATED FULLMETAL ALCHEMIST VOLUME 24--COMING SOON!!

THE HOHENHEIM FAMILY TREE
HOHENHEIM
TRISHA
KIDS ?
KIDS
FATHER
ED
AL
KIDS
WRATH
GLUTTONY
SLOTH
GREED
ENVY
LUST
PRIDE

WHICH MEANS...

UNCLE ED, UNCLE AL.
GIVE US SOME POCKET MONEY!!
HEY!!

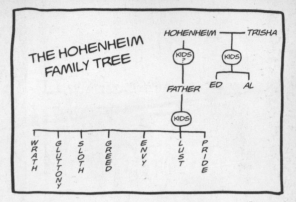

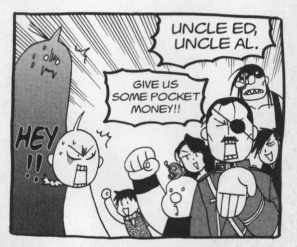

...IS THIS HOW THINGS COULD BE?

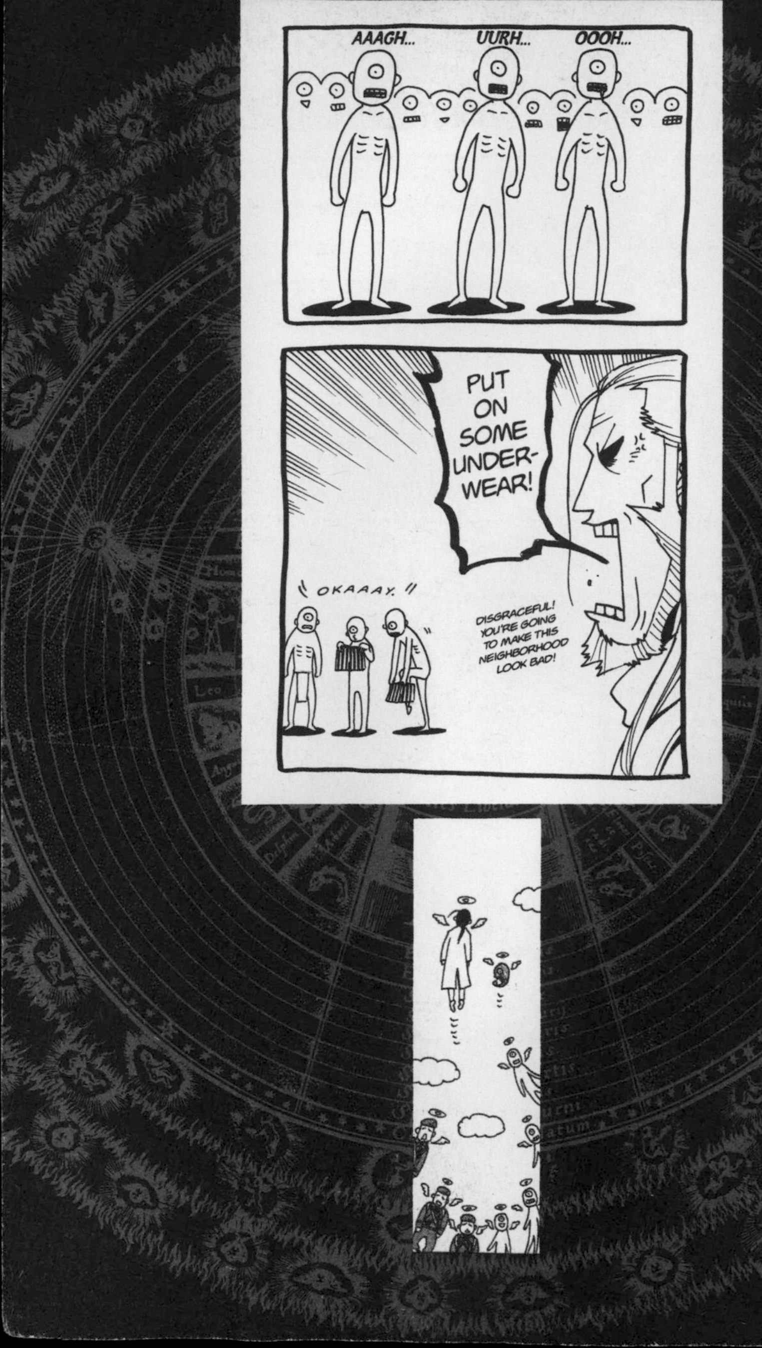
OOOH...
UURH...
AAAGH...
PUT ON SOME UNDER-WEAR!
DISGRACEFUL! YOU'RE GOING TO MAKE THIS NEIGHBORHOOD LOOK BAD!
OKAAAY.

TLE

ALITA Last Order™

In this epic story spanning two complete manga series, a powerful cyborg struggles to make sense of her mysterious past. But every answer only leads to more questions. Will she uncover the truth before it's too late?

Find out in the *Battle Angel Alita* and *Battle Angel Alita: Last Order* manga—buy yours today!

By Yukito Kishiro

"Excellent... intense action and combat, detailed renderings of inventive super-technology, unpredictable storyline, surprisingly deep philosophical bent, and cute heroine."

—*Library Journal*

On sale at store.viz.com
Also available at your local bookstore and comic store.

RATED T+ FOR OLDER TEEN ratings.viz.com

VIZ media www.viz.com

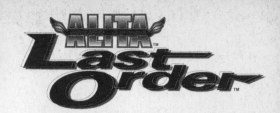

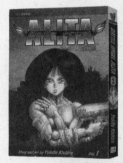

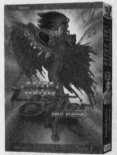

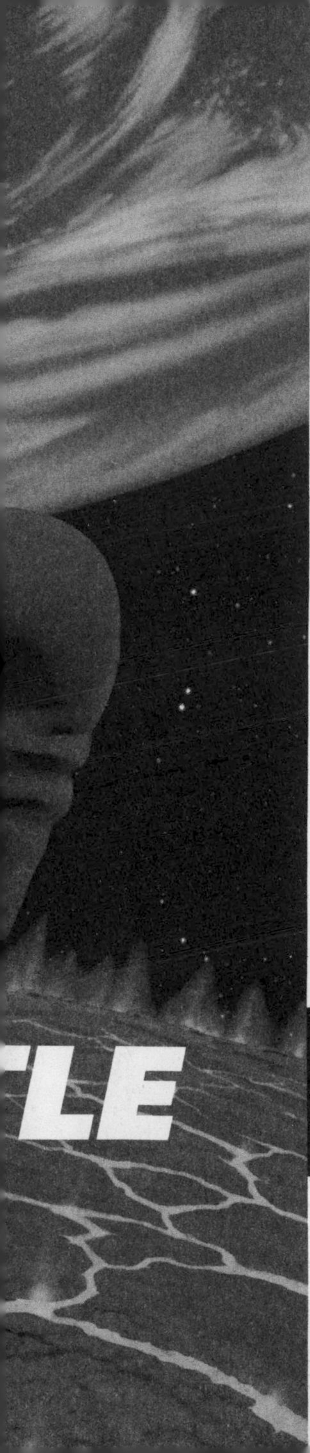

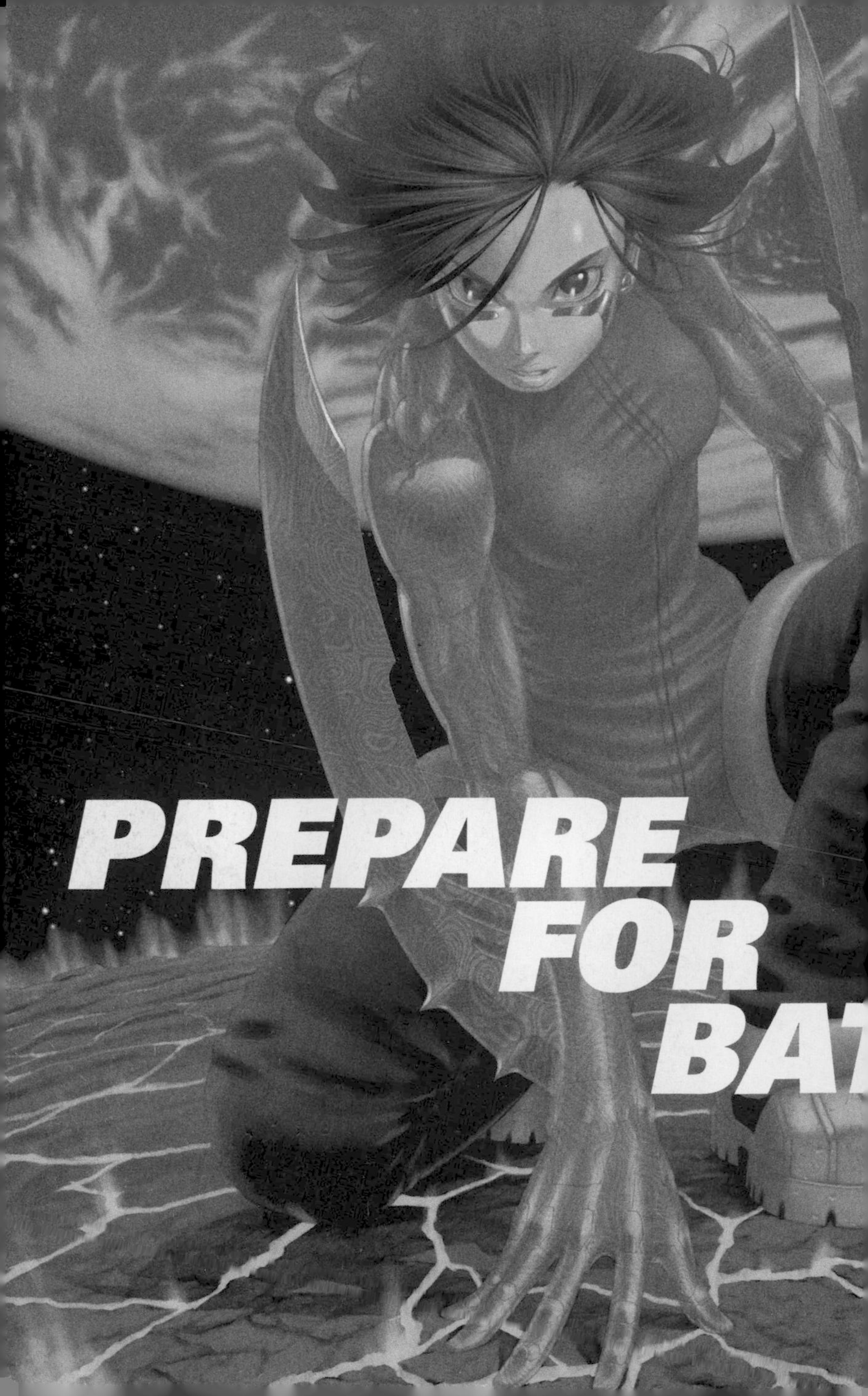

PREPARE
FOR
BAT

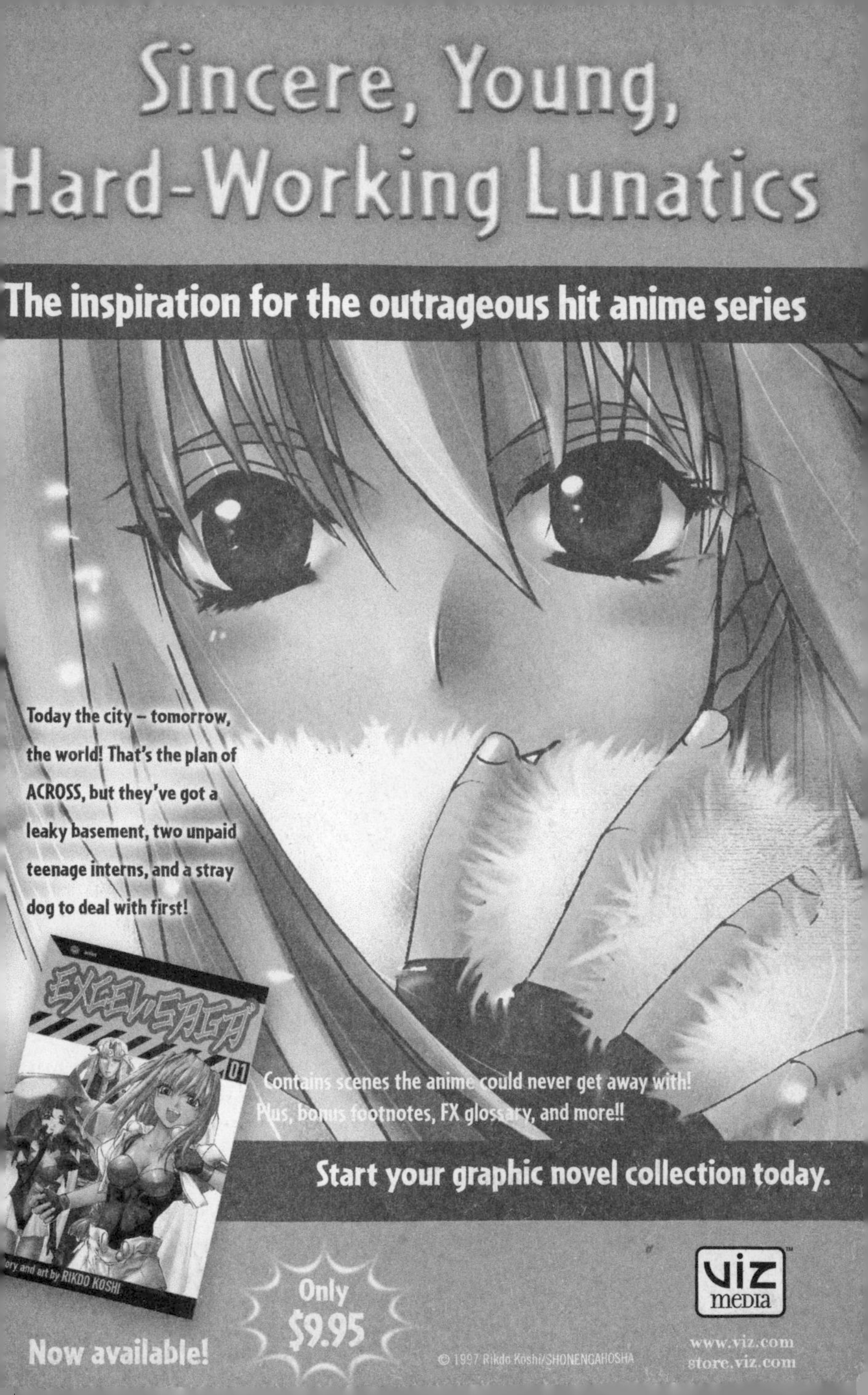
Sincere, Young, Hard-Working Lunatics
The inspiration for the outrageous hit anime series
Today the city – tomorrow, the world! That's the plan of ACROSS, but they've got a leaky basement, two unpaid teenage interns, and a stray dog to deal with first!
EXCEL SAGA
01
ory and art by RIKDO KOSHI
Contains scenes the anime could never get away with!
Plus, bonus footnotes, FX glossary, and more!!
Start your graphic novel collection today.
Only $9.95
Now available!
© 1997 Rikdo Koshi/SHONENGAHOSHA
viz media
www.viz.com
store.viz.com

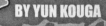

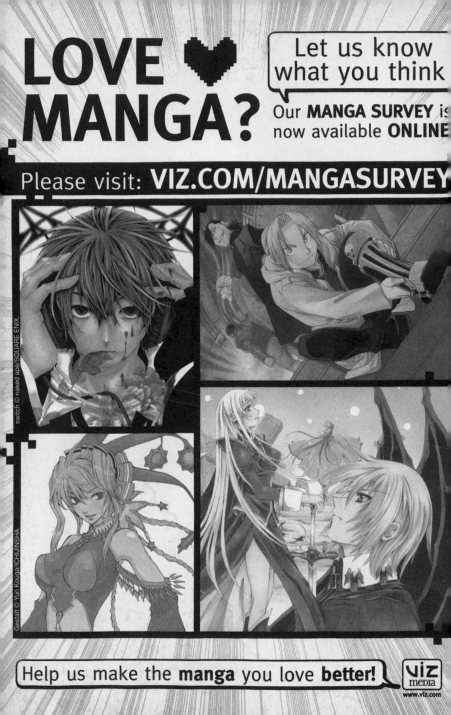

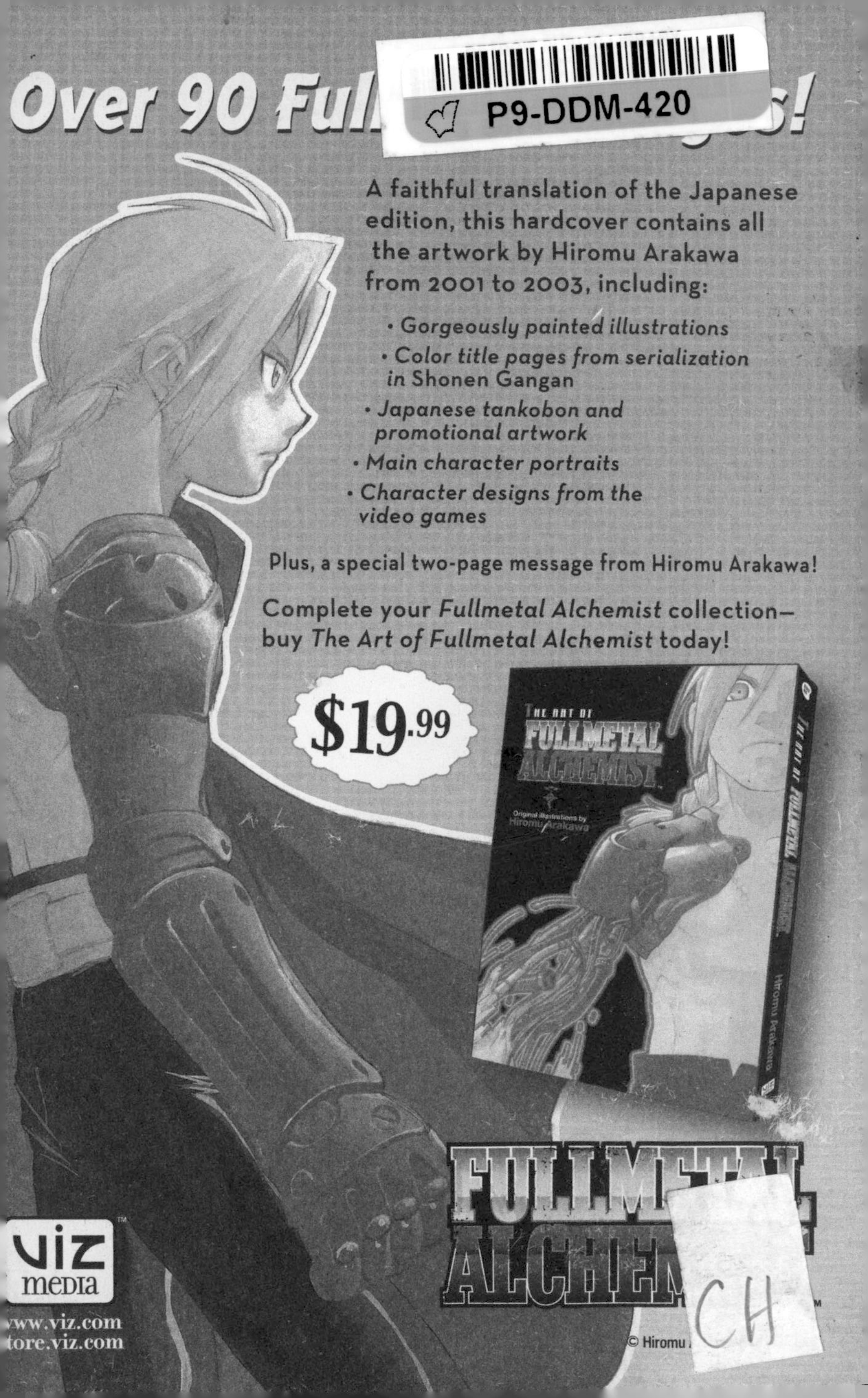
Over 90 Ful
s!
P9-DDM-420
A faithful translation of the Japanese edition, this hardcover contains all the artwork by Hiromu Arakawa from 2001 to 2003, including:
• Gorgeously painted illustrations
• Color title pages from serialization in Shonen Gangan
• Japanese tankobon and promotional artwork
• Main character portraits
• Character designs from the video games
Plus, a special two-page message from Hiromu Arakawa!
Complete your Fullmetal Alchemist collection—buy The Art of Fullmetal Alchemist today!
$19.99
The Art of Fullmetal Alchemist
Original illustrations by Hiromu Arakawa
FULLMETAL
ALCHEM
CH
viz media
www.viz.com
store.viz.com
© Hiromu